Publishing Research in English as an Additional Language

This book is available as a free fully-searchable ebook from
www.adelaide.edu.au/press

Publishing Research in English as an Additional Language:
Practices, Pathways and Potentials

edited by

Margaret Cargill and Sally Burgess

THE UNIVERSITY
of ADELAIDE

UNIVERSITY OF
ADELAIDE PRESS

Published in Adelaide by

University of Adelaide Press
Barr Smith Library
The University of Adelaide
South Australia 5005
press@adelaide.edu.au
www.adelaide.edu.au/press

The University of Adelaide Press publishes peer reviewed scholarly books. It aims to maximise access to the best research by publishing works through the internet as free downloads and for sale as high quality printed volumes.

© 2017 The Contributors

This work is licenced under the Creative Commons Attribution-NonCommercial-NoDerivatives 4.0 International (CC BY-NC-ND 4.0) License. To view a copy of this licence, visit http://creativecommons.org/licenses/by-nc-nd/4.0 or send a letter to Creative Commons, 444 Castro Street, Suite 900, Mountain View, California, 94041, USA. This licence allows for the copying, distribution, display and performance of this work for non-commercial purposes providing the work is clearly attributed to the copyright holders. Address all inquiries to the Director at the above address.

For the full Cataloguing-in-Publication data please contact the National Library of Australia: cip@nla.gov.au

ISBN (paperback) 978-1-925261-51-6
ISBN (ebook: pdf) 978-1-925261-52-3
ISBN (ebook: epub) 978-1-925261-53-0
ISBN (ebook: kindle) 978-1-925261-54-7
DOI: http://dx.doi.org/10.20851/english-pathways

Editor: Rebecca Burton
Editorial support: Julia Keller
Book design: Zoë Stokes
Cover design: Emma Spoehr
Cover image: iStockphoto

Contents

List of contributors	vii
Acknowledgements	xiii
Foreword	xv
Mary Jane Curry and Theresa Lillis	
Introduction: Unpacking English for Research Publication Purposes [ERPP] and the intersecting roles of those who research, teach and edit it	1
Margaret Cargill and Sally Burgess	

1. Accept or contest: 13
   A life-history study of humanities scholars' responses to research publication policies in Spain
   Sally Burgess

2. Introducing research rigour in the social sciences: 33
   Transcultural strategies for teaching ERPP writing, research design, and resistance to epistemic erasure
   Kate Cadman

3. Blurring the boundaries: 55
   Academic advising, authors' editing and translation in a graduate degree program
   Susan M. DiGiacomo

4. The delicate art of commenting: 71
   Exploring different approaches to editing and their implications for the author-editor relationship
   Oliver Shaw and Sabrina Voss

5. The CCC Model (Correspondence, Consistency, Correctness):   87
   How effective is it in enabling and assessing change in text-editing knowledge and skills in a blended-learning postgraduate course?
   John Linnegar

| 6 | How credible are open access emerging journals? A situational analysis in the humanities | 121 |
| | *Ana Bocanegra-Valle* | |

| 7 | Disseminating research internationally: Intra-subdisciplinary rhetorical structure variation in immunity and allergy research articles | 151 |
| | *Pedro Martín and Isabel K. León Pérez* | |

| 8 | Scientists publishing research in English from Indonesia: Analysing outcomes of a training intervention to inform institutional action | 169 |
| | *Margaret Cargill, Patrick O'Connor, Rika Raffiudin, Nampiah Sukarno, Berry Juliandi and Iman Rusmana* | |

| 9 | 'The one who is out of the ordinary shall win': Research supervision towards publication in a Chinese hospital | 187 |
| | *Yongyan Li* | |

| 10 | The geopolitics of academic plagiarism | 209 |
| | *Karen Bennett* | |

| 11 | Training 'clerks of the [global] empire' for 21st-century Asia? English for Research Purposes (ERP) in Vietnam | 221 |
| | *Thuc Anh Cao Xuan and Kate Cadman* | |

| 12 | Standardisation and its discontents | 239 |
| | *John M. Swales* | |

Reflections and future directions in publishing research in English as an Additional Language: An afterword   255

Laurence Anthony

List of contributors

Laurence Anthony is professor of applied linguistics at the Faculty of Science and Engineering, Waseda University, Japan. He has a BSc degree (Mathematical Physics) from the University of Manchester, UK, and MA (TESL/TEFL) and PhD (Applied Linguistics) degrees from the University of Birmingham, UK. He is a former director and the current co-ordinator of graduate school English in the Center for English Language Education in Science and Engineering [CELESE]. His main research interests are in corpus linguistics, educational technology and English for Specific Purposes [ESP] program design and teaching methodologies. He serves on the editorial boards of various international journals and is a frequent member of the scientific committees of international conferences. He received the National Prize of the Japan Association for English Corpus Studies [JAECS] in 2012 for his work in corpus software tools design. He is the developer of various corpus tools including *AntConc*, *AntWordProfiler*, *FireAnt*, and *ProtAnt*.

Karen Bennett lectures in translation and academic writing at the Nova University in Lisbon. She has an MA and PhD in Translation Studies from the University of Lisbon, and researches the translation and transmission of knowledge (amongst other things) with the Centre for English, Translation and Anglo-Portuguese Studies [CETAPS] and University of Lisbon Centre for English Studies [ULICES/CEAUL]. She has published three books and numerous articles and book chapters, and is also currently co-editing a special issue of *The Translator* with Rita Queiroz de Barros on the subject of international English and translation.

Ana Bocanegra-Valle is a senior lecturer at the University of Cadiz, Spain, where she teaches Maritime English to undergraduates and master's students. She has conducted research on needs analysis, Maritime English discourse, academic English and English for research publication purposes. She was editor of the LSP journal *Ibérica* between 2006 and 2014 and is at present book review editor for the journal *ESP Today*.

Sally Burgess is a lecturer in English at the University of La Laguna, Spain. Her main research interests are in cross-cultural rhetoric, the contribution of language professionals to the preparation of research publications, the teaching of writing in the university context and, most recently, the effects of research evaluation policies on Spanish scholars' publishing practices. She has published on all of these topics. Sally was also a member of the Spanish Team for Intercultural Studies on Academic Discourse, based at the University of León and led by Ana Moreno. With Margaret Cargill she organised the first PRISEAL conference in early 2007 and has since that time also been a regular participant in the Mediterranean Editors' and Translators' Meetings. Apart from her interest in academic discourse studies and English for Research Publication Purposes, Sally has also published a number of literary translations in collaboration with the University of La Laguna's Literary Translation Workshop.

Kate Cadman is a senior adjunct lecturer at the University of Adelaide in Australia where she specialises in English for Research Publication Purposes [ERPP], and transcultural research education in the humanities and social sciences. She has conducted international consultancies on the writing of theses and articles for international publication in many Asian countries and Africa. She has continued to review for several international journals including the *Journal of English for Academic Purposes* for which she has been an Editorial Board Member for many years. Among her ERPP research activities is a project entitled *Bridging Transcultural Divides: Asian Languages and Cultures in Global Higher Education*, resulting in a co-edited book (University of Adelaide Press, 2012, with Xianlin Song).

Thuc Anh Cao Xuan is currently a lecturer in the English department of Hanoi University, where she specialises in English communication skill training for first- and second-year students. She was a postgraduate research student in the MTESOL course run jointly by Victoria University, Melbourne, and Hanoi University, Vietnam. Her special research interest is in teaching English language research methods and writing in Asian contexts. She gave a presentation on the autonomy of students in the English classroom at the PRISEAL conference in Coimbra, Portugal in November, 2015.

Margaret Cargill holds an adjunct senior lectureship in the School of Agriculture, Food and Wine at the University of Adelaide and is Principal Consultant at SciWriting — Communicating science effectively in English. She is an applied linguist specialising in the development of research communication skills for scientists who use English either as a first or an additional language, and has over 25 years' experience working with early career researchers and their supervisors. Her current research and teaching interests lie in developing, delivering and evaluating appropriate collaborative pedagogies to enable scientists and language specialists together to assist inexperienced authors in getting their research published in the international refereed literature. She is co-author, with Dr Patrick O'Connor, of *Writing Scientific Research Articles: Strategy and Steps* (Wiley-Blackwell 2009, 2013, www.writeresearch.com.au).

Susan M. DiGiacomo is professor of anthropology at the Universitat Rovira i Virgili, Tarragona, Catalonia, where she teaches graduate courses in medical anthropology and one course in the English department's MA program in professional English-to-Spanish and Spanish-to-English translation. She also holds an appointment as adjunct professor of anthropology at the University of Massachusetts Amherst, USA. In addition to several years working as a biomedical translator, she has published numerous translations (Catalan and Spanish to English, and English to Catalan) in her own field of anthropology over the past 25 years, as well as one literary translation of a short story by the late Catalan writer Montserrat Roig, and articles theorising translation from ethnography. She offers a departmental publication support service for her colleagues and graduate students in the URV anthropology department that includes critical review of manuscripts, author's editing, and translation.

Berry Juliandi is a biologist with special interests in animal structure and development. His current research theme is regulation of neural stem cell differentiation and specification. He is currently head of the Veterinary Stem Cell Laboratory at Bogor Agricultural University [IPB] and chief editor of *HAYATI Journal of Biosciences*.

Isabel K. León Pérez, PhD, tenured lecturer (University of La Laguna, Spain), has done research in applied linguistics: cross-disciplinary/-linguistic discourse analysis, ESP and EMP. She has published in *ASp* (journal of the Groupe d'Etude et de Recherche en Anglais de Spécialité, GERAS), *IBÉRICA* (journal of the European Association of Languages for Specific Purposes), *Revista Canaria de Estudios Ingleses*, and as a co-author with Pedro Martín (2014) in *English for Specific Purposes*. She belongs to the ULL research group on Contrastive Academic Discourse Analysis, and also worked in the Multidisciplinary and Multilingual Research Group on Scientific Discourse Analysis, conducted by Françoise Salager-Meyer (ULA, Venezuela).

Yongyan Li is an associate professor at the Faculty of Education, University of Hong Kong, China, where she teaches in the areas of written discourse, academic writing, qualitative research methodology, and literacy development in school contexts. Her scholarship focuses mainly on English as an Additional Language [EAL] scholars writing for international publication and English as a Second Language [ESL] university students writing and publishing in disciplines. Her recent research projects explore issues related to writing in postgraduate professional development programs, writing from sources, and the teaching of academic writing in varied contexts. She has published in the *Journal of English for Academic Purposes*, *Journal of Second Language Writing*, and *Science and Engineering Ethics*.

John Linnegar has been a writer, copy-editor, proofreader and translator for 35 years, and a trainer of editors and proofreaders since 2000. He specialises in improving academic texts for publication, a pursuit in which he encounters the many linguistic challenges non-native speakers of English experience. He is a co-author of *Text Editing: A Handbook for Students and Practitioners* (UPA, 2012). As a member of the Society of English-language professionals in the Netherlands [SENSE] and the Mediterranean Editors and Translators [MET], as well as of societies in Australia and South Africa, he remains active in education and training — both as a lifelong learner himself and in order to transfer knowledge and skills to new generations of language practitioners. John also teaches English proficiency and academic writing skills at undergraduate and postgraduate levels at the University of Antwerp [UA] in Belgium. His postgraduate research at UA is on the development of a model for learning (self-)editing skills and for evaluating the competence of editors in training or being mentored online.

Pedro Martín is a tenured lecturer in EAP at the University of La Laguna (Spain). His main area of interest is intercultural and cross-disciplinary academic discourse. He has published a number of articles on this issue. He is also the author of the book *The Rhetoric of the Abstract in English and Spanish Scientific Discourse* (2005), and co-editor of the monograph *English as an Additional Language in Research Publication and Communication* (2008). He is currently a team member of a multidisciplinary project (ENEIDA) on the rhetorical strategies used by Spanish scholars when seeking to publish in English-language journals.

Patrick O'Connor is managing director of the consulting company O'Connor NRM and associate professor at the University of Adelaide. Patrick's consulting and research work focuses on the design, creation, implementation and evaluation of markets for ecosystem services. Patrick works on projects aimed at overcoming negative environmental externalities from agricultural production systems and has created markets for the conservation of soil and biodiversity and for carbon sequestration. Patrick also has an interest in applied linguistics and is co-author of the book *Writing Scientific Research Articles: Strategy and Steps*.

Rika Raffiudin is an entomologist specialising in molecular study of insects and the sensing behaviour of social insects such as bees, termites and ants. She uses molecular techniques for rapid detection of several agriculturally important insects and invasive species. She has been teaching, researching and supervising students working on arthropods and insects for 18 years. She is experienced in constructing DNA markers and DNA barcodes for tropical insects and has published several papers in international peer-reviewed journals. Dr Raffiudin has served as Chief Editor for *HAYATI Journal of Biosciences*, indexed in Crossref and EBSCO and currently hosted by Elsevier.

Iman Rusmana is a microbiologist specialising in nitrogen cycling and N_2O emission in tropical estuaries and agricultural systems, and methanotrophic and methanogenic bacteria in rice fields and aquatic ecosystems. He has been working for Bogor Agricultural University [IPB] for over 25 years. Dr Rusmana served as chief editor (2007-13) for *HAYATI Journal of Biosciences* and as review editor of the *Intergovernmental Panel on Climate Change (IPCC): 2013 Supplement to the 2006 IPCC Guidelines for National Greenhouse Gas Inventories: Wetlands*. He is the current head of the department of biology, IPB.

Oliver Shaw is a translator, editor, interpreter and language instructor at the Hospital Universitario Fundación Jiménez Díaz and the healthcare-management firm Quirónsalud. In addition to his work as a practitioner, he is currently pursuing his PhD in applied linguistics at the *Universidad de Zaragoza* in Zaragoza, Spain. Oliver's research explores the phenomenon of international English-medium academic publishing by native-Spanish-speaking researchers in the field of biomedicine. He is based in Madrid, Spain.

Nampiah Sukarno is a mycologist specialising in tropical fungal diversity and the biology of fungal symbionts and their application in food, agriculture, health and the environment. She has been teaching, researching and supervising students working on tropical fungi for over 25 years. She is experienced in exploring tropical filamentous fungi and has published several papers in international refereed journals. She is also a co-author and research member of *Taxonomic and Ecological Studies of Fungi and Actinomycetes in Indonesia* and was rated highly among Indonesian scientists in the Google Scholar Citations public profiles edition January-June 2015.

John M. Swales was appointed visiting professor of linguistics and acting director of the ELI in 1985, positions that were confirmed two years later. Prior to this, he worked at the University of Aston in Birmingham, UK and, before that, at the University of Khartoum. Among his numerous publications are *Genre Analysis: English in Academic and Research Settings* (Cambridge, 1990), *Other Floors, Other Voices: A Textography of a Small University Building* (Erlbaum, 1998) and, with Christine Feak, *Academic Writing for Graduate Students* (U-M Press, 2012). He officially retired in 2007, but continues to work on various projects.

Sabrina Voss is a Canadian freelance translator, editor and educator based in Barcelona, Spain. She works almost exclusively within the university sphere, providing language support to non-native-English-speaking authors seeking journal publication. Many of her clients are researchers in the biomedical field.

shadow of doubt over the OA model and impinges on the reputation of certain journals, particularly those accessed or published exclusively online; young, small or peripheral journals (that is, published by developing or peripheral countries and outside the scope of mainstream publishing houses, as defined by Salager-Meyer, 2015); or those that are not (or not yet) abstracted or indexed in reputable databases and lists. Fear of plagiarism, concerns pertaining to copyright and digital archiving, scepticism about the maintenance of research quality and integrity, fear of the absence of the controls resulting from peer review (hence, poor quality control), or the claim that the very existence of scholarly journals is threatened — these are all reasons that work against the OA model (Salager-Meyer, 2012).

OA journals in the humanities are arguably more likely to be impacted by these factors than are journals in the hard or natural sciences, probably because the latter have a longer tradition in the dissemination of research findings and possess well-established quality benchmarks that are overtly accepted by the academic community — one of them being the impact factor, as discussed in a later section. Moreover, if peripheral, OA journals are faced with additional problems, like the need to strive for improved quality (Salager-Meyer, 2015).

This chapter examines OA emerging journals within the humanities and seeks to identify those features which might boost or threaten their information credibility — thereby posing a challenge to the OA movement itself and today's academic publishing industry. By 'emerging journals', I refer to scholarly journals that are not published by mainstream publishing houses and that lack a demonstrated citation impact but aim at gaining some kind of academic reputation and becoming relevant in a particular scientific field. I begin by providing a more detailed account of the OA model and how journal credibility in the field of the humanities is established and maintained. Next, I describe the work carried out by the Spanish Foundation of Science and Technology in order to arrive at criteria for quality assessment in scientific publishing (Delgado López-Cózar, Ruiz-Pérez & Jiménez-Contreras, 2006), identifying those formal features which have, in Spain at least, come to be considered as mandatory for a quality journal — features now referred to as quality requirements [QRs]. I then go on to explore a collection of OA humanities journals, with the aim of investigating the extent to which such mandatory QRs are met by each individual journal in the collection. I then group and discuss the results with respect to their compliance or non-compliance in terms of the information quality of the journal as a means of scientific communication, the quality of the editorial process, the journal scientific quality, and the quality of dissemination and visibility of the journal. My conclusions are intended to raise awareness of the existence of these QRs for journal assessment; findings may be helpful to both editors and researchers alike. It is hoped that they might provide insights applicable to other contexts where it is seen as desirable to establish similar quality assurance measures.

6

How credible are open access emerging journals?

A situational analysis in the humanities

Ana Bocanegra-Valle

1. Introduction

Open access [OA] scholarly publishing has grown rapidly over the last decade and has succeeded in consolidating its position as a valid vehicle for the publication of journal articles and the dissemination of research findings (Laakso et al., 2011; Salager-Meyer, 2012). At its most basic, OA journal publishing refers to the free and unrestricted online access to full-text articles published in academic journals. Unfortunately, alongside the increase in numbers of OA journals, academic publishing has also seen the emergence of predatory publishers — that is, those 'which publish counterfeit journals to exploit the open-access model in which the author pays' (Beall, 2012, p. 179). These journals not only impact the OA movement and confidence in peer-reviewing (Beall, 2012; Bohannon, 2013; Bartholomew, 2014), but also put the credibility of rigorous research at risk, while fomenting confusion among unsuspecting novices seeking a target journal for their work. OA can claim to offer authors and their research 'vast and measurable new visibility, readership, and impact' (Budapest Open Access Initiative, 2002, n.p.). Clearly, free unlimited access to journals enhances the visibility of an article — thus, raising its impact and increasing citation counts (in some cases by as much as 250%, according to Harnad, 2008). The deleterious influence of predatory practices casts a

III.5. Level E: Presentation

Presentation is perhaps the aspect of a text least considered by author-editors. This is possibly because wordsmiths do not necessarily have a well-honed visual aptitude, but also because most of them do not receive formal education or training in the fundamentals of text or book design. Its explicit inclusion in the CCC Model is therefore important for drawing attention to a critical aspect of effective written communication: how it presents to the reader.

EP13 requires the writer or text editor to assess the quality of a text according to its presentation in print or digitally. Do the layout, font style and size, line spacing and arrangement of the text on the page help the reader make better sense of the writer's message? A knowledge of design, layout and typography (added in the latest edition) is indispensable here.

EP14 seeks to evaluate the consistency of the layout and whether it is in harmony with the text. The design elements must not only convey visual messages consistently but also support the messages being conveyed by the text. There must be congruence or synergy between text and layout that guides or supports the reader.

EP15 was originally confined to an assessment of the spelling and punctuation, regarded as highly visible elements of texts. In the current edition, layout and typography have been added, commensurate with the changes to EP13 and EP14. So visually noticeable, such errors can send out negative impressions of a text as having been carelessly put together. They can also create a negative impression of the content and the author.

III.3. Level C: Structure

EP7: If a written piece is poorly structured, with paragraphs in the wrong sequence or incorrectly constructed, and with subheadings missing or incorrect, it will lack cohesion. The reader will find it difficult to follow the text, and could even be misled by it. The text editor who focuses too intently on errors of grammar, spelling and punctuation could overlook structural errors, leaving the text fundamentally flawed. They therefore have to learn not to overlook structure, by attending to this aspect before wording and presentation.

EP8: Once a writer decides upon a certain structure, they should maintain it consistently throughout a document, otherwise the text as a whole will not make complete sense to a reader. For instance, if every chapter is supposed to open with 'Introduction' and end with 'Summary', omitting either of these features or labelling them differently in some chapters will confuse the reader. Similar confusion could reign if the reader is confronted with a mixture of thematic and chronological structuring. The text editor's role here is to identify structural inconsistencies and convince the writer to remedy them.

EP9 helps writer-editors to consider the effectiveness of the linkages used to help the readers follow the narrative or argumentation. Because the authors of *Text Editing* consider linking words to be only a part of the bigger picture of an author's argumentation, the latest edition of the CCC Model labels EP9 'Argumentation (linking)' rather than Renkema's 'Linking words'.

III.4. Level D: Wording

EP10 forces the editor to examine the writer's use of wording: Is it appropriate to the readers, the medium and the intention in writing the piece? Using wording that is unfamiliar to readers (jargon, in particular) without explaining its particular usage in context will not help the readers to fulfil their needs or expectations in reading the text. The text editor can ensure that such words are either contextualised or explained carefully.

EP11 considers the consistent use of words — their meaning and their spelling, capitalisation, hyphenation or closed or open forms. When the writer does not use words precisely and consistently to convey the same meaning, or fails to apply house style consistently, the text editor should step in.

EP12: Originally, Renkema asked whether the author's syntax and word choice were correct. In the new edition, the focus is on the preciseness of the meaning being conveyed through correct grammar, vocabulary and sentence construction.

Appendix III

The Text Facets or levels and evaluation points [EPs] of the CCC Model

Renkema has claimed that 98% of all possible comments about texts can be reduced to 15 EPs (1999a, p. 2). The EPs are described below. (Refer to Table 5.1.)

III.1. Level A: Text type

EP1 requires the writer or the text editor to respond to the question: Is this text, as a whole, appropriate to its readers and the medium? If, fundamentally, it does not meet the needs or expectations of its intended readers, then it will fail on this criterion alone (Renkema 2002, p. 180). Similarly, if it is not suited to the identified medium (for instance, an academic journal, a website), then it will not succeed either. For example, an academic text must have an appropriate degree of formality, a structure and suitable word usage; text intended for a website should comprise short sentences and paragraphs, bulleted items, many subheadings. In Table 5.1, the original 'Appropriateness', regarded as too vague a label for this EP, has been replaced with the English wording 'Appropriate text'.

EP2 evaluates a text in terms of the genre it is written in: Does it adhere consistently to the characteristics of fiction writing as opposed to those of an academic textbook, for instance?

EP3: There are certain rules of composition that pertain to each genre; does the text adhere to them? If not, the text is not of an acceptable quality. In this instance, all the text editor can do is to refer the problem to the author for revision.

III.2. Level B: Content

In line with the English edition of the CCC Model, EP4 requires the practitioner to evaluate whether the content of a text is sufficient and/or adequate or appropriate: Has the writer supplied enough information on the topic? Is the information in itself adequate or appropriate? Again, the text editor should point out such weaknesses to the author.

EP5 has to do with whether the content the author has provided is consistent, whether it concurs, and whether it is not contradictory: for example, spellings of names may vary; key dates may be at odds in different places of the text. The author-editor is expected to correct these, otherwise the reader may not regard either the author or their book as credible.

EP6: The correctness of the information provided by the writer is critically important: dates, names, measures and other facts should be correct, otherwise the text will not pass muster. The text editor should be alert to such errors and either correct or query them.

the Gulf Wars. New in the construction of identity in the new media is the West's

Comment [jd73]: EP6, 10 Gulf War.

view of the Arabic media, the exact opposite of the oriental's idea of Edward Said

Comment [jd74]: EP10, 11 Arab media'
Comment [jd75]: EP12 Word choice appropriate? Meaning? EP12 Is this Said's idea of the oriental or the oriental's of Said? Unclear.
Comment [jd76]: EP12 The reader needs to know what this 'idea' was to understand 'the exact opposite'.

(*Orientalism*, 1969). Due to all these contradictory and polemical phenomena there

Comment [jd77]: EP3, 11 Incorrect and inconsistent form of citation for this genre.
Comment [jd78]: EP4, 6 Incorrect date (should be 1973).
Comment [jd79]: EP13 Should read "Owing to ..."
Comment [jd80]: EP12 Ambiguous referent. To what does 'these' refer?
Comment [jd81]: EP10, 12 Correct word choice? Meaning?
Comment [jd82]: EP10, 12 Correct word choice? Meaning?

has been important changes: on the one hand, from an elitist public sphere based on

Comment [jd83]: EP12 Incorrect verb form ("have" is correct).
Comment [jd84]: EP12 Passive voice could be improved by conversion to active voice.
Comment [jd85]: EP9, 12 'he change from'
Comment [jd86]: EP10, 12 'elite'?
Comment [jd87]: EP10, 12 Delete 'sphere'?

press readership and reduced to this lobby which is the most educated and

Comment [jd88]: EP10, 12 'who read the press avidly'?
Comment [jd89]: EP10, 12 Unclear what is intended with this phrase. Could it be deleted? What is 'his lobby'?

Occidentalized social group to a new public sphere transformed through TV and, on

Comment [jd90]: EP10, 12 'westernised'?
EP15 UK or US spelling
Comment [jd91]: EP10, 12 Delete 'sphere'?
Comment [jd92]: EP7, 9, 12 Sentence too long and convoluted. Split here, delete the conjunction 'and' and restart sentence at "On the other hand."

another hand, the Occidentalized elite was diminished and the effects were really

Comment [jd93]: EP10, 12 Should read 'the other'
Comment [jd94]: EP10, 12 'westernised'?
EP15 UK or US spelling
Comment [jd95]: EP10, 12 'elitist'? (see comment re 'elitist' above).
Comment [jd96]: EP10, 12 Word choice appropriate?

difficult to calculate. For instance, opinion polls were often wrong, as occidental

Comment [jd97]: EP7, 9, 15 To what does this assertion relate? The effects of what? Vague and ambiguous.
Comment [jd98]: EP7, 9 There is an error of logic between these two sentences.
Comment [jd99]: EP10, 12 "Western"?

means of measuring voting intentions did not work in Arabic society.

Comment [jd100]: EP10, 11, 12 'Arab society'?
Comment [jd101]: EP1, 3, 4, 7, 9 Author, is this is the end of your introduction, it does not end effectively. The final sentence seems to be a digression from the topic, where a more effective concluding statement that refers back to your opening statement and then goes on to introduce your article as a whole (or the main thrust of your thesis or argumentation).

important consequences of this change are the emergence of: Tabloid press in the

Comment [jd43]: EP12, l2 Is this the correct word? "effects"?
Comment [jd44]: EP13 Delete colon; lowercase "T"
Comment [jd45]: EP1, 12 What do you mean by "tabloid press"?

Anglo-Saxon area, new audiovisual media, lead by Al Jazerra, other channels and

Comment [jd46]: EP10, 12 Why is this term used? What is the "Anglo-Saxon area"?
Comment [jd47]: EP10, 12, 15 Incorrect usage; should be simple past tense for "led"
Comment [jd48]: EP13 Misspelling of Al Jazeera.
Comment [jd49]: EP9, 12 "Al Jazeera and other channels"?

the Internet, which is arguably an unregulated universe. There have also been

Comment [jd50]: EP4, 12 Is this opinion even relevant here?
Comment [jd51]: EP1, 12 Unclear what the three consequences are because the sentence is poorly constructed.
Comment [jd52]: EP7, 9 Use the linking words: "first", "second", "third" to make it clear what the three are.

changes in media content: a vastly increased flow of informations; an increase in

Comment [jd53]: EP10, 15 Incorrect plural form of a mass abstract noun.

TV serial fiction; new modes of reflection (debates) and audience's participation

Comment [jd54]: EP10, 12 "expression" or "expressions and reflection"?
Comment [jd55]: EP10, 12 "for example, debates" OR "in the form of debates"
Comment [jd56]: EP10, 15 Should be "audience participation".

(audience studies and direct or non-direct participation); the use of humour and

Comment [jd57]: EP10, 12 Do you mean "indirect", or simply not direct? What is either of these?
Comment [jd58]: EP11, 15 Unclear what is meant by this.
Comment [jd59]: EP11 US or UK spelling?

satire via the Internet; the SMS communication; and the new audiovisual media.

Comment [jd60]: EP10, 12 How do these differ? Do you define them?
Comment [jd61]: EP10 Delete - incorrect use of definite article here.
Comment [jd62]: EP15 Preferably a comma here.

Some identity problems have derived from this situation: The Eastern World

Comment [jd63]: EP13, 14 Correct paragraphing style?
Comment [jd64]: EP10, 12 Either "have arisen" or "are derived".
Comment [jd65]: EP15 "the" - lowercase letter after a colon. Or "The." after a full stop!

view is reconstructed in an aggressive way, especially after 9/11 (ELLIOT, 2003),

Comment [jd66]: EP10, 15 "worldview".
Comment [jd67]: EP10 Word choice: "reconstituted"?
Comment [jd68]: EP9, 12 Meaning unclear here: Do the Western view Of the East or the view BY the East of the West?
Comment [jd69]: EP9, 11, 15 "Elliot".
Comment [jd70]: EP11 Tenses a problem here. Either "has been reconstructed — since 9/11" or "was reconstructed — after 9/11".

and the West is being also reconstructed in the Arabic world through war images of

Comment [jd71]: EP10, 12 See common above.
Comment [jd72]: EP10, 11 Arab world?

they representing not only a formal modification in practices but an integral

Comment [jd21]: EP12 Syntax problem; should be "they are".
Comment [jd22]: EP12 Should the verb form not be "represent" (how they represent)?
Comment [jd23]: EP10, 12 "change in" or "modification of"?

permutation of the content which is thus modified and how they present new

Comment [jd24]: EP10, 9 Word choice?
Comment [jd25]: EP12 Archaism or inappropriate usage in media studies?

themes. There have been several important changes to the Arabic and Islamic

Comment [jd26]: EP12 Lack of parallel construction.
Comment [jd27]: EP12 Syntax/voice: rephrase as "Several important changes have been introduced into".
Comment [jd28]: EP10, 12 The distinction between these two terms should be explained somewhere.

media, press and audiovisual, during recent years.

Comment [jd29]: EP10, 12 Insert "both" before "press"?
Comment [jd30]: EP7, 9 This sentence is misplaced. It should be the topic sentence of this introductory paragraph. It should also be followed by a supportive sentence that links it to the sentence commencing "This paper explores ...". Consider following it with "The changes that we are studying in this paper ..."

Public Opinion has been transformed through changes to the media system

Comment [jd31]: EP7, 8 ,9 Reposition this paragraph elsewhere?
Comment [jd32]: EP11, 15 Why treated as a proper noun? Lowercase the "o".
Comment [jd33]: EP10 Delete "system"? Or replace with "setup"?

arising from the death of the old colonial or postcolonial system with a reduced

Comment [jd34]: EP10 "demise"?
Comment [jd35]: EP15 Insert comma after "system" EP10, 12 Meaning unclear; explain what the terms "colonial" and "postcolonial" refer to.
Comment [jd36]: EP10, 12 Is "reduced" the correct word? Diminished? Smaller?

elite and the use of the Western World languages such as English or French as the

Comment [jd37]: EP15 Lowercase "world"? Delete altogether?
Comment [jd38]: EP7, 10, 12 "and"?

languages of power.

The changes that we are studying in this paper come from new Satellite

Comment [jd39]: EP13, 14 Correct paragraphing style?
Comment [jd40]: EP10 Article?
Comment [jd41]: EP11, 15 Lowercase "s".

channels which introduce globalization in an old National system. The three most

Comment [jd42]: EP11, 15 US or UK spelling?

Appendix II

The 'Arab Media' passage with EPs (evaluation points) identified

Introduction

> **Comment [jd1]:** EP1, 3, 7 This text does not follow the structure of a typical introduction to an academic paper. It is surely an abstract?

This paper explores the hypothesis that is not possible to adopt a new more formal

> **Comment [jd2]:** EP12 The word "it" is missing; this affects the meaning and syntax of this sentence
>
> **Comment [jd3]:** EP15 A comma should separate two qualitative adjectives.

model of communication without changing the contents of the communication

itself. The practices implicated to a change of media modulate new uses and new

> **Comment [jd4]:** EP10, 12 Incorrect word choice affecting meaning.
>
> **Comment [jd5]:** EP10, 12 Incorrect word choice affecting meaning.
>
> **Comment [jd6]:** EP10 Necessary to repeat "new"?

models of thinking in the societies where they are based. The TV channnel Al

> **Comment [jd7]:** EP9 Link between ideas/sentences missing. Insert "For instance," at the start of this sentence.
>
> **Comment [jd8]:** EP15 Misspelling of "channel". Insert comma after "channel" for noun appositional construction.
>
> **Comment [jd9]:** EP7 Structure: This sentence should support the next topic sentence and therefore follow it. Otherwise it should be moved to the third paragraph to illustrate the changes taking place in the Arab media.

Jazerra, not only is creating a new public sphere, but also is shaping and leading the

> **Comment [jd10]:** EP15 Misspelt. Should be Al Jazeera.
>
> **Comment [jd11]:** EP12 Syntax problem: transpose "not only is".
>
> **Comment [jd12]:** EP12 Syntax problem: transpose "also is".

changes in the narative strategy of the news, introducing themes, provoking

> **Comment [jd13]:** EP15 Misspelling of "narrative".
>
> **Comment [jd14]:** EP3, 4, 10, 12 What does this mean? Clarify to your reader.

debates, working on the language of the public sphere and introducing new

> **Comment [jd15]:** EP3, 4, 10, 12 What is meant by "public sphere" and "private sphere"?

relationships with the private sphere (EL-NAWAWY, 2002). Our aim is to analyze

> **Comment [jd16]:** EP3 Non-adherence to genre (intext referencing). EP1 Inconsistent referencing style.
>
> **Comment [jd17]:** EP7, 9 Start new paragraph here? And follow with "The changes that we are studying ..."?
>
> **Comment [jd18]:** EP3, 10 If a single author, use "I".
>
> **Comment [jd19]:** EP15 Should this be UK or US spelling style?

Université catholique de Louvain Graduate School of Management Research Institute. (2011). DSM Doctoral Programme. Retrieved 9 May 2016 from https://www.uclouvain.be/en-349675.html.

University College Dublin. (2015). Education theory: Constructivism and social constructivism. Retrieved 30 November 2015 from http://www.ucdoer.ie/index.php/Education_Theory/Constructivism_and_Social_Constructivism.

Van de Poel, K., Carstens, W.A.M., & Linnegar, J. (2012). *Text editing: A handbook for students and practitioners*. Brussels: University Press Antwerp.

Wadee, A., Keane, M., Dietz, T., & Hay, D. (n.d.). Effective PhD supervision — Mentorship and coaching. *Rozenberg Quarterly: The Magazine*. Retrieved 12 May 2016 from http://rozenbergquarterly.com/effective-phd-supervision-mentorship-and-coaching-2.

Appendix I

The 'Estuary Villa' passage

The Villa is situated in very secure surroundings on a Country Estate, a short stroll to the beach. All three bedrooms are en-suite with a shower and a toilet. The kitchen is fully equipped with a glasstop stove, oven, microwave, fridge/freezer, dishwasher, kettle, toaster, pots, pans and cooking utensils. Cutlery, crockery and glassware are provided for 6 guests. The bedrooms are fully equipped with sheets, blankets, duvets and pillows. Please bring your own towels. There is a TV with a DSTV decoder, please bring your own smart card. Braai facilities are situated outside the villa. Strictly no pets allowed. No Smoking.

Port Edward and the surrounding district have a large variety of activities that cater to all tastes and requirements. The close proximity to the Wild Coast Sun Country Club (10 minutes) and San Lameer Country Club (15 minutes), keeps the pros and amateurs out of mischief. Port Edward also has a nine-hole golf course that is a great way to relax.

There is a game reserve Lake Eland (35 minutes) and the Umtamvuna Nature Reserve offers a variety of trails for outdoor enthusiasts and those keen to get fit . The flora and fauna in this reserve is outstanding and the scenery is spectacular. There is horse riding in the vicinity and a huge variety of adventure activities ranging from 4x4 trails to the highest abseil in the country.

There is on-site parking for 2 cars. A full or part-time maid service and laundry arrangements can be made sheets and towels are changed twice a week for longerstaying guests. Culinary afficonados and nightclub-'jollers' are also catered for with a large variety of restaurants and eateries. The Wild Coast Casino (5 minutes) also offers something for the young and old, big and bold!

Port Edward has all the necessary daily shopping facilities with two large supermarkets, bottle stores, garages, a post office and a variety of other shops and restaurants.

In V. Damoiseaux, & B. Van Ruler (Eds.), *Effectiviteit in het communicatiemanagement* (pp. 39-54). Deventer: Samson.

Renkema, J. (1998b). De C3-analyse. *Tekst[blad]*, *4*, 29-31.

Renkema, J. (1999a). Een raamwerk voor tekstdiagnose: Het CCC-model (Deel 1). *Ad Rem: Tijdskrif voor Zakelijke Communicatie*, *13*(4), 1-5.

Renkema, J. (1999b). Een raamwerk voor tekstdiagnose: Het CCC-model (Deel 2). *Ad Rem: Tijdskrif voor Zakelijke Communicatie*, *13*(5), 1-5.

Renkema, J. (2000). Pretesten testen. De CCC-analyse en de beperkte plus-en-minmethode vergeleken. In R. Neutelings, N. Ummelen, & A. Maes (Eds.), *Over de grenzen van de taalbeheersing: Onderzoek nar taal, tekst en communicatie gepresenteerd op het achste VIOT-congres aan de TU-Delft* (pp. 371-380). Den Haag: SDU.

Renkema, J. (2001). Undercover research into text quality as a tool for communication management: The case of the Dutch tax department. In D. Janssen, & R. Neutelings (Eds.), *Reading and writing public documents* (pp. 37-57). Amsterdam: John Benjamins.

Renkema, J. (2002). Over smaak valt goed te twisten: Een evaluatiemodel voor tekstkwaliteit. In F. van Eemeren, P. van den Hoven, C. Jansen, & .P.J. Schellens (Eds.), *Tussenstand: 25 jaar Tijdschrift voor Taalbeheersing* (pp. 177-190). Assen, Netherlands: Van Gorcum.

Renkema, J. (2012). Tekstkwaliteit scoort: Het CCC-model als hulpmiddel bij het beoordelen van (onderwijs)teksten. In E. Mijts (Ed.), *Seminar Publicaties Universiteit van Aruba* (pp. 9-21). Oranjestad: Aruba.

Renkema, J., & Cleutjens, B.I. (1997). Van herformuleren naar beschrijven: Een modelmatige aanpak voor het verbeteren van teksten. In P. Schellens, O. Scholten, D. Vloeberghs, & C. van Woerkum (Ed.), *Jaarboek Onderzoek Communicatiemanagement* (pp. 103-118). Houten: Bohn Stafleu Van Loghem.

Renkema, J., & Kloet, L. (2000). De toestand van een tekst: Een diagnose volgens het CCC-model. *Management & Communicatie*, dossier, *6*, 25-36.

Renkema, J., Sanders, T., Sanders, J., & Van Wijk, C. (1994). Praktykondersoek naar tekstkwaliteit: Een standaardvoorbeeld. *Communicatief*, *7*(4), 13-22.

Renkema, J., & Schellens, P. (1996). Tekstevaluatie, oftewel het raadsel van de Bosch-kabouter. *Tijdschijft voor Taalbeheersing*, *18*, 305-309.

Schellens, P.J., & Steehouder, M. (Eds.). (2008). *Tekstanalyse: Methoden en toepassingen*. Assen: Van Gorcum.

Sherry, L. (1996). Issues in distance learning. *International Journal of Educational Communications*, *1*(4), 337-365.

Society for Editors and Proofreaders [SfEP]. (2014). *Editing theses*. London: SfEP.

Society for English-language Professionals in the Netherlands [SENSE] UniSIG. (2016). Guidelines for proofreading of student texts: Definitions and proofreader tasks. Retrieved 22 February 2017 from https://www.sense-online.nl/editing-guidelines.

Sonesson, A., & Karlsson, L. (2010, April 13-15). A study program for doctoral supervisors — A vehicle for development. Paper presented at the *9th Quality in Postgraduate Research Conference: Education Researchers for the 21st Century, Adelaide*, South Australia. Retrieved 15 May 2016 from http://lup.lub.lu.se/luur/download?func=downloadFile&recordOId=4437869&fileOId=4437870.

Taylor, S., & Beasley, N. (2005). *A handbook for doctoral supervisors*. London & New York: Routledge.

2016 from http://www.fu-berlin.de/en/sites/promovieren/drs/resources/Guidelines_Doctoral_Supervision.pdf.

Great Schools Partnership. (2013). Blended learning. *The glossary of educational reform*. Retrieved 1 December 2015 from http://edglossary.org/blended-learning.

Hvistendahl, M. (2015, November 20). China pursues fraudsters in science publishing. *Science*. Retrieved 8 May 2016 from http://www.sciencemag.org/news/2015/11/china-pursues-fraudsters-science-publishing.

Institute for Higher Education Policy [IHEP]. (2000). *Quality on the line: Benchmarks for success in internet-based distance education*. Washington, DC: IHEP. Retrieved 7 January 2015 from http://www.ihep.org/sites/default/files/uploads/docs/pubs/qualityontheline.pdf.

Institute of Professional Editors Ltd [IPEd]. (2014). Editing research theses. Retrieved 5 November 2014 from http://iped-editors.org/About_editing/Editing_theses.aspx.

Knowles, M.S. (1970). *The modern practice of adult education: Andragogy versus pedagogy*. New York: Associated Press.

Knowles, M.S. (1975). *Self-directed learning: A guide for learners and teachers*. Englewood Cliffs: Prentice Hall/Cambridge.

Knowles, M.S. (1984). *Andragogy in action*. San Francisco: Jossey-Bass.

Knowles, M.S., Holton, E., & Swanson, R. (2005). *The adult learner: The definitive classic in adult education and human resource development*. Oxford: Butterworth-Heinemann.

Learning Theories. (2015). Constructivism. Retrieved 30 November 2015 from http://www.learning-theories.com/constructivism.html.

Lieb, S. (1991). Principles of adult learning. *Vision* — South Mountain Community College, Phoenix, AZ. Retrieved 1 March 2017 from https://docs.google.com/document/d/1IXTZcjv_2VzAzmuLSrSP6LDBzSc_EMwO1vO9yW1jCtU/edit#.

Mackenzie, J. (2011). *The editor's companion*. Port Melbourne: Cambridge University Press.

Manning Murphy, E. (2012). *Working words*. Canberra: Canberra Society of Editors.

Martinez, A.S. (2016, January 20-21). The doctoral candidate's perspective on 'engaging and training supervisors'. Paper presented at the *9th EUA-CDE Workshop: Doctoral supervision — practices and responsibilities*, Delft University of Technology, Netherlands. Retrieved 11 May 2016 from http://www.eua.be/Libraries/default-document-library/thursday-21_plenary-session-iii_alexandra-samper-martinezc3c465ca84b96a879ce5ff00009465c7.pdf?sfvrsn=0.

Max Planck Society. (n.d.). Guidelines for doctoral training at Max Planck Institutes. Retrieved 13 May 2016 from https://www.mpg.de/guidelines_doctoral_training.

McGillivray Linnegar Associates. (2013). *Copy editing and proofreading for academic purposes: A short, skills-based training course*. Cape Town: McGillivray Linnegar Associates.

Mossop, B. (2010). *Revising and editing for translators*. Manchester: St. Jerome Publishing.

Nystrand, M. (1986). *The structure of written communication: Studies in reciprocity between writers and readers*. Orlando, FL: Academic Press.

Pinta, E., Hytönen, K., Mäkinen, J., & Vuorio-Lehti, M. (2015). Training programme for doctoral thesis supervisors in University of Turku. Presentation for the University of Turku, Finland. Retrieved 10 May 2016 from http://www.eua.be/Libraries/default-document-library/1-paper-session-i-a-pinta-elise_new.pdf?sfvrsn=0.

Renkema, J. (1994). Het beoordelen van tekstkwaliteit. *Onze Taal*, *63*, 82-84.

Renkema, J. (1998a). Correspondentie, consistentie en correctheid in schriftelijke communicatie.

for the student learning text-analysis and text-editing skills, it should be applicable also to the mentoring of text editors in the craft of improving texts — a further use that should form the subject of a separate study.

References

Bach, S., Haynes P., & Lewis-Smith, J. (2007). *Online learning and teaching in higher education.* London: Open University Press.

Bandura, A. (1977). Self-efficacy: Toward a unifying theory of behavioural change. *Psychological Review, 84*(2), 191-215.

Bandura, A. (1982). Self-efficacy mechanism in human agency. *American Psychologist, 37*(2), 122-147.

Brabazon, T. (2010, September 22). How to get students through their PhD thesis. *Times Higher Education.* Retrieved 12 May 2016 from https://www.timeshighereducation.com/news/tara-brabazon-just-what-the-doctorate-ordered/413566.article.

Brabazon, T. (2013, July 11). 10 truths a PhD supervisor will never tell you. *Times Higher Education.* Retrieved 10 May 2016 from https://www.timeshighereducation.com/features/10-truths-a-phd-supervisor-will-never-tell-you/2005513.article.

Brown, A., & Thompson, H. (1997). Course design for the WWW: Keeping online students onside. In R. Kevill, R. Oliver, & R. Phillips (Eds.), *14th annual conference proceedings for the Australian Society for Computers in Tertiary Education: What works and why?* (pp. 74-81). Perth: Curtin University of Technology.

Cadman, K., & Cargill, M. (2007). Providing quality advice on candidates' writing. In C. Denholm, & T. Evans (Eds.), *Supervising doctorates down under: Keys to effective supervision in Australia and New Zealand.* Camberwell, Victoria: Acer Press.

Carstens, W.A.M., & Van de Poel, K. (2010). *Teksredaksie.* Stellenbosch: SUNMedia.

Clayton Christensen Institute for Disruptive Learning [CCIDL]. (2015). Blended learning definitions. *Christensen Institute.* Retrieved 15 October 2015 from http://www.christenseninstitute.org/blended-learning-definitions-and-models.

Daniëls, W. (2011). *Teksten redigeren.* Houten: Prisma.

Editors' Association of Canada. (2014). Toronto branch mentorship program (including Application form for mentees and Mentor information sheet). Retrieved 16 July 2014 from http://www.editors.ca/branches/toronto/mentoring_program.html.

Ellis, K. (2000). A model class. *Training, 37*(12), 50-57.

European University Association [EUA]. (2006). *EUA-BFUG doctoral programmes follow-up project report from the workshop on 23-24 March 2006, Brussels.* Brussels: EUA. Retrieved 10 May 2016 from http://www.eua.be/eua/jsp/en/upload/report_on_EUAtemplate.1158143779501.pdf.

Fidishun, D. (2000, April 9-11). Andragogy and technology: Integrating adult learning theory as we teach with technology. Paper presented at the *5th Annual Instructional Technology Conference,* Middle Tennessee State University, USA. Retrieved 20 February 2017 from http://pdfsr.com/pdf/andragogy-and-technology-integrating-adult-learning-theory-as-we-teach-with-technology.

Freie Universität Berlin. (2014). *Guidelines for good doctoral supervision.* Retrieved 13 May the students became increasingly familiar with through repeated use. By redefining text analysis or improvement as error detection and breaking errors down into 15 labelled criteria, the model has made the process of improving texts more tangible, focused and systematic. This fostered a constructivist, problem-based and practical approach to acquiring specialist knowledge and skills through 'mastery experiences' (Bandura, 1977) by using an empowering rubric.

Importantly, the model also served to eliminate vague, ad hoc and subjective diagnoses when evaluating students' ability to detect errors and improve a text: the EPs provide precise and comprehensive data and a 'common language' for critiquing and improving texts (Renkema, 1998a, p. 40). The model also made the analysis of text-editing skills and the monitoring and assessment of proficiency considerably more systematic. This is borne out by the findings from iterations AM1 to AM3, corroborated by EVF to EVM. Moreover, all of Renkema's stated purposes were successfully fulfilled in teaching (self-)editing skills to postgraduate students through familiarising them with and applying the CCC Model.

The model is not without its limitations, however. First, its first-time users have to be inducted into the meaning and use of the EP labels to ensure that they fully understand the kinds of error they refer to, and then apply them correctly. When, for example, should information be classified as not 'appropriate and sufficient' (EP4), as opposed to factually incorrect (EP6)? Is 'congruence of facts' (EP5) as a particular class of error obvious at first reading? And if characters in a text have not been italicised or bolded as they should have, which EP does one allocate to this error type, EP13 or EP15? Similarly, the use of upper-case initial letters when sentence case should have been used also has, at face value, no EP clearly allocated to it (is it a problem of a lack of correspondence to the medium, inconsistency or incorrectness?). Furthermore, where does 'appropriate wording' (EP10) end and 'meaning' (EP12) begin, or are they simply two sides of the same coin? (In my view, they often are very close yet different, an inappropriately chosen word usually not conveying the author's intended meaning.) And it is not obvious where 'grammar' errors are located in the model: EP12? Further elucidation of the precise meanings and intentions of some of the EPs, and their refinement, is therefore necessary. Such refinement will form the basis of my future analysis of the students' interpretation of the EPs in this and other case studies as well as further discussion with the CCC Model's creator. Nevertheless, the data derived from this 2015 study provide strong support for the assertion that the model is an effective tool for (self-)improving texts — whether it is by student writers, authors, text editors or doctoral supervisors — and assessing improvements systematically.

Based on the present case study tracking students' progress, the CCC Model has proved to be a systematic way of guiding, enabling and assessing the development of learners' proficiency. It has done so both as a self-assessment rubric and as a tool with which teachers can monitor and assess learners' progress. Since the model lends itself to a systematic pedagogical approach and a learning path that leads to positive outcomes for these groups, where the total of all Correspondence and Consistency errors was 702; combined EP12+EP15 errors totalled 489. This indicates that in fact a much wider range of errors was detected in May than in February and also that the students were detecting errors at higher levels of the CCC Model. The increase in the detection rate of the less common and less obvious Correspondence and Consistency errors is more than threefold (220.6%), most likely as a direct outcome of new knowledge having been acquired about them between EVF and EVM. This is in contrast to the much more modest increase in combined EP12+EP15 errors (8.4%), which started from a higher base. This is largely attributable to a decline in the number of EP15 errors detected (from 171 to 113), possibly as a result of a greater focus on other error types (an intended trend that the CCC Model attempts to encourage).

So far as the 'Arab media' text is concerned, the total Correspondence and Consistency errors almost doubled (113.2%) between AM1 (250) and AM3 (533). While this is certainly a substantially more modest increase than between EVF and EVM, it is indicative of a similar trend between the February and May iterations: the spread of the errors detected into these EPs as a result of the acquisition of editing knowledge and skills and sharpened awareness.

Regarding changes in the number of Correctness errors (EP3, 6, 9) detected between February and May, a comparison of the data from the two texts indicates some congruence: whereas the scores in question rose from 50 to 79 (58.0%) in 'Estuary Villa', they rose from 138 to 246 (78.3%) in 'Arab media'. Both increases were significant.

6. Conclusions

By all the measures used, the students' performance in the two assignments would seem to indicate that this group of student editors-in-training were capable of both increasing their overall rate of error detection and of identifying a wider range of the errors included in the rubric as a result of the training they received and a raised awareness. In other words, given a systematic rubric to enable them to identify errors in a text (supported by relevant in-class teaching), they were capable of improving their (self-)editing skills.

What is evident through this case study involving the use of a largely non-didactic blended-learning approach to teaching as a strategy for improving the writing skills of a group of 30 master's students is this: through a combination of learning approaches effective, measurable learning did take place. Through these approaches, the students constructed their own understanding and knowledge actively, not passively, through experiencing errors in poorly written texts, using a rubric to label them and reflecting on those experiences. Generating knowledge and meaning themselves and reflecting on their experiences therefore constituted an integral part of the course (Learning Theories, 2015).

Whether used for guidance, self-assessment or evaluation by the teacher, the CCC Model, its hierarchy of Text Facets and its EPs formed the basis of the course, a rubric media' assignment. I start with a comparison of the total errors detected in the two assignments (see Table 5.7). In 'Estuary Villa', the initial total errors detected was 820 (in EVF) versus 1270 in EVM, an overall increase of 54.9%. In 'Arab media', between AM1 (965) and AM3 (1764) the overall increase was 82.8%.

I next wanted to ascertain whether there had been a concomitant increase in the spread of the types of error detected, both into the EPs in the Correspondence and Consistency columns and also extending up the Correctness column. I also wanted to know whether in this respect there was concordance between the outcomes of the two assignments. These overall trends are presented in Table 5.7.

'Estuary Villa'				'Arab media'		
EVF totals	EVM totals	% increase		AM1 totals	AM3 totals	% increase
820	1270	54.9		965	1764	82.8
EVF EP12+EP15	EVM EP12+EP15			AM1 EP12+EP15	AM3 EP12+EP15	
451	489	8.4		577	985	70.7
EVF EP3+6+9	EVM EP3+6+9			AM1 EP3+6+9	AM3 EP3+6+9	
50	79	58.0		138	246	78.3
EVF Corres+ Consis	EVM Corres+ Consis			AM1 vs AM3 Corres+ Consis	AM1+AM3 Corres+ Consis	
219	702	220.6		250	533	113.2

Table 5.7: Trends in error-detection rate and spread of errors in 'Estuary Villa' and 'Arab media' compared.

Two possible reasons for the generally higher rates of error detection in the 'Arab media' text versus the 'Estuary Villa' passage are, first, that with a total of 103 possible errors to detect 'Arab media' provided greater scope for increased error detection than 'Estuary Villa' (with 73 possible errors to detect); second, that there was a more direct link between the content taught and each attempt at error detection.

In the 'Estuary Villa' assignment, a distinct spread in the kind of errors away from EP12 and EP15 was detected. First, in EVF the total of all Correspondence and Consistency errors combined (EP1, 2, 4, 5, 7, 8, 13, 14) in the first iteration was 219 as opposed to the 451 combined EP12+EP15 errors. This is in contrast to the EVM scores

What is evident from this tabulation of the increases in error detection for the three types of criteria is that they were in all instances greater for Correspondence and Consistency than for Correctness. It is highly probable that these increases were associated with both theoretical input and practical work on each of the Text Facets plus the support of the CCC Model.

An interesting development at this juncture is that at least some students must have reflected upon and reconsidered their previous decisions (or lack of a decision) regarding Text Type (EP3) and Content (EP6), the scores for which appear to be evidence of further errors having been detected in these criterion. EP3 increased from 78 to 96 between AM2 and AM3 (23.1%), effectively increasing the detections in AM1 threefold. From a base of 6 in AM1, through 12 in AM2, the detections of EP6 rose to 19 (58.3% increase between AM2 and AM3, a 216.7% increase between AM1 and AM3). EP6 in AM3 is now more than threefold the first score. Such reflection and reconsideration are characteristic of self-directed or autonomous learning in the sense Knowles intends it to be understood (1975; Knowles, Holton & Swanson, 2005).

The trends in the Correctness errors detected are discussed next and summarised in Table 5.6.

Between ...	EP3+EP6+EP9		EP12+EP15	
	Errors detected	% increase	Errors detected	% increase
AM1 & AM2	138-207	50.0	577-897	55.5
AM2 & AM3	207-246	18.8	897-985	9.8
AM1 & AM3	138-246	78.3	577-985	70.7

Table 5.6: Trends in error detection between Correctness errors EP3+EP6+EP9 and EP12+EP15 compared.

Notably, at first the increases in the errors detected in these two groupings of errors were almost equal (50%; 55.5%), but between AM2 and AM3 (18.8%; 9.8%) and AM1 and AM3 (78.3%; 70.7%) the EP3+EP6+EP9 errors detected increased by more than their equivalents for EP12+EP15. These increases suggest that the learning process had borne fruit by increasing both the knowledge and the skills of the students and also raising their awareness of the kinds of error a text editor should detect.

5.3. Comparison of the error-detection rates and ranges between 'Estuary Villa' and 'Arab media'

There are some instructive concordances between the error-detection scores in the two exercises that serve to validate the findings and conclusions drawn concerning the 'Arab was therefore interested in discovering whether the data drawn from AM3 reflected their acquisition of this new knowledge.

Overall, the total errors detected showed an increase of 82.8% between AM1 (965) and AM3 (1764) (see Table 5.4). This trend occurred before the group presentations on Presentation (print and digital). The EP12 and EP15 errors detected in AM3 continued the trend between AM1 and AM2, although at a slower rate: EP12 increased from a base of 455 through 657 to 710 (8.1% from AM2 to AM3, an overall increase from AM1 to AM3 of 56.0%); EP15 increased from a base of 122 through 240 to 275 (14.6% from AM2 to AM3; an overall increase from AM1 to AM3 of 125.4%). These findings would seem to support the outcome of the students' 'mastery experiences' resulting from the successful performance of tasks (Bandura, 1977, p. 192).

At this stage in the course, some significant increases in error-detection rates are also evident under Correspondence, Consistency and Correctness, in the Text Facets Structure and Wording. Between AM2 and AM3, under Correspondence, EP7 increased from 58 to 79 (increasing by 36.2%; by 31.6% between AM1 and AM3); EP10 increased from 62 to 85 (increasing by 37.1%; by 80.9% between AM1 and AM3). Under Consistency, EP8 saw an increase in detected errors from 6 to 11 (increasing by 83.3%; AM3 almost four times AM1); under EP11 errors increased from 128 to 157 (increasing by 22.7%; by 145.3% between AM1 and AM3). Under Correctness, EP9 increased from 117 to 131 (increasing by 12.0%; by 31.0% between AM1 and AM3); EP12 increased from 657 to 710 (increasing by 8.1%; by 56.0% between AM1 and AM3). The mean increase in the detection of Correspondence, Consistency and Correctness errors between AM2 and AM3 was 33.2%; that between AM1 and AM3 was 101.9% (more than double). It can be concluded, therefore, that the expected increase in the detection of Structure and Wording errors between AM1 and AM3 in the three criteria did occur as a direct result of exposure to these two Text Facets.

The increase in error-detection rates for the three criteria columns is summarised in Table 5.5.

Between ...	CORRESPONDENCE		CONSISTENCY		CORRECTNESS	
	Errors detected	% increase	Errors detected	% increase	Errors detected	% increase
AM1 & AM2	171-284	66.1	79-153	93.7	715-1104	54.4
AM2 & AM3	284-330	16.2	153-203	32.7	1104-1231	11.5
AM1 & AM3	171-330	93.0	79-203	157.0	715-1231	72.2

Table 5.5: Error-detection trends between AM1, AM2 and AM3 for the three criteria compared.

the increase in EP12+EP15 errors, a greater number of errors associated with the other EPs was detected than previously. A particularly noteworthy increase in Correspondence errors between AM1 and AM2 was registered for EP4 (a greater than threefold increase, from 39 to 135), the total Correspondence errors increasing by 66.1% between AM1 (171) and AM2 (284).

Under Consistency, EP5 registered a fivefold increase in errors detected between AM1 and AM2 (from 3 to 15). Moreover, EP8 saw a doubling from a modest 3 to 6 errors detected, and EP11 saw a doubling (from 64 to 128), despite the formal input on Structure and Wording not having been presented yet. Indeed, taken together, the total Consistency errors almost doubled between AM1 and AM2 (79 to 153). Under Correctness, the EP3 errors detected more than doubled (from 32 to 78, or 129.4%) and the EP6 errors doubled (from 6 to 12, or 100%). Moreover, the total EP3+EP6+EP9 scores increased by 56.8% between AM1 (138) and AM2 (207). The increase in the range of this category of errors away from EP12 and EP15 was already noticeable at this early stage, even though Structure and Wording had not been taught yet; nor had Presentation, yet the errors classified under EPs12 and 15 increased simultaneously at a similar rate (55.46%; AM1: 577, AM2: 897).

This is evidence of an early increase in the detection rate of the less common and less obvious Correspondence, Consistency and Correctness errors, most likely as a result of new knowledge having been acquired about them between AM1 and AM2 and the students' awareness of the variety of errors having been raised.

I was also interested in ascertaining the impact, if any, of the students' exposure to these two Text Facets on their scores for EPs1-6. For this reason, I analysed the number of errors detected between AM1 and AM2 only. For Text Type, the scores for EP1 Appropriate text remained unchanged at 15; EP2 Unity of genre saw a decline from 8 to 2 errors (the students were permitted to change the labels they had assigned to particular errors, and this may be an EP for which they reversed their previous decisions, possibly relabelling some as EP3s after the inputs from the teaching session); for EP3 Application of genre rules, there was an increase in errors detected from 32 to 78 (an increase of almost 2.5 times). Where we witness the more consistent and significant changes in errors detected after the teaching and awareness-raising class is in the level of Content: here, EP4 scores increased by 2.5 times (from AM1 39 to AM2 135); EP5 scores increased fivefold (from AM1 3 to AM2 15) and EP6 scores doubled (AM1 6 to AM2 12). This would tend to indicate that the teaching sessions on Text Type and Content had a direct impact on the nature and range of the errors that the group detected.

5.2.2. Impact of teaching the Text Facets Structure and Wording

The students undertook iteration 3 of 'Arab media' (AM3) after having received theoretical input and completed practical exercises on Structure and Wording (Weeks 5 and 7). I

D. Wording	EP10. Appropriate wording			EP11. Unity of style			EP12. Syntax, vocabulary & meaning		
	47	62	85	64	128	157	455	657	710
E. Presentation	EP13. Appropriate layout & typography			EP14. Congruence of text & layout			EP15. Spelling, punctuation, layout & typography		
	10	14	27	1	2	19	122	240	275
Totals	171	284	330	79	153	203	715	1104	1231
Total AM1 vs AM2 vs AM3							965	1541	1764
	15 Evaluation points								

Table 5.4: Scores (error detection) in each EP on iterations 1 (AM1), 2 (AM2) and 3 (AM3) of 'Arab media'.

Typically, in line with the findings in the 'Estuary Villa' exercise, the highest number of errors detected upon initial exposure to the passage (AM1) were those of EP12 (455), and EP15 (122). As with 'Estuary Villa', I was interested in ascertaining whether the range of errors would broaden out to include more of the Correspondence and Consistency errors and also to include a wider range of the Correctness errors as a result of the training provided.

5.2.1. Impact of teaching the Text Facets — Text Type and Content

The students undertook iteration 2 of 'Arab media' (AM2) after having received theoretical input and completed practical exercises on Text Type and Content (Weeks 2 and 4). I was first interested in whether the range of errors detected in the 'Arab media' text had broadened beyond EP12 and EP15; and then in determining whether the teaching of these Text Facets had had any impact on the students' awareness of the types of error they could have corrected at these levels. An analysis of the data reveals that the total of all Correspondence and Consistency errors detected in the first iteration (AM1) was 250 as opposed to the 577 combined EP12+EP15 errors. This contrasts with the AM2 scores: the total of all AM2 Correspondence and Consistency errors was 437 (74.8% increase over AM1); EP12+EP15 totalled 897 (55.45% increase over AM1). This higher rate of increase in the detection of Correspondence and Consistency errors would tend to indicate that there was a broadening of the types of error detected: besides

— the highest increase of all 15 EPs; EP9 errors increased by 16%, from 44 to 51. At the same time, EP12 errors increased by 34% (280 to 376), and EP15 errors decreased by 33% (171 to 113), for the reasons explained above.

More revealing are the trends displayed by the groupings of Correctness errors: for EVF, 50 EP3+EP6+EP9 errors were detected as opposed to 451 EP12+EP15 errors; by EVM, the totals were 79 (58% increase) versus 489 (a modest 8.43% increase) respectively. This would suggest that the learning process had borne fruit by increasing both the knowledge and the skills of the students as well as their sensitivity to the kinds of error an editor has to detect and correct over and above grammar, spelling and punctuation.

5.2. Student performance in 'Arab media'

Second — and perhaps more significantly in view of the more direct association between theoretical input, practical exercises and the three iterations of 'Arab media' (AM) than could be seen in 'Estuary Villa' — there is the students' cumulative detection of errors in this text. A total of 103 possible errors could have been detected. These data are summarised in Table 5.4, which compares the students' scores in iterations AM1, AM2 and AM3. Appendix II presents the 'Arab Media' text and the errors that could have been identified, labelled with EP numbers.

The students completed iteration AM1 before receiving any formal theoretical or practical input other than being introduced to the CCC Model and its 15 EPs. This introduction was necessary to enable them to use the model to detect and label errors. AM2 was timed to occur after the students had received input and completed practical exercises on Text Type and Content (Weeks 2 and 4).

TEXT FACETS	CRITERIA FOR QUALITY ANALYSIS								
	CORRESPONDENCE			CONSISTENCY			CORRECTNESS		
	AM1	AM2	AM3	AM1	AM2	AM3	AM1	AM2	AM3
A. TEXT TYPE	EP1. Appropriate text			EP2. Unity of genre			EP3. Application of genre rules		
	15	15	8	8	2	1	32	78	96
B. CONTENT	EP4. Appropriate & sufficient information			EP5. Congruence of facts			EP6. Facts		
	39	135	131	3	15	15	6	12	19
C. STRUCTURE	EP7. Sufficient cohesion			EP8. Uniformity of structure			EP9. Argumentation (linking)		
	60	58	79	3	6	11	100	117	131

The total errors detected in EVF (before teaching commenced) was 820, whereas that in EVM (Week 11) was 1270, an overall increase of 54.9%. This substantial increase is indicative both of the acquisition of editing knowledge and skills which took place during the course and also of the fact that, using the rubric as a guide, the students were prompted to detect many more errors than would otherwise have been the case.

Any decreases in the errors detected can be attributed either to students' reversing earlier decisions about errors or not carrying them over to subsequent iterations (having started afresh with a new iteration, without accumulating, or having deleted an earlier comment in error). It is also possible that some students overlooked these errors while focusing instead on errors of other types. Reversals of decisions are evident in the Comments inserted in the two iterations. Where a student detected an error but assigned an incorrect EP to it, in my analysis I reassigned the correct EP or EPs to such an error so as to reflect the nature of the error detected correctly.

In line with my previous unpublished findings, the highest number of errors detected upon initial exposure to the passage (EVF) was those of EP12 (280) and EP15 (171). A much wider range of errors was detected in May than previously, as indicated by other increases. First, the total of all Correspondence and Consistency errors (EP1, 2, 4, 5, 7, 8, 10, 11, 13, 14) in EVF was 219 as opposed to the 451 combined EP12+EP15 errors. This contrasts with the equivalent total EVM scores for these groups: 702 versus combined EP12+EP15 errors totalling 489. This is also evidence of a more than threefold increase in the detection rate of the less common, less obvious Correspondence and Consistency errors (220.55%), most likely as a direct outcome of new knowledge having been acquired about them between February and May. This contrasts with the modest increase in combined EP12+EP15 errors (8.43%) during this period.

Noteworthy increases in the detection of Correspondence errors were registered in EP1 (a more than fourfold increase, from 19 to 88 errors detected), EP4 (a more than fourfold increase, from 43 to 188), EP10 (a more than threefold increase, from 49 to 155) and EP13 (a more than sixfold increase, from 3 to 19). Under Consistency, EP5 registered a more than threefold increase in errors detected (from 6 to 21), EP11 a more than twofold increase and EP14 a notable increase from 0 to 14.

Considering the total errors detected in each of the criteria columns, the following noteworthy trends emerge: total Correspondence errors detected increased more than threefold (155 to 544) between EVF and EVM, total Consistency errors more than doubled (64 to 158), and total Correctness errors increased by a modest 13.4% (501 to 568), though off a high base.

The Correctness errors detected in this exercise require analysis. I anticipated that between EVF and EVM there would be an increase in the Correctness errors detected at the EP3, EP6 and EP9 levels, without there being a concomitant reduction in the EP12 and EP15 errors detected. The scores obtained in May bear this out: detected EP3 errors slightly more than doubled, from 3 to 7; EP6 errors increased sevenfold, from 3 to 21 rendering it suitable for an online environment. A total of 73 error types could have been detected in this text, covering all 15 EPs (the passage is provided in Appendix I; none of the students identified all of the errors, in either the February or the May iteration). The students' performance in detecting errors in the 'Estuary Villa' text in Week 1 ('EVF') and again at the end of the course ('EVM') is summarised in Table 5.3.

TEXT FACETS	CRITERIA FOR QUALITY ANALYSIS					
	CORRESPONDENCE		CONSISTENCY		CORRECTNESS	
	Feb (EVF)	May (EVM)	Feb (EVF)	May (EVM)	Feb (EVF)	May (EVM)
A. TEXT TYPE	EP1. Appropriate text		EP2. Unity of genre		EP3. Application of genre rules	
	19	88	1	0	3	7
B. CONTENT	EP4. Appropriate & sufficient information		EP5. Congruence of facts		EP6. Facts	
	43	188	6	21	3	21
C. STRUCTURE	EP7. Sufficient cohesion		EP8. Uniformity of structure		EP9. Argumentation (linking)	
	41	94	3	8	44	51
D. WORDING	EP10. Appropriate wording		EP11. Unity of style		EP12. Syntax, vocabulary & meaning	
	49	155	54	115	280	376
E. PRESENTATION	EP13. Appropriate layout & typography		EP14. Congruence of text & layout		EP15. Spelling, punctuation, layout & typography	
	3	19	0	14	171	113
Totals	155	544	64	158	501	568
Totals EVF vs. EVM					820	1270
	15 EVALUATION POINTS					

Table 5.3: Scores (error detection) in each EP of the CCC Model in the 'Estuary Villa' ('EV') passage by the students (n = 30): February (EVF) and May (EVM) 2015 compared.

Some errors could be allocated to more than one EP. For example, an incorrect in-text reference, according to the Harvard system of in-text referencing, '(EL NAWAWY 2010)', could be labelled as three different errors: EP3 (not following genre rules), EP11 (inconsistent style for in-text references) and EP15 (using capital letters instead of initial capital followed by lowercase letters). If the student also pointed out that a specific page number was missing from the citation, EP4 (lack of appropriate or sufficient information) could also be cited as an error according to the Harvard system. Similarly, if the student detected an instance of incorrect or inappropriate word usage (EP10) that could affect the author's intended meaning, then EP12 could also be assigned to the error. In addition, the matter of italicising characters that needed such treatment could be regarded as an EP11, EP14 or EP15 error. A few of the students did assign more than one EP to an error.

To ensure that errors were consistently attributed to the same EPs, and also that no errors detected by a student escaped allocation to an EP, an editor-colleague familiar with the CCC Model reassessed a random sample of one-third of each batch of iterations to ensure rater reliability. I then compared the two evaluations. Where variations occurred between the two readings, the text was revisited and adjustments to the affected scores were made accordingly. It is crucially important that the EPs be allocated to detected errors both systematically and consistently: this is what the model intends to inculcate in practising text editors. Once each batch had been scored and scores adjusted where necessary, the scores were consolidated. The scores per iteration for the entire group were then totalled.

5. Findings and discussion

The main findings are, first, those that reflect the students' performance in detecting errors in the 'Estuary Villa' text in Week 1 and again at the end of the course (Week 11). Second, and more significantly, there are the three iterations of their cumulative error detection in the academic text, 'Arab media'. As indicated by my third research question, what I was most interested in discovering from these two sets of data is whether there is any concordance between the error-detection results in the two exercises. In other words, if the precursor to improving text is detecting and labelling errors of various kinds, did the students display evidence of the same or a similar improvement in their editing knowledge and skills when they applied the 15 EPs of the model similarly in the 'Estuary Villa' and the 'Arab media' exercises? If there was concordance, then the model can be considered reliable as a means of measuring student performance. I consider the students' scores on the 'Estuary Villa' passage first, then those on the 'Arab media' text. Finally, I compare the two sets of data, before drawing some conclusions.

5.1. Student performance in 'Estuary Villa'

This passage of unedited text was composed with the intention of having it published on a tourism website after a team of professional editors and web designers had been assigned to

8	Students sat in on 'conversation' between two practising text editors about challenges and opportunities they face in their working world. Q&A session.	Generated informative discussions about editor's craft, three students expressing interest in editing/publishing as career. Students again wrote up and posted their reflections.	Introduced constraints and challenges editors face: e.g. when making informed improvements not interfering with author's 'voice'; and dealing with sensitivities when communicating with authors.
11	Learning completed. Students to computer lab for online detection of errors in unedited 'Estuary Villa' text a second time. Q&A session.	Students put through same exercise to enable teacher to measure their pre- and post-course error-detection rates and ranges.	To determine editing knowledge and skills post-teaching.
12	Concluding remarks, reinforcement of role of CCC Model.	Overall reflection on entire course and what participation had meant to the students.	Feedback and evaluation.

Table 5.2: Teaching and learning components of the 'Aspects of Writing and Speaking' course.

4.4. The study

First, the students' error detections in the pre- and post-teaching 'Estuary Villa' exercises were analysed, then those for 'Arab media'. For the purposes of this article and to facilitate comparison, only data drawn from the first three iterations of 'Arab media' are considered. In the fourth iteration, a number of the students resorted to rewriting the passage, or parts of it; this made evaluating their progress in detecting errors difficult or impossible.

The 15 EPs were used to categorise the errors the students detected in the two texts (using Microsoft Word's 'Track Changes' and/or 'Comments' functions). One point was allocated for each error detected, whether a student labelled it at all according to the EP or even labelled it incorrectly (incorrect labels were not altered). It was decided from the outset that the teacher would not remediate such incorrect labels with individual students, but some students did self-correct their earlier decisions in later iterations. In the case of the 'Estuary Villa' text, the prescribed textbook includes commentary on, and illustrations of, the editorial interventions required to improve the text to a publishable form; the students were referred to this chapter as a guide. In each iteration, the total Correspondence, Consistency and Correctness errors detected were also calculated and the total number of errors overall was recorded.

Week	Teaching	Assignment	Use in this study
1	No prior teaching or induction before error-detection assignment completed. Post-assignment, presentation in class on role and functions of text editor, including application of CCC Model. Students given course textbook and printout of model. Briefed students on presentations ('teaching moments') and practical exercises they would put their peers through to illustrate chosen Text Facet.	Onscreen in computer lab, detecting errors in a passage of text ('Estuary Villa', Appendix I). Used Microsoft Word's Track Changes and Comments to indicate errors they identified. Then assessed by the teacher. Students divided into 6 groups of 5; each group chose a Text Facet to team teach.	Determine editing knowledge and skills prior to learning.
2, 4, 5, 7, 9 & 10	Group presentations on Text Facets: PowerPoint presentation on topic with in-class exercises to test peers' understanding of issues and concepts. Teacher facilitated, critiqued and evaluated presentations.	Students reflected on group presentations orally in class and subsequently in writing (uploaded). After presentations, students re-analysed the same text ('Arab media') to detect further errors: a total of 4 iterations.	Knowledge and skills transfer; testing understanding of Text Facets. Attempt to discern effect, if any, of presentations on students' ability to improve a text through error detection.
3 & 6	Skype Video presentations by 2 'guest lecturers': the first introduced students to academic text, 'Arab media', written in English by an EFL/L2 author; the second spoke on challenges of standardising Australian English for foreign authors.	Students wrote reflections on content of session: the relationship between text editor and author and how much the editor may alter an author's words. Students detected and labelled errors in the passage, as described above.	Introduction to editing academic texts by a professional editor (here text type = abstract). Exposure to another facet and constraint of editing texts; building on previous knowledge.

4.2. Sample group

The group comprised 30 MA students (7 male, 23 female) registered for the semester course 'Aspects of Writing and Speaking'. They were all ESL or EFL speakers, with Dutch as the L1 of the majority; none had previously received formal training in text editing. All had had prior experience in writing essays, term papers and a bachelor's thesis as undergraduates, having had to self-edit their own writing without formal input in editing skills; and most reported that they had registered for the course partly to improve their writing skills in English.

4.3. Course implementation

The course comprised weekly three-hour sessions held between February and May 2015 (see Table 5.2). It aimed to give the students hands-on exposure to the art and science of (self-)editing texts through modalities that included team-teaching practice, two assignments requiring the detection of errors in two previously unedited passages, and presentations on the editor's craft by expert practitioners. Chapters 6 to 10 of their prescribed text, *Text Editing* (Van de Poel, Carstens & Linnegar, 2012), deal with each of the Text Facets, and they formed the basis of each group's preparation and further reading. Beyond that, the student groups were given free rein to present their chosen topics using media of their choice deemed appropriate to teaching their peers about their chosen Text Facet. Their teacher was present at each presentation to facilitate their peers' critiquing, to provide further comments and to evaluate the quality and content.

Besides the error-detection task performed on the 'Estuary Villa' text in a computer laboratory, the main online component entailed identifying the errors in the 'Arab media' passage of academic text through four iterations — each of which was timed to be done after the group presentations on a Text Facet. These were completed using Microsoft Word (including the 'Track Changes' and 'Comments' functions, which some of the students had to learn). They were then uploaded to BlackBoard, the institution's online repository for announcements, assignments, feedback and grades. The students were also encouraged to communicate their queries about their assignments to the teacher by email; the teacher also played the role of 'proxy author' for the purposes of answering the students' queries directed at the 'author' of the academic text (the real author having intentionally been kept anonymous).

The students produced one group presentation each on one of the Text Facets, three reflections on presentations by experienced text editors and a final reflection on what the course had meant to, or achieved for, them (Week 12). There were also two attempts to evaluate the 'Estuary Villa' text, plus their iterations of the 'Arab media' text. Taken together, these data provided a rich measure of the students' progress through the course, their development of text-editing knowledge and skills, and their evaluations of the impact on their writing and (self-)editing abilities.

editors must refer to external reference resources (1999a, p. 2) such as encyclopaedias, atlases, online dictionaries and style guides.

These three criteria work together to give meaning to the five 'Text Facets': 'Text Type' (EPs1, 2, 3), 'Content' (EPs4, 5, 6), 'Structure' (EPs7, 8, 9), 'Wording' (EPs10, 11, 12) and 'Presentation' (EPs13, 14, 15). Ideally, if a text satisfies all 15 EPs, then it is of optimal quality (2000, p. 25; 2012, p. 9). To get it to that state often requires eyes other than those of the supervisor or the writer: those of the text editor, whom the model guides systematically towards optimal quality. However, the model also offers a systematic pedagogical approach that is by definition blended and self-directed and constitutes a learning route that potentially leads to a positive outcome for the student editor-in-training. Its value as an assessment or evaluation tool should therefore also be put to the proof and recognised.

3.1. The CCC Model as an aid to teaching editing skills

Renkema has spoken of the fact that the relative simplicity of the model makes it a very manageable tool to use in teaching and language training, as well as in situations in which texts have to be appraised (1994, 1998a, 1999a, 1999b, 2012). It is therefore likely that the CCC Model will lend itself to being used to measure a change in text-editing knowledge and skills. This claim was investigated in the study reported here.

4. Methodology and method

4.1. Course design

At the start of the course, the students completed an onscreen error-detection exercise ('Estuary Villa'; see Appendix I) and were then introduced to the model, each of the five facets of text evaluation and the three columns of criteria described in Table 5.1, with the support of a textbook based largely on the model. Regularly, over a period of 12 weeks' teaching/contact time, the editorial issues concerning Text Type, Content, Structure, Wording and Presentation were covered, both as take-home online assignments and as in-class presentations. During this period, the students edited a difficult passage from an actual academic text written by an L2 English speaker (dubbed 'Arab media'; see Appendix II). The excerpt contained errors of many kinds; the students were required to label the errors they detected according to the 15 EPs of the model, but not necessarily to correct them. In this manner, they were exposed to the kinds of real error a writer-editor has to identify and diagnose when evaluating a real text (Knowles's Principles 4 and 5). Student reflections formed an important component of the design: reflections on knowledge and insights acquired, the course as a whole, and their editing experience through it. Analysis of this component will be the subject of a forthcoming article.

The relative weight of each EP in the hierarchy is best expressed when one reads the rubric from top to bottom and from left to right: EPs in the first level or facet ('Text type') carry the most weight, as do those in the first column ('Correspondence'). For Renkema, the higher up the facet level, the more fundamentally critical is the error to be remedied (Renkema & Cleutjens, 1997, pp. 107-8; Renkema, 1999a: p. 3), so errors or weaknesses at levels A, B and C (for example, EP4) must be resolved before any other problems are attended to (Renkema, 1998b; 2001, p. 44). Thus, trying to remedy wording and punctuation at levels D and E (for example, EP12 or EP15) would be a pointless exercise (1998b; 2001, p. 44) if there are errors at levels A, B or C. Also, where an error has more than one EP attached to it (for example, EPs 3, 4, 11, 15), the highest of them should take precedence. In this way, the model makes it possible to identify systematically the factors influencing the ineffectiveness of a particular text type (Renkema, 2001, p. 44). This weighting encourages the text editor to approach a text logically and consider macro-flaws before working on the micro-errors and weaknesses. It therefore offers a thorough, structured approach to analysing a text and to detecting, labelling and correcting the errors in it. The students were introduced to this approach in the first week of the course.

The EPs are described in detail in Appendix III. Briefly, the first column, the criterion of Correspondence, concerns the alignment of the author's intention and the needs and expectations of the reader (Renkema, 1999a, p. 2). Accordingly, the writer-editor or supervisor has some freedom to choose the type of text and whether they stay true to the characteristics of the type throughout (1999a, p. 1; 2002, p. 178). Renkema regards Correspondence as the most important criterion, since text quality is fundamentally affected by the extent of the alignment between writer and reader, and of the text to the medium. To be optimal, such alignment should be achieved at all five levels in this column.

The second column concerns the criterion of 'Consistency'. A text meets this requirement when the choices a writer-editor makes (for example, a certain structure, particular choice of words, style of punctuation) are maintained consistently throughout (Renkema, 1999b, p. 2). For example, it is not good for an author to divide their text on the basis of both thematic and chronological schemas: that will only confuse or alienate the reader (2002, p. 178). To resolve consistency problems, the vigilant text editor will always compare at least two parts of a text, because it is between them that any discrepancy may have occurred (1999a, p. 2).

The third column, 'Correctness' or correct usage, concerns genre rules, facts, argumentation (linking), syntax, vocabulary and meaning, and spelling, punctuation and typography. Normative linguistics and factual accuracy play a central role here, making the evaluation of text quality somewhat easier. This is often the novice text editor's instinctive starting point, but through its structure the CCC Model tries to persuade them to consider aspects of correctness last. To check for correctness, writer-supervisors are often criticised for providing this kind of unsystematic evaluation (Taylor & Beasley, 2005; Cadman & Cargill, 2007; Brabazon, 2013).

Renkema has produced a framework for systematic error analysis, one incorporating even aspects that seasoned text editors sometimes overlook. He also required his model to be independent of text type or genre (Renkema & Cleutjens, 1997, p. 107; Renkema, 2002, p. 182). His matrix for systematically evaluating text quality comprises 'criteria' and 'levels' (or Text Facets; see Table 5.1). The intersections of criteria and Text Facets, or evaluation points [EPs], form 15 criteria. These are applied to any text in order to diagnose and pinpoint errors or weaknesses systematically, and the editor then either effects or suggests appropriate changes to improve it. The EPs are presented within a coherent, hierarchical rubric (Renkema, 1998a, p. 43; 2001, p. 40), illustrated in Table 5.1. The version presented here and used in the study is a second generation away from Renkema's, the English language version itself having been adapted from an Afrikaans language adaptation. Problems in translation were one of the reasons for the adaptation (*ijkpunt* becoming 'evaluation point', not 'calibration point', for instance); another was that the authors of the English text felt that some of the Dutch and Afrikaans labels for the evaluation points [EPs] were not entirely appropriate (according to research of my own that is as yet unpublished).

TEXT FACETS	CRITERIA FOR QUALITY ANALYSIS		
	CORRESPONDENCE	CONSISTENCY	CORRECTNESS
A. TEXT TYPE	EP1 Appropriate text	EP2 Unity of genre	EP3 Application of genre rules
B. CONTENT	EP4 Appropriate & sufficient information	EP5 Congruence of facts	EP6 Facts
C. STRUCTURE	EP7 Sufficient cohesion	EP8 Uniformity of structure	EP9 Argumentation (linking)
D. WORDING	EP10 Appropriate wording	EP11 Unity of style	EP12 Syntax, vocabulary & meaning
E. PRESENTATION	EP13 Appropriate layout & typography	EP14 Congruence of text & layout	EP15 Spelling, punctuation, layout & typography
	15 EVALUATION POINTS		

Table 5.1: CCC Model: Criteria for text-quality analysis, as adapted for use in *Text Editing* (2012). Source: Renkema, as cited in and adapted by Van de Poel, Carstens & Linnegar, 2012.

to learn (Knowles, 1984). Critical reading of the two imperfect texts on this course required the students to be both enquiring and resourceful. The implications for the present approach to transferring text-editing skills are these: the students are motivated to put their skills and knowledge into practice, learn more about the craft, gain in self-efficacy and feel capable of performing work to a high standard.

Principle 2: Adults bring life experiences and knowledge to new learning experiences: Adult learners should be exposed to reflective learning opportunities that enable them to examine any existing habits or biases and 'move them towards a new understanding of information presented' (Fidishun, 2000, p. 4). Reflection as a key aspect of this learning experience will be reported on elsewhere.

Principles 3 and 5: Adults are goal-oriented and practical: They become ready to learn when 'they experience a need to learn [something] in order to cope more satisfyingly with real-life tasks or problems' (Knowles, 1984, p. 44). Nurturing a student's readiness for problem-based learning is best achieved through real case studies and practical exercises as a basis from which to learn — on this course, (self-)editing skills, plus a knowledge of normative linguistics, text linguistics and document design (Van de Poel, Carstens & Linnegar, 2012). The practical experiences facilitated in this case study helped the students to recognise firsthand how what they are learning applies to life and a work context.

Principle 4: Adults are relevancy-oriented: The course content and the reflections built into this course catered to the learners' expectation to be able to apply their new knowledge and skills, which helped them appreciate the value of their observations and practical experience. These editors-in-training engaged with real texts that clients had supplied for improvement (the 'Estuary Villa' and 'Arab media' texts — see the Appendices). The skills and knowledge acquired and assessed through these assignments are both useful and directly applicable to text editing.

3. The CCC Model and systematic editing

Text editing is essentially about systematically identifying and eliminating the flaws in writing to improve it so that it not only conveys the authors' intended meaning as clearly and correctly as possible but also meets the readers' needs or expectations (Renkema, 1999b, p. 5). Text analysis is a first step that 'helps us to form well-considered judgements about the quality of a text ... to discuss texts on the basis of sound arguments' (Schellens & Steehouder, 2008, p. 3). But what is 'quality', and how do different errors affect it?

Since 'quality' is a particularly vague notion, precisely how does one evaluate text quality in a manner that is meaningful, systematic and helpful to a writer (Renkema, 1999a, p. 1; Renkema & Schellens, 1996)? Examples of unsystematic evaluation include vague, subjective statements such as 'too unstructured', 'this paragraph doesn't work' and 'word choice inappropriate' (Renkema, 1998a, p. 40). The interventions of doctoral to Bandura, there are four major sources of self-efficacy: mastery experiences, social modelling, social persuasion and psychological responses. In the approach adopted to learning (self-)editing skills in this instance, these four sources were largely taken into account, through group work, student reflections and several iterations of error detection in the 'Arab media' text (discussed below).

'The most effective way of developing a strong sense of efficacy is through mastery experiences,' Bandura explained (1977, p. 192). Using a text-analysis tool (such as the CCC Model), I believe, provides the student with a means of approaching texts systematically and more meaningfully, which inculcates a sense of mastery over texts. Witnessing other people (either peers or a mentor) successfully completing a task is another important source of self-efficacy. If '[s]eeing people similar to oneself succeed by sustained effort raises observers' beliefs that they too possess the capabilities to master comparable activities' (p. 194), then the group-work approach served to expose students to this process.

Bandura (1977) also asserted that people can be persuaded to believe that they have the skills and capabilities to succeed: provide them with a tool that helps them to make sense of the nebulous and they can begin to feel empowered and able to succeed. The CCC Model can serve this purpose, offering a form of logical 'common language' within a group.

2.2. Knowles's andragogy or self-directed learning

Part of being an effective educator involves understanding how adults learn best (Lieb, 1991, p. 1). Andragogy (or adult learning) emphasises the value of the process of learning, which it regards as internal and self-directed (Knowles, 1970; Knowles, Holton & Swanson, 2005). Its approaches to learning are problem-based and collaborative rather than didactic; they also emphasise greater equality and collaboration between teacher and learner (Lieb, 1991, p. 2). On the present course, I was as interested in the learning process facilitated by the CCC Model (helping students to identify and make sense of errors in texts) as I was in the outcomes for the students. Five of Knowles's six principles of andragogy that relate to the needs of the student text editors are briefly described here.

Most text editors are adults by the time they require formal (self-)editing skills. They are also single-minded in improving their own or others' texts, bring a wealth of life experiences and knowledge to their work, and tend to set store by the practical application of their knowledge and skills in enhancing texts to a required standard (Mackenzie, 2011, pp. 49, 51; Manning Murphy, 2012, pp. 4-6). Knowles's principles are therefore apt for this group:

Principle 1: Adults are internally motivated and self-directed: Adult learners resist learning when they feel others are imposing information, ideas or activities on them (Fidishun, 2000), so the educator's role should be to facilitate a student's becoming more self-directed and responsible in order to foster the student's internal motivation for teaching. These learning experiences provide some degree of student control over time, place, path and/or pace (Great Schools Partnership, 2013; Brown & Thompson, 1997). The modalities along each student's learning path within a course or subject are connected to provide an integrated learning experience (Clayton Christensen Institute for Disruptive Learning [CCIDL], 2015; Bach, Haynes & Lewis-Smith, 2007). For example, students might attend a class taught by a teacher in a traditional classroom setting while independently also completing online components of the course outside of the classroom (Sherry, 1996; Institute for Higher Education Policy [IHEP], 2000). Blended-learning experiences may vary widely in design and execution: online learning may be a minor component part of a classroom-based course; or video-recorded lectures, live video and text chats, and other digitally enabled learning activities may constitute primary teacher-student instructional interactions. The rotation model most closely describes the blended-learning experience described in the present study: students rotate on a fixed schedule or at the teacher's discretion between learning modalities, at least one of which is online learning (Ellis, 2000, p. 52). Other modalities might include small-group or full-class instruction, group projects, individual tutoring or pencil-and-paper assignments. The students learn mostly on the brick-and-mortar campus, except for any homework or other assignments (CCIDL, 2015).

Because the course was a learning process for a group of young adults, and since specialised text-editing skills were being learned, I considered Bandura's (1977, 1982) self-efficacy mechanism and Knowles's adult learning theory (andragogy), self-directed learning and learner autonomy (1970, 1975, 1984) to be appropriate theoretical underpinnings for the learning experience described here.

2.1. Bandura's self-efficacy mechanism

Bandura and others have found that an individual's self-efficacy plays a major role in how goals, tasks and challenges are approached. Accordingly, people with a strong sense of self-efficacy tend to view challenging problems as tasks to be mastered, develop a deeper interest in the activities in which they participate, form a stronger sense of commitment to their interests and activities, and recover quickly from setbacks and disappointments (1977). Those with a weak sense of self-efficacy tend to avoid challenging tasks, believe that difficult tasks and situations are beyond their capabilities, focus on personal failings and negative outcomes, and lose confidence in their personal abilities quickly (1977). Because text editors are expected to work semi-independently or independently in close collaboration with authors, taking editorial decisions and often persuading authors and other role-players of their correctness (Mossop, 2010, p. 23; Mackenzie, 2011, pp. 1-2, 49, 51, 201; Manning Murphy, 2012, pp. 4-9), it is necessary that they possess a strong sense of self-efficacy. Being guided by a logical rubric or model can contribute to an editor's self-efficacy.

Self-efficacy beliefs that form in early childhood evolve throughout life as people acquire new skills, experiences and understanding (Bandura, 1982, p. 124). According it is also a solid tool for teaching a systematic approach to (self-)editing texts. However, its use as a teaching tool has not been formally assessed to date.

An opportunity arose in 2015 for me to investigate the effectiveness of the CCC Model as a training tool with a group of 30 postgraduate 'editors-in-training'. To my knowledge, this was the first attempt at using the model for this purpose in a postgraduate academic setting. This chapter reports on a study in which this group learned text-editing skills either to improve their own writing or to enhance that of others. For this group of young adults, the approach adopted for skills and knowledge transfer was that of blended learning with a strong social constructivist emphasis (University College Dublin, 2015) based on the ideas of two influential learning theorists, Knowles and Bandura. Participants were encouraged to generate knowledge and meaning from an interaction between their experiences and their ideas while presenting relevant topics to their peers as groups. They also did so through engaging in error detection in, and analysis of, unedited texts based on the CCC rubric, with minimal formal teacher intervention. Because the quality of systematic editing can be measured according to both the number and the range of errors detected in a text, the goal was for students to learn to identify not only an increasing *number* of errors overall as they worked through each of three iterations of an editing assignment, but also an increasing *range* of error types. The errors they detected typically moved from only commonly detected errors of word choice, syntax, meaning, spelling, punctuation, layout and typography to a wider range of errors involving text type, content and structure, especially those concerning the criteria of correspondence and consistency (see Table 5.1). My experience has shown these to be the less obvious errors to practitioners new to editing.

What I set out to determine in this study is expressed in these research questions:

- To what extent is the CCC Model for text analysis, evaluation and improvement an effective tool for facilitating systematic (self-)editing by novices?

- To what extent is the CCC Model an effective rubric for systematically monitoring and assessing a change in editing knowledge and skills? Used across sequential iterations, can it be used to indicate

    1. an overall increase in errors detected?

    2. a spread in the range of error types detected, from those intuitively identified by untrained editors to those at a deeper level?

- How reliable is the CCC Model as a monitoring or assessment tool, as identified through a comparison of students' performance on two different editing passages across the duration of the course?

2. Theoretical framework

The term 'blended learning' (or hybrid or mixed-mode learning) is generally applied to the practice of using both online and in-person supervised learning experiences to the skill of writing as being something supervisors should be trained in (European University Association, 2006). Typical of most of this batch, one states vaguely that '[t]hesis supervisors will have regular consultations with their doctoral students about the progress of their thesis work' (Max Planck Institutes, n.d.) — which is more about process than product, it would seem. Another stipulates, without any mention of actual writing or editing skills, that '[s]upervisors should carefully review the submitted materials and identify weaknesses in the argumentation. This allows doctoral candidates to address problems as they arise' (Freie Universität Berlin, 2014). An exception is the Université catholique de Louvain's Graduate School of Management Research Institute, which specifically mentions editing as 'one of the research training activities ... that support the individual research work that the thesis constitutes' (2011). Brabazon (2013), a doctoral-student-turned-supervisor as a professor of education in Australia, asserts that not reading a candidate's writing is one of the characteristics of the worst supervisors; she herself begins 10 interactive editing cycles with a candidate when their first draft is complete (2010). Finally, a chapter on 'encouraging early writing and giving feedback' in a handbook for doctoral supervisors focuses entirely on process to the neglect of actual writing or editing skills (Taylor & Beasley, 2005).

In response to this situation, a number of universities, training establishments and professional bodies for editors worldwide have been offering skills-based programs or courses and mentorships in text editing, particularly editing academic writing (see course descriptions at Editors' Association of Canada, 2014; Institute of Professional Editors [IPEd], 2014; McGillivray Linnegar Associates, 2013; Society of English-Language Professionals in the Netherlands [SENSE] UniSIG, 2016; Society for Editors and Proofreaders [SfEP], 2014). However, there is a dearth of published literature on teaching or mentoring text editors or on enhancing their skills; even the offerings of professional bodies remain unreported. In my 35 years' experience, none of them has used a universal standard tool against which to measure the level of editing knowledge or skills of those who complete programs or mentorships — or even the quality of text editors' interventions in texts.

One such rubric does exist, however: the Correspondence, Consistency, Correctness [CCC] Model devised by Dutch linguist Professor Dr Jan Renkema (1999a, 1999b, 2000). By 2011, it had been published only in Dutch and Afrikaans (Carstens & Van de Poel, 2010), rendering it largely unknown outside the Netherlands until it appeared in English in 2012, in an international publication on text editing (Van de Poel, Carstens & Linnegar, 2012). This text has since reached editors and proofreaders worldwide. Through applying his refined model in a variety of contexts, Renkema has been able to demonstrate its effectiveness in analysing text quality, as have other adopters or modifiers of the model (Daniëls, 2011; Carstens & Van de Poel, 2010; Van de Poel, Carstens & Linnegar, 2012). They have either devised alternatives or refined it further as an aid to text editing. Since 2011, I have become fully acquainted with the model, rediscovering it as more than an aid for writers and text editors who need help with perfecting writing:

5

The CCC Model (Correspondence, Consistency, Correctness):

How effective is it in enabling and assessing change in text-editing knowledge and skills in a blended-learning postgraduate course?

John Linnegar

1. Introduction

A growing need for text editors worldwide has been created by the increasing importance of English as the *lingua franca* of academic and scientific publishing, combined with growing pressure in these communities to 'publish or perish' in English as a foreign or second language (Hvistendahl, 2015) and a greater number of students who lack academic writing skills. An allied problem that places an additional burden on text editors is the failure of academic supervisors of postgraduate researchers to intervene appropriately when their wards display an inability to express themselves clearly or correctly in their writing (Cadman & Cargill, 2007), or even an unwillingness to do so. A recent informal survey of eight online sites addressing the training of academic supervisors to cater better to doctoral researchers' needs[1] revealed that only one refers

---

1 The first eight sites listed in response to a web search on 'training of supervisors of doctoral candidates' were these: European University Association, 2006; Martinez, 2016; Pinta, Hytönen, Mäkinen & Vuorio-Lehti, 2015; Freie Universität Berlin, 2014; Université catholique de Louvain's Graduate School of Management Research Institute, 2011; Max Planck Institute, Hamburg, Germany, n.d.; Sonesson & Karlsson, 2010; RozenbergQuarterly.com, n.d. (SANPAD scheme for developing supervisory-mentoring-coaching skills in South Africa and the Netherlands; see Wadee, Keane, Dietz & Hay, n.d.).

Shashok, K. (2001). Author's editors: Facilitators of science information transfer. *Learned Publishing, 14*, 113-121.

Sheldon, E. (2011). Rhetorical differences in RA introductions written by English L1 and L2 and Castilian Spanish L1 writers. *Journal of English for Academic Purposes, 10*(4), 238-251. DOI: http://dx.doi.org/10.1016/j.jeap.2011.08.004.

Swales, J.M. (1990). *Genre analysis: English in academic and research settings.* Cambridge: Cambridge University Press.

Tardy, C. (2004). The role of English in scientific communication: Lingua franca or Tyrannosaurus rex? *Journal of English for Academic Purposes, 3*(3), 247-269. DOI: http://dx.doi.org/10.1016/j.jeap.2003.10.001.

University of Chicago Press staff. (2010). *The Chicago manual of style* (16th ed.). Chicago: The University of Chicago Press.

Uzuner, S. (2008). Multilingual scholars' participation in core/global academic communities: A literature review. *Journal of English for Academic Purposes, 7*(4), 250-263. DOI: http://dx.doi.org/10.1016/j.jeap.2008.10.007.

Ventola, E., & Mauranen, A. (1991). Nonnative writing and native revising of scientific articles. In E. Ventola (Ed.), *Functional and systemic linguistics: Approaches and uses* (pp. 457-492). Berlin: Mouton de Gruyter.

Willey, I., & Tanimoto, K. (2012). 'Convenience Editing' in action: Comparing English teachers' and medical professionals' revisions of a medical abstract. *English for Specific Purposes, 31*(4), 249-260. DOI: http://dx.doi.org/10.1016/j.esp.2012.04.001.

Yli-Jokipii, H., & Jorgensen, P.E.F. (2004). Academic journalese for the Internet: A study of native English-speaking editors' changes to texts written by Danish and Finnish professionals. *Journal of English for Academic Purposes, 3*(4), 341-359. DOI: http://dx.doi.org/10.1016/j.jeap.2004.07.006.

Burrough-Boenisch, J. (2003). Shapers of published NNS research articles. *Journal of Second Language Writing, 12*(3), 223-243. DOI: http://dx.doi.org/10.1016/S1060-3743(03)00037-7.

Curry, M.J., & Lillis, T. (2004). Multilingual scholars and the imperative to publish in English: Negotiating interests, demands, and rewards. *TESOL Quarterly, 38*(4), 663-688. DOI: http://dx.doi.org/10.2307/3588284.

Curry, M.J., & Lillis, T.M. (2010). Academic research networks: Accessing resources for English-medium publishing. *English for Specific Purposes, 29*(4), 281-295. DOI: http://dx.doi.org/10.1016/j.esp.2010.06.002.

Ferguson, G.R. (2007). The global spread of English, scientific communication and ESP: Questions of equity, access and domain loss. *Ibérica, 13*, 7-38.

Flowerdew, J. (2000). Discourse community, legitimate peripheral participation and the nonnative-English-speaking scholar. *TESOL Quarterly, 34*(1), 127-150.

Gosden, H. (1995). Success in research article writing and revision: A social-constructionist perspective. *English for Specific Purposes, 14*(1), 37-57. DOI: http://dx.doi.org/10.1016/0889-4906(94)00022-6.

Harwood, N., Austin, L., & Macaulay, R. (2009). Proofreading in a UK university: Proofreaders' beliefs, practices, and experiences. *Journal of Second Language Writing, 18*(3), 166-190. DOI: http://dx.doi.org/10.1016/j.jslw.2009.05.002.

Huang, J.C. (2010). Publishing and learning writing for publication in English: Perspectives of NNES PhD students in science. *Journal of English for Academic Purposes, 9*(1), 33-44. DOI: http://dx.doi.org/10.1016/j.jeap.2009.10.001.

Kerans, M.E. (2013). Writing process research: Implications for manuscript support for academic authors. In V. Matarese (Ed.), *Supporting research writing: Roles and challenges in multilingual settings* (pp. 39-54). Oxford: Chandos Publishing.

Knorr-Cetina, K.D. (1981). *The manufacture of knowledge: An essay on the constructivist and contextual nature of science*. Oxford: Pergamon.

Kourilova, M. (1998). Communicative characteristics of reviews of scientific papers written by non-native users of English. *Endocrine Regulations, 32*, 107-114.

Koyalan, A., & Mumford, S. (2011). Changes to English as an Additional Language writers' research articles: From spoken to written register. *English for Specific Purposes, 30*(2), 113-123. DOI: http://dx.doi.org/10.1016/j.esp.2010.10.001.

Li, Y., & Flowerdew, J. (2007). Shaping Chinese novice scientists' manuscripts for publication. *Journal of Second Language Writing, 16*(2), 100-117. DOI: http://dx.doi.org/10.1016/j.jslw.2007.05.001.

Lillis, T., & Curry, M.J. (2006). Professional academic writing by multilingual scholars: Interactions with literacy brokers in the production of English-medium texts. *Written Communication, 23*(1), 3-35. DOI: http://dx.doi.org/10.1177/0741088305283754.

Lillis, T., & Curry, M.J. (2010). *Academic writing in a global context: The politics and practices of publishing in English*. London: Routledge.

Mišak, A., Marušić, M., & Marušić, A. (2005). Manuscript editing as a way of teaching academic writing: Experience from a small scientific journal. *Journal of Second Language Writing, 14*(2), 122-131. DOI: http://dx.doi.org/10.1016/j.jslw.2005.05.001.

Second, the fact that we selected the passages to be used in the editing exercise, together with the brevity of these passages, limits the extent to which the results can be extrapolated beyond the experiment, as the choice of text was clearly made to illustrate our beliefs rather than randomly test a hypothesis. Third, in circumscribing the blinded edit to a particular passage rather than revising the entire manuscript, we limited the possibility for each of us to demonstrate how we propose improvements in the text as a whole. These textual samples might have displayed greater focus on non-surface issues if we had revised the entire article rather than just a small part. Lastly, this experiment cannot account for the influence of the existing author-editor relationship on the type and frequency of margin comments, and this relationship is not to be underestimated. In one comment made to the author, the freelance editor raised doubt as to the author's usage of a particular term, indicating that the only other example of this particular language was found in a paper written by someone whom the editor knew to be a collaborator of the author in question. Such situatedness is a key element in editing work and may be the subject of further study.

With this chapter, we hope to have contributed to the ongoing research on the challenges faced by language services providers who work with NNES authors in specialised fields of discourse. Based on the analysis of our own previous work and our attempt to determine how the other would have handled the points of difficulty in the texts, we believe our findings show a varied palette of tools upon which editors can call as they help authors improve the quality of their research publications. Considerations on the use of these tools by each editor raise interesting questions as to the remit of each type of professional and are useful in suggesting ways in which both types of editor may add value to their services while at the same time highlighting the factors that may limit the viability of these strategies.

References

Belcher, D.D. (2007). Seeking acceptance in an English-only research world. *Journal of Second Language Writing, 16*(1), 1-22. DOI: http://dx.doi.org/10.1016/j.jslw.2006.12.001.

Benfield, J.R., & Feak, C.B. (2006). How authors can cope with the burden of English as an international language. *Chest, 129*(6), 1728-1730. DOI: http://dx.doi.org/10.1378/chest.129.6.1728.

Bisaillon, J. (2007). Professional editing strategies used by six editors. *Written Communication, 24*(4), 295-322.

Burgess, S., & Lillis, T.M. (2013). The contribution of language professionals to academic publication: Multiple roles to achieve common goals. In V. Matarese (Ed.), *Supporting research writing: Roles and challenges in multilingual settings* (pp. 1-15). Oxford: Chandos.

Burrough-Boenisch, J. (2002). *Culture and conventions: Writing and reading Dutch scientific English*. Utrecht: Netherlands Graduate School of Linguistics.

English teacher. Indeed, it has been reported that editing work that focuses exclusively on the textual surface is unsatisfying to NNES writers, even though a majority of editing done by native-English-speaking editors was found to be limited to basic aspects in texts (Ventola & Mauranen, 1991). However, studies of conversations around texts have found that authors experience great difficulty in articulating their desired meaning (Willey & Tanimoto, 2012), often because authors and language professionals do not share a common metalanguage (Burgess & Lillis, 2013). Therefore, editors must hone their skills in communicating with authors so as to maximise the efficiency of these meetings and limit the complications that this extra time spent creates for issues of billing, in the case of the freelance editor, and for potentially longer waiting times for other authors of the institution in the case of the in-house editor.

In spite of the potentially negative effects of the limited contact that the in-house editor has with clients, it is of interest that few writers in the institution instigate meetings to discuss their work and the editor's sometimes extensive commentary included in their texts. Although the in-house editor often encourages writers to meet for a conference in case of doubt, not many seize this opportunity. There may be a number of reasons for this, and the nature of the present study is not conducive to assessing this matter. One possible explanation for this reluctance, however, may be that the margin comments appear in English, giving the authors pause at the prospect of discussing these ideas in English despite the fact that the in-house editor is a proficient speaker of Spanish and generally able to discuss matters in either language. Another explanation may be that scholars work under tight deadlines, often balancing clinical work, teaching and research, and the added delay involved in scheduling and holding a meeting with the editor may be unfeasible given the imperative to publish as much and as quickly as possible. Lastly, we have noted in our experience that most criticism of language quality levied by journal reviewers encourages NNES authors to have their manuscripts revised by a native English speaker without providing much detail as to what precisely must be improved. Such blanket instructions may lead NNES authors to adopt a *satisficing* strategy of their own, arranging to have their manuscripts edited by a native English speaker only to comply with journal reviewers, even when it is clear that editing work done under suboptimal circumstances produces texts of lesser quality.

In addition to the implications of the study's scope mentioned previously, this research has a number of limitations. First and foremost, we, as the authors of this chapter, having undertaken the study partially to identify certain differences in our approach to editing, are likely to have introduced some degree of performance bias in their data. Though we intended to replicate our approach to the highest degree of accuracy possible, it is likely that the very question that brought us to conduct the study — that is, how it is possible that two types of editor working toward the same goal and for very similar clients display a notable degree of difference in the way we go about our task — interfered in the blinded editing. Further studies along these lines should seek to limit the influence of this bias.

inclined to invest in this effort than the in-house editor. We compensated for potential areas of incorrect interpretation of the authors' intended meaning by using a number of strategies, which included calls for the authors to confirm reformulated text, queries requesting the scholars to indicate whether the gist was what we understood it to be, indications of problematic language with little or no further commentary, and other remarks which sought to focus the authors' attention on the clarity or appropriateness of certain stretches of text. In employing these tactics at different points in the articles, we displayed sensitivity to both the many levels on which language works and the difficulty of isolating linguistic form and scientific content.

The differences highlighted in this study in terms of author involvement and time devoted to the text, didactic editing as an opportunity to both educate the author and defer responsibility, and diplomacy in the relationship with the author are an indication not only of personal style but also of the way in which each editor manages the constraints of their situation. Editors adapt their methods to factors such as their expected output and the number of projects they are obliged to, or able to, take on; the implications of this output on the profitability of their work; the loyalties they must honour when collaborating with authors; and the explicit or implicit remit they are given. Freelancers strive to maximise their time because of the implications of output on their financial bottom line, while also maintaining relations with the clients who entrust them with their work and holding themselves to high professional standards. While similarly maintaining the highest level of professional integrity, in-house editors have somewhat greater leeway to employ such strategies as *satisficing* (Burrough-Boenisch, 2003) — that is, focusing more on surface-level issues rather than deeper problems found in the text, or commenting on, rather than correcting, flaws in author manuscripts (Harwood et al., 2009; Li & Flowerdew, 2007; Ventola & Mauranen, 1991).

The question of how well these different approaches meet the expectations of NNES scholars is complex and would require feedback from the clients of both editors in order to reach a well-founded conclusion. Studies of editing practices in institutional contexts have revealed that, when asked, authors report that they expect revisers to directly intervene in their texts and query the author little or not at all (Flowerdew, 2000; Harwood et al., 2009; Willey & Tanimoto, 2012), thus suggesting that the approach taken by the freelance editor may be more pleasing to clients. This view has been challenged, however, by Ventola and Mauranen (1991). Other research, meanwhile, has found that insufficient contact with the author may be detrimental to the quality of the finished product (Burrough-Boenisch, 2003) and that a lack of author contact is demoralising for the editor (Willey & Tanimoto, 2012).

The freelance editor complements editing with face-to-face meetings, discussing a number of issues that arose while revising the text. These encounters are directed at going beyond obvious errors to provide added value to the client, and the editor has noted that clients are usually amenable to such instruction, often referring to the editor as their throughout the process of editing and revising, most often when working together for the first time in a designated coaching session. The freelancer may also have to 'read' the client and determine whether such added-value services, like teaching, are welcome.

As mentioned above, there was a marked difference in the way each editor treated a situation in which two forms of English, US and UK, were being mixed, a sign that could raise suspicion of plagiarism or micro-plagiarism. In this instance, the freelance editor made no comment and revised the entire manuscript according to one variant of English, while the in-house editor clearly stated that such a mistake could be taken as a red flag by the journal gatekeepers. In situations like this, the freelance editor proceeds with caution, opting to edit the text without mentioning this potentially delicate subject. Meanwhile, the in-house editor, whose only employer is the institution, did not feel the need to be quite so concerned about the author taking exception to such remarks. This example highlights how freelancers must nurture more carefully the working relationship with the author, exercising greater diplomacy than in-house editors.

4. Conclusion

In this comparative intervention study of two professional editors' approaches to biomedical editing for NNES authors, we have examined the way in which an in-house editor and a freelance editor interact with texts and with their author-clients. Taking margin comments as key data points and situating these comments within writing intended for international publication, we show how different approaches can be taken when problem areas in texts require communication with the author. The interventions we made during this study were first examined according to a framework that follows in the tradition of Lillis and Curry (2006) and then evaluated using a fit-for-purpose empirical scheme that classified the particular calls to action conveyed by these messages. To our knowledge, no previous studies have examined this para-textual correspondence produced during the editing process, choosing rather to focus on language facilitators' contributions to writing from the vantage point of the finished product.

In revising the texts, we activated a varied set of knowledge and skills. These interventions were mostly applications of linguistic knowledge, helping the author to produce error-free English to the extent of our abilities. Knowledge of the genre of the research article was also evident in our revisions, although because of the text-wide implications of genre and other discourse-related features, contributions aimed at helping the author produce discoursally effective texts is a substantially more ambitious project, albeit one that other editors may undertake by accompanying authors more closely as they design research, perform experiments, and then draft their texts (Kerans, 2013). As we are not members of the authors' discourse communities, our interventions reflected less control over field knowledge, and we deferred these matters to our author-clients. We attempted to compensate for this lack of expertise by researching problematic passages in the literature, although we have seen how the freelance editor was more the text in which the editor, having doubts as to whether they interpreted the author's meaning accurately, invites the author to evaluate the proposed edit for conceptual accuracy.

When offering alternatives to the author to improve a text without including such edits in the text proper, the freelance editor was much more inclined than the in-house editor to use the third category, clarifying the gist of the passage by offering an alternative. In interventions like these, proposals are most often phrased in terms of '*Do you mean ... ?*', as recommended in *The Chicago Manual of Style* (section 2.66). This strategy is more diplomatic, as it simultaneously highlights a problem and provides a solution while avoiding a critical or otherwise potentially offensive tone. Commenting on problems in the text without offering actionable solutions may lead to lengthy, difficult-to-invoice queries in order to negotiate the intended meaning of the author, if not the comment itself. The freelancer must weigh carefully the extra time spent researching content in order to get the edit right against the time that might be spent on follow-up queries, emails or phone calls from the client if a simple highlighting comment had been used. As stated earlier, time spent on follow-up is perhaps less of an issue for the in-house editor, who is not often approached after delivery of the work and who, in any case, receives a regular salary.

In the fourth of these categories, the editor comments on direct interventions in the text or indicates possible solutions to the problem. Though this strategy is similar to those used in the second and third categories, here the editor either mentions his or her justification for the intervention or provides evidence that the author may consult, often in the form of a hyperlink to a Google search or a specific paper in the literature where the author may find alternative ways of conveying ideas using more appropriate language. In the six texts studied, the freelance editor tended to refer to linguistic usage 'in the literature', indicating to their client that this assessment had been informed by research into the topic. The in-house editor, in contrast, opted to use hyperlinks so that the author could consult actual examples of the issues highlighted for commentary.

Examining the two professionals' work broadly, the observed use of comments to direct self-correction in in-house editing reflects a more didactic approach at this stage of the process, which is associated with the fact that few in-house clients meet with the editor to discuss their papers. When deficiencies noted in the text would require either highly specialised field knowledge to interpret the intended meaning or lengthy searches in the literature, feedback of this nature not only shortens the time required to revise the text but also invites authors to rewrite these passages, thereby creating the opportunity for them to identify their own weaknesses and act on them. Indeed, in certain comments the in-house editor extends this practice even further by clearly indicating a more appropriate alternative to excerpts containing errors, placing these comments deliberately in the margin for the author to type in themselves. The freelance editor, in contrast, often reserves remarks like this for face-to-face conferences held editor, and that the analysis we undertook during the research for this chapter showed them all to be unfounded.

One salient difference revealed during this study was in the way margin comments represented both the editor-author relationship and the role played by the editor in improving the text. To assess possible differences in editing style in general and, in particular, the correspondence embodied in margin comments, we analysed all comments that were related to sentence-level or paragraph-level problems, coming up with a four-category system to describe what action was requested of the author.

Author action indicated in editor comment	In-house editor	Freelance editor
Responsibility deferred to author; no change proposed	26 (57.8%)	1 (6.7%)
Confirmation of proposed edit made in text	4 (9%)	5 (33.3%)
Confirmation of proposed edit with no edit in text (e.g., Do you mean … ?)	11 (24.4%)	6 (40%)
Comment refers to edit made directly in text or edit required; evidence mentioned or provided in comment	4 (9%)	3 (20%)
TOTAL	45	15

Table 4.4: Types of author action requested in margin comments targeting sentence-level or paragraph-level problems detected by the in-house editor and the freelance editor.

The four categories of editorial strategies appear in Table 4.4, along with the frequency of each strategy and the percentage of all comments made by each editor. As can be seen, the first category of editor comment — in which the editor encourages the author to rewrite the text — was used with much greater frequency by the in-house editor. These comments included indications that the original text was difficult to comprehend, which in some instances was marked only with question marks, comments such as 'I don't follow this', or other remarks flagging problematic passages but not offering alternatives. Interventions of this nature approach the text from a distance, with the editor implicating themself only to detect language requiring improvement and, at times, to comment on the problems, though without venturing any possible solution.

Regarding the second category of comments requesting confirmation of direct interventions, both editors made use of this strategy, although the freelance editor did so with greater frequency. This tactic is used by both to signal direct interventions in

Detecting the same error in the original, the two editors take different paths to solve the problem. While the in-house editor chooses to flag the problem, the freelance editor assumes responsibility to both detect and remedy the error.

When the 62 passages that elicited editor commentary were analysed and coded to establish the orientation of the editor in the comment, we found 78 instances of these messages. Most of these remarks were aimed at just one of the four categories, although some comments were assigned two, as in the following comment in which the freelance editor intervened directly by proposing a change to the text and also explained how, if accepted, the change in the text had implications beyond the section of the manuscript where the fragment was found.

Original text	Freelance editor's proposed edit	Commentary on the edit
21 paired samples were analysed by western blot and it was found 10/21 (48%) showed UNR overexpression while 1/21 (4%) presented downregulation.	Western blot analysis revealed that 10 out of 21 pairs (48%) showed UNR overexpression while 1 out of 21 pairs (4%) presented downregulation.	You need to first explain that only 21 of the 31 samples underwent western blot analysis, if that is the case, both here and in the methods section.

Table 4.3: Passage in which the freelance editor made a correction to the text and added a margin comment.

In addition to proposing a change to the text, the freelance editor defers responsibility to the author to explain more clearly the concepts conveyed in this sentence and also displays sensitivity to genre issues here and beyond.

The most common type of margin comment had to do with sentence-level issues (50), followed by discipline-specific discourse (6), target-publication concerns (6), and knowledge content and claims (3). Many of the comments addressing sentence-level issues were concerned with writing clarity, terminology, and other aspects in which the editors brought their language expertise to bear on the text, either after having researched possible solutions to the problem or not. Comments addressing discipline-specific discourse referenced citation practices, discourse-level flow beyond the sentence level, genre appropriateness, and other issues interpreted as limiting the text's degree of adaptation to the genre of the research article. Remarks made by the two editors regarding target-publication concerns urged the authors to consult the journals' standards for citing works in the literature, use of abbreviations, and warnings on what could constitute copy-paste writing and be interpreted as plagiarism. Lastly, references to knowledge content and claims challenged the author to review certain passages where the editor believed the ideas conveyed by the text contradicted scientific fact. Here, it is of interest to note both that all three of these comments were made by the in-house

Article	Comments by in-house editor in a single paragraph	Comments by freelance editor in a single paragraph
1	8	6
2	5	2
3	6	3
4	9	2
5	19	3
6	9	3
mean	9.3	3.2

Table 4.1: Total number of margin comments made by each editor in the selected paragraph of each article. The mean number of comments appears in the bottom row.

Turning now to the perceived deficiencies or other issues that sparked these comments, the editors made observations on 62 text fragments, consisting of single words, terms, clauses, sentences, or even stretches of text comprising more than one sentence. Twelve of these passages (that is, 19%) saw both editors writing remarks in the margin, although in many of the remaining comments the editor who intervened directly rather than indirectly did so to address the same problem perceived by the other editor. An example of this divergent approach to resolving the same difficulty appears in the three excerpts appearing below. The text highlighted for commentary by the in-house editor appears in italics.

Original text	Comment from in-house editor	Direct intervention by freelance editor with no comment made
It is known that the Cln3 levels are controlled *by the phosphorylation state of its destruction box, the PEST region, by Cdk1, and the subsequent proteosomal degradation.*	Parallel grammar. When I read a list like this, 'by' tells me that I'm at a new item. How many items are in this list? Revise.	It is known that the Cln3 levels are controlled by the phosphorylation state of the destruction box, or PEST region, through Cdk1, with subsequent proteasomal degradation.

Table 4.2: Passage from a text illustrating the different approaches taken by the in-house editor and the freelance editor.

high concentration of margin comments, sending both the original text and our edited version to the other co-author. Each editor then blindly edited this section, replicating as closely as possible the editing approach used in their regular practice with such authors and making comments to the author as per usual. When performing this experimental edit, the entire text was made available in order to provide the normal range of resources (for example, references, tables) to carry out a complete revision.

Once these experimental edits were performed, the six sets of two edited texts were examined both quantitatively and qualitatively. First, the total number of comments made by each of the two researchers was calculated to determine each editor's tendency to make such comments as evidenced in the three-article sample. Then, each text segment that had triggered commentary by one editor was studied to establish whether the second editor had also remarked on the passage or, alternatively, had opted to propose changes directly in the text or make no change or commentary. While direct interventions in the text constitute a potentially rich focus of inquiry, they were disregarded if both editors had proposed changes to the same passage as the study was concerned with the specific implications of comments and not with the nature or quality of direct interventions.

All observations were evaluated qualitatively to classify the field of knowledge applied by the editor in each case. These assignments were made according to the four different orientations found by Lillis and Curry (2006) — that is, sentence-level edits, knowledge content and claims, discipline-specific discourse, and target-publication concerns. As a second step, all instances in which one or both editors included a margin comment were assessed to codify the strategy used by the editor when faced with passages that were problematic enough to warrant further communication with the author. For both of these analytical procedures, all comments made in a single paper were placed sequentially in tables containing three columns: the comments of the original editor, those of the second editor, and analytical findings arrived at by comparing the two sets of results. The analyses were discussed by the two authors of this chapter to arrive at a consensus on the goals behind these comments.

3. Results

The results of the study revealed significant differences in terms of involvement in the text, didacticism and diplomacy. The first of these differences was seen in commenting frequency. While the in-house editor showed a greater tendency to use comments to flag passages requiring improvement, the freelance editor was substantially more likely to make considerable changes directly in the text, even when doing so involved extensive research in order to decipher the author's intended meaning. As shown in Table 4.1, the in-house editor made margin comments three times as frequently as the freelance editor.

1.3. 'Unfinished business' in edited text and its relevance to the author-editor relationship

One editing strategy that is particularly illustrative of how editors respond to the many factors inherent to the editor-author relationship is the author query. Unlike direct interventions in texts, where authors are invited to either accept or reject the proposed edit, the interactions we are referring to often appear as margin comments (Ventola & Mauranen, 1991). The actions requested in these comments vary substantially and may call on the author to confirm the editor's supposition, revise a problematic passage, review the edited passage with particular care, or reconsider broader aspects of the paper as a whole, among others. The signals transmitted by these comments can be an indication of what Burrough-Boenisch refers to as editor assertiveness (2003) and, by extension, how the editor views their relationship with the author. When this stance toward the author is contextualised against the backdrop of the editor's working arrangement with the author — be it freelance or in-house — new insights on this relationship can come into focus.

The authors of this chapter — an in-house editor and a freelance editor — carried out a comparative intervention study to explore their respective approaches to revising NNES texts. In performing this analysis, we were particularly interested in seeing where our different styles of editing might lead us to either intervene directly in the text or defer responsibility, urging the author to revisit particular passages in light of our comments or questions. As in the Willey and Tanimoto study, these consultation points often signalled problems within the text, at times encouraging the author to take action, although margin comments could also be intended to educate the author about language, the genre of the research article, or other issues related to academic literacy. By examining the nature of these messages for the author and the editing work they reflect, we sought to describe the way in which we oriented toward the text, and to map these approaches against the categories of literacy brokers described by Lillis and Curry (2006). We thus aimed to illustrate the way in which we moved along a continuum between superficial copyediting at one extreme and highly substantive editing at the other.

2. Methods

We each chose a set of three research articles written by a single past or current client and sent to us for editing. Each of the two authors we selected had drafted and prepared their three respective research articles for submission to biomedical journals as original contributions following the IMRD format (introduction, methods, results and discussion), and each had published. After obtaining written consent from both authors to participate anonymously, we chose what we believed to be a particularly rich section from each text for the purposes of this study because of its comparatively

Others, however, adopt a broader perspective, as in the case of Knorr-Cetina (1981), whose work tracked and categorised changes across different versions of a single academic publication, finding two categories of changes geared toward content — deletion and reshuffling — and one category foregrounding rhetoric (that is, changes in modality). Gosden (1995) later expanded on Knorr-Cetina's work, studying seven different texts produced by novice NNES writers of research articles from first draft to final draft by examining the redrafting along the arc of each text and also taking into account more substantive modifications that are made during text production. Gosden concluded that aside from deletion and reshuffling, the writers who contributed texts to his corpus also added technical detail, polished language (generally below the clause level), and engaged in what Swales refers to as 'rhetorical machining' (1990) — that is, altering discourse structure, modifying claims, and carrying out changes related to purpose.

For their part, Willey and Tanimoto (2012) used an abstract written by a novice NNES academic writer to perform a comparative study of intervention patterns among four groups, comprising inexperienced and experienced editors of academic medical texts from outside the medical profession, scientists working within the medical profession, and a control group. Their analysis grouped these interventions into seven different categories: rewriting, recombining, mechanical changes, substitution, deletion, reordering and addition. Lastly, in their multi-year text-ethnographic study of the genesis and development of academic texts by NNES writers, Lillis and Curry (Curry & Lillis, 2010; Lillis & Curry, 2006) have found the interventions of 'language brokers' to vary in terms of involvement, ranging from the sentence level to deeper issues specific to the author's academic field, with language professionals focusing more on textual surface issues and academic professionals showing a greater tendency to rework content for journal audiences.

One aspect of particular interest in the aforementioned paper by Willey and Tanimoto is their inclusion of consultation points signalled by editors when revising. To study this approach to problematic stretches in texts, the authors examined all points marked by editors for clarification in face-to-face meetings with authors, calculating both the frequency with which these points arose across the different groups of editors and the characteristics that sparked this uncertainty, thus allowing for a more precise description of textual hurdles as perceived by different types of revisers and the decisions they made to address these difficulties. This entry point into the editing process resembled the findings of Bisaillon (2007) and, especially, Flower (as cited in Willey & Tanimoto, 2012), who concluded that when confronted with such problems, editors may revise when the problem is well defined, rewrite the problematic part of the text based on gist, delay action/search for a solution, or ignore the problem.

knowledge and language expertise on successful NNES writing have found that it is more advantageous for both scientific peers and language professionals to collaborate in the editing process (Benfield & Feak, 2006) as non-scientists' lack of field knowledge may make them better equipped to evaluate whether the ideas expressed in the manuscript come across effectively (Willey & Tanimoto, 2012).

The initial quality of NNES writing can also impact the degree to which editors intervene in texts. While some editing tasks involve fairly straightforward improvements of syntax, orthography, punctuation and other issues, other papers require much broader reworking or rewriting to overcome shortcomings in discourse and rhetoric (Burrough-Boenisch, 2003; Shashok, 2001). Although editors are most often expected to orient exclusively toward language, it is nearly impossible for them to draw a clean line between linguistic form and content (Flowerdew, 2000; Lillis & Curry, 2006), and this may increase the invasiveness required to improve manuscripts (Bisaillon, 2007). Studies on language facilitation have found that these higher-order problems with writing require great time and effort due to the uncertainty caused when the editor must try to discern the author's intended meaning or when attempting to improve flow between sentences (Li & Flowerdew, 2007). This raises the question of whether a substantial gap in an author's writing proficiency can be remedied by a language services provider (Harwood, Austin & Macaulay, 2009).

1.2. Previous research on language facilitation

To better understand the work carried out by editors and the way in which they orient their services to texts, a number of studies have analysed the act of editing from a variety of perspectives. Much of this scholarship has examined self-editing, and less is known about the ways in which providers of language support orient themselves to texts (see Bisaillon, 2007, for an overview). Some studies have based their analyses either fully or partially on the work done in writing centres and other institutional contexts (Koyalan & Mumford, 2011; Li & Flowerdew, 2007; Ventola & Mauranen, 1991; Willey & Tanimoto, 2012), offering certain insights on intervention strategies despite the fact that some of the data come from writing support provided to university students rather than academics (Harwood et al., 2009). Outside of academic contexts, some of the research looking at the impact of editors on texts has been based on genres other than strictly academic work, including 'journalese' (Yli-Jokipii & Jorgensen, 2004).

In addition to the socio-cultural context in which editing takes place, some studies on practice have examined a number of linguistic and textual features, while others have observed the phenomenon of editing and self-revision from a wider perspective. Searching to classify changes related to register, Koyalan and Mumford (2011) observed five different intervention types concerned with nominalisation, subordination, non-finite clauses, prepositional phrases as post-modifiers, and noun premodification.

funds, and other factors. Assistance can come from individuals in researchers' personal or professional environments, and the background and experience of these facilitators may vary widely (Burrough-Boenisch, 2003; Lillis & Curry, 2010; Shashok, 2001).

Professional language support provided to NNES researchers who have access to such services may come in a variety of forms. While some authors have their manuscripts translated into English from their mother tongue, others call on collaborators to improve texts already drafted in English. This type of work has been described using a number of terms, including revising, proofreading and editing, with each term subject to a range of interpretations. For the sake of simplicity, we will refer to the process of improving written work as editing, and its practitioners as editors.

1.1. Factors influencing approach and orientation in editing

When presented with English language research papers, editors may take any one of a number of approaches that reflect the many constraints inherent to the author, the editor, the context of their collaboration, the type and quality of the original draft, and the explicit and perceived relationship between the two. Some institutions hire in-house editors to support staff researchers in their attempts to publish their papers. These institutional editors may be found in a number of private and public organisations, including universities, hospitals, research institutes, national and international agencies, and a range of enterprises. The responsibilities of these salaried employees are often clearly outlined in institutional guidelines (Shashok, 2001), although, as in the case of one of the co-authors of this chapter, this remit is sometimes developed more organically over time, evolving through practice. In recent years, more and more editors have established themselves as freelancers, working with clients who pay them to collaborate on specific projects with no lasting contractual obligation to the author or the author's institution (Shashok, 2001). Though working toward the same goal of improving English language manuscripts to meet the requirements of journal gatekeepers, these two types of editor must align themselves to very different loyalties due to their physical circumstances, with the in-house editor answering to the administrators of the institution that employs both the service provider and client, while the freelance editor maintains a more flexible yet fragile relationship with each client in their portfolio and experiences greater exposure to changes in clients' circumstances and satisfaction with the work done.

Editors come from diverse backgrounds: some have previous experience in the author's field, while others enter the profession with expertise in language teaching, translation and linguistics, among others. Subject knowledge may sometimes limit how an editor can intervene in a text (Burrough-Boenisch, 2002; Flowerdew, 2000; Mišak, Marušić & Marušić, 2005; Willey & Tanimoto, 2012), although in some circumstances, NNES authors prefer for editors to be from other backgrounds (Flowerdew, 2000). Beyond this insider-outsider dichotomy, certain studies on the influence of content

4

The delicate art of commenting:

Exploring different approaches to editing and their implications for the author-editor relationship[1]

Oliver Shaw and Sabrina Voss

1. Introduction

The premium placed on English-medium international publications for career advancement in academia has been widely documented, and this virtual English-only playing field creates a substantial burden for academics who are non-native English speakers [NNES] (Belcher, 2007; Lillis & Curry, 2010; Sheldon, 2011; Uzuner, 2008). While NNES scholars are widely published in many scientific journals and acceptance rates for these academics are similar to those of native-English-speaking authors (Benfield & Feak, 2006; Burrough-Boenisch, 2003; Ferguson, 2007; Kourilova, 1998), this success often comes at a substantial cost in terms of effort, time and other resources (Curry & Lillis, 2004; Huang, 2010; Swales, 1990; Tardy, 2004). Many scientists who wish to publish in international journals seek language support for their manuscripts, although the availability of these services can vary substantially depending on the researcher's location, network of international researchers available to assist them, availability of

---

1 This chapter is based on a presentation given at the October 2015 meeting of Mediterranean Editors and Translators in Coimbra, Portugal.

Calvino, I. (1974/1972). *Invisible cities* (W. Weaver, Trans.). New York: Houghton Mifflin Harcourt.

Comelles, J.M. (2006). *Stultifera navis. La locura, el poder y la ciudad*. Lleida, Catalonia: Editorial Milenio.

Cover, I. (2016). *Open walls: The experience of psychiatric institutionalization through Egyptian women's drawings* (unpublished doctoral thesis, Universitat Rovira i Virgili, Catalonia).

DiGiacomo, S.M. (1987). Biomedicine as a cultural system: An anthropologist in the kingdom of the sick. In H.A. Baer (Ed.), *Encounters with biomedicine: Case studies in medical anthropology* (pp. 315-346). New York and London: Gordon and Breach Science Publishers.

DiGiacomo, S.M. (2013). Giving authors a voice in another language through translation. In V. Matarese (Ed.), *Supporting research writing: Roles and challenges in multilingual settings* (pp. 107-119). Oxford: Chandos Publishing.

Foucault, M. (2006/1961). *History of madness* (J. Murphy, Trans.). London and New York: Routledge.

Frank, A. (1991). *At the will of the body: Reflections on illness*. Boston and New York: Houghton Mifflin.

Geertz, C. (1973). *The interpretation of cultures*. New York: Basic Books.

Geertz, C. (1983). *Local knowledge: Further essays in interpretive anthropology*. New York: Basic Books.

Geertz, C. (1988). *Works and lives: The anthropologist as author*. Stanford, CA: Stanford University Press.

Goffman, E. (1991/1961). *Asylums: Essays on the social situation of mental patients and other inmates*. London: Penguin Books.

Rosaldo, R. (1989). Grief and a headhunter's rage. In R. Rosaldo, *Culture and truth: The remaking of social analysis* (pp. 1-21). Boston: Beacon Press.

Stoller, P. (2004). *Stranger in the village of the sick: A memoir of cancer, sorcery and healing*. Boston: Beacon Press.

sessions as data and analytic points of departure; in her use of literary mirrors in addition to anthropological theory — her own short story composed while she was in the field, and Italo Calvino's book *Invisible Cities* — and in her identification and interpretation of the paradoxical character of the Alexandria psychiatric hospital as both a prison and a refuge for Egyptian women. I have deliberately used two text examples from the thesis that demonstrate the paradox.

The challenges for the academic adviser/author's editor/translator are substantial. My contributions to the final product were those of the anthropologist as well as the language professional, but both involved teaching. The goal was both to help Ilaria create an account of her research that is a positive contribution to knowledge in medical anthropology and more broadly to anthropology in general, and to help her develop as a scholarly writer in English, learning to frame her ideas syntactically in English, not as Romance-language calques; to move away from writing in English as literal translation and toward greater command of English as a literary instrument; and to develop an ethnographic voice that establishes her authorial presence in her own text. The complexity of this work suggests that a single doctoral thesis supervisor is insufficient in cases in which the student is pursuing the European or International Doctorate and is writing even a part of the thesis in English. Linguistic form is closely connected to analytic content, and this points to a need for start-to-finish involvement in the thesis writing process by an academic adviser from the student's own discipline or a related discipline who is also a language professional, rather than the use of end-stage translation or 'proofreading' services.

Every level of the 'vertical continuum of editing' (Burrough-Boenisch, 2013, p. 146) is present here, from 'light' to 'heavy', from copyediting to developmental editing, which, in the context of doctoral work, is part of what thesis supervision entails. I have been careful, however, as Joy Burrough-Boenisch warns (p. 148), not to 'hijack the author's role'. This thesis is Ilaria's work, but what I have tried to do is to help her achieve the most credible ethnographic voice possible in English.

References

Allué, M. (1996). *Perder la piel*. Barcelona: Planeta/Seix Barral.

Behar, R. (1996). *The vulnerable observer: Anthropology that breaks your heart*. Boston, MA: Beacon Press.

Bennett, K. (2013). The translator as cultural mediator in research publication. In V. Matarese (Ed.), *Supporting research writing: Roles and challenges in multilingual settings* (pp. 93-106). Oxford: Chandos Publishing.

Burrough-Boenisch, J. (2013). Defining and describing editing. In V. Matarese (Ed.), *Supporting research writing: Roles and challenges in multilingual settings* (pp. 141-155). Oxford: Chandos Publishing.

obscured by the fact that the student appears as the sole author. What, then, constitutes 'authorship' in the writing of doctoral theses? There is no single answer to this question, only multiple answers that vary by discipline, but in no discipline can the measure of authorship be that the student wrote every single word alone and without guidance because the doctoral thesis is the final stage of a professional apprenticeship. It is also the first stage of the research publication process, in which newly minted PhDs also require assistance, and in anthropology, the goal is increasingly to move away from the thesis as an unpublished academic exercise and toward the thesis as the first draft of a full-length published ethnographic study.

One of the criteria for the granting of the doctorate is that the research and the textual account of it be original work. Originality in ethnography means not a new 'discovery' but fresh insight into a previously analysed problem that can lead to its reframing or redefinition, and a willingness to experiment with ethnographic method and form and to push the boundaries of the analytic vocabulary of anthropology. This is experimentation not for its own sake but in search of those new insights, and in the interest of reaching audiences in other disciplines with shared concerns, even audiences outside the academy.

Ethnographic writing is closer to literary than to scientific discourse, grounded in knowledge that is empirical, but not in an empiricist methodology. Unlike biomedical knowledge, which represents itself as a copy of biological facts, anthropological knowledge is framed as a close critical reading, an interpretation of social actions that are themselves first-order interpretations of the shared structures of meaning and feeling that shape them without determining them. Clifford Geertz (1973, pp. 6-7) famously characterised ethnography as 'thick description': an explication of other cultural experience that renders it accessible to us in its own terms, 'from the native's point of view' (1983, p. 55). The 'density' of ethnographic texts consists not simply in a wealth of detailed description, but in contextualisation. This is achieved through an intellectual movement characteristic of all ethnographic writing: a tacking back and forth between what Geertz (1983, p. 57) calls 'experience-near' concepts — local cultural knowledge — and 'experience-distant' concepts, those that form part of the anthropologist's analytic vocabulary, bringing them simultaneously into view in such a way that they shed light on each other (see DiGiacomo, 2013, p. 111). This is how ethnographic writing produces its effects: familiarising the strange, and defamiliarising the taken-for-granted.

In anthropological writing, the way the ethnographer holds her data up to the mirror of theory in such a way that the resulting reflections allow her to trace a methodological pathway through it, and the extent to which that method grapples successfully with what Clifford Geertz (1988, p. 16) called the 'signature dilemma' — 'how far, and how, to invade one's text' (p. 20) — produce an authorial voice, which is part of its originality. Ilaria's thesis is original in all the ways that count: in her treatment of the drawings and collages that she and her informants made in the art expression

I do not mean to imply that the staff of a psychiatric hospital should not watch over the patients and make sure that the hospital is a safe place. Accidents and even tragedies can happen in a context so imbued with suffering, be it the prison, the school or the home. The point I want to stress is the tendency to misrepresent patients' acts and words — in a word, their agency — in the context of the psychiatric hospital. This misrepresentation, in order for the staff members to be at peace with themselves, usually slants towards perceiving threats and problems where there are none, and towards considering patients' behaviors as consequences of their illness rather than meaningful statements about their condition in the institutional context.

... In Rosenhan's words: 'The hospital itself imposes a special environment in which the meaning of behavior can easily be misunderstood ... the magnitude of distortion is exceedingly high in the extreme context that is a psychiatric hospital' (Rosenhan 1973: 257). ... During a collage session held with Group 1, a male patient took a pair of scissors and walked [a] few steps away from the group. The psychiatrist and I exchanged worried glances. Yussef calmly sat down on a rickety chair, pulled a foot out of his broken shoe, and started to cut his toenails. Dr. Mirvat and I looked at each other with relief; neither of us had the courage to tell him that the scissors were meant for another use.

This passage captures important elements of the tragedy of psychiatric institutionalisation in a first-person narrative that shows how the logic of the asylum engulfs and penetrates everyone, even the anthropologist, who is enlisted unwillingly, even unwittingly, into its service as yet one more border guard. It conveys with great immediacy what is at stake for patients in an institution that is ostensibly dedicated to their care and healing, yet systematically undermines their selfhood, identity and agency, by allowing readers to share the anthropologist's painful recognition of her own complicity in this logic. This narrative strategy is by now familiar (if still contested) territory in ethnography as a literary genre (see DiGiacomo, 2013). The use of personal experience as analytic category, thanks to the courage of writers like Renato Rosaldo (1989) and Ruth Behar (1996), is now recognisable as one of those 'theaters of language' (Geertz, 1988, p. 21) in which other authors perform. It is a theatre to whose construction I have also contributed from the subfield of medical anthropology (DiGiacomo, 1987), as have my colleagues in Tarragona (Allué, 1996; Comelles, 2006) and elsewhere (Frank, 1991; Stoller, 2004). Decades ago, Clifford Geertz (1973, p. 16) invoked 'the power of the scientific imagination to bring us into touch with the lives of strangers' and, citing Thoreau, continued, 'It is not worth it ... to go round the world to count the cats in Zanzibar'. What *is* worth going round the world for is, in Ruth Behar's (1996) words, 'anthropology that breaks your heart'.

3. Conclusion

It is not unusual for thesis advisers to intervene significantly in the texts produced by their graduate students, but this process is seldom examined explicitly, and it is

When working with the women of Group 2 in the hospital library I found myself in the unpleasant situation of asking the psychiatrists to subject all the patient participants to a body search. We dedicated the session to the collage technique, using scissors with rounded tips to cut images out of newspapers. Aware of the hospital rule prohibiting patients from possessing potentially harmful objects, I counted the pairs of scissors I placed on the table: at the end of the session I counted them again to make sure they were the same number. At the beginning of the session there were nine, but when we finished work, there were only eight. Count, recount. Look everywhere: on the table, under it, between the pages of the newspaper. No trace of the ninth pair. While I started to doubt whether I had counted them correctly at the beginning of the session, two patients told us — a female psychiatrist, a female psychologist and I were coordinating that session — that they had shared the same pair during the entire session. If we had believed them, the 'case' would have been solved. It would have explained why the nine participants of the workshop managed to work with the eight pair of scissors that were now gathered on the table. This would also have meant that my count was wrong, something I was increasingly less sure about. But we did not believe them; we wanted to, but we could not, we thought, take the responsibility of trusting them without verification.

To be precise, I was more worried than the psychiatrist and the psychologist about the disappearance of the ninth pair, and insisted on conducting the search. I was aware that this might change the patients' feelings toward us and our work, and confirm a truth that, with my work, I was trying to dismantle: that 'the patient is shorn of credibility by virtue of his psychiatric label' (Rosenhan 1973: 256). The patient's word was, once again, deemed meaningless or untruthful by the staff — and by the anthropologist as well! I asked my 'colleagues' to undertake the search in a separate room, in order for the patients not to be embarrassed in front of the group because of the exposure of their bodies or in case the missing scissors were found on one of them. As there was no available space near the hospital library to perform such action, the psychiatrist searched every patient in a corner of the room. No pair of scissors came out of the search; after having expressed repeated regrets, I let the patients go back to their wards. During the two days that passed before I returned to the hospital for the next session, this pair of scissors was constantly in my thoughts. It was with both relief and irritation that I finally discovered that it had been taken by a social worker who needed it for work outside the library: he took it without asking permission.

This episode is instructive of the imbalances of power and credibility that characterise the psychiatric hospital. Someone like me, who was committed to creating a space impermeable to institutional dynamics through her artistic sessions, found herself reproducing a typical institutional logic, that of control and distrust towards the less empowered. My action was motivated more by fear than by the desire to exert force on patients. However, fear and distrust towards patients can also operate as institutional tools that maintain distance between the supposedly sane and those whose insanity is guaranteed by their psychiatric label. It did not even occur to me that the person responsible for the 'theft' could have been a member of the staff.

she confirms to me an hypothesis that I had been developing during the second half of my fieldwork period: that the psychiatric hospital can work, for lower and middle-lower class Egyptian women, as a 'leeway space'. In other words, the hospital can be described as a *marginal space* in which, to a certain extent, its inhabitants dispose of a *margin* of action that is greater than the one accorded to them in their communities. The room of maneuver of which they dispose is guaranteed by the very marginality of the space.

The lee of a ship it is the sheltered side of it, the one that it is not reached by the shacking force of the wind. If we borrow the metaphor of the asylum as a ship of fools anchored within the city limits (Martínez-Hernáez, 2013) and we use the wind as the metaphor for social constraints, we can affirm that for some female inpatients the psychiatric hospital embody a 'lee-way space'. Or, better said, we can affirm that for some aspects or in some moments of their life, for diagnosed women to stay at the hospital it is the equivalent of staying in the sheltered side of a ship that is being slammed by a storm. Of course, the hospital has its kinds of 'tempests', but they are tempests of a different order.

she confirmed a hypothesis I had been developing during the second half of my fieldwork period: that the psychiatric hospital can work, for lower and lower-middle class Egyptian women, as a 'leeway space'. In other words, the hospital can be described as a *marginal space* in which, to a certain extent, its inhabitants have at their disposal a *margin* for action that is greater than the one accorded to them in their communities. This room to maneuver is guaranteed by the very marginality of the space.

The lee of a ship is the sheltered side of it, the one that it is not reached by the force of the wind. If we borrow the metaphor of the asylum as a ship of fools anchored within the city limits (Martínez-Hernáez, 2013) and we use the wind as a metaphor for social constraints, we can say that for some female inpatients the psychiatric hospital embodies a 'leeway space'. For some aspects or in some moments of their life, for diagnosed women being in the hospital is the equivalent of staying on the sheltered side of a ship that is being slammed by a storm. Of course, the hospital has its own kinds of 'tempests', but they are tempests of a different order.

Finally, there are long passages toward the end of the thesis in which I changed nothing at all. One of these focuses on how the logic of the asylum as a 'total institution' inhabits patients, penetrating their bodies and their selves so that over time they come to resemble it. The sociologist Erving Goffman (1961/1991), to whom we owe the concept of the total institution, called attention to the systematic humiliations and degradations to which inpatients are subjected: 'contaminative exposure' that may be either physical or social, and is sometimes both. One such practice — the body search — is the subject of Ilaria's account of an art expression session devoted to collage, at the end of which one pair of scissors — a dangerous object to which patients normally do not have access — was missing (Cover, 2016, pp. 227-9).

So far I have focused on the linguistic shortcomings of the text. At this point, however, I would like to explain that, despite the problems of the initial draft, the thesis always had the power to engage and persuade the reader. Whenever I started working on a new section of Ilaria's thesis, I read straight through it without stopping because it was hard to put down, even if there were other urgent claims on my time. This was not a case in which stock phrases and technical jargon were embedded in elementary English; it was a nuanced and compelling account of suffering — alien suffering, but suffering rendered both intelligible and moving. A colleague of mine, someone whom I have often translated, once remarked that while it is possible to write a medical article in English with a vocabulary of 300 words, the power of ethnographic writing depends on shades of meaning. Lest anyone be tempted to see that as a social scientist's prejudice, let me point out that the colleague in question is both a doctor and an anthropologist.

As time went on, Ilaria became a more confident writer in English, especially during and after her stay as a visiting scholar in the US. The analytic strands developed in the chapters began to come together in a coherent narrative, and the last two chapters seemed to write themselves through her. The following text example, taken from one of these chapters, illustrates Ilaria's control of the expressive power of English through the extension of an existing analytic metaphor for the insane asylum — the ship of fools — in order to advance an argument of considerable subtlety. The text is not without minor problems, but they can be fixed easily with only light editing. What is important in this passage is its use of an image linked to the nautical metaphor in a way that obliges us to question accepted wisdom about psychiatric institutions. The sources of this wisdom are highly authoritative; they include Michel Foucault's (1961/2006) work on the history of madness and Erving Goffman's (1961/1991) theorisation of the asylum as a total institution, both of which have shaped generations of work in medical sociology and anthropology.

ILARIA

In the hospital, many things of the outside world are not present. There are some, however, whose lack is missed by no one. Stigmatisation on the basis of people's mental condition and lack of social pressures are one such instance. 'The psychiatric hospital is a poor but not a terrible place. Families, most of the time, reject their mentally ill member, while the hospital offers acceptance to them'. This is Dr. Manal talking, a female psychiatrist who works at the Alexandria hospital. When I interviewed her, in October 2014,

SUSAN

In the hospital, many things of the outside world are not present. There are some, however, that no one misses: for example, stigmatisation of the mentally ill and social pressure to conform to narrow expectations. 'The psychiatric hospital is a poor but not a terrible place. Families, most of the time, reject their mentally ill member, while the hospital offers acceptance to them'. This is Dr. Manal, a female psychiatrist who works at the Alexandria hospital. When I interviewed her, in October 2014,

I received a common worried and deceived comment from my acquaintances (especially from the women): 'Enti khassiti ghidan … Leeh? Enti kowaysa?' ('You lost a lot of weight … Why? Are you okay?'). I did not more fit with the conventional idea of beauty and the people who had now the confidence to make remarks about my look told me that I needed to gain back the kilos I had lost.

my acquaintances (especially the women) greeted me with concern: 'Enti khassiti ghidan … Leeh? Enti kowaysa?' ('You've lost a lot of weight … Why? Are you okay?'). For them the problem was not only aesthetic; my weight loss was possible evidence of illness, and because we shared a sufficient degree of social intimacy they had the confidence to tell me that I needed to gain back the kilos I had lost.

Ilaria is a very good storyteller, and at the beginning it was in telling stories that her English was the most fluid and the least labored. It was when she reached for an academic voice that her writing got bogged down. Despite one's best intentions, when working in a language in which you are not native, and when you are conscious that in the last analysis a doctoral thesis is an academic exercise in which you have to demonstrate your competence in your chosen field of study — as Ilaria put it (personal communication, 25 January 2016), 'mak[ing] [the data] "square" with theory' — it can be all too easy to fall back on familiar academic conventions, styles and techniques learned during one's undergraduate years, or even earlier, in secondary school. One of these was the use of numbered sections and subsections in chapters (1.1, 1.2, and so forth), which had the unfortunate effect of turning Ilaria into a sort of traffic cop in her own text, intruding on it to point the reader's attention backward or forward to other sections ('As I observed in section 3.2 of Chapter X … '). This was much more distracting than helpful to the reader, so I strongly urged her to dispense with it, and she did. Another was the tendency to write defensively, explaining herself constantly in formal diction and abstruse vocabulary, both in advance and retrospectively, while hedging all the way. This kind of writing forces the reader to hack her way through thickets of unnecessary verbiage to get at the meaning. What I tried to preserve in my edit was the storytelling voice that Ilaria deploys so effectively elsewhere in the thesis.

ILARIA

I will now try to describe the composite ways in which this mixing can take shape. The boundaries between the three delineated worlds are fluid both from the perspective of whom is dealing with a distress, and of whom works to solve it. Patients can resort to different kinds of healing figures (meaning here psychiatrist, religious or traditional healers) in a diachronic or synchronic line and without perceiving this action as contradictory.

SUSAN

The boundaries between psychiatric, religious and traditional healing are fluid from both the afflicted person's and from the healer's perspective. Patients may resort to different kinds of healing figures serially or simultaneously without perceiving this as contradictory.

exhibitionism and an unwarranted use of the cultural Other as a detour back to the Self (see Behar, 1996, pp. 170-1), it is increasingly evident that the anthropologist is as much a positioned subject as her informants are, and that the credibility of the analysis depends on making one's positioning (and repositioning) explicit in the text. Our department of anthropology has a long history of mining the ethnographer's personal experience for analytic insight, and we encourage our students to do so as well. This produces work that is more accessible to readers outside the discipline of anthropology and even outside the academy. The resulting thesis is less like an academic exercise and more like a book … and certainly more easily transformed into a publishable document. This is not, however, an easy voice to use effectively (see Behar, 1996, pp. 16-19). Some students are both more receptive to it and deploy it more skillfully than others, and Ilaria was one of these. It helped, perhaps, that she was highly conscious that her limited control of Arabic was an important limitation for her thesis, and had to be compensated for by other means of knowing; in her case, through participating with her informants in the art expression sessions she organised in the Alexandria psychiatric hospital. Whatever the case, she responded to my urging to write in the first person, and to find the strength in her own vulnerability.

ILARIA	SUSAN
A drawing can represent a situation that <u>their</u> creator <u>experimented</u>; one that they wish to experiment or even … a situation (or a person, an object) whose meaning or knowledge <u>is by them unknown</u>.	A drawing can represent a situation that <u>its</u> creator <u>experienced</u>, one that they wish to experience, or even … a situation (or a person, or an object) whose meaning <u>is unknown to them</u>.
The setting in which the tests were performed was the room adjoining the charity ward psychiatrists' office. Crossing the ward in the company <u>of Yosra</u> I understood that <u>it was the first time, for her, to access</u> a public psychiatric hospital. As we <u>moved forward in the hallway,</u> <u>her look became disoriented</u> and her bodily attitude stiffened. When I asked her if I could <u>assist</u> the performance of the tests, she accepted with enthusiasm.	The setting in which the tests were performed was the room adjoining the charity ward psychiatrists' office. Crossing the ward in <u>Yosra's</u> company I understood that <u>it was the first time she had been inside a public psychiatric hospital</u>. As we <u>walked down the hallway,</u> <u>she began to look disoriented</u> and her bodily attitude stiffened. When I asked her if I could <u>be present</u> during the administration of the tests, she accepted with enthusiasm.
After <u>having completed</u> the first part of my research, I went back to Italy for the summer, where <u>I slam down</u> considerably. When I returned to the field for the second part of my research,	After <u>completing</u> the first part of my research, I went back to Italy for the summer, where <u>I slimmed down</u> considerably. When I returned to the field for the second part of my research,

... the distance between what I wanted to write and what I was actually able to write was unbridgeable. While producing a PhD thesis one can experience moments of inspiration but, for the most part, it is hard work. I remember *feeling* what I wanted to write, feeling it in a pre-verbal sense. I subsequently started to think about the main points I wanted to mention and in what sequence I could present them. This inner dialogue happened in Italian, but it needed to be rendered in English. Apart from the Word document, four other windows were omnipresent on my computer screen: an Italian-English dictionary, a Spanish-English dictionary (because sometimes expressions came to mind in this language), antonyms and synonyms, and an automatic translator of set phrases. I used to slip from one webpage to another, trying not to lose sight of the content because of the form. But the two aspects are actually deeply intertwined; so intertwined that, if you have difficulty with one of them, the other will inevitably be affected.

In the first example, the plural possessive pronoun 'their' does not agree in number with its antecedent, 'a drawing', although I retained 'them' to refer to a person, 'its creator', in order to avoid the clumsiness of 'he or she' or, worse still, 'he/she' or 's/he', or an uncomfortable choice between 'he' and 'she' as a generic pronoun. The word order at the end of the sentence ('is by them unknown') also needed rearranging. In the second example, 'assist' was initially hard to detect as a false cognate, because it was entirely plausible that Ilaria might have offered to help, and this in fact was what I initially thought. On reading my edited text, Ilaria caught the misinterpretation and we were able to correct it.

The second example contains another Romance calque: 'in the company of Yosra' instead of 'in Yosra's company'. I altered the word order and usage in the rest of the sentence; while one may access information on the internet, one doesn't 'access' a hospital. Similarly, people walk down hallways rather than 'move forward in' them, and look disoriented rather than being in possession of 'a look' that becomes disoriented.

The third example contains many other problems besides the false cognate ('deceived'). Ilaria's story about gaining weight in the field and then — to her relief — losing it during a summer visit to her home in Italy, only to face the disapproving and worried reactions of her informants on her return to Egypt (see Cover, 2016, p. 170), is part of a discussion of her emotional and cognitive adjustments to the field and how her perception of Egyptian women moved from 'distance and incomprehension' to 'proximity and understanding'. The discussion includes not only Egyptian canons of feminine beauty but also dress, veiling, learning to embody an ideal of feminine modesty, being a single woman in Egypt, and situations in which Ilaria was mistaken for an Egyptian woman both by Egyptians and, disorientingly and upsettingly, by Italian tourists visiting Alexandria. These topics are not simply 'background' to the thesis; they are part of the reflexivity that is important in a discipline in which the instrument of knowledge production is not a research technique but the person of the ethnographer. Although there are still voices in the discipline that challenge the inclusion of the anthropologist as a character in her own ethnography as solipsism, mere self-indulgent

The majority of psychiatrists I interviewed maintained that religion has a supreme power and significance in Egyptian society: overlooking this aspect in the treatment of a patient would be, in their view, illogical.	The majority of psychiatrists I interviewed maintained that religion has a supreme power and significance in Egyptian society, and overlooking this fact in the treatment of a patient would be, in their view, illogical.

Interference from the writer's native language can produce syntactic calques. One example of such calques is the construction of sentences containing strings of 'ofs'. This is inevitable in Romance language syntax, but in English it is clumsy and slows down the text. Again, this is not the only problem in the following example. The sentence is also repetitive ('were used' … 'was used') and wordy ('to contemporary society or to its members', 'Egyptian citizens'); the passive verbs slow the text down even further; the second clause has a gerund, 'conveying', instead of a main verb; and the hedge ('probably') makes it sound unnecessarily tentative. The context here is the absence of a single clearly defined therapeutic itinerary for Egyptians suffering from mental illness. In order to convey this apparent asystematicity, Ilaria invoked two expressions — 'there is no system' and 'there is no conscience' — widely used in everyday Egyptian conversations to express (and censure) chaos at many levels, from monumental traffic jams to politics (Cover, 2016, pp. 56-7). In this case I opted to strip out all the unnecessary elements, shorten the sentence by about 50 percent, and move the text on quickly to examples of chaotic events, institutions and processes that contextualise the multiple and partially overlapping medical cultures that constitute Egyptian mental health care and their historical sources.

ILARIA	SUSAN
Both expressions were usually used in reference to contemporary society or to its members and the frequency by which this expression was used probably conveying the high level of frustration of Egyptian citizens towards an unfair economic and political system.	Both expressions, and the frequency of their use, reflect Egyptians' high level of frustration with an unfair economic and political system.

False cognates are the bane of writers struggling with an additional language. There are several examples of these in the text, and they reveal the problems of trying to write in one language while thinking in another. 'Experimented' should be 'experienced'; 'assist' should be 'be present'; and 'deceived' should be 'disappointed', although in this case I rewrote the sentence without it. Again, the examples contain other problems as well. Ilaria is a skilled and confident writer in Italian, but facing the blank computer screen in English was different. In her own words (personal communication, 25 January 2016, emphasis in the original):

say whether this is true or not, but in English the colon serves only two purposes: introducing a series; and explaining, expanding upon or clarifying what precedes it.

Punctuation is not the only problem in the following examples; I also removed unnecessary words to lighten the prose so that it would carry the reader along more easily. In the first example, in Egypt the relationship between religious and traditional healing is 'complex' because, as Ilaria's thesis explains, these two domains of belief and practice partially overlap, but institutional Islam regards some traditional healing beliefs and practices as quackery at best and immoral at worst: a way to take sexual advantage of vulnerable women (Cover, 2016, pp. 64-6). 'Elaborate', however, simply gets in the reader's way and adds nothing to our understanding of this. Similarly, in the second example, I changed 'religious-related' and 'the religious realm' to 'religious' and 'religion' respectively. These are examples of what Ilaria explains as a tendency in Italian academic writing to wordiness. As Karen Bennett (2013, p. 98) argues, for ideological and cultural reasons in the countries of southern Europe, a preference for a Baroque rhetorical style — 'verbal copiousness and complexity as signs of intellectual sophistication' — prevailed until well into the 20th century, and this influence is still present even beyond the humanities in scientific discourse.

What I aimed for with Ilaria's thesis was to adjust her style to English academic discourse without denaturing it, something that I hope will become clear in later text examples. I eliminated redundancies, but retained the poetic and emotive features of the text because there is room for them in ethnographic writing, where analytic metaphors abound. In some cases I shortened sentences, but not always; in the third example, I substituted a comma for the colon and left the sentence structure intact. As in the other text examples, I have underlined the problematic parts of the original text as well as the changes I made.

ILARIA

My research focused on the world of Egyptian psychiatry: I did not venture into the complex and elaborate areas of religious and traditional healing.

To resort to religious verbal expressions and to religious-related images while drawing was quite common between female patients during the art expression sessions: one may think that the condition of suffering from a mental illness and the very context of the psychiatric hospital could induce patients to frequently draw upon the religious realm as a way for founding solace.

SUSAN

My research focused on the world of Egyptian psychiatry; I did not venture into the complex areas of religious and traditional healing.

During the art expression sessions, it was quite common for female patients to resort to religious expressions or images. One might think that the condition of suffering from a mental illness and the very context of the psychiatric hospital could induce patients to draw frequently upon religion as a way of finding solace.

in order to resolve them or explain them away but to explicate the reasons for their presence and continued existence in social life.

Ilaria's is a literary thesis in more than one sense. In addition to the inclusion of her own short story as a source of analytic metaphors, she also makes use of Italo Calvino's book *Invisible Cities* (1972/1974). She transforms a number of the imaginary cities Calvino describes into creative ways of reconceptualising the psychiatric hospital and its relationship to the society in which it is embedded. Ilaria thus brings to her thesis a number of abilities and interests in art and literature that have shaped the text and imbued it with a distinctive authorial style and voice.

When we began working together, Ilaria's written English was uneven. In some places, it demonstrated a command of the language that some native speakers would envy, and in other places there were startlingly elementary mistakes — things like verb tenses out of sequence, and nouns and verbs that disagreed in number. With practice and with immersion, it evened out. The months she spent at Boston University [BU] as a visiting scholar, writing in an English-speaking academic context, talking about her work with faculty members at BU and Harvard, attending classes and seminars in English, and living with an American family, refined her control of the language. In the chapters written near the end of her stay at BU and following her return, there are long passages of beautiful prose (as well as analytic depth) that I hardly touched.

Our method of working was for Ilaria to send me a chunk of text — sometimes a whole chapter, sometimes part of a chapter, in the order in which they were written, which was not necessarily the order in which all the pieces were assembled in the final text of the thesis. I then edited each submission using the 'track changes' function to make all alterations to the text, questions and comments visible, and sent it back to her. Next, Ilaria accepted some of the changes and did some rewriting; after this, we met to read through the text together so that we could discuss and resolve together any remaining concerns. Sometimes two rounds of this were necessary. We spoke English.

My three intersecting roles — academic adviser, author's editor and translator — form the basis of this chapter. The extent and nature of this overlap are examined through a narrative about the development of the thesis that is structured around paired examples comparing Ilaria's original text with my edited text. Text examples that needed no editing, drawn from later chapters of the thesis, are also included, in order to show the degree of control Ilaria achieved not only over the mechanics of English but also over the analytic and expressive possibilities of ethnographic writing.

2. Blurring the boundaries: Editing as advising; advising as editing

In the beginning, one of the first problems we had to deal with was punctuation. The colon, in Ilaria's writing, tended to take the place of full-stops [periods], commas, and semicolons. When we talked about this, Ilaria said that she had learned to use the colon this way because this was how it was normally used in Italian academic writing. I cannot and we have since worked together on many occasions, both as author and translator and as co-authors. We shared responsibility for advising the conceptual, theoretical and ethnographic aspects of Ilaria's thesis, but I was the only person in my department who could be Ilaria's editor, a role that included correcting her translations of material quoted from sources in Italian and Spanish and also the third-party translations of two chapters, one originally written in Spanish and the other in Italian.

Ilaria did her fieldwork in Egypt in the public psychiatric hospital of the city of Alexandria, with mostly women inpatients. Many of her important insights about the experience of Egyptian women both inside the hospital and in the wider society emerge from her analysis of drawings and collages by her informants — both inpatients and hospital staff — and her own drawings produced in the art expression workshops she organised and led in the hospital. In her thesis, these are not treated simply as illustrations, but are given analytic value as materialisations of the positioned subjectivity of all the participants in these sessions. Approached in this way, the artwork is a source of analytic concepts that challenge received ideas about gender in the Muslim world, mental illness, and the nature of the psychiatric hospital as a total institution.

This thesis experiments with ethnography as a literary genre to the extent that it includes a short story Ilaria wrote during her fieldwork, which furnishes one of the guiding metaphors of the text, that of the asylum as a fish tank: a space of confinement in which both the inpatients and the ethnographer are out of their natural element. Her thesis also experiments with method. Ilaria's Arabic is limited and she did much of her interviewing and conversing with patients through a translator, but she compensated for this (more than compensated, in my view) by using a projective technique to elicit experiences and emotions: art expression through various drawing techniques and collage. She organised, with the hospital's approval and assistance, a number of workshops for the inpatients in which she and members of the hospital staff also participated, and the drawings and collages they — and she — produced are part of her data. Several of them also figure in the thesis.

The inclusion and analysis of Ilaria's own artwork is an innovative form of the reflexivity that is characteristic of contemporary ethnography, which is grounded in the understanding that the instrument through which anthropological knowledge is created is the person of the ethnographer. Her central argument is that the public psychiatric hospital, despite its marginal location in Alexandria on a dirt road far from the city centre, is not a place isolated from the rest of the city or from Egyptian society more generally. In complex ways, it both reflects and reproduces social, economic and political forces that contribute to destabilising the mental health of the inpatients: what anthropologists call structural violence. She documents forms of covert and occasionally overt resistance to the hierarchy of power relations in the hospital, heartbreaking forms of quiet suffering, and even moments of self-realisation. Her thesis demonstrates that the hospital is, paradoxically, experienced by the inpatients both as a prison and as a refuge. The identification and analysis of such paradoxes is central in ethnography, not

3

Blurring the boundaries:

Academic advising, authors' editing and translation in a graduate degree program

Susan M. DiGiacomo

1. Introduction

The spread of English as a global *lingua franca* affects not only established scholars who use English as an additional language in order to publish their work in international journals. It has also created pressure on doctoral students at universities in non-English-speaking EU member countries to avail themselves of the European Doctorate and International Doctorate options introduced under the Bologna Plan. These options require PhD candidates to spend a period of at least three months in a university outside the country in which they will obtain their degree, and to write part of their PhD thesis in English so that outside examiners can read it. This requirement poses special challenges for both the students and their thesis supervisors.

This chapter is based on a doctoral thesis in cultural anthropology that I co-advised with another colleague in my department. The student in question is Ilaria Cover (I include her name with her permission). She is a native Italian speaker and a competent speaker and writer of Spanish who opted for the International Doctorate and decided to write her thesis entirely in English. Ilaria's co-supervisor, Angel Martínez-Hernáez, is a specialist in cultural studies of psychiatry and mental health with whom I have participated in two competitively funded research projects on depressive distress in adolescents and their strategies for managing it. We met 25 years ago, when I translated the book he published from his doctoral thesis on the concept of 'symptom' in psychiatry,

Mertkan S., Arsan, N., Cavlan, G.I., & Aliusta, G.O. (2016). Diversity and equality in academic publishing: The case of educational leadership. *Compare: A Journal of Comparative and International Education*. DOI: http://dx.doi.org/10.1080/03057925.2015.1136924.

Nguyen, P.-M., Elliott, J.G., Terlouw, C., & Pilot, A. (2009). Neocolonialism in education: Cooperative learning in an Asian context. *Comparative Education, 45*(1), 109-130.

Paltridge, B. (2014). What is a good research project? *Language Education in Asia, 5*(1), 20-27.

Pennycook, A. (1997). Vulgar pragmatism, critical pragmatism, and EAP. *English for Specific Purposes, 16*(4), 253-270.

PRISEAL. (2015, October 30-November 1). Conference program. *PRISEAL 3, Coimbra 2015*, University of Coimbra, Portugal. Retrieved 6 March 2016 from https://ppriseal.webs.ull.es/ Abstracts_and_programme.html.

Qi, J. (2015). *Knowledge hierarchies in transnational education: Staging dissensus*. London: Routledge.

Santos, B.S., Nunes, J.A., & Meneses, M.P. (2007). Introduction: Opening up the canon of knowledge and recognition of difference. In B.S. Santos (Ed.), *Another knowledge is possible: Beyond Northern epistemologies*. London: Verso.

Schostak, J., & Schostak, J.F. (2013). *Writing research critically: Developing the power to make a difference*. London: Routledge.

Shehzad, W. (2008). Move two: Establishing a niche. *Ibérica, 15*, 25-50.

Smith, B. (1998, September). 'It doesn't count because it's subjective!' (Re)conceptualising the qualitative researcher role as 'validity' embraces subjectivity. Paper presented the *AARE Annual Conference*, Adelaide, Australia. Retrieved 18 April 2016 from www.aare.edu.au/ data/publications/1998/smi98278.pdf.

Smyth, R., & Maxwell, T.W. (2010). *The research matrix: An approach to supervision of higher degree research students*. Crawley, WA: HERDSA.

Swales, J.M. (1990). *Genre analysis: English in academic and research settings*. London: Cambridge University Press.

Swales, J.M., & Feak, C.B. (2012). *Academic writing for graduate students: Essential tasks and skills* (3rd ed.). Ann Arbor, MI: University of Michigan Press.

Weissberg, R., & Buker, S. (1990). *Writing up research: Experimental research report writing for students of English*. Englewood Cliffs, NJ: Prentice Hall Regents.

Wisker, G. (2015). *Getting published: Academic publishing success*. London: Palgrave Macmillan.

Clerehan R., & Moodie, J. (1997). A systematic approach to the teaching of writing for supervisors of international candidates: Perspectives from genre theory. In R. Murray-Harvey, & H. Silins (Eds.), *Learning and teaching in higher education: Advancing international perspectives — Refereed proceedings of the HERDSA National Conference* (pp. 73-89). Adelaide: Flinders University Press.

Connell, R. (2007). *Southern theory: The global dynamics of knowledge in social science.* Sydney: Allen & Unwin.

Corcoran, J., & Englander, K. (2016). A call for critical pragmatic pedagogical approaches to English for Research Publication Purposes. *Publications, 4*(6). Retrieved 1 May 2016 from www.mdpi.com/2304-6775/4/1/6/pdf.

Fenton-Smith, B. (2014). The place of Benesch's critical English for academic purposes in the current practice of academic language and learning. *Journal of Academic Language and Learning, 8*(3), A23-A33.

Flowerdew, J. (2008). Scholarly writers who use English as an additional language: What can Goffman's '*stigma*' tell us? *Journal of English for Academic Purposes, 7*, 77-86.

Flowerdew, J. (2013). English for Research Publication Purposes. In B. Paltridge, & S. Starfield (Eds.), *The handbook of English for Specific Purposes* (pp. 301-321). London: Wiley & Sons.

Harwood, N., & Hadley, G. (2004). Demystifying institutional practices: Critical pragmatism and the teaching of academic writing. *English for Specific Purposes, 23*, 355-377.

Hewings, M. (2006, November). English language standards in academic articles: Attitudes of peer reviewers. *Revista Canaria de Estudios Ingleses, 53*, 47-62.

Holliday, A. (2007). *Doing and writing qualitative research* (2nd ed.). London: Sage.

Huang, Q., Rozelle, S., Wang, J., & Huang, J. (2009). Water management institutional reform: A representative look at Northern China. *Agricultural Water Management, 96*(2), 215-225.

Hyland, K. (2016a). Academic publishing and the myth of linguistic injustice. *Journal of Second Language Writing, 31*, 58-69.

Hyland, K. (2016b). *Academic publishing: Issues and challenges in the construction of knowledge.* Oxford: Oxford University Press.

Kwan, B.S.C. (2010). An investigation of instruction in research publishing offered in doctoral programs: The Hong Kong case. *Higher Education, 59*, 55-68.

Lillis, T.M., & Curry, M.J. (2006). Professional academic writing by multilingual scholars: Interactions with literacy brokers in the production of English-medium texts. *Written Communication, 23*(1), 3-35.

Lillis, T., & Curry, M.J. (2010). *Academic writing in a global context: The politics and practices of publishing in English.* London: Routledge.

Lillis, T., & Curry, M.J. (2015). The politics of English, language and uptake: The case of international journal article reviews. *AILA Review, 28*, 127-150.

Lillis, T., Magyar, A., & Robinson-Pant, A. (2010). An international journal's attempts to address inequalities in academic publishing: Developing a writing for publishing program. *Compare, 40*(6), 781-800.

Matthews, S. (2005). Crafting qualitative research articles on marriage and families. *Journal of Marriage and Family, 67*(4), 799-808.

McNiff, J. (2012). Travels around identity: Transforming cultures of learned colonization. *Educational Action Research, 20*(1), 129-146.

evaluation has been convincingly displayed in penetrating oral critique, in submitted written documents I have seen only the operations of what Schostak and Schostak (2013, p. 9) have called 'the real-politic that suppresses, represses, erases voices'.

Nevertheless, I am still confident that using the Research Writing Matrix in this way allows ERPP to fulfil a dual role for periphery novice researchers in the social sciences. First, it structures an in-depth learning of both the epistemological assumptions of anglophone research and the language in which the dominant methodological criteria are realised; second, it simultaneously makes a small but strategic step towards Qi's (2015) 'staging dissensus'. That is, using the Research Writing Matrix offers us the opportunity 'to rise above the unilateral knowledge transfer of western concepts and enable knowledge co-construction that better addresses local needs' (p. 9).

References

Bennett, K. (2014). Discourses of knowledge: Cultural disjunctions and their implications for language industries. *Ibérica, 27*, 35-50.

Bennett, K. (2015). Towards an epistemological monoculture: Mechanisms of epistemicide in European research publication. In R. Plo Alastrué, & C. Perez-LLantada (Eds.), *English as a scientific and research language: Debates and discourses* (pp. 9-36). Berlin: De Gruyter Mouton.

Burgess, S., & Cargill, M. (2013). Using genre analysis and corpus linguistics to teach research article writing. In V. Matarese (Ed.), *Supporting research writing: Roles and challenges in multilingual settings* (pp. 55-71). Cambridge: Woodhead.

Cadman, K. (2002). English for academic possibilities: The research proposal as a contested site in postgraduate genre pedagogy. *Journal of English for Academic Purposes, 1*(2), 85-104.

Cadman, K. (2005). Towards a 'pedagogy of connection' in research education: A 'REAL' Story. *Journal of English for Academic Purposes, 4*(4), 353-367.

Cadman, K. (2014). Of house and home: Reflections on knowing and writing for a 'southern' postgraduate pedagogy. In L. Thesen, & L. Cooper (Eds.), *Risk in academic writing: Postgraduate students, their teachers and the making of knowledge* (pp. 166-200). Bristol: Multilingual Matters.

Cadman, K., & Song, X. (2012). Embracing transcultural pedagogy: An epistemological perspective. In X. Song, & K. Cadman (Eds.), *Bridging transcultural divides: Asian languages and cultures in global higher education* (pp. 3-26). Adelaide: University of Adelaide Press. DOI: http://dx.doi.org/10.1017/9781922064318.

Cargill, M., & O'Connor, P. (2013). *Writing scientific research articles: Strategy and steps* (2nd ed.). Oxford: Wiley-Blackwell.

Casanave, C.P. (2008). The stigmatizing effect of Goffman's stigma label: A response to John Flowerdew. *Journal of English for Academic Purposes, 7*(4), 264-267.

Clavero, M. (2010). Awkward phrasing. Rephrase: Linguistic injustice in ecological journals. *Trends in Ecology and Evolution, 20*, 1-2.

how these are carried out or how their outcomes are analysed and written about. Nevertheless, a research design is dawning. Figure 2.3 illustrates the self-questioning that the dialogic process has stimulated, as the writer asks themselves, 'Is it [the RQ] still broad?' The mixed-method study proposed here will clearly need more analysis and language work for both conducting and writing about the different kinds of analysis proposed.

In a learning context like this, 'in theory', as Corcoran and Englander (2016, p. 7) suggest, researchers can make 'informed choices of compliance, resistance or amalgam' (p. 5, citing Benesch, 2001) when they present their draft Matrix as well as their resulting manuscript for assessment. However, despite my own learners' active and critical oral discussions, when it has come to producing written accounts of their thinking, their 'informed choices' have not produced strategic variation from anglophone norms (as evident in Figures 2.2 and 2.3). In writing, participants have universally chosen to approximate prevailing values and processes in order to be found acceptable at the intersection of their own and the global anglophone criteria for epistemological rigour. Perhaps they have followed the trend described by Nguyen et al. (2009, p. 112) in which 'Western theories and practices … are thought to give a competitive edge and are considered to be fashionable and modern'. Alternatively, they may just have had doubt about my personal opinion, or a well-founded mistrust in my subservient 'pencil'. Either way, their written responses may be clearly seen to demonstrate the 'learned colonization' identified by McNiff (2012). Qi (2015, p. 198) offers a piece of challenging advice: 'Critique-based multilingual knowledge co-construction (CMKCC) starts with valuing and soliciting non-Western actors' knowledge, preferably *before* western … educators offer their concept, framework and model' (emphasis in the original). As has often been noted, to make this happen would need new vision and commitment from anglophone institutional policy makers, which in my view we are unlikely to see soon. For ERPP teachers, then, our imperatives are beautifully summarised by the Schostaks (Schostak & Schostak, 2013, p. 9): 'In the end there are no recipes to create public lives in mutual respect, only gestures towards writing'.

5. Conclusion

In this chapter, I have argued that in the social sciences it is both relevant and important for ERPP teachers to engage in what I have called 'methodology brokering' in order to facilitate learners' language development in direct relation to the global epistemological expectations of rigorous social research. Negotiating the expectations of a Research Writing Matrix for their own research project can greatly enhance EAL learners' chances of getting their research published in today's anglophone academy. I have shown here how in a transcultural, critical-pragmatic pedagogy, inexperienced research writers can demonstrate their understanding of research rigour by evaluating the relevance of our knowledge-making requirements for their own communities, including data collection, analysis and expected language structures. In my experience, however, while this

WHAT? [NB Focus & Scope]			WHY?	HOW? ['WHY of HOW' & 'HOW of 'HOW']		ANALYSIS & CLAIMS [Focus & Scope]
Question	Information from literature needed to answer question	Type of data needed to answer question	Key literature/ keywords	Methodology and/or paradigm framework	Methods (1) data collection (2) data analysis	Using evidence from data to answer question, solve problem, or support argument
1. Do NTU students of Architecture have positive attitudes to learning ESP? ~ is it still biased by linguistics?	Real situation (context) of teaching and learning ESP program at NTU. Definition of attitudes by linguistics.	Curriculum of English of Architecture program at NTU. Students answers in terms of survey/interview questions	ESP, Oral presentation, learning vocabulary in ESP, Teach vocabulary in ESP, Attitudes to ESP learning	Qualitative Quantitative — Mixed —	Teacher's journal Interview data Survey collection → Descriptive statistics to analyse data	
2. Can oral presentation improve skill in learning English, especially vocabulary of ESP NTU students, comprehend vocabulary and methodology taught by ESP in ESP class?	Real benefits of presentation skill in learning English, especially ESP. Teacher's journal notes on students performance in ESP class					

Figure 2.3: An example draft Research Writing Matrix in TESOL.

	WHAT? [NB Focus & Scope]		WHY?	HOW? ['WHY of HOW' & 'HOW of 'HOW']		ANALYSIS & CLAIMS [Focus & Scope]
Question	Information from literature needed to answer question	Type of data needed to answer question	Key literature/ keywords	Methodology and/or paradigm framework	Methods (1) data collection (2) data analysis	Using evidence from data to answer question, solve problem, or support argument
1. What are the impacts of using Jigsaw as a co-operative learning technique on reading comprehension skills of the first year student who/without English as their major at HANU? 2. What are the students' views towards the use of Jigsaw as a cooperative learning technique in reading classes?	- Definition of Co-operative learning (Characteristics, activities, in Reading the recording) - Observation of teacher. - Definition and of teacher tests - the use of Jigsaw activity in Reading classes - benefits & limitations of this method.	- Students' opinions gained from the interviews. - Reading comprehension skills - Journal writings of Vietnam students after each Reading lesson using this method.	- Co-operative learning → Qualitative - EFL students - EFL student in paradigm framework - Jigsaw activity → Constructivist	Methodology: - Semi-structured interviews - Journal Writing	- Observational, Semi structured + Clarification (Click up students on purposes to see the specimen) - I am going to observe students during the lessons using this activity, then I am going to pick up 3 students to conduct the interviews (from the observation - students who enjoy the lesson, students who'll in the middle & students who got bored with the lesson) Next, I am going to collect the journal writings of the 3 same students who from the interviews to analyse.

Figure 2.2: An example draft Research Writing Matrix in TESOL.

My conclusions from the broad range of ERPP courses that I have drawn on for this paper are that in each setting learners, individually and in groups, have actively engaged in vocal interrogation and often well-reasoned rejection of the global academy's required methodological procedures. Particularly probing questions have repeatedly emerged, such as the following:[4]

- Do research processes and outcomes need to be secular, not acknowledging God or any spiritual dimension to knowledge?

- Why can't knowledge be generated by an 'extra-academic' community, one that hasn't had any academic training? (See also Cadman, 2014; Cadman & Song, 2012)

- Does 'scientific' method have to follow abstract principles? Can't it just be practical?

- Does research involve love, of any kind? Can it be mentioned in a research report?

- Why can't doctoral research be collaborative, if publications can?

- Are Aristotelian logics the only way to argue 'empirically'?

- Is there such a thing as 'Standard Academic English'? Does research have to be written in a particular style for a particular methodology? Isn't it enough for it to be clear and communicable?

To me, it has been conclusively demonstrated that this kind of transcultural critical-pragmatic ERPP pedagogy works effectively to engage a learner's situated, intellectual and affective position as a researcher. Using the Matrix in this way not only increases their evidence-based knowledge of the expectations for research rigour we require, but it also raises their doubts, frustrations and resistances, and encourages them to articulate these to each other and to me in trusted dialogic exchanges. Drafting and redrafting their own Matrix stimulates these discussions.

A brief examination of a couple of learners' Matrix drafts reflecting the proposal stage in TESOL shows some of the ways in which design elements have been taken up by learners. The work-in-progress learner ownership of the research ideas in these documents is immediately apparent in deletions, bracketed selections, insertions and self-corrections. Significantly, these participants are beginning to see how the information they have to gain from existing literature in terms of 'definition[s]', 'benefits and limitations' and the 'real situation (context) of teaching', differs from what they need to learn from their data. In Figure 2.2, for example, the researcher has worked out that they need to understand the broad concept of 'co-operative learning' before they narrow its application to a particular activity. For data collection, observations and interviews labelled in words such as 'semi-structured' may not mean that the learner understands

---

4   Please note that, while the focuses of these questions are here related faithfully, the language they are expressed in is mine.

hardly any of my ERPP participants have failed to understand and align themselves with professional imperatives like these. In our discussions, however, I am quite honest and open in expressing my personal opinions about the mores of the global academy (which are by no means necessarily favourable; see Cadman, 2014). Most significantly, my classroom curiosity about how the expectations of an anglophone research study are thought to be appropriate, or not, by novice researchers for their own communities, is entirely authentic. My sincerity in these dialogues derives from my genuine position as a non-believer in the universal superiority of anglophone knowledge making. In an earlier study, I have explained my teaching values in this way (Cadman, 2005, p. 359, emphasis in the original):

> I try to avoid approaching target genres and communication practices as a *believer* in them, converted to their purposes, without offering scope for interrogation of their assumptions or potential critique of their conventional forms. This approach closes off opportunities for the production of alternative, more representative practices. (See Canagarajah, 2001)[3]

For me, this non-believing stance underpins my initiatives with many of the strategies proposed by Corcoran and Englander (2016, p. 6), especially that of presenting all the elements in the Matrix discussed above 'from a critical angle that examines [them] in terms of increasing global English hegemony in knowledge production ... ' and notably discussing variability in these elements (p. 5). Questions that have stimulated particular interest for my EAL researchers have been ones such as:

- Is there literature in your own language which throws light on these issues? How do these studies differ from the anglophone ones?

- Will these data sources work in your context? Are there others which are not typical in the dominant literature? Will these data collection procedures cause any interpersonal problems for you with your participants?

- Are there philosophical approaches or beliefs in your culture that would throw light on these issues?

- These tightly interconnected logical criteria, do you feel they constrain or limit you? In what ways?

- How could your research journey be imagined differently? What is missing in your view from the 'story' that your research will tell?

---

3   The potential for education to 'convert' came home to me when one of my children, being particularly interested in comparative religion, was disappointed to learn that his school was only 'allowed' by the relevant Department of Education and Children's Services [DECS] to teach religion for one half-day per semester. On investigating the situation, I was advised that this was an error: in fact, 'Religion Studies' was taught as a full elective subject at several different year levels; the curriculum limitation was imposed only on the teaching of religion by 'a believer in it'. Clearly, the DECS administrators saw 'believers' as the problem, and that was when I started to question the relationship between a teacher's 'beliefs' and their capacity to 'convert'.

is possible where time in a program permits. However, for reciprocal teaching and learning in a *trans*cultural, critical-pragmatic ERPP as described above, it is vital to ensure that time and effort are assigned to integrating activities for item (4).

For me, the primary purpose of using the Matrix is not to imprint or demand adherence to its assumptions and its logic, but rather to learn more about how mutually acceptable social research may be conceptualised and practically carried out in my learner-researchers' own contexts. This means creating a dialogic classroom environment for deliberately generating critical questions about the relevance for the learners of the norms represented by the Matrix, even as they are being clarified. This process is not new for me; I have shaped my EAP teaching in this critical-pragmatic way for many years (see Cadman, 2002, 2005). I now see such an approach to be especially crucial in ERPP today, as recently advocated by Corcoran and Englander (2016), for resisting 'the centripetal pull towards normative writing practices' (p. 4). In doing this myself, my interest has primarily been on ways in which I, as an employed teacher, can best create teacher-learner relationships on a footing that is as authentically open, sincere and 'connecting' as possible. This means that, for developing 'acceptable' research designs, to which my teaching through the Matrix leads, my goal is for us all, teacher and learners, to enjoy learning about how each others' research interests might be fulfilled in our different contexts.

My ways of doing this in my own practice relate to Pennycook's (1997) early arguments against the discourses of 'neutrality' which continue to surround the teaching of English internationally. Recently, in exploring this issue in detail for his own EAP teaching, Fenton-Smith (2014) has cited a range of scholars who believe that 'a position of impartiality with respect to course themes is possible on the part of the instructor' (p. A26). Fenton-Smith himself disagrees, arguing that this so-called 'neutrality' is 'ultimately feigned' (citing Santos, 2001) because it 'underplay[s] the power and influence of teachers over students' (p. A26). When I hear this, I feel I immediately want to say, 'Well, while I totally endorse the non-neutrality of English, my personal neutrality is *not* feigned, and it *does not* fail to interrogate my power as a teacher'. In trying to analyse this response, I draw an explicit distinction for my students between me, the human, embodied, situated and opinionated person in the classroom, and me, the representative of an institution, and spokesperson for a preordained set of intellectual values and a historically determined academic culture.

While I can obviously see some slight overlap in these personae, the distinction is clear to me and I make it quite transparent to my ERPP learners. To do this I bring to life and characterise my *pencil*: if, for example, you ask me to read and evaluate a piece of writing, *I* do not evaluate *you*; my pencil evaluates the document before it exactly as required by the target institution. If you would like, we can work together to address your skill development with extensive time and effort by me, but my 'pencil' represents my best judgement of the prevailing values, whether or not I share them. In practice,

She makes the point that:

> It is much easier for a reviewer to doubt the veracity of the first statement, much more difficult to doubt the second because it makes clear that the assertion is based on data provided by the wives included in the study. (p. 806)

Matthews also points to the difference between the discursive structures of aiming to present facts (as in 'John was unfairly treated by his parents') and those reporting perceptions (as in 'John felt strongly that he had been unfairly treated by his parents'), especially when 'analysts are tempted to make causal statements' (p. 806). In my teaching, it is exactly these kinds of methodologically linguistic pointers that inexperienced researchers, of both EAL and English language [EL] backgrounds, have been especially glad to investigate and practise.

Notably, however, when we work with diverse disciplines and methodologies in ERPP, our teaching focus is not on delivering direct academic advice of this kind, but rather on raising questions for training in text analysis and composing. Nevertheless, I have come to feel that for research writing in the social sciences we need to bring a scholarly perspective into our curricula. For successful rigour, knowledge claims must be seen, *in the language of the manuscript*, to fulfill certain criteria. They must

- be clearly supported by a sufficient amount of appropriately collected data
- emerge from an academy-recognised and validated data analysis procedure
- provide specific answer/s to the driving research question/s and/or fulfil stated objectives
- be directly related to established anglophone knowledge bases and theoretical positions.

The vital relationships across and among these criteria are explored and clarified by working dialogically through the columns of the Matrix.

4. A critical-pragmatic pedagogy

In this way, the Research Writing Matrix generates a systematic and 'academically' relevant ERPP which comprises the following activities:

1. genre-based descriptive input
2. teacher-led deconstruction of provided materials
3. learner-led deconstruction of self-chosen materials
4. dialogic critical evaluation for learners' own research contexts
5. learner-led joint composition of manuscript sections.

A further stage:

6. independent construction and assessment

Then, in a section called 'Descriptive analysis', they present extremely hedged claims such as:

> Our data *suggest* that the nature of a village's water resources *may play* an important role in reform …

> Descriptive analyses also *suggest* that the quality or the complexity of the irrigation infrastructure *seem to matter* …

> … the system *seems* more likely …

> … leaders *appear to be* more willing …

> … policy *appears to play* an important role …

> and so on. (pp. 221-2, emphases added)

It is noteworthy that our confidence in these authors' analytical intellect is not weakened by all this hedging because all the main comments are related back to data and so accurately reflect the 'story' that the data are telling. In fact the authors here make a strong, confident claim for the importance of their hedged conclusions: 'The finding that reform *seems to occur* in areas with relatively more available water resources *has important implications*' (p. 223, emphases added). From a methodological perspective, it is particularly interesting that this hedging is predominantly evident in the section on 'Descriptive analysis'; in the subsequent 'Multivariate analysis', unhedged assertions also occur, expressed in simple tenses and immediately tied directly to specific columns in a data table as shown below:

> Villages with relatively more water available in 1995 (*row 1, column 2*) … *were* more likely to form WUAs …

> Similarly, policy also *plays* a positive role in promoting WUAs (*row 6*) …

> The positive and significant coefficient on canal length means that villages with longer canal systems *have* a greater propensity to reform (*row 5*) … (pp. 223-4, emphases added)

Clearly, the different data analysis method employed here allows for generalised assertions requiring different language structures from the previous method.

Blurring the 'language' and 'academic' boundaries in this way has also been carried out by published academic brokers in methodology- or discipline-targeted guides (as in Holliday, 2007). In sociology, Matthews (2005, p. 806), for example, advises would-be publishing authors to 'keep attention focused on the actual data [so] write in the past tense … in order to keep in check the temptation to generalize inappropriately'. She quotes the difference for an article reviewer reading the following sentences:

> S1: Wives *are* critical of husbands who *do not do* their share of the housework.

> S2: The wives *criticized* their husbands for not doing their share of the housework. (emphases added)

procedures of data collection and analysis, are much more straightforwardly revealed in deconstruction of exemplars, both teacher- and learner-provided. These deconstructions offer opportunities for teaching to specific grammar points, especially subject-verb agreements and active/passive verb forms as appropriate for the methodology involved. The language required for writing the researcher's own project procedures — whether in the future tense for learners at the 'proposal' stage, or in the past tense for those who have already collected and analysed data — is thus made comprehensible and accessible to ERPP participants.

3.4. Analysis and claims

The final element in research design as we know it represents what kinds of claims can be made from data analysis, and in what language structures they may occur. These issues can be considered hypothetically and conceptually by learners who have not yet analysed data, and in real terms by those who have. Continuing to follow the deconstruction-to-co-construction process, activities and questions are designed to focus on key aspects of presenting results and expressing analysis or 'discussion' of them:

- Are the results and discussion of data separated or presented together in the example article(s)? And in your own writing?

- In what ways has the analysis clearly fulfilled the research objectives in the *WHAT?* and 'occup[ied] the niche' established earlier in the *WHY?*

- Is it appropriate to present findings in tables or figures?

- How are the analysis assertions grouped and organised? Are subheadings used to name the themes that have been developed for discussion?

- What is the final take-home message of this article? And of your own analysis? To what extent does it directly answer the Research Question(s)? By what explicit statements in 'discussion' has the author shown that the data analysis has led directly to this 'message'?

Two extremely important language features which are able to be examined at this stage are how modality is constructed to represent an appropriate strength of claim supported by the data, and how past and present tenses are used to create parameters of generalisation. Tense change, for example, can indicate a move from reporting 'results' to presenting an author's generalised claims from analysis, and this can be highly significant in building a reliable take-home message and research contribution. In my example article here, in reporting their results, Huang et al. (2009) develop strong assertions with past simple verbs:

> [O]ur data *show* that management under WUAs (Water User Associations) was more transparent. Nearly 40% of WUAs *shared* three types of information … (p. 221, emphases added)

showing the basic principles of positivist, constructivist, critical and post-structural research paradigms in activities which stimulate probing dialogic discussion amongst the learners. The goal is for them to begin to appreciate that for us a contribution to knowledge in the social sciences requires an established theoretical perspective and/or approach, and that researchers may aim to contribute to theory as distinct from, or as well as, to contextual social knowledge. The ways in which methodologies are written in social sciences are diverse: conceptual frameworks may be presented in figures, diagrams or text; in some disciplinary contexts, paradigms and methodologies can be assumed without specific reference, while in others they need to be named, explained and justified with scholarly support. Significantly, how quantitative and qualitative methodologies are valued is signalled through language choice: 'validity' is not evaluated on the same principles as 'trustworthiness'; research 'subjects' are not discussed in the same language as 'participants'; 'measuring' outcomes based on 'variables' is not to be confused with 'interpreting' people's perceptions and feelings. The boundaries between our conceptual criteria for research rigour and the language of its expression are patently blurred.

My ERPP learners thus analyse their own target journal articles to try to understand the extent to which, and how, the authors have expressed theoretical approaches and goals. My own role in this is not to provide technical or informed theoretical information but rather to question, clarify and facilitate each learner's understanding of their own theoretical framework, or lack of it. Without any attempt to influence a writer's own choice or construction of theoretical approach, I feel it is my business in ERPP to demonstrate the role that theory plays in a globally successful social study. In my view, it is especially significant to address how for us the theoretical lens we adopt influences our choice of qualitative and/or quantitative methodologies, data collection and analysis methods, and even our selection of literature to review. Above all, and specifically for language work, the methodology can affect macro-rhetorical choices: the logical structure of a piece of writing, its inductive or deductive argument logic, the accepted conventions of its argument expression and subheadings. At a more micro-level, it can determine rhetorical style in terms of, for example, first- or third-person authorial construction[2] (such as in a reflexive analytical narrative as distinct from impersonal, author-evacuated prose), vocabulary choice (as in the difference between 'subject' and 'subjectivity'), even singulars and plurals (as in 'literacy' or 'literacies', and 'identity' or mandated 'identities'). My teaching goal is primarily to enhance participants' control over their own writing in direct relation to the 'methodology' that they aim to use.

In this way the *WHY of HOW?* is conceptually and linguistically distinguished from the procedural writing required for research 'methods', named in the Matrix as the *HOW of HOW?* The typical elements of methods' writing such as the site, participants,

---

2   In my view, in contrast to that of Harwood and Hadley (2004), it is more appropriate in the social sciences to base an investigation into the use of first-person/third-person pronouns on a study's methodology rather than on its discipline.

reveal these 'moves' (Wisker, 2015), though often with the goal of amending previous research outcomes in relation to a different context, or presenting counterarguments by applying diverse sources or theories. Scaffolded analysis of each of Swales's 'moves' opens opportunities for exemplifying the language in which the rhetorical purposes are realised. For example, to clarify 'Move 2: Establishing a niche' — that is, the 'gap' or limitation in existing scholarship — the Huang et al. (2009) example article demonstrates fairly typical expressions: 'In addition to the *limited* number of existing studies, most research focuses on villages that span *narrow* geographic areas. Zhang (2001) studies *only* World Bank project sites ... There is *little, if any*, nation-wide research ...' (p. 216, emphases added). If learners are supported through guided deconstruction to compose the relevant function for their own study — this latter step in co-construction with me and their classmates — then the interactive process effectively provides experience in analysing texts as well as writing them. Significantly, this interaction has also built novice researchers' confidence in sharing hesitant ideas and drafts with colleagues.

It is worth mentioning here that other important focuses can be introduced into teaching at the *WHY?* stage, especially, for example, activities to clarify anglophone concepts of plagiarism, or relevant referencing and citation styles and practices, or the art of writing topic sentences or rhetorical 'maps'. Crucially, however, in terms of research rigour, it is vital for novice social researchers to recognise the difference between their own lack of knowledge about the social problem which drives the research question (that is, the *WHAT?*), and the gap in pertinent, previously published research in the global academy that addresses their research question (that is, the 'niche' established in the *WHY?*). Above all, each set of linguistic 'moves' needs to be conceptualised and related both forwards and backwards to all the elements in the whole research journey being mapped on the Matrix.

3.3. 'HOW?'

In my experience, perhaps the most significant element of the Matrix for periphery researchers is located in the *HOW?* of a study, as demanded by anglophone social-scientific traditions. Almost without exception, the most unexpected and challenging aspect of rigour for my ERPP participants has been the way in which an established theoretical lens fundamentally drives analysis of social data and the analytical claims that can eventually be made, not to mention the language in which those claims are expressed. The ontological and epistemological implications of different research paradigms and 'systems of inquiry' are rarely familiar to my EAL learners. It is this which has led me to include teaching to the *WHY of HOW?* in the Matrix.

Initially, I create teaching input, materials and readings through which I can demonstrate how authors have presented, validated and then applied or amended a well-established methodology. This most often first involves diagrammatised information through language elements within its research question in terms of tense, modality, singulars/plurals, prepositional links, use of the English article to mark countable as distinct from conceptual entities, and so on.

My own genre analysis of articles in many social science disciplines shows that they usually identify early a social or contextual problem that needs to be solved. In the Huang et al. (2009) case, the problem looks like this:

> Increasing demand for China's limited water resources from *rapidly* growing industry, urban populations and agriculture implies *potentially dire* consequences for the sustainability of water resources, especially in Northern China (Zhang, 2001) … *Problems* in the water sector will *no doubt* affect China's future trade position in *key* crops and incomes in the farming sector. (Huang et al., 1999, p. 215, emphases added to show modality)

This kind of authentic example provides material for learners to discuss issues such as: 'Where, and how, is the RQ and/or social problem presented in this article? What modality is used to show how serious the problem is? Is there a clear statement of the information or specific data that are needed to answer this author's question?' Learners can then scan their own chosen example papers for answers to similar questions. Finally, they work with each other and with me to interrogate these rhetorical functions in relation to their own study and its context, so moving from deconstruction to critical co-construction.

At this point, it is extremely important for novice research writers to be able to see the two distinct kinds of information they need to gain for themselves: first, established factual material to inform their understanding of their topic and the context of their social problem; and second, exactly what they will need to learn from primary data in order to answer their research question and arrive at a potential contribution to the solution. In my experience, seeing this distinction has not been easy for learners educated in non-anglophone contexts. Consequently, they have greatly valued being involved in crafting and re-crafting their own RQ and problem statement so that these express exactly and 'reliably', in anglophone terms, the original contribution that they want their study to make.

3.2. 'WHY?'

The *WHY?* of a study lies in its scholarly justification. The rhetorical logic of this process was famously established in the 'CARS [Creating a Research Space]' model by Swales in 1990, and is greatly valued by EAL research writers today. The basic elements of this model involve a series of logical 'moves' which have been well explained in genre-based pedagogic literature in the natural and applied sciences (see Weissberg & Buker, 1990; Shehzad, 2008; Swales & Feak, 2012; Cargill & O'Connor, 2013). In the social sciences, learners' investigations into their target journal articles still very often

A RESEARCH WRITING MATRIX FOR ANALYSIS OF SOCIAL DATA						
WHAT?			**WHY?**	**HOW?** ['WHY of HOW' & 'HOW of 'HOW']		**ANALYSIS & CLAIMS**
Research Question (emerging from a social problem)	*Information from* literature needed to answer question	*Type of data* needed to answer question	Key literature/ keywords Research gap?	Methodology – theoretical/ conceptual framework	Methods of (i) data collection (ii) data analysis	Using evidence from data *with theory* to answer question, solve problem or support argument
1.						

Figure 2.1: A Research Writing Matrix for discussing research rigour in the social sciences.

1.   '*What* are the *main factors* … ' = the research contribution
     [*Q — What form, logically, would the contribution of this study take?*]

2.   ' … that influence' = the defining verb, the condition or action to be analysed
     [*Note the <u>tense</u> and <u>modality</u> of the verb.*
     Q — What is the implication for data collection of this present simple verb form as distinct from alternatives such as 'have influenced' or 'can influence', 'could influence', 'might influence?]

3.   ' … the implementation' = the target of the observation and analysis
     [*Q — How will this concept be captured and understood?*]

4.   ' … of water management reform' = the focus of the field topic
     [*Q — How much interest has been shown on this topic in recent publications? Why is it timely?*]

5.   ' … in China' = the scoping phrase
     [*Q — What are the content and language implications of alternatives: in Asia? in Northern China? in Beijing?*]

In a further activity, I present learners with a few topics relevant to their disciplines and ask them to come up with interesting questions that could potentially make 'drivers' for research. In this way, the focus and scope of a study can be demonstrated relating to research questions and goals, generalisation of findings, data collection and methodological legitimacy. As a result, and most significantly for my ERPP teaching, I have inadvertently conceptualised a refinement of Lillis and Curry's (2006, 2010) 'brokering' model as I work at 'methodology brokering' by taking a self-conscious step to design teaching materials which integrate so-called 'academic' structures into social science learners' language work.

3. A Research Writing Matrix

To address these issues directly, I have created a 'Research Writing Matrix' (Figure 2.1) as a tool to generate dialogues with learners around the currently dominant criteria for assessing the reliability or trustworthiness of their social research, and how it might be written.[1] Through this Matrix, it is possible to teach appropriate English language structures through the learner's own research study design and thereby clarify our anglophone expectations of each of the necessary conceptual stages in the research journey. This process requires that every learner is actively engaged in a research project, even if they are just starting out; they work to fill in and update their own Matrix as the course or workshop proceeds. They are asked to provide pre-course information about their project so that I can provide them with suitable published examples of relevant structures and language as exemplars. In this way, they participate in the well-established 'deconstruction' phase of the genre pedagogy cycle (see Clerehan & Moodie, 1997). If they are also required to bring to class an example of an article from their own target journal (as described in Cargill and O'Connor, 2013), they can then actively investigate how authors in their specific field and/or methodology effect each epistemological stage. The Matrix itself structures the teaching/learning process. It basically promotes a focus on the individual elements expected in a conventional social science study, in order gradually to throw light on how they relate to each other.

3.1. WHAT?

The *WHAT?* of the study is driven by the design of a research question [RQ]. In teaching, stimulus activities can begin by playing games with question words, their grammar and their logics, with questions such as: 'If "How?" is the question word used, what form will its answer logically take?' This can then lead to the analysis of a published example RQ specially chosen for its relevance to as many discipline areas as possible (see also Paltridge, 2014). An example I have used, from Huang, Rozelle, Wang and Huang (2009) is: 'What are the main factors that influence the implementation of water management reform in China?' This example can be used to make explicit the following elements:

---

1 This Matrix is developed out of an idea put forward for research supervision by Smyth and Maxwell (2010).

'the zeitgeist of a research community' (p. 58). Hyland (2016b, p. 190) describes this as 'the practices surrounding the route to … publication' which 'may seem out of place in an ERPP course', in that 'most writing for publication courses focus on rhetorical aspects of the RA'.

As noted above, however, the significance of study design in the publication uptake of international journals is well established. Hyland (2016a, p. 62) elsewhere conducts a substantial analysis of literature on academic publishing, which leads him to state: 'Research shows that a key issue for many novices is the lack of a disciplinary appropriate conceptual framework that allows them to speak with authority'. He cites many specific studies in drawing the conclusion that there is little evidence for the scale-tipping effects of EAL language issues, but rather that 'reviews … tend to focus strongly on aspects of the research itself, rather than its presentation' (p. 65). More specifically, Lillis and Curry's (2006) in-depth analysis of mediation activity separates the work of 'academic professionals' from that of 'language professionals' (p. 14), defining the former group as one which 'orients to knowledge content and claims, [and] discipline-specific discourse' whereas the latter 'tend to focus on sentence level revisions and direct translations' (pp. 15-16); English language specialists and teachers of English fall naturally into the second group. In this 2006 study, they report that 73% of all text brokers were 'academic professionals' and 24% were 'language professionals', again showing the significance of this 'academic' work. They conclude that 'a large amount of brokering is carried out by academic professionals and … although scholars tend to frame these brokers' interventions in terms of language or discourse, in fact they tend to orient to content' (p. 29). The blurred boundaries between the language of research writing and its content are also noted by Hewings (2006, p. 52) in his analysis of journal article reviews. He defines 'comments on language' as opposed to 'comments on content', saying that 'for the most part, this was unproblematic' but he later identifies cases where 'It was not always possible, however, to determine whether a comment was referring to language or content' (p. 53).

This language/content dilemma feeds directly into my own professional question: Is it appropriate for an ERPP teacher to engage with a learner's study design? For teaching social science research writing I believe that it is, basically because I do not have an easy answer to the related question: At what points do epistemological 'credibility', rhetorical logic and language structure diverge? In thinking like this, I find myself transgressing the boundaries of Lillis and Curry's (2006, 2010) mediation categories: as a disciplinary 'academic professional' supervising researchers' drafts and reviewing journal submissions, I often act as a 'language broker' by straying into detailed advice on the logical structures of English, rephrasing subheadings to maintain the focus and scope of subsections, restructuring paragraphs, suggesting topic sentences to improve flow and readability, and so on; conversely, as a 'language professional', I find myself acting as an 'academic' broker in terms of unavoidably straying into questions and comments reviewer, doctoral supervisor and thesis examiner. This albeit idiosyncratic experience with both first and additional English language users in the social sciences has led me to realise that it has very rarely been a novice scholar's variant English language that has resulted in failure and/or rejection. Recent ERPP studies have been raising similar issues. Lillis and Curry (2015), for example, have expressed a central concern with 'whether English or language figures at all as a significant issue' in a journal's uptake of an article (p. 133). Their Text History data reveal that gatekeepers' critical comments focus on 'concerns about methodology, analytical tools used, and forms of analysis', or on 'epistemological and methodological issues' (p. 140); they finally assess that 'language by itself does not act as a warrant for dismissal or rejection' (p. 147). My own observation is that, even where inappropriate language forms have been seen to impede successful communication, a much more critically significant issue has been whether or not the prevailing criteria for methodological rigour in research design are met. Reflecting on my own international journal reviewing over the last five years, I note over 30 comments related to authors' crucial failure to meet anglophone expectations of research rigour. Fairly typical quotations from my reviews are (and I have noted very consistent agreement with my blind co-reviewers):

> One serious issue for me is the loose tendency to generalise the findings: when the base sample of the study is a very small number of participants, generalising to any group is not possible.

> There is no explanation of what was aimed to be learned from each of these data sets, nor how and why they were selected.

> … data discussion does not convince us of a lack of bias in the data collection and analysis.

> We would need to know much more methodological detail … including what steps were taken in data analysis and what theoretical principles were applied.

> … these claims are much too sweeping to be supported by the data.

> To introduce the results of the study in the introduction, and to present arguments which have not yet been validated by data analysis, compromises our trust in the study's methodology.

For me, these issues are as much about the writing as they are about the methodology. In this respect, it seems I don't share the view of many ERPP scholars, who have touched on the centrality of study design issues for publication writing but have rarely seen them as significant for writing teachers. Several authors refer to Kwan's (2010) study of ERPP courses, in which she states that for a piece of research to be published successfully it must demonstrate 'command of disciplinary academic rigour' (p. 58; see Flowerdew, 2013; Corcoran & Englander, 2016; Hyland 2016b) — yet none of them, including Kwan herself, elaborates on this. She places this competence in an umbrella framework of 'Strategic research conception', which is largely taken to refer to and instead proposes a moral base of reasoning' which 'embraces subjectivity' (p. 6). In this way, Smith establishes 'trustworthiness' as the fundamental criterion for reflexivity: 'The central moral imperative, backed by evidence and argument making the account compelling, is a virtue to be nurtured not a prejudice that distorts' (p. 5).

It is just such a moral imperative that creates the tensions for me in my research writing and teaching (see Cadman, 2014). Particularly in my ERPP role, I am deeply challenged by the question: Am I primarily a part of the neocolonial problem or a contributor to its solution? Working to address this disquiet and implement an effective and ethically acceptable ERPP, I have recognised that for me it is important to engage three distinct yet interacting elements:

- appropriate teaching materials for students' target texts, in order to represent and throw light on today's dominant disciplinary and even journal-sensitive textual practices
- a well-informed, genre-theoretical knowledge base such as those developed by Swales and Feak (2012), Burgess and Cargill (2013) and Paltridge (2014), among others
- a 'transcultural', dialogic pedagogy (see Cadman, 2005) which aims, in the critical pragmatist tradition, to interrupt the notion of education as 'a unidirectional flow' through which 'the ignoramus must receive the benefits of "our culture" … [to] change and become one of "us"' (Malinowski as cited in Cadman & Song, 2012, p. 11).

Importantly, 'engaging with confrontation' in Pennycook's (1997) terms does not mean ignoring or reducing emphasis on the first two of my priorities above — that is, making explicit the currently dominant 'practices of the academy'. For a consciously *trans*cultural and critical-pragmatic pedagogy, it is vital to develop appropriate lesson materials and teacher/student relationships, both in order to fulfil students' thirst for training in anglophone research skills, and to engage their agency in the learning opportunities we offer them.

My aim in this chapter, then, is to propose an original framework and pedagogic approach for teaching research writing in the social sciences, in order to address what I see as a major lacuna in this field today in relation to ERPP teaching materials. In proffering these materials, I want to suggest ways in which exemplars of prevailing genres may be used to open up epistemological dialogues with EAL researchers, thus making our anglophone expectations completely transparent while simultaneously disrupting the process of extinguishing learners' culturally diverse ways of knowing.

2. Teaching to methodological rigour

In designing these teaching materials, I have drawn insights from my practice as gatekeeper in the global academy as a teacher-assessor, international journal editor and

In parallel to these findings, among Asian scholars too is a belief that 'an obsession with theoretical knowledge from the West reproduces Euro-American intellectual dominance in the global-local knowledge hierarchies' (Qi, 2015, p. 195). Nguyen, Elliott, Terlouw and Pilot (2009, p. 109) draw specific attention to Asian contexts 'where rapid reforms in education may run the risk of "false universalism"' involving the relatively uncritical adoption of various Western approaches. This is seen to open the way for 'mental colonialism to continue and neocolonialism to triumph' (p. 112). From a European perspective, Bennett (2014) also argues that this process 'ultimately represents the colonisation of one culture by another — in this case, the "imposition of new 'mental structures' through English"' (pp. 45-6, citing Phillipson; see also Bennett, 2015). And for me too, despite the obvious diversity of contextual outcomes, the strong form of this argument remains convincing (see Cadman, 2014). It is from this position that I walk into a classroom as a research writing teacher, holding the same view as the Schostaks (Schostak & Schostak, 2013, p. 11) when they say 'rhetoric is more than just ornament since it provides an underlying structuring of the thought processes where data is transformed into evidence ... ' For ERPP teachers, employed as often as not by anglophone metropolitan institutions, such a process takes a simple but indomitable form, in that, as Fenton-Smith (2014, p. A29) points out, these institutions 'recommend that instructors assimilate international students into the academic, sociocultural and linguistic norms of the host nation'.

The call for teachers to resist this enforced assimilation process in the context of English for Academic Purposes (EAP) has continued regularly since Pennycook (1997) brought Dewey's concept of 'critical pragmatism' to EAP, and it has recently been taken up by Corcoran and Englander (2016) in ERPP. For Pennycook, a successful and ethical pedagogy

> ... seeks to do more than just tolerate difference, but moves towards a more direct engagement with the confrontation between the cultural, educational and linguistic practices of the students and the practices of the academy. (p. 266)

A similar 'engagement with confrontation' has recently been characterised by Qi (2015) as 'staging dissensus' — that is, aiming to deliberately disrupt educational norms that are 'characterised by one epistemology dominating others, thus marginalizing and ruling out dissensus' (p. 198). How to stage dissensus and effect this disruption then becomes the challenge for an ethical ERPP practice.

In this chapter, I will describe how I try to meet this challenge in practical teaching strategies. I will here present a reflexive analysis which involves my researcher's attitudes and approaches, engagement with theory, and with my academic and teaching experience over the last 15 years. Building on the groundbreaking work of Lincoln and Guba in 1985, Smith (1998) demonstrates the reliability of this research approach in education when he endorses the critical pragmatist stance, which, he says, 'rejects the dominant empiricist goal of research as generating knowledge or adding to scientific theorising,

2

Introducing research rigour in the social sciences:

Transcultural strategies for teaching ERPP writing, research design, and resistance to epistemic erasure

Kate Cadman

1. Introduction

A recurring theme of scholarly work in English for Research Publication Purposes [ERPP] has been the potentially causal relationship between the global dominance of English for 'international' publication and the suppression of alternative knowledges. The titles of presentations in the recent PRISEAL conference on international publication reflect support for this view in phrases such as 'English as *the* international language of science' (emphasis in the original), ' … domain loss and the erosion of specialized discourse in non-Anglophone cultures', 'English-monolinguist research policies in Spain', and so on (PRISEAL, 2015, n.p.). The perceived disadvantages experienced by researchers in non-mainstream contexts have been richly analysed (Lillis & Curry, 2010; Clavero, 2010) and contentiously debated (Flowerdew, 2008; Casanave, 2008; Hyland, 2016a). Meanwhile, quantitative studies such as those by Mertkan, Arsan, Cavlan and Aliusta (2016) in educational management have drawn some resonant conclusions about today's academy: '[T]he complexity of knowledge-production … is marked by disproportionate influence of an exceptionally small set of core inner-circle Anglophone and non-inner-circle Anglophone settings' (p. 13; see also Lillis & Curry, 2015).

López-Navarro, I., Moreno, A.I., Quintanilla, M.A., & Rey-Rocha, J. (2015). Why do I publish research articles in English instead of my own language? Differences in Spanish researchers' motivations across scientific domains. *Scientometrics*, *103*, 939-976. DOI: http://dx.doi.org/10.1007/s11192-015-1570-1.

Lorés-Sanz, R., Mur-Dueñas, P., Rey-Rocha, J., & Moreno, A.I. (2014). Motivations and attitudes of Spanish Chemistry and Economics researchers towards publication in English-medium scientific journals. *Revista Canaria de Estudios Ingleses*, *69*, 83-100.

Martín, P., Rey-Rocha, J., Burgess, S., & Moreno, A.I. (2014). Publishing research in English-language journals: Attitudes, strategies and difficulties of multilingual scholars of medicine. *Journal of English for Academic Purposes*, *16*, 57-67. DOI: http://dx.doi.org/10.1016/j.jeap.2014.08.001.

Moreno, A.I., Rey-Rocha, J., Burgess, S., López-Navarro, I., & Sachdev, I. (2012). Spanish researchers' perceived difficulty writing research articles for English-medium journals: The impact of proficiency in English versus publication experience. *Ibérica*, *24*, 157-184.

Pérez-Llantada C., Plo, R., & Ferguson, G.R. (2011). 'You don't say what you know, only what you can': The perceptions and practices of senior Spanish academics regarding research dissemination in English. *English for Specific Purposes*, *30*(1), 18-30.

Plummer, K. (2001). *Documents of life 2: An invitation to a critical humanism*. London: Sage.

Ramos-Torre, R., & Callejo-Gallego, J. (2013). 'El español en las ciencias sociales'. In J.L. Gacría-Delgado, J.A. Alonso, & J.C. Jiménez (Eds.), *El español, lengua de comunicación científica* (pp. 29-74). Madrid: Ariel and Fundación Telefónica.

Swales, J.M. (2004). *Research genres: Explorations and applications*. Cambridge: Cambridge University Press.

Whitehand, J.W.R. (2005). The problem of Anglophone squint. *Area*, *37*(2), 228-230. DOI: http://dx.doi.org/10.1111/j.1475-4762.2005.00625.x.

Ylijoki, O.H. (2005). Academic nostalgia: A narrative approach to academic work. *Human Relations*, *58*(5), 555-576.

Englander, K., & Uzuner-Smith, S. (2013). The role of policy in constructing the peripheral scientist in the era of globalization. *Language Policy, 12*(3), 231-250. DOI: http://dx.doi.org/10.1007/s10993-012-9268-1.

Feng, H., Beckett, G.H., & Huang, D. (2013). From 'import' to 'import-export' oriented internationalization: The impact of national policy on scholarly publication in China. *Language Policy, 12*(3), 251-272. DOI: http://dx.doi.org/10.1007/s10993-013-9285-8.

Flowerdew, J. (1999). Problems in writing for scholarly publication in English: The case of Hong Kong. *Journal of Second Language Writing, 8*(2), 243-264.

Flowerdew, J. (2008). Scholarly writers who use English as an additional language: What can Goffman's '*stigma*' tell us? *Journal of English for Academic Purposes, 7*(2), 77-86.

Flowerdew, J. (2009). Goffman's stigma and EAL writers: The author responds to Casanave. *Journal of English for Academic Purposes, 8*(1), 69-72. DOI: http://dx.doi.org/10.1016/j.jeap.2009.01.001.

Flowerdew, J., & Li, Y. (2009). English or Chinese? The trade-off between local and international publication among Chinese academics in the humanities and social sciences. *Journal of Second Language Writing, 18*(1), 17-29. DOI: http://dx.doi.org/10.1016/j.jslw.2008.09.005.

Gea-Valor, M.L., Rey-Rocha, J., & Moreno, I. (2014). Publishing research in the international context: An analysis of Spanish scholars' academic writing needs in the social sciences. *English for Specific Purposes, 36*, 47-59. DOI: http://dx.doi.org/10.1016/j.esp.2014.05.001.

Hanauer, D.I., & Englander, K. (2011). Quantifying the burden of writing research articles in a second language: Data from Mexican scientists. *Written Communication, 28*(4), 403-416. DOI: http://dx.doi.org/10.1177/0741088311420056.

Hyland, K. (2016a). Academic publishing and the myth of linguistic injustice. *Journal of Second Language Writing, 31*, 58-69. DOI: http://dx.doi.org/10.1016/j.jslw.2016.01.005.

Hyland, K. (2016b). Language myths and publishing mysteries: A response to Politzer-Ahles et al. *Journal of Second Language Writing, 34*, 9-11. DOI: http://dx.doi.org/10.1016/j.jslw.2016.09.001.

Jiménez-Contreras, E., De Moya, F., & Delgado, E. (2003). The evolution of research activity in Spain: The impact of the National Commission for the Evaluation of Research Activity (CNEAI). *Research Policy, 32*(1), 123-142.

Lee, H., & Lee, K. (2013). Publish (in international indexed journals) or perish: Neoliberal ideology in a Korean university. *Language Policy, 12*(3), 215-230. DOI: http://dx.doi.org/10.1007/s10993-012-9267-2.

Li, Y., & Flowerdew, J. (2009). International engagement versus local commitment: Hong Kong academics in the humanities and social sciences writing for publication. *Journal of English for Academic Purposes, 8*(4), 279-293.

Lillis, T.M., & Curry, M.J. (2006). Professional academic writing by multilingual scholars: Interactions with literacy brokers in the production of English-medium texts. *Written Communication, 23*(1), 3-35.

Lillis, T.M., & Curry, M.J. (2010). *Academic writing in a global context: The politics and practices of publishing in English*. London: Routledge.

Lillis, T.M., & Curry, M.J. (2015). The politics of English, language and uptake: The case of international academic journal article reviews, *AILA Review, 28*, 127-150. DOI: http://dx.doi.org/10.1075/aila.28.06lil.

References

Ammon, U. (2000). Towards more fairness in international English: Linguistic rights of non-native speakers? In R. Phillipson (Ed.), *Rights to language: Equity, power and education* (pp. 111-116). Mahwah, NJ: Lawrence Erlbaum.

Ammon, U. (2001). *The dominance of English as a language of science: Effects on other languages and language communities.* Berlin: Mouton de Gruyter.

Ammon, U. (2006). Language planning for international scientific communication: An overview of questions and potential solutions. *Current Issues in Language Planning, 7*(1), 1-30. DOI: http://dx.doi.org/10.2167/cilp088.0.

Anderson, L. (2013). Publishing strategies of young, highly mobile academics: The question of language in the European context. *Language Policy, 12,* 273-288. DOI: http://dx.doi.org/10.1007/s10993-013-9272-0.

Bernal Triviño, A. (2016, May 30). El cajón sastre del profesor universitario. *Público.* Retrieved 23 January 2017 from http://www.publico.es/sociedad/cajon-sastre-del-profesorado-universitario.html.

Burgess, S., & Fagan, A. (2006). From the periphery: The Canarian researcher publishing in the international arena. In J.I. Oliva, M. McMahon, & M. Brito (Eds.), *On the matter of words: In honour of Lourdes Divasson Cilveti* (pp. 45-54). La Laguna: Publicaciones Institucionales, Universidad de La Laguna.

Burgess, S., Gea-Valor, M.L., Moreno, A.I., & Rey-Rocha, J. (2014). Affordances and constraints on research publication: A comparative study of the language choices of Spanish historians and psychologists. *Journal of English for Academic Purposes, 14,* 72-83. DOI: http://dx.doi.org/10.1016/j.jeap.2014.01.001.

Casanave, C.P. (2009). The stigmatizing effect of Goffman's stigma label: A response to John Flowerdew. *Journal of English for Academic Purposes, 7*(4), 264-267. DOI: http://dx.doi.org/10.1016/j.jeap.2008.10.013.

Chan, L.T-K. (2016). Beyond non-translation and 'self-translation': English as lingua academica in China. *Translation and Interpreting Studies, 11*(2), 152-176. DOI: http://dx.doi.org/10.1075/tis.11.2.02cha.

CNEAI. (2014). *Boletín Oficial del Estado.* Resolution de 26 de noviembre de 2014: Núm. 290, Sec. III, 12482 (pp. 98204-98219). Spain: BOE. Retrieved 23 February 2017 from https://boe.es/boe/dias/2014/12/01/pdfs/BOE-A-2014-12482.pdf.

Connell, R.W. (2006). Core activity: Reflexive intellectual workers and cultural crisis. *Journal of Sociology, 42*(1), 5-23.

Connell, R.W. (2010). Building the neoliberal world: Managers as intellectuals in the peripheral economy. *Critical Sociology, 36*(6), 777-792.

Connell, R.W., & Wood, J. (2002). Globalization and scientific labour: Patterns in a life history study of intellectual workers in the periphery. *Journal of Sociology, 38*(2), 167-190.

Connell, R.W., Wood, J., & Crawford, J. (2005). The global connections of intellectual workers: An Australian study. *International Sociology, 20*(1), 5-26.

Curry, M.J., & Lillis, T.M. (2004). Multilingual scholars and the imperative to publish in English: Negotiating interests, demands, and rewards. *TESOL Quarterly, 38*(4), 663-688.

Curry, M.J., & Lillis, T.M. (2013). Introduction to the thematic issue: Participating in academic publishing — Consequences of linguistic policies and practices. *Language Policy, 12*(3), 209-213. DOI: http://dx.doi.org/10.1007/s10993-013-9286-7.

potential conflicts of interest. Even FDV expresses mild irritation with the university's lack of interest in his insider knowledge of evaluation procedures in the humanities.

MAC would like to see the powerful baronial full professors who hold such sway over some areas of his discipline contained or dethroned. JD, likewise, would be happy to see only those who are 'genuine researchers' achieving status and success. PCR, too, hints that some gain undeserved credit simply as a result of accumulating multiple citations of their work. For JD and PCR, at the moment, the CNEAI is not a likely agent of positive change. The linguists share both a mistrust of the competence of the committee in their area to judge their work and serious doubts about the criteria used and their implications for the nature of research.

All the interviewees understand that a successful review means making certain changes to their approach to publication, possibly abandoning practices they consider correct or desirable. This might mean accepting a lower standard of written expression as a result of having to write in English. Membership of editorial boards and certain research genres such as the book-length text or monograph also have to be sacrificed to meet the criteria. Working methods, too, are affected, because multiple authorship is frowned upon or even castigated, thus potentially limiting teamwork and skills exchange across disciplines.

The willingness of the historians to adapt to and accept these circumstances was surprising, as many who participated in the ENEIDA survey (see Burgess et al., 2014) reported resentment of the implicit privileging of English. Here it is the linguists who voice this view — even PCR, whose own language skills allow him to write and publish without much recourse to literacy brokers.

The research evaluation policies and restructuring in the universities themselves, as a result of the Bologna Accord along with the economic downturn, are undoubtedly bringing pressure to bear, particularly on those who do not have a current favourable assessment. For these people, there is the fear that English will gain even more territory, pushing their own research further underground, where it will be read and cited even less.

None of the scholars in this small sample seems keen to contest the policies, either because they lack the will or because they do not consider it to be necessary. At the same time, none of them wholeheartedly accepts the policies, seeing them as part of a neoliberal project where marketisation of university work is the main aim. Even if they are not adversely affected, they see harm being done to their friends and colleagues, and this distresses them. In the end, it is not a question of contesting or accepting but of learning how to work the system. The growing industry in preparation for research reviews suggests that this is the approach most Spanish scholars are taking. In Spain at the moment one grins — or perhaps grimaces — and bears it.

just after she gained tenure, but it also coincided with major structural changes in the university as a result of the Bologna Accord. These she sees as having had more serious implications for her than the changes in research evaluation policies — thus sharing a view expressed by both MAC and PCR.

One consequence of the restructuring is that her department has now been combined with three other departments. An annual research seminar that her old department once ran no longer takes place because the support of the new department is required and has not been forthcoming. This, for IB, is just one of the many examples of the university 'putting up barriers to research activity'. She looks back with considerable nostalgia to the collegial atmosphere she contends existed in the past, observing sadly, 'We all feel completely isolated and very disillusioned with the institution'.

Added to restructuring, for IB, is the burden of a different style of teaching in which continuous assessment is imposed from above. This she finds time consuming and of questionable merit. IB particularly dislikes the various forms of online delivery of content, observing that students are just 'snacking on the discipline', whereas she, she says, read six or seven books for every course she took as an undergraduate.

What IB perceives as impositions and barriers result in a sense that she is left with little time for research, though she remains involved in several projects. These, too, she feels take her time away from her own individual work and prevent her from being able to start a book she intends to write. With a book under her belt, she feels, she would be guaranteed a third positive assessment. Though publication in English is not the *sine qua non* of success it is elsewhere (IB cites sociology as an example), she acknowledges that her last positive assessment was probably granted on the basis of a publication in English in a US gender studies journal. In this case, the publisher commissioned and paid for a professional translation.

6. Accept or contest: Common ground and difference in the narratives

In all but one of the narratives — that of FDV — the participants see specific institutions as responsible for the pressures they experience as part of contemporary academic life. For the historians, the source of these pressures is not located in the CNEAI and their criteria, which they see as transparent and manageable. Instead, MAC, IB and PCR share resentment of top-down curriculum reforms and, in the case of the two historians, MAC and IB, their implications for teaching. They see a shift away from traditional methods of presenting content and assessing students as creating extra pressures for them both inside and outside the classroom, and as taking precious time away from research. They level blame at European institutions that are seen as having given unwarranted power to educationalists.

IB additionally perceives the university itself as not only having failed to provide sufficient support for academics with children, but also as having created barriers to research activity through fusing departments and indeed faculties, with little regard for

PCR had gained tenure and was well on the way to becoming a full professor when I interviewed him in 2002. Since that time, he has led three consecutive national research projects, and he collaborates closely with an erstwhile mentor in the north of Spain who leads another large team with strong connections to researchers in the US and Russia. It was this person who essentially launched PCR's career by inviting him to give a keynote speech at a major symposium — a daunting prospect for PCR but ultimately a positive experience that, in his words, 'put me on the map'.

Despite his success, PCR is distrustful of the research evaluation system, which he sees as both pressuring people to publish in JCR journals and as confounding citations and quality. His particular area is one he sees as having a smaller 'clientele' than others such as pragmatics and discourse analysis, and he is therefore concerned that his work may not receive the credit it deserves.

A particular cause of resentment for PCR is the fact that the assessors remain anonymous. Although the names of the 12 members of the committee for Area 11 are published, PCR assumes that each application is assessed by a smaller number of people or even by a single individual. Without knowing who that individual is, he contends, it is very difficult to successfully contest a negative review.

The limitation on including, among the five chosen publications, articles in journals the editorial boards of which one is a member is another of the criteria PCR finds obnoxious. There are a limited number of appropriate journals in his field and he was proud to have been invited to become a member of several editorial boards. He has had to ask the editors to remove him so as to be able to include his publications in those journals among his five merits.

In my earlier interview with PCR, he commented that he continued to publish in Spanish because he wanted non-English-speaking Spanish researchers to be able to read his work. At that time, publication exclusively in Spanish was still a reasonable strategy. This is no longer the case, according to PCR. Now he sees anyone who is limited to publishing only in Spanish as at a great disadvantage, especially in a context where an increasing number of Spanish linguistics journals are now published in English.

PCR attributes his own success to a kind of tenacity. Less ambitious individuals opt out in part because the university system places greater and greater demands on them. Like MAC, PCR bewails the bureaucratisation of university work and the frequent reforms of the university curriculum.

5.7. IB: 'We all feel completely isolated and very disillusioned with the institution'

The last participant, IB, is less indignant about research evaluation policy than JD, PL or PCR, but is also even less sanguine about the state of the university. Her immediate response to my question about what had changed since our last interview was to gesture towards a photograph on her desk of her child. She sees the institution as offering little or no support for researchers with small children. The birth of IB's own child came the vehicular language of publication, Romance languages such as Spanish and Italian are more appropriate choices. PL quoted an instance where a prestigious conference held in Germany had refused to accept papers in Spanish while accepting presentations in German. After a formal protest was made, the conference organisers were forced to back down. This event marked a kind of watershed and since then PL has seen a tendency for conferences and journals in her field to accept papers in a number of languages. She notes that 'there is even a kind of backlash against the use of English'.

Her administrative and teaching commitments have made it difficult for PL to continue to publish. She was forced to turn down an invitation to participate in a lexicography project with colleagues from the English department, in part because she felt that she did not have a good enough command of English to participate fully, but also because of time constraints. PL, without a strong publications record, lacks the confidence to apply for a research assessment. She characterises her fear of receiving a humiliating negative review as 'cowardly'.

Like her colleague JD, PL considers the CNEAI criteria unclear. As she puts it, 'I just don't know what the parameters are'. She also holds the view that some criteria are unjust and counterproductive. The particular instance of this she cites is the fact that co- or multiple-authored papers receive lower numbers of points. This she sees as going against a positive trend in her field towards interdisciplinary research. She is also particularly resentful of the fact that changes in the criteria are sometimes made *post hoc*, so that a particular publishing strategy one has adopted might turn out to be erroneous in the light of newly published criteria. She expresses this resentment in particularly strong terms: 'How can you sit in judgement on me and my work produced over a period of five years with your criteria created last week?'

In PL's field, it has apparently been difficult to reach an agreement on how the relevant Spanish journals should be ranked. This makes targeting the right journals in order to achieve a positive evaluation difficult. Although PL has completed courses offered by the university library on how to develop a publishing strategy with a view to presenting a successful application, she sums up her current position as one of feeling 'completely lost'.

5.6. PCR: 'How many curriculum reforms have we been subjected to?'

PCR shares several of PL's views. In his field, working with teams made up of members with different areas of expertise is essential, something he notes is unusual in fields such as literary studies. He echoes JD's position that linguistics does not sit comfortably in a humanities area at all. In response to the CNEAI's current criteria, PCR now finds himself trying to write some individually authored papers so as to prepare for his fourth research assessment. This also forces him to partially abandon a mentoring and supportive role in relation to colleagues with less robust CVs.

towards publishing in English, but says, 'There's no point bewailing the fact; it's just the way things are'.

FDV recognises that publication in English is fundamental since, ultimately, 'it is impact that matters and impact in English is far greater'. The writing in English of an entire monograph — the genre that would earn the highest number of points in the humanities — is too great a challenge for many Spanish historians, according to FDV. He observes that the literary capacities involved are beyond the reach of most, and that translation of a book-length text could cost in the vicinity of €12 000. As a result, more and more Spanish historians are opting to publish research articles. Thus, like his colleague MAC, FDV sees the CNEAI criteria as conditioning research publication practices. His tactic, however, is to write and publish specifically in order to satisfy the criteria while still publishing in other languages and in the contexts the CNEAI criteria proscribe.

There is no sense of nostalgia in FDV's account. He is an active participant in various social media and considers that researchers have to learn to make themselves visible in this way, strategically promoting their work and attracting readers and citers who might thus help them to gain a positive assessment.

5.4. PL: 'There's a kind of backlash against the use of English'

PL, the fourth participant, had recently finished her PhD when I interviewed her in 2002. At that time, she was more concerned with acquiring a reading competence in German than with issues surrounding publication in English. Now, she attends English classes at the university's language services department — classes which, she says, have allowed her to develop 'a good passive knowledge but there are still many things I can't do'. She considers that people who work with language are far more respectful of and reticent about writing and publishing in English than their counterparts in other disciplines. In some cases, and PL cites historians, there is 'a willingness to abandon literary elegance in favour of just getting your work out there'.

When I first interviewed PL, she was secretary of the philology faculty and is now one of three sub-deans. She has a number of administrative roles, among them sole responsibility for all the faculty's European student exchange programs. One reason she has agreed to form a part of the current faculty team is that there is a small salary bonus paid. However, a strategy common to those who opt out of the research evaluation process, who seek to establish their usefulness for the institution, is to take on what for many is the least appealing aspect of university work. PL also teaches more hours than many of her colleagues and is obliged to prepare and teach different courses almost every year.

She shares with many others in classics a resentment of the growing dominance of English, which she says 'tramples on other languages'. In her view, if Latin itself is not view, lack intellectual curiosity and bring to the classroom fewer resources in terms of language and background knowledge than the students of the past. He 'really suffers' in the classroom some years, as a result of having to work with students he perceives as having embarked upon a degree as a result of 'a kind of inertia'. For someone who was the first member of his rural working-class family to attend a university, this is particularly galling. He bewails the fact that 'the habit of reading has been lost'.

5.3. FDV: 'Did I ever say I was a native speaker?'

FDV, also a historian, had already achieved a great deal of prominence in his field when I first interviewed him in 2010. Although he struggled with English, journals invited him to publish and paid for his work to be translated, and when that was not the case he was able to draw on funds from research projects to pay professional translators and authors' editors. FDV's strong second language is French. He was already fluent before he was given a grant to spend a year at the Sorbonne, thanks to primary and secondary education at a French Lycée in mainland Spain. As he puts it, 'If I were to feel any resentment, it would be towards French for becoming a secondary language of academic communication'.

FDV has forged new paths for a discipline which, at the time he entered it in Spain at least, was still vexed by controversies over putting a plural s on the word 'religion'. As an innovator and trailblazer, he was sought after internationally by those wanting to do comparative research examining their own contexts and his. These individuals were also non-first-language users of English. FDV is unconcerned about achieving proficiency in English, since it is these researchers with whom he needs to communicate. 'Between you and me', he confides, 'there is a *lingua franca* spoken by people in my field — Norwegians, Italians and so on — and it's not standard English'. He feels none of the fear or stigma that Flowerdew (2008, 2009) suggests Chinese academics experience. On one occasion, when a reviewer said that FDV's paper required revision because it was 'obvious that the author is not a native speaker', FDV responded, 'Did I ever say I was?'

FDV was quick to debunk any suggestion that the work of the evaluation committees was mired in subjectivity or arbitrariness. As a former member of the Area 10 Committee, he has insider knowledge of how that committee operates and is anxious to share that knowledge with colleagues, noting with an air of bemusement that the university administration did not seem interested in drawing on his expertise.

As FDV puts it, success depends on 'studying the criteria carefully in the same way you'd look carefully at the style guide before submitting to a journal'. If the system is unjust, it is so in two ways: first, through apportioning status and prestige to journals with high rejection rates; and second, in failing to recognise that citations are accrued much more slowly in the humanities than they are in the hard sciences. He acknowledges that people have to tailor their research activity to the demands of the agencies and that this may involve a shift away from publishing in Spanish or other European languages

5.2. MAC: 'The baronial full professors are a bigger problem'

MAC, a historian working in contemporary history, historiography and the history of ideas, shares at least one element in JD's narrative — namely, 'the rogue'. For MAC, 'baronial' full professors in the Spanish university system, who may not themselves be particularly productive as researchers, still control departments and even whole branches of the discipline. He considers that it is these individuals who should be the target of resistance and not the apparent privileging of English by the research evaluation agencies.

MAC was, when I first interviewed him, devoting time and effort to learning English, spending most of the summer vacation every year in the UK. He had grown frustrated with the work of the translators he had paid to prepare an English version of a monograph he had written in response to a commission from a prestigious UK publisher. On seeing a draft of the translation, he detected, to his horror, a series of errors that would have caused him enormous embarrassment. The potential disaster he succeeded in averting is something he says he can still 'hardly bear to think about'. Since that time MAC has never relinquished control of his work in the same way, often preferring to use online translators to produce English versions which he then edits.

In 2015 MAC finds himself more at ease with his own position and more relaxed about his English, while still choosing to publish in Spanish from time to time. This he does not see as 'a mission', noting that that there are others who do and who often limit themselves to local concerns and local publication in a bid to defy the growing encroachment of English. Unlike the historians in the ENEIDA survey (see Burgess et al., 2014), MAC is not resentful of the dominance of English. He sees it as simply a *fait accompli* that he has learned to accept with considerable grace. If he does feel mildly resentful, it is not in relation to the implicit privileging of English but rather to the fact that real research productivity is not, in his view, what is being assessed. Instead, he sees researchers increasingly tailoring their activities to the demands of the CNEAI and abandoning worthwhile book-length projects in favour of articles.

MAC celebrates a certain level of solidarity among Spanish historians at home and abroad, such that those working in the United States invite their Spain-based colleagues to contribute chapters to books produced by prestigious publishers. One of MAC's most recent publications was a review article in a major US-based journal. He wrote the paper in Spanish and the journal paid for an expert translator, with whom he was able to negotiate a process which resulted in a highly satisfactory outcome. MAC places a great value on the contribution of skilled authors' editors and translators.

Like the historians in Ylijoki's (2005) study of academic nostalgia, MAC harks back to a better time — in his case, before the Bologna Accord and the creation of the European Educational Space. While he maintains his enthusiasm for research, he is disillusioned with teaching and with the increasing bureaucratisation that accompanies it. He resents the fact that this takes time away from research. Today's students, in MAC's less competent and hard-working researchers sometimes achieved positive assessments merely on the basis that their work had appeared in English. More recently, she has made several attempts to publish in English herself, largely in response to the CNEAI guidelines but also because she believes it is of benefit to younger researchers whom she mentors and who are also her co-authors. She has generally turned to family members or colleagues in the English department as translators rather than to specialised professionals. JD's limited competence in English makes it difficult for her to assess the quality of these translations and she is thus forced to relinquish control of her work. This practice has produced mixed results. Her most recent submission to a journal with an impact factor was rejected partly on the grounds that technical terms used in the article were confusing.

In 2015, JD remains indignant about the research assessment policies and procedures, particularly in the humanities, still contending that undeserving people who are not 'real researchers' succeed whereas those with merit do not always get recognition. As she puts it: 'This country is a rogue's paradise'.

She sees the consequences of the research evaluation policies as impacting not only individual scholars but also the status of particular disciplines in Spain. JD considers that her field does not receive due recognition because it has been 'lumped together' with the other humanities disciplines which, she rightly observes, have different methods, values and standards of excellence. JD sees her research area, experimental phonetics, as having more in common with the sciences and indeed feels she has more of a sense of fellowship with scientists than she does with others in her own faculty. At a doctoral school board meeting shortly before the interview, someone from the hard sciences had assumed her resentment of the CNEAI to be the result of her failure to achieve positive reviews. When JD explained that she had four '*sexenios*', the scientist's response had been, 'You're one of us; one of the elite'.

Despite her satisfaction in receiving what she deemed to be a compliment, JD sees holding on to this elite status as an uphill battle that takes her attention away from work she enjoys and considers her duty — namely, mentoring younger colleagues and students. As she puts it, 'I never rest and now I have to deal with this as well'. In the lead-up to receiving her fourth positive evaluation, she had experienced high levels of anxiety because she believed herself to be subject to the whims of the evaluation committee rather than to objective measures of productivity and quality. Had the outcome of her application been negative, she said, the potential impact on her self-esteem and her sense of herself as an extremely hard-working, elite researcher would have been so great that she would have considered applying for early retirement.

JD bewails the fact that the humanities criteria are open to interpretation. In contrast, in the sciences, as she puts it, 'it's just a question of mathematics'. What she sees as vagueness in the Area 11 criteria plays into the hands of the 'rogues' who, as she perceives it, surround her in many aspects of her professional life.

in Spanish in the participants' offices, under conditions of privacy. I was the only interviewer.

I had interviewed each of the six researchers on one of two previous occasions. Three of the participants had been interviewed in 2002 and three in 2010. Both these rounds of interviews were part of two earlier projects. The 2002 interviews formed a part of the study reported in Burgess and Fagan (2006), and the 2010 interviews were conducted in the initial stages of the ENEIDA [Spanish Team for Intercultural Studies on Academic Discourse] project, reported in Moreno, Rey-Rocha, Burgess, López-Navarro & Sachdev (2012), Burgess et al. (2014), Martín et al. (2014), Lorés-Sanz et al. (2014), Gea-Valor et al. (2014) and López-Navarro et al. (2015).

I began the 2015 interviews by reminding the researchers of the themes that we had discussed in the earlier interviews and asking them what had changed for them over the ensuing period. I then raised the issue of the research assessment procedures and how they felt these had impacted their lives. The interviews, each approximately two hours long, were conducted at a time when these issues were particularly pertinent, since the current application period for research evaluation had closed shortly before, and the results of the previous review had just been sent out to applicants. This was also a time of the year when teaching allocations for the following year were being decided upon and the consequences of positive or negative assessment were very much at the forefront of people's minds.

The participants are 3 women and 3 men, ranging in age from their early 40s through to their late 50s. In terms of seniority, 5 out of the 6 are tenured and 4 are full professors. Three are members of the two history departments in our faculty and 3 are members of philology departments and are linguists working with English, Spanish and Latin. Three are graduates of the University of La Laguna and did their doctorates there. Three were trained in mainland Spain.

In each case I make use of my own translations of key comments or observations made by the interviewees in both the titles and the account of the experience of each participant. I use only their initials to identify them so as to preserve their anonymity.

5. Chapters in life histories: The impact of research evaluation policies

5.1. JD: 'This country is a rogue's paradise'

The first life history is that of JD, a full professor in the Spanish philology department who describes herself as being 'completely immersed in research'. She is the director of one of the university's research facilities, the phonetics laboratory, leads a research team and engages with other similar teams in Cuba, Colombia, Venezuela and other parts of the Spanish- and Portuguese-speaking world.

Since Spanish is her object of study, JD sees little academic justification for publishing in English, and in the earlier interview she had expressed the opinion that

Foundation for Science and Technology in accrediting emerging journals (see Bocanegra-Valle, this volume). There are also specific instructions for music, art and geography, and a list of items that do not even merit consideration, including chapters in festschrifts and articles published in journals produced by the scholar's home institution. Applicants are also warned that fewer points will be given to multiple papers published in the same journal.

The guidelines for Area 11 (philosophy, philology and linguistics) are somewhat less specific, though a number of indices for the humanities are listed. Applicants are told that RAs in journals the editorial boards of which the author forms a part will not be considered. There is some general guidance on how one might gain a positive assessment: it is stated that, ideally, at least one of the five publications should be a research monograph published internationally. Failing that, applicants are told that they should present at least two RAs published in journals 'of international standing' or, alternatively, one RA in a journal with an impact factor and a book chapter in an international publication.

4. The life-history approach as a method

Perusal of the CNEAI Criteria (2014) and participant observation amply demonstrate both the mechanisms of research evaluation and their consequences for humanities scholars. My aim in this chapter was to map these observations onto accounts of the implications of research evaluation by individual scholars by using the life-history interview (Plummer, 2001). This approach Connell (2010) describes as appropriate when one is seeking to 'unite close-focus analysis of a labor process with broad questions of cultural dynamics' (p. 779). The life-history approach, as Connell and her colleagues Wood and Crawford have employed it, involves semi-structured interviews intended to draw out stretches of narrative in which the interviewee might provide information on personal background, training and career, current work and workplace, international connections, travel and use of technology. The researcher considers each interview individually before making statements about the group (Connell, 2006, p. 8).

My focus is on the research evaluation policies and how these affected the participants' work, their attitudes to the Spanish university system, the European Educational Space and their position in the wider world. In each case, I also used a recent instance of research writing as a starting point for discussion as well as the interviewee's most recent application for research assessment, where applicable. The applications are essentially narratives that reflect key incidents in academic and intellectual life, but they also provide the backdrop for other narratives of labour processes and personal circumstances.

The interviews were conducted in February 2015. The interviewees were all members of staff at the University of La Laguna, a large provincial university where I am also employed. I recorded and transcribed the interviews, which were conducted

3 for the social sciences, and that engineering and architecture are divided into a further 3 subcommittees, whereas only 2 committees assess humanities scholars over a wide range of disciplines, often with very different practices and values. The disciplinary areas are the following:

1. Mathematics and physics
2. Chemistry
3. Cellular and molecular biology
4. Biomedical sciences
5. Natural sciences
6. Engineering and architecture (broken down into three subcategories: mechanical, communications, construction)
7. Social, political and behavioural sciences and education
8. Economics and business studies
9. Law and jurisprudence
10. History, geography and arts
11. Philosophy, philology and linguistics.

The CNEAI publishes general guidelines for preparation of the summary and the evidence of quality and impact but also offers specific instructions for each of the 11 areas in the state gazette (CNEAI Criteria, 2014). The general guidelines emphasise scientific rigour, innovation and creativity and explicitly proscribe descriptive accounts, applications of research findings (for example, in textbooks) and popularisations. Journals included in the Thompson-Reuters ISI index are clearly seen as a key target for publication of one's work, although in fields where emerging Spanish journals are contexts for publication the guidelines stipulate that these journals must demonstrably operate under the same quality criteria as the established international journals (Bocanegra-Valle provides an account of these quality criteria in this volume).

A proviso that the involvement of multiple authors will only be regarded as justifiable in the case of complex topics or longer publications is common to the two humanities areas, 10 and 11. Similarly, in both areas evidence of the quality of books or book chapters is established by the number of citations received, the prestige of the publishing house, the fact that the work has been reviewed in academic journals, that it has been translated into other languages and that it has been included in bibliographies produced independently of authors and the institution where they are employed. Journal articles are evaluated in terms of whether or not the journal is included in international databases such as Web of Science or the Humanities and Social Sciences citation reports of the JCR.

For Area 10 (history, geography and arts) more specific guidance is given in which a series of databases are mentioned as well as acknowledgment of the role of the Spanish in the rankings and where there is considerable public resentment of what is sometimes perceived as another corrupt institution where nepotism and a culture of 'jobs for the boys' prevail (see, for example, the comments by Bernal Triviño, 2016).

3. Research productivity and quality assessment procedures in Spain

There are two national agencies involved in research assessment. The first is the *Agencia Nacional de la Calidad y la Acreditación* [the National Quality Assurance and Accreditation Agency, or ANECA]. The ANECA assesses and accredits those applying for non-tenured university positions, those already in these positions who wish to obtain tenure, and tenured staff seeking promotion to full professorships. This accreditation is granted largely in terms of research productivity, although teaching and administrative work are also considered. Once the summit of full professorship is attained, this agency is no longer relevant to one as an individual researcher.

Of more pressing concern to most university and research institute staff is the *Comisión Nacional Evaluadora de la Actividad Investigadora* [the National Commission for the Evaluation of Research Activity or CNEAI], a commission under the auspices of the Spanish Ministry for Education, Culture and Sport. The CNEAI is responsible for reviewing scholars' research productivity and quality over six-year periods. People opt to take part in the review process and, if successful, receive a relatively modest salary increment, though in some universities this is not paid to non-tenured staff. One might think that for staff on contracts there would, therefore, be little incentive to apply for assessment but, although the economic benefits of a successful application are not entirely negligible, they are far less important to most scholars than the prestige attached to obtaining a '*sexenio*', as the productivity assessments are known. Holding two or more *sexenios* means admission to a privileged club where one has considerably reduced teaching loads, more involvement with postgraduate teaching and supervision, a growing incentive and entitlement to engage in more research, greater access to funding and professional status.

Those wishing to be reviewed present a dossier which includes their curriculum vitae and a summary of their research activity over the previous six years, highlighting their five best publications and providing evidence of the quality of these publications. The CNEAI publishes guidelines on the publication types most likely to be regarded as indicators of research productivity and what kinds of evidence of quality should be provided. Scholars prepare the dossier on the basis of the criteria the CNEAI publishes (see below) but also often draw on the expertise of senior scholars and librarians in their institutions. There is also a burgeoning fee-paying service industry offering assistance in the preparation of applications.

The CNEAI consists of 12 committees, each of which is responsible for reviewing in 1 of 11 disciplinary areas. A 12th committee reviews in the area of knowledge transfer. It is worth observing that there are 5 separate committees for the hard disciplines and

The chapter is divided into five sections. First, I describe the ways in which negative and positive research productivity reviews affect scholars. In the second section, I provide an overview of the current research assessment procedures in Spain. The third section, devoted to research methodology, briefly reviews the various projects in which Connell and her colleagues made use of the life-history methodology, explaining how and why the current study used that methodology. The fourth section explores each of the life histories; and the final section charts the various patterns that emerge.

2. Consequences of positive and negative assessments

The first, and most obvious, way in which research assessment can impact a scholar's life is in terms of job security. Although not all Spanish universities have implemented redundancies during the economic downturn, the threat of job loss has weighed heavily on non-tenured staff. Some institutions have opted for a freeze on promotions to tenured or full professor status so as to maintain existing levels of permanent staff, with few of those who retire being replaced and only then with staff on short-term contracts. For junior staff on such temporary contracts, a formal accreditation by either the national or a local agency is a crucial step on the path to obtaining a permanent position.

For established members of university staff, positive assessments of research activity may protect one from increased teaching loads, particularly in heavily subscribed programs, and ultimately may provide a scholar with the necessary credentials for a full professorship. Positive assessments also raise scholars' status in departmental hierarchies so that they are able to choose the courses they teach, usually opting for final-year and elective courses in undergraduate degrees or graduate-level teaching. Those without these positive assessments tend to be lumbered with compulsory courses taught to large undergraduate groups in the first years of the degrees and consequently have a heavier workload, not only in terms of contact hours but also because of increasingly burdensome administrative work in relation to continuous assessment of large cohorts.

Negative reviews, or opting out of the review process altogether, ultimately bar one from taking part in the teaching of doctoral courses and from the supervision and assessment of PhD students. Those in this situation, given their increased teaching and administrative workload, become less and less likely to find time to participate in research and may see themselves excluded from research activity altogether. Invitations to join research teams dry up or, if they are issued, have to be turned down because scholars are overcommitted in other areas of their university work (typically administrative work as secretaries of departments and faculties). Since funding for conference attendance is now scarce and often entirely drawn from research project grants, a serious consequence of the lack of a positive assessment is decreasing participation and engagement with peers and more senior researchers, particularly those outside Spain. Finally, and as a result of all of the above, there are important affective consequences in terms of the scholar's prestige, self-esteem and general wellbeing — this, in a climate where the Spanish universities are low criteria, especially if the author has a professional connection with the publisher such as being employed by the same institution. Even in disciplines in which monographs are still regarded as the most highly valued contributions, it can seem a profligate waste of precious time and even more precious research findings to put one's efforts into a publication of this length and complexity when producing one or more research articles in a Journal Citation Report [JCR] journal can guarantee a successful research evaluation report. Thus humanities scholars frequently face a task that is challenging on two fronts. First, they may see themselves as obliged to make the change to writing shorter, more rhetorically constrained texts — that is, research articles [RAs]. Second, they are under increasing pressure to produce these texts in a foreign language.

Pragmatists in Spain, as elsewhere, while not necessarily welcoming the research evaluation policies that implicitly encourage publication in English and publication of less lengthy research process genres such as the research article, generally see it as being in their interests to change their publishing behaviours (López-Navarro, Moreno, Quintanilla & Rey-Rocha, 2015). Recent survey findings (Lorés-Sanz, Mur-Dueñas, Rey-Rocha & Moreno, 2014; Martín, Rey-Rocha, Burgess & Moreno, 2014; Gea-Valor, Rey-Rocha & Moreno, 2014) suggest that this pragmatist approach is more common among hard science and social science academics in Spain. The picture is less clear for scholars working in the humanities.

Humanities scholars have received attention in a number of studies, including Burgess, Gea-Valor, Moreno & Rey-Rocha (2014) and Chan (2016), but also earlier in the work of Li and Flowerdew (2009), Flowerdew and Li (2009), Curry and Lillis (2004) and Lillis and Curry (2010). 'Niche subjects', as Ammon (2006) terms those humanities fields in which publication in languages other than English remains at least a principled choice if not a practical option, merit our attention still. It is these disciplines — disciplines such as history, literary and cultural studies and even linguistics — which represent sites of potential resistance to the implicit privileging of publication in English, a privileging that is encoded in current Spanish national research evaluation policies and procedures.

Although quantitative research provides important insights into the responses of scholars to the pressures to publish in English (for example, Hanauer & Englander, 2011), qualitative data provide a means of understanding and appreciating the various ways in which policies of this kind impact individual scholars, how these individuals respond, and how both the implications of the policies and individual responses vary across disciplines, relative academic status and gender. In this chapter, I use the life-history approach adopted by Connell and Wood (2002) and endorsed by Connell, Wood and Crawford (2005) and Connell (2006, 2010) to explore the experiences of six Spanish humanities scholars and the impact that research evaluation policies which implicitly privilege English have had on their lives.

Although the view that non-first-language users of English face an anglophone bias when presenting their work for publication is often challenged (Swales, 2004; Casanave, 2009; Hyland, 2016a, 2016b), few would suggest that the status of English as the current *lingua franca* of international academic communication does not present users of other languages and of English as an additional language [EAL] with a greater challenge than that faced by those for whom it is a mother tongue. Scholars whose first language is not English devote more time and economic resources to producing publications than do their anglophone counterparts (Ammon, 2000, 2001). Funds may be used to pay for language training or periods of time spent in English-speaking countries. Once scholars have achieved competence in English, many continue to rely at least partially on support (usually paid) from specialised translators, editors and other 'literacy brokers' (Lillis & Curry, 2006; Chan, 2016). Journal editors and peer reviewers may recommend that EAL authors avail themselves of these services, especially those offered by first-language users of English, to revise their papers (Lillis & Curry, 2015). Scholars who write without any such support or assistance comment on the greater amount of time and effort it takes them to produce text in English and talk of feeling frustrated with their inability to express their meanings as they might have done in their first language (Pérez-Llantada, Plo & Ferguson, 2011). Others talk of the stress they experience when obliged to communicate in English (Flowerdew, 2009).

The situation I describe pertains to all contexts where English is a foreign or second language and where it is not the principal medium of instruction in the education system (see Anderson, 2013; Curry & Lillis, 2013; Englander & Uzuner-Smith, 2013; Feng, Beckett & Huang, 2013; Lee & Lee, 2013). The privileging of English holds true even in contexts in which other 'big' languages with claims to global status are used, which one might expect to be sites of resistance (see Feng et al., 2013 and Chan, 2016). Spain is a case in point. Spanish scholars, like their counterparts elsewhere in the world, now find themselves under increasing pressure to publish in English. This is a situation that has prevailed for some time in the natural and social sciences (Jiménez-Contreras, De Moya & Delgado, 2003), but which now impacts research publication in the humanities as well.

The fact that evaluation agencies privilege publication in international high-status journals and use citations accrued as proof of quality not only implies a shift for humanities scholars away from publishing largely in their first language but may also mean changes in terms of the usual vehicles of publication. Thus genres that might once have been considered the most appropriate for their work, such as the book, may be partially or wholly abandoned. One important reason for this is that books — and indeed chapters in books — are less likely to attract citations, especially if there is limited online access and no permission to place the text in a repository. Second, books are often published by smaller, local publishing houses, many of them university presses, and these are less readily viewed by the agencies as satisfying quality control

1

Accept or contest:

A life-history study of humanities scholars' responses to research evaluation policies in Spain

Sally Burgess

1. Introduction

The adoption of globalised forms of knowledge production in a climate of economic downturn has led to greater pressures being brought to bear on academics in many contexts around the world. Access to research funding, academic status, promotion and employment security are dependent on providing evidence of research productivity. The pressure to quickly and objectively assess and compare scholars, who compete for ever-scarcer resources, has led to a situation in which academic evaluation agencies are likely to look to quantifiable measures of research productivity, both in terms of output and in terms of the value of that output and the quality of the research. The most obvious evidence of the impact of a scholar's research, and ostensibly of its quality, is acceptance for publication in an elite journal and the number of citations accrued. It is well known that research publications in English attract a wider readership than do publications in other languages and that, as a result, these publications are more likely to garner citations (see, for example, Whitehand, 2005, and Ramos-Torre & Callejo-Gallego, 2013). Therefore, when research quality is measured in terms of citations, publication in English is implicitly favoured and publication in other languages can become a dispreferred option.

Hyland, K. (2016a). Academic publishing and the myth of linguistic injustice. *Journal of Second Language Writing, 31*, 58-69.

Hyland, K. (2016b). Language myths and publishing mysteries: A response to Politzer-Ahles et al. *Journal of Second Language Writing, 34*, 9-11.

Institute of English, University of Silesia. (2009). Occupying niches: Interculturality, cross-culturality and aculturality in academic research. Retrieved 19 January 2017 from http://ija. us.edu.pl/sub/prisealweb/.

Kuteeva, M., & Mauranen, A. (2014). Writing for publication in multilingual contexts: An introduction to the special issue. *Journal of English for Academic Purposes, 13*, 1-4.

Lillis, T., & Curry, M.J. (2006). Professional academic writing by multilingual scholars: Interactions with literacy brokers in the production of English-medium texts. *Written Communication, 23*(1), 3-35.

Lillis, T., & Curry, M.J. (2010). *Academic writing in a global context: The politics and practices of publishing in English.* London: Routledge.

Lillis, T., & Curry, M. (2015). The politics of English, language and uptake: The case of international academic journal article reviews. *AILA Review, 28*(1), 127-150.

Matarese, V. (Ed.). (2013). *Supporting research writing: Roles and challenges in multilingual settings.* Oxford: Chandos Publishing.

Moreno, A.I., Rey-Rocha, J., Burgess, S., López-Navarro, I., & Sachdev, I. (2012). Spanish researchers' perceived difficulty writing research articles for English medium journals: The impact of proficiency in English versus publication experience. *Ibérica, 24*, 157-184.

Politzer-Ahles, S., Holliday, J.I, Girolamo, T., Spychalska, M., & HarperBerkson, K. (2016). Is linguistic injustice a myth? A response to Hyland (2016). *Journal of Second Language Writing, 34*, 3-8.

PRISEAL. (2007). The Tenerife statement. Retrieved 19 January 2017 from http://ppriseal. webs.ull.es/tenerife_statement1.pdf.

Salager-Meyer, F. (2015). Peripheral scholarly journals: From locality to globality. *Ibérica, 30*, 15-36.

Santos, B.S., Nunes, J.A., & Meneses, M.P. (2007). Introduction: Opening up the canon of knowledge and recognition of difference. In B.S. Santos (Ed.), *Another knowledge is possible: Beyond northern epistemologies* (pp. xviv-lxii). London: Verso.

Swales, J.M. (1990). *Genre analysis: English in academic and research settings.* Cambridge: Cambridge University Press.

Swales, J.M. (2004). *Research genres: Explorations and applications.* Cambridge: Cambridge University Press.

Tönnies, F. (2002/1887). *Community and society* (C. Loomis, Trans.). New York: Dover Publications.

van de Poel, K., Carstens, W.A.M., & Linnegar, J. (2012). *Text editing: A handbook for students and practitioners.* Brussels: University Press Antwerp.

factors affecting publication in English by multilingual authors is provided. In as much as the authors arrive at new understandings, they also raise many questions and provide an impetus for further reflection. New participants are drawn into the conversations around these questions and fruitful dialogue is established between academic researchers and practitioners at the chalk- and text-face. With that comes the recognition that any barriers to participation in these conversations based on notions of hierarchy and institutional exclusion serve little purpose. The ways in which we can learn from and inform one another are the unspoken thread that binds the chapters together. We will no doubt see scholars continue to weave rich patterns through responses to what is published here and through future contact between PRISEAL and MET and other groups. Fittingly, Laurence Anthony's Afterword provides the first of what we hope will be many more such responses and is an example of the ways in which the conversation can be continued and expanded.

References

Bennett, K. (Ed.). (2014). *The semiperiphery of academic writing: Discourses, communities and practices*. London: Palgrave Macmillan.

Cargill, M., & Burgess, S. (2008). Introduction to the special issue: English for Research Publication Purposes. *Journal of English for Academic Purposes, 7*(2), 75-76.

Connell, R.W. (2006). Core activity: Reflexive intellectual workers and cultural crisis. *Journal of Sociology, 42*(1), 5-23.

Connell, R.W. (2007). *Southern theory: The global dynamics of knowledge in social science*. Sydney: Allen & Unwin.

Connell, R.W., & Wood, J. (2002). Globalization and scientific labour: Patterns in a life-history study of intellectual workers in the periphery. *Journal of Sociology, 38*(2), 167-190.

Curry, M. J., & Lillis, T. (2013). Introduction to the thematic issue: Participating in academic publishing — Consequences of linguistic policies and practices. *Language Policy, 12*(3), 209-213. DOI: http://dx.doi.org/10.1007/s10993-013-9286-7.

Delgado López-Cózar, E., Ruiz-Pérez, R., & Jiménez-Contreras, E. (2006). *La edición de revistas científicas. Directrices, criterios y modelos de evaluación*. Madrid: FECYT.

Directorate Generale of Higher Education-Indonesian Ministry of Education. (2012). Surat Edaran No. 152/E/T/2012 tentang Publikasi Karya Ilmiah. Indonesia: Indonesian Ministry of Education.

Engeström, Y. (2000). Activity theory as a framework for analyzing and redesigning work. *Ergonomics, 43*, 960-974.

Ferguson, G. (2007). The global spread of English, scientific communication and ESP: Questions of equity, access and domain loss. *Ibérica, 13*, 7-38.

Freire, P. (1970). *Pedagogy of the oppressed*. New York: Continuum.

Hanauer, D.I., & Englander, K. (2013). *Scientific writing in a second language*. Anderson, South Carolina: Parlor Press.

homage and signalling respect, while in the newer social system it is seen as intentional or unintentional theft of intellectual property and therefore as plagiarism.

Bennett concludes by suggesting a questioning of social pressures and dominant value systems that influence action. A context-embedded response to externally imposed pressure is demonstrated in Chapter 11, by Thuc Anh Cao Xuan and Kate Cadman. Their research context is Vietnam, and the pressure is for English language teachers to become researchers and conduct and publish research in ways accepted by the Western academy (an intersection of Clusters A and B). This necessitates developing a culture of research through effective training (Cluster C), and teachers of English for Research Purposes [ERP] are expected to be important contributors. In the light of the limited amounts of research actually being conducted, Cao and Cadman's study investigates how Vietnamese ERP teachers conceptualise their roles as educators of English language research skills and writing, and how learning and teaching are actually experienced in ERP classrooms. In particular, they seek to understand how Freire's (1970) distinction between transmissive and transformative pedagogies is playing out in three sophomore classrooms, through the interplay between newly encouraged innovative practices and traditional practices in which teachers keep student learning under their own control. Findings demonstrate both student agency in their responses to the teaching they receive, and local priorities determining teachers' decisions about the applicability of Western best practice in this Asian context.

The questioning of an orthodoxy — in Hyland's (2016a, b) paper, that of 'unjust' treatment of EAL authors — is mirrored in the final chapter of this book, which questions orthodoxies of other kinds. In his chapter, John Swales illustrates, in both playful and serious ways, a number of instances where published authors deliberately flout the established English for Research Publication Purposes [ERPP] conventions and thus reveal their lack of willingness to quietly toe the line represented by journal requirements in Figure 1.1's Cluster B. These acts of rhetorical and stylistic rebellion, he concludes, are not only the province of established key figures whose status licenses them to step outside the narrow confines of disciplinary discourse practices. Instead, he notes a number of such instances in the writing of people at the beginning of their academic publishing careers. The fact that Swales draws on the published work of these erstwhile relative novices, now themselves high-profile researchers in their field, suggests that there were few if any negative consequences of these breaches of convention for the writers concerned. Swales ends with a call for more 'experimentation in both style and substance' in the face of 'excessive and stultifying standardisation' in ERPP contexts — a call reflected in different ways throughout the volume.

The mirroring and extension of research findings and experiences of practice across the clusters depicted in Figure 1.1 are shared characteristics of the chapters in this volume. They also share a strong theoretical focus, often drawing on other disciplines in the social sciences to use theory as a prism through which a new perspective on the very complete account of the theory, noting that if the nodes in the theory are viewed hierarchically, goal-directed activity can be seen as comprising sequences of goal-oriented *actions*, which can include rhetorical actions such as the types of comments a supervisor makes in the context of a student's oral presentation of research. What gives coherence to these actions is the macro-level motive-carrying object (Engeström, 2000): here, progress in research and quality work. Using this analytical approach, Li identifies a clearly 'power-over' relationship between the 'big boss' (Director) and his cohort of research students, which nevertheless is shown to be both successful in terms of completions and publications, and highly valued by the students. Li's analysis shows that the supervisor invokes 'rules' from five surrounding activity systems to contribute to 'tools' for conducting the main activity, research supervision. The five are the world of evaluation at the policy level, the publishing world, the scientific research world, competitive society-at-large, and Chinese culture, the last exemplified by the supervisor's saying incorporated in the chapter title: 'The one who is out of the ordinary shall win'. This chapter, in which mentoring is embedded in the busy world of a hospital surgery department, provides an instructive counterpoint to DiGiacomo's study of mentoring a PhD student's writing in the field of cultural anthropology, reflecting two very different outcomes of interaction between the clusters labelled A and C in Figure 1.1.

One of Li's key conclusions is that, in a particular local context, a supervisory style that contrasts markedly with practices found to support learning effectively in Western contexts may be both 'natural and potentially productive'. In Chapter 10, Bennett applies a similar lens to the issue of plagiarism, a concern relevant to all three of the Figure 1.1 clusters. The orthodoxy that there are clear-cut and unambiguous norms of citing, referencing and quoting that run across all circumstances, languages and cultures is one that Swales, too, questions in Chapter 12, discussed below. Bennett draws on Tönnies's (2002/1887) influential 19th-century sociological model and argues that what is regarded as cheating or theft in social systems where looser ties among members privilege competition and a belief in individual inviolable ownership of resources, will, in small closer-knit communities where resources are owned communally, be regarded as appropriate behaviour. When applying the model to the context of the university, Bennett observes that the once predominant culture of patronage and protection, in which professional advancement and security were dependent on allegiance and tutelage, has now given way to an academic culture in which originality and the notion of intellectual property predominate. Bennett is careful to point out that while one or other system might characterise university education in a particular country, individual institutions or departments, in fact in many cases the two systems operate in parallel and often in conflict. Where this is the case, older established academics may still hold fast to the norms of the manorial system, while 'young turks' strive to publish original research and attract citations of their work. In the older system, reiteration of the words and ideas of an authoritative source without explicit citation may well be regarded as paying

Chapter 7 maintains a primary focus in Cluster B in Figure 1.1, 'Journal conventions and practices', but shifts the context to the broad area of medical research. Martín and León Pérez take up the challenge of providing ERPP teachers and authors' editors with information about changes in features of the prime research genre, the research article [RA]. In this case, their concern is to show how journal audience issues may condition the rhetorical organisation of the RA at macro-structure level but also at the level of preferences for individual moves and steps (Swales, 1990, 2004). For their analysis, they construct a corpus of RAs drawn from the five top-ranked journals in the field of immunology and allergy. Where the journal is narrow in scope, Martín and León Pérez find that the preferred macro-structure is the IMRD [Introduction, Methods, Results and Discussion] while journals with a broader focus use the pattern IRDM [Introduction, Results, Discussion and Method]. Giving greater prominence to the results of a study in this way is also reflected at the level of move and step in both the introduction and discussion sections of the paper, with principal results being presented in the introduction and their importance boosted in the discussion section. Findings such as these potentially offer important information to teachers of ERPP, authors' editors and other mentors.

Mentor training and development (Cluster C, Figure 1.1) is a key focus of Chapter 8, by Cargill, O'Connor, Raffiudin, Sukarno, Juliandi and Rusmana, working in an Asian context, Indonesia (Cluster A). Here also, the pressure to publish research findings in international journals is being felt to an increasing degree, with a publication requirement for PhD graduation having recently been introduced (Directorate Generale of Higher Education, 2012). The biology department where this research took place sought training from long-term collaborators from Australia to develop staff skills as both article authors and mentors of student article writing. The chapter reports outcomes recorded immediately post-intervention and findings from an interview study conducted after the participants had spent 12 months applying the learning *in situ*. Participants reported significantly increased confidence both to write a paper in English and to mentor their students in writing one immediately after the five-day workshop, with the gains maintained or increased 12 months later. The workshop materials had been used widely, including as a complete package for student teaching. However, teaching and administrative workloads were identified as factors affecting the conversion of a highly positive training experience into published papers at the level desired by the Indonesian higher education sector, a finding echoing those from other comparable contexts (for example, Hanauer & Englander, 2013).

Another Asian context, in this case an orthopaedics department in a major Chinese hospital, is the context for Li's study, in Chapter 9, of mentoring interactions between a research supervisor and a group of master's and PhD students. The students are required to publish research articles in order to obtain their degree, and the chapter examines the supervision of this research through a novel application of activity theory. Li provides a

Linnegar, 2012) is used. The model provides criteria for assessment of quality in text editing across five levels of intervention (text type, content, structure, wording and presentation) and in terms of the dimensions of 'correspondence', 'consistency' and 'correctness'. The first of these dimensions concerns the degree to which interventions are a response to a perceived lack of appropriateness across the five levels, while the consistency allows an assessor to evaluate uniformity of the interventions across the text as a whole. Finally, judgements can be made in terms of how correct the interventions are. Linnegar's chapter also demonstrates that the CCC model is effective as a teaching tool in a blended-learning environment, enabling postgraduate students to successfully acquire skills for editing across all the levels, not just the basic level often accepted as sufficient. This locates Linnegar's contribution at the intersection of Clusters B and C (Figure 1.1) but with a very different pedagogical focus from the other contributions considered in the volume.

The function of the editing skills to be developed using Linnegar's procedures is to make texts fit for purpose — in the context of this volume, for submission to, and ultimate acceptance by, the journal selected as most appropriate by the manuscript's author(s). Factors affecting the selection of appropriate journals by scholars in the humanities is the focus of Chapter 6. Bocanegra-Valle explores open access journals in the humanities, an area of research publication practice involving the intersection of the Figure 1.1 clusters around journals (B) and author disciplines and drivers (A). She begins by noting that open access publication was once seen as a somewhat suspect challenger to privatised academic publishing, where large profits accrue through subscription fees and, more recently, payment for individual downloads. The need to establish the viability for authors and credibility for institutions of open access publication was one of the key themes in the first PRISEAL conference, a theme that was addressed again in Poland in 2011 through a panel discussion including a paper by Françoise Salager-Meyer, a major champion of the movement. Bocanegra-Valle cogently argues that open access publication has now achieved acceptability. Like Salager-Meyer (2015), she notes that for smaller journals which function as organs for institutions and associations, open access is clearly a means of maintaining the existence of the journal by attracting contributions from authors who recognise that their work is far more likely to attract interest and citations if it is freely available. Nevertheless, as she observes, the old orthodoxy that open access publications are somehow less credible threatens to re-emerge with the rise of predatory journals which solicit papers from authors, often on a pay-to-publish basis. Drawing on the framework recently developed by the Spanish Foundation of Science and Technology regarding quality assessment in scientific publishing (Delgado López-Cózar, Ruiz-Pérez & Jiménez-Contreras, 2006), Bocanegra-Valle examines a series of Spanish humanities journals in terms of how far they meet these criteria. Observing that orthodox measures of the status of journals still rely heavily on impact factor, she concludes her chapter by positing alternative means of determining quality for the smaller journals that still play an important role in the humanities.

to be submitted in English in the context of the European Doctorate program. Just as Cadman observes tensions in her role as an ERPP teacher, DiGiacomo sees challenges in the multiple roles she performs as co-supervisor of the thesis, author's editor, post-translation editor and translator (Figure 1.1, Cluster C). The 'blurred boundaries' between these roles ultimately involve helping the student to produce a thesis which makes a contribution to the field while also developing the specific literary skills needed in the writing of ethnography — skills which also involve the acquisition of genre knowledge. At the same time, and through the interventions and her discussions with DiGiacomo, the doctoral candidate gains a greater command of English. In this way, DiGiacomo shares with Cadman the view that epistemological questions, genre knowledge and language are inextricably linked. By providing a highly nuanced account of this particular instance of mentoring, DiGiacomo makes it clear that, without insider knowledge of the discipline concerned, the language professional is unlikely to be able to bring about the desired outcome.

One function that DiGiacomo performs is the institutionally authorised role of academic supervisor. In Chapter 4, Shaw and Voss examine the differences in the kinds of interventions made by an institutionally authorised editor — in this case Shaw himself, who works in-house in a medical research facility in Madrid — and those made by Voss, a freelance language professional. For their analysis, located at the intersection of Clusters B and C (Figure 1.1), they draw on Lillis and Curry's (2006) classification of levels of change, namely sentence-level changes, discipline-specific discourse changes, and changes in terms of knowledge claim or contents. They also examine how much consultation with the author about the interventions is articulated through margin comments. Shaw and Voss's results indicate that the institutional editor makes more interventions at the levels of discipline-specific discourse and in terms of knowledge claim and content. While for the most part the freelance editor makes the changes with no consultation, the institutional editor often puts the ball back in the author's court, and thus effectively educates while editing. Voss, when she does seek the author's opinion, tends to provide an alternative wording in her comment. These results parallel those of Lillis and Curry (2006), who found that academic professionals are more inclined to address content and journal audience questions while language professionals often see their remit as restricted to textual surface issues.

But how are higher-order text-editing skills acquired and how should they be systematically evaluated? These are the questions addressed by Linnegar in Chapter 5, in an account of an approach in which editing quality is assessed in terms of how far text interventions correspond to five key levels, only one of which ('Wording') is strictly speaking on the surface of the text. The other four all involve reworking of content and even direct engagement with the scientific accuracy of the text, which, as Shaw and Voss have shown, is a level of engagement many freelance language professionals would find challenging. Linnegar describes a training program employing blended-learning methodology in which a model termed 'the CCC model' (van de Poel, Carstens &

to the present volume critique aspects of this claim, each locating themselves more in some of the Figure 1.1 clusters than others in so doing. Hyland (2016a) himself concedes that 'difficulties with English syntax, lexis, or discourse … greatly complicate the task of non-Anglophone academics' (p. 66), and it is multiple experiences of working in this space that inform the chapters in the present volume.

The focus of Chapter 1 is ways in which scholars respond to the changes in national and institutional policies that occur as a result of the increasing pressure to publish in English. Burgess investigates changes in publication practices in Spain and the implications of these changes in the context of research assessment. While noting that the impacts of these policies on Spanish scholars closely reflect the experience of their counterparts in many other contexts, she draws on the life-history approach adopted by Connell and Wood (2002) and endorsed by Connell (2006) in a series of case studies of Spanish humanities scholars. Burgess uses two sets of interview data collected at different points in time to chart the effects of the changes in research evaluation procedures and the impact of language planning and policy decisions on the scholars' professional lives over time. She suggests that while some scholars continue to regard these measures of productivity as neoliberal affronts resulting in the erosion of local knowledge production practices, others are more inclined to accept the change, while recognising the need for support when preparing work for publication in English. Burgess's chapter concludes with a critical examination of how the researchers worked with translators and editors and the degree to which these relationships helped them make the kinds of contributions they sought to make to their disciplines. Her chapter thus demonstrates interaction among all three of the Figure 1.1 clusters.

Like Burgess, Cadman in Chapter 2 draws in part on the work of Connell, in this case her (2007) critique of hegemonic knowledge production and epistemic erasure, and on Santos, Nunes and Meneses's (2007) notion of the 'epistemicide' of Southern intellectual traditions (Figure 1.1, Cluster A focus on authors, cultures and drivers). Cadman shares with Bennett (2014) and Lillis and Curry (2015) an acute awareness of the dangers of epistemicide, dangers which she sees as creating a number of 'tensions' for the ERPP teacher (Figure 1.1, Cluster C focus on pedagogy). One of these tensions is the degree to which it is their province to intervene in questions of research design. Cadman considers such intervention to be an essential component of principled ERPP training, noting that a failure to meet anglophone expectations of epistemological rigour is a more common reason for research paper rejection than perceived deficiencies in the language used (a concern of Cluster B). She describes a 'Research Writing Matrix', in which language issues are addressed through the dialogic development of epistemologically credible research questions and an increased understanding of the underlying logic of the structure of research genres in the social sciences.

In Chapter 3, DiGiacomo also addresses the issue of intervention by examining the degree and nature of such interventions in a text produced by a novice author, in this case a doctoral candidate in the field of cultural anthropology preparing a thesis

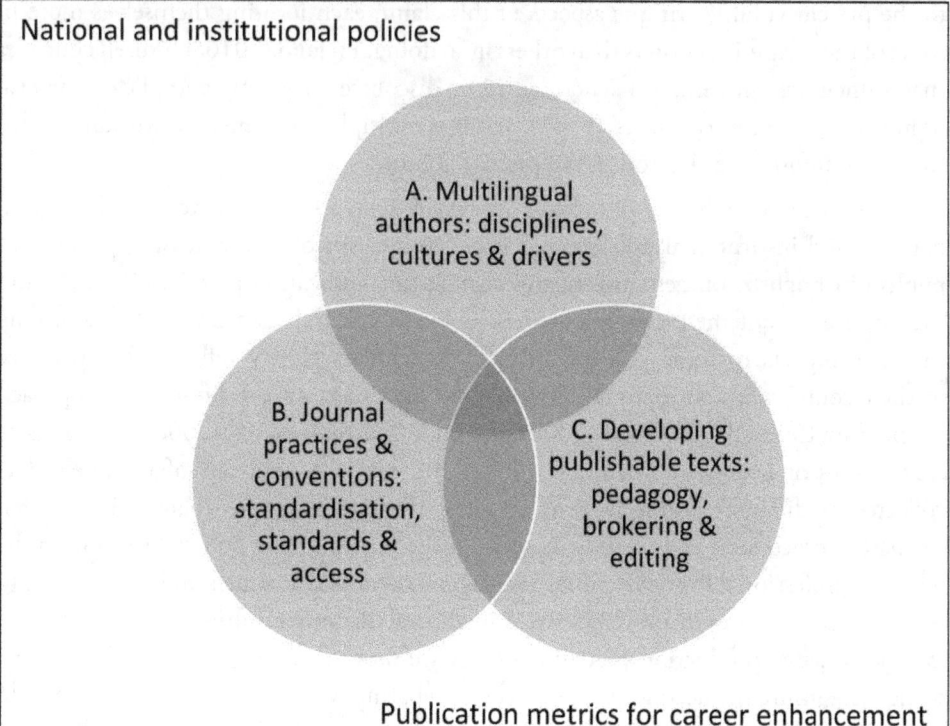

Figure 1.1: Intersecting factors affecting academic publishing by linguistically diverse authors in the early 21st century: one potential model.

emanating from PRISEAL 1, described above. The third cluster gathers issues around developing publishable texts, including pedagogical approaches and activities, brokering (Lillis & Curry, 2006) and editing, including authors' editing (Matarese, 2013).

We argue that seeking to understand the relationships between the clusters (however described) is important, so that conclusions reached in necessarily restricted contexts can be appropriately synthesised or their contrasts and limitations debated. A recent article has claimed that the idea of disadvantage for authors using English as an additional language [EAL] in the realm of academic publishing has become an orthodoxy now understood as 'injustice', and that this is 'a myth' which both downplays the very real difficulties experienced by novice academic authors who use English as a first language [EL1] and serves to demoralise those who use it as an additional language, telling them 'to look for prejudice rather than revision' (Hyland, 2016a, p. 66).[1] Several contributors

1   We note that subsequent to the publication of Hyland (2016a), a response to his position has appeared (Politzer-Ahles, Holliday, Girolamo, Spychalska & HarperBerkson, 2016), calling for empirical studies of the response to EAL authors' submissions. Further to this, Hyland (2016b) has responded, reiterating his initial position but also stating that research is needed across disciplines.

in Coimbra, Portugal: PRISEAL [Publishing and Presenting Research Internationally: Issues for Speakers of English as an Additional Language] and MET [Mediterranean Editors and Translators]. The conference collaboration was the most recent outcome of a growing cross-fertilisation of ideas and perspectives between the two groups, represented in members of both authoring chapters in the 2013 book *Supporting Research Writing: Roles and Challenges in Multilingual Settings* (Matarese, 2013).

Issues around academic publishing in multilingual contexts are attracting increasing interest worldwide (Hanauer & Englander, 2013; Kuteeva & Mauranen, 2014; Lillis & Curry, 2010; Moreno, Rey-Rocha, Burgess, López-Navarro & Sachdev, 2012), and the progression of focus concepts featured in the PRISEAL conferences since 2007 is instructive in tracking a development. Peripherality was the defining framework of the inaugural gathering in Tenerife, Spain in 2007 (PRISEAL 1). This included specifically

> how peripherality is manifested on the surface of the text, how outcomes of research into these features can inform ERPP materials design, the social and geopolitical impacts of peripherality, attitudes to the status of current norms around English language use in publication contexts, and the role of other languages in research communication. (Cargill & Burgess, 2008, p. 75)

A spontaneous outcome of that conference, in a move to address issues of peripherality, was a call for greater inclusivity, equity and access in academic publishing within the disciplines represented, expressed in the Tenerife Statement (PRISEAL, 2007). Four years later at the University of Silesia, Poland, the focusing theme was 'occupying niches'. The Call for Papers highlighted

> the activity of the academic discourse community in terms of niches occupied by users of English as an Additional Language. How much of what is done in the niche gets outside? Is what is done in the niche what gets outside? To what extent is English a distorting mirror of the original ideas? Are these niches isolated linguistic and cultural cavities or are they connected by channels of English, or perhaps Englishes, and other languages? What part of culture is gained or lost in the process of publishing in English? (Institute of English, University of Silesia, 2009)

In 2015, in Coimbra, the theme that united the two conferences could perhaps best be described as 'complexity'. The chapters presented here represent this complexity across many of the relevant dimensions. We propose here one model for clustering the factors that intersect to produce this complexity: broadly, multilingual authors, publishable texts, and journal practices (Figure 1.1). The multilingual author cluster (A in Figure 1.1) includes factors to do with authors' disciplinary homes, the cultures within which they live and work, and the national, institutional and personal goals that direct their efforts. The volume includes contributions grounded in disciplines from humanities, social sciences and natural sciences, and from cultural contexts in Europe, Asia, North America and Australia, all responding to a widespread and growing pressure to publish academic research 'internationally', and therefore in English. The journal practices and conventions cluster (B in Figure 1.1) incorporates issues of standardisation, standards or requirements, and access to published work, reflecting the concern with this topic

Introduction

Unpacking English for Research Publication Purposes [ERPP] and the intersecting roles of those who research, teach and edit it

Margaret Cargill and Sally Burgess

Regardless of where academics work or which languages we use, the pressures to publish in English are considerable and now extend to all disciplines. Gaining an understanding of the multiple roles that English performs and its place in academic publishing has therefore become a major concern for many researchers. The statistics supporting the dominance of English as the language of academic publication worldwide are well reported (for example, Ferguson, 2007; Swales, 2004). Yet, as the numbers of new authors submitting articles to journals grow, new cohorts of editors and reviewers meet issues of variation across the full range of lexico-grammatical, socio-pragmatic and discoursal dimensions. The variable nature of the texts submitted for publication affects the practices of these editors and reviewers in subtle and profound ways. Most know little of the debates that have been conducted around this situation over many years in the field of applied linguistics and its related disciplines, and may often regard language as a transparent conduit for the researcher's meaning (Lillis & Curry, 2015). The remedy commonly recommended by the journal publishers is the use of an editing or language polishing service, now, for those able to pay the fees, increasingly just a click away on the journal's website.

But does a 'quick fix' of this kind adequately address the wide range of issues arising from the use of a variety of academic English perceived as non-standard? We would argue that it does not, and that the expanding field of research and practice in academic publication has much to contribute to a better understanding of the complexities. The chapters in this volume represent work from established and emerging scholars and practitioners involved in investigating the interconnections between linguistically and culturally diverse authors, published research texts, processes for supporting the production of the texts, the social conditions surrounding publication, and critical investigation and reflection on the current trends in all these areas. The chapters developed as a result of a fruitful conjunction of two related groups which held overlapping conferences in 2015

Lillis, T., & Curry, M.J. (2015). The politics of English, language and uptake: The case of international academic journal article reviews. *AILA Review*, *28*(1), 127-150. DOI: http://dx.doi.org/10.1075/aila.28.06lil.

Sheridan, C.L. (2015). National journals and centering institutions: A historiography of an English language teaching journal in Taiwan. *English for Specific Purposes*, *38*, 70-84. DOI: http://dx.doi.org/10.1016/j.esp.2014.12.001.

Swales, J.M. (1990). *Genre analysis: English in academic and research settings*. Cambridge: Cambridge University Press.

Swales, J.M., & Feak, C.B. (2012). *Academic writing for graduate students: Essential tasks and skills: Vol. 3*. Ann Arbor, MI: University of Michigan Press.

We commend the organisers of these conferences as well as the founders of the two organisations (PRISEAL and MET), who have guided their members towards such creative collaborations. The chapters in this book illustrate the nature of the conversations currently taking place and exemplify the products of this cross-fertilisation in thinking. By engaging in theoretical and interventionist conversations from a range of disciplinary, institutional and geographical contexts, the book makes a major contribution to the field of academic writing for publication and signals important new directions for future work.

References

Bennett, K. (2014). *The semi-periphery of academic writing: Discourses, communities and practices.* Houndmills, UK: Palgrave Macmillan.

Burrough-Boenish, J. (2003). Shapers of published NNS research articles. *Journal of Second Language Writing, 12*(3), 223-243.

Cargill, M., & O'Connor, P. (2006). Developing Chinese scientists' skills for publishing in English: Evaluating collaborating-colleague workshops based on genre analysis. *Journal of English for Academic Purposes, 5,* 207-221.

Cargill, M., & O'Connor, P. (2013). *Writing scientific research articles: Strategy and steps* (2nd ed). Oxford, UK: Wiley-Blackwell.

Curry, M.J., & Lillis, T. (2013). *Academic writing for graduate students: Essential tasks and skills.* Bristol, UK: Multilingual Matters.

Curry, M.J., & Lillis, T. (2014). Strategies and tactics in academic knowledge production by multilingual scholars. *Educational Policy Analysis Archives, 22*(32). Retrieved 2 March 2017 from http://epaa.asu.edu/ojs/article/view/1561/1238.

Curry, M.J., & Lillis, T. (Eds.) (in press). *Global academic publishing: Policies, perspectives, pedagogies.* Bristol, UK: Multilingual Matters.

Feng, H., Beckett, G.H., & Huang, D. (2013). From 'import' to 'import-export' oriented on scholarly publication in China. *Language Policy, 12,* 251-272.

Hanauer, D.I., & Englander, K. (2013). *Scientific writing in a second language.* Anderson, SC: Parlor Press.

Huang, J.C. (2010). Publishing and learning writing for publication in English: Perspectives of NNES PhD students in science. *Journal of English for Academic Purposes, 9,* 33-44.

Lee, H., & Lee, K. (2013). Publish (in international indexed journals) or perish: Neoliberal ideology in a Korean university. *Language Policy, 12*(3), 215-230.

Lillis, T. (2012). Economies of signs in writing for academic publication: The case of English medium 'national' journals. *Journal of Advanced Composition, 32*(3-4), 695-722.

Lillis, T., & Curry, M.J. (2006). Professional academic writing by multilingual scholars: Interactions with literacy brokers in the production of English-medium texts. *Written Communication, 23*(1), 3-35.

Lillis, T., & Curry, M.J. (2010). *Academic writing in a global context: The politics and practices of publishing in English.* London: Routledge.

a number of issues, including important questions about the multiple and sometimes conflicting roles of those involved as 'experts' and instructors in such programs.

As we have noted in relation to journal gatekeepers, the ideologies that inform attitudes about writing and language (English) as embodied in research articles are often implicit and hegemonic (Lillis & Curry, 2010, 2015). That is, language/English is seen as a stable, monolithic resource and as such English-medium text is often evaluated for how closely the language used approximates the 'standard' English valued by many high-status journal gatekeepers. Some of these ideologies are at play in the approaches of different types of experts involved in supporting writers — whether 'academic literacy brokers' (Lillis & Curry, 2006, 2010), in-house or freelance authors' editors (Burrough-Boenisch, 2003), writing centre tutors, workshop leaders, or PhD supervisors. Important questions to consider, therefore, include: Who is given responsibility for designing and implementing pedagogies to support multilingual writers' practices of writing for publication? Where should support programs be housed? What expertise do those responsible for supporting writers have, or need to have? What ideologies of language, English and academic writing do they uphold? What are the aims of such programs — for example, are they meant primarily to assist scholars to conform to the dominant norms of anglophone-centre journals or to be empowered to challenge these hegemonies? Should pedagogical approaches entail supporting scholars only to publish in English or also to write for publication in local languages, or indeed, in a number of languages? How are different pedagogies evaluated and circulated? How might pedagogical designs and experiences be used to inform policies on writing for publication?

Rarely have researchers of academic writing for publication and language professionals working in this area come together to discuss issues of mutual interest. The joint conference held between the Publishing and Presenting Research Internationally: Issues for Speakers of English as an Additional Language [PRISEAL] and Mediterranean Editors and Translators [MET] groups in Coimbra, Portugal, in 2015 realised the desire to bring together researchers and practitioners dedicated to understanding writing for publication by multilingual scholars and students, as well as the dynamics of global academic publishing in the range of contexts where writers and language professionals are working. This collaboration signals greater understanding on the part of members of both groups that important and generative points of contact exist between those who create research findings about the publishing experiences of multilingual scholars and those who engage in the daily practices of supporting scholars — language professionals including translators, teachers, authors' editors. This conversation goes beyond any simplistic notion of 'translating' research findings from academic studies into 'implications' to be used by practitioners. (Indeed, many in this field engage in both research and practice.) Instead, it recognises that expertise exists within both groups and knowledge areas and embodies a decentring of knowledge as stemming only from the academy in order to recognise the expertise of language professionals in the field.

Foreword

Mary Jane Curry and Theresa Lillis[1]

It has practically become a commonplace that, in the past two decades, pressures for multilingual scholars to publish their work in English continue to intensify and to spread across global contexts. Even more recently, in many locations acceptable target journals have been identified as those included in high-status citation indexes — in other words, target journals have become sanctioned and explicitly linked to the evaluation of and rewards for scholars' academic work (Curry & Lillis, 2014; Lillis & Curry, 2010). Pressures have also heightened for postdoctoral students to publish before finishing their degrees (Huang, 2010). The research field that investigates various aspects of academic writing for publication has burgeoned, from early studies deconstructing texts in order to analyse generic features (Swales, 1990) to research exploring a wide range of aspects, including the pressures on scholars living and working in specific contexts, their responses to pressures, their writing practices, and their perspectives on all of these aspects (Bennett, 2014; Hanauer & Englander, 2013; Lillis & Curry, 2010). A small but growing strand of research has also explored the impact of national and institutional policies about publishing (Feng, Beckett & Huang, 2013; Lee & Lee, 2013), and the changing nature of scholarly journals (including open access), the practices of journal editors and reviewers, and scholar-writers' interactions with these powerful gatekeepers (Lillis, 2012; Lillis & Curry, 2015; Sheridan, 2015).

The unrelenting pressure to publish has generated two important trends in relation to supporting multilingual writers in publishing:

1. a growing demand for service from those who support research writers on an individual basis — often called 'authors' editors'
2. the development of a raft of pedagogical supports for multilingual writers (both scholars and graduate students).

These approaches range from writing and publishing guides (for example, Cargill & O'Connor, 2013; Curry & Lillis, 2013; Swales & Feak, 2012), to individual consulting through writing centres, to dedicated workshops, to face-to-face and online modules or full-credit courses on writing for publication (Cargill & O'Connor, 2006; see also Curry & Lillis, in press). The emergence of these interventionist/pedagogical approaches raises

---

1   Mary Jane Curry, University of Rochester, NY, US; Theresa Lillis, Open University, UK.

Acknowledgements

We owe a special debt of gratitude to many people for their contributions to this volume, and for the gracious and enthusiastic way in which they have each played their part in its development.

First and foremost we would like to thank our fellow authors, based in many different countries and coming from many different backgrounds and perspectives. We warmly acknowledge their expertise and professionalism and their ongoing commitment and contributions to the research field we share.

Our appreciation goes also to the anonymous reviewers of our chapters and the book as a whole, for their insightful suggestions and judgements. Special thanks go to the University of Adelaide Press for their support of this project, and in particular to our editors Rebecca Burton and Julia Keller.

Finally, we wish to extend warm thanks to all the organisers and participants of the paired 2015 conferences in Coimbra, Portugal, that saw initial presentations of the research studies included in this volume: PRISEAL3 (Publishing and Presenting Research Internationally: Issues for Speakers of English as an Additional Language3) and METM16 (Mediterranean Editors and Translators Meeting16). The fruitful interaction between the two communities hosting these conferences has had ongoing and important implications for the development of both research and practice, and this volume stands as additional evidence of this joint contribution.

Margaret Cargill and Sally Burgess
November 2016

2. Open access, quality assurance and credibility in the humanities

Open Access implies broad access to scholarly work via the internet without financial, legal or technical constraints as long as the integrity of the research reported and authorship are safeguarded. It was created 'by scholars for scholars to increase the dissemination of knowledge and the impact of new research and its social utility' (Zuccala, 2009, p. 359). Though its clearest benefits are in terms of peer-to-peer communication, it also embraces the 'social value of science' by making 'the global pool of scientific knowledge' available for the benefit of the general public that funds the research (Salager-Meyer, 2012, p. 65). The OA movement arose in the late 1990s (Laakso et al., 2011) but, as Salager-Meyer (2012) explains, it began to gain real traction after the release of the Budapest Open Access Initiative [BOAI] in 2002 (also known as the Budapest Declaration). This was a public statement of commitment to removing access barriers to scientific and scholarly literature, by virtue of which OA has been defined and accepted worldwide.

Two further initiatives followed the BOAI, both intended to strengthen the OA model: the Bethesda Statement on Open Access Publishing (released in June 2003 by the Howard Hughes Medical Institute in Chevy Chase, Maryland, USA) and the Berlin Declaration on Open Access to Knowledge in the Sciences and Humanities (released in October 2003 by the Max-Planck Institute, Germany). These three initiatives together endorse a number of OA principles, two of which are relevant to this study:

1. Traditional scholarly publishers should endeavour to move gradually to the OA model (Budapest Declaration).

2. The existing model of quality assurance needs to be challenged so that OA is compatible with the high standards and the high quality expected of non-OA scholarly publications; therefore, it is important 'to make progress by developing means and ways to evaluate open access contributions and online-journals in order to maintain the standards of quality assurance and good scientific practice' (Berlin Declaration, 2003, n.p.). In the same vein, it is a prerequisite

> to advocate changes in promotion and tenure evaluation in order to recognize the community contribution of open access publishing and to recognize the intrinsic merit of individual articles without regard to the titles of the journals in which they appear. (Bethesda Statement, 2003, n.p.)

Response to the first of these OA initiatives is already evidenced in information search practices and in the use of scholarly literature (Zuccala, 2009). Today, regardless of whether academic journals are purely electronic publications or still maintain a print run, it is through the internet that researchers worldwide access them. They may be open access and free to any reader, or accessed through subscription databases, the costs of which are borne by university or institutional libraries. Many journals have initiated the transition from print to digital, and others — known as 'hybrid journals', with digital editions supplemented by traditional or print editions — are on the increase in the humanities (Adema & Ferwerda, 2014). All but one of the sample journals in this study are hybrid, and this journal (J5) is online only.

It should be noted that the humanities, unlike other scientific fields, still occupy a middle ground in terms of the second initiative above, in that they engage in new digital communication practices while still applying the norms, values and accepted institutional practices which give prominence to print publication (Adema & Ferwerda, 2014). It would seem, therefore, that humanities scholars need time to respond to this print-to-digital shift and, as Dávidházi (2014) suggests, minimise the inevitable collateral damage that this may cause. In so doing, the OA model has much to offer these disciplines. This study supports the way forward mapped out by Adema and Ferwerda (2014, p. 136) towards a more transparent, robust and fair publication model. As they put it:

> Open Access publishing can also play a role in changing scholars' scepticism concerning the quality and trustworthiness of online publications. One way Open Access publishers can do this is by being fully transparent with regards to their peer-review policies and by stressing the fact that they adhere to the same quality standards as in the past. Open Access initiatives can also push forward the discussion on new standards and rules in terms of establishing the quality and ensuring the integrity of the text if one wishes to do so. The same holds true for scholars' concerns pertaining to copyright and digital preservation. Fears concerning these issues need to be addressed, and this can only be done by discussing and implementing new standards based on digital practices.

Credibility is a construct which has stimulated the interest of scholars from many disciplines. The wide range of sources of scholarly information available on the internet obliges researchers to make use of 'filters' when locating information and determining how believable, trustworthy, reliable, well-founded and authoritative — that is to say, 'credible' — such information might be. Disciplinary differences have yielded diverse trust criteria for credibility assessment.

Liu (2004, p. 1028) defines 'information credibility' at an operational level as 'the extent to which users think that information is truthful, unbiased, accurate, reputable, competent, and current'. Enhancing Tseng and Fogg 's (1999) study, Liu (2004, p. 1028) provides a framework to explain users' perceptions of the credibility of scholarly information available online. He identifies six types of credibility:

1. 'presumed credibility' — that of 'information hosted in a well-respected website'
2. 'reputed credibility' — that provided by an 'author's affiliation with a prestigious institution'
3. 'surface credibility' — that provided by the layout of documents
4. 'experienced credibility' — that pertaining to prior publication in a printed journal

5. 'verifiable credibility' — that referring to the inclusion of references and contact information in documents
6. 'cost-effort credibility' — that relating to the easiness in accessing free scholarly information.

Thus, in the particular case of journal selection for the publication of research, it may be said that journals are perceived as credible if scholars are able to positively assess online information in terms of presumed, reputed, surface, experienced, verifiable and cost-effort credibility. Such diversity is addressed in Section 4 below, when discussing the results of this work; however, 'experienced credibility' needs further exploration at this stage.

One important measure of credibility is the impact factor [IF]. The IF was first proposed by Eugene Garfield and Irving H. Sher in 1955, with the aim of eliminating the uncritical citation of papers in science literature (for an update of its proper and improper uses in scholarly publishing, see Garfield, 2005). Today's academic journals are ranked by their IF, a measure of journal prestige and influence (impact) in a particular field over time regardless of the target discipline or research domain. 'Experienced credibility', in my view, is a quality associated with a journal particularly through IFs. An IF provides evidence of the journal's experience and support of research in a specific domain over time. It is through IFs that many journals build a reputation, thus coming to be known in the literature as 'mainstream', 'top-tier', 'reputable', 'high-ranking', 'high-status' or 'elite', or even as 'the epitome of excellence' (Salager-Meyer, 2015, p. 17) in scholarly publishing. Once this level of prestige has been attained, experienced credibility is virtually inviolable.

That said, it is also the case that in many contexts IFs have erroneously come to be equated by research assessment authorities and funding and accreditation agencies with a measure of article quality, researcher productivity or prestige, research program achievements or even allocation of financial support. This metric has come to be seen as the guiding light for many scholars seeking a journal in which to publish their work, despite the fact that both publishers and editors question the fairness of a system they see as riddled with limitations and shortcomings — for more information, see the statement on inappropriate use of impact factors (European Association of Science Editors [EASE], 2007) or, more recently, Gruber (2014). There is also variation in terms of publication cultures across disciplines and research domains (Dávidházi, 2014), such that the blanket acceptance of IFs as quality indicators regardless of disciplinary area seems foolhardy. Even so, in the humanities, where the IF is a recent phenomenon, it is already having an effect on publishing procedures.

This raises the question of how an OA journal lacking an IF and unsupported by prestigious international publishers might establish credibility and reliability for researchers as an outlet for their publications. In other words, is there a publication life for emerging journals in coexistence with mainstream journals? As stated in the Berlin Declaration, it is obviously necessary to explore alternative models of quality assurance and identify those quality indicators that may qualify a journal as a credible source of scholarly information.

It is with this clear goal in mind that I explore the ways to make quality and trustworthiness compatible with the publication practices of emerging OA journals within the humanities on the basis of the achievements on journal quality criteria attained in Spain, which are discussed in detail in Sections 3.3 and 4. The effort carried out in Spain on this matter is a case in point and makes a compelling example for a need to assure quality in research publication. Similar indicators for quality assurance are in place and applicable around the world via databases, reference systems or academic information centres, and some countries have adopted them as an evaluation measure for research recognition and scholarly accreditation. Although in most cases they are not limited to the humanities, most of them have an explicit focus on this area. Two of the examples that follow are taken as a reference by educational authorities and research agencies in two focus regions — first, Latindex, used in part of America, Spain and Portugal; and second, ERIH PLUS, used in Europe. The last example, Scopus, is also relevant in accreditation systems and has a more global orientation.

Latindex[1] is an online information system focused on scientific journals published in Latin America, the Caribbean, Spain and Portugal. It covers all journals, either electronic or in print, published in any languages used in the target regions and related to any of the following disciplinary groups: arts and humanities, social sciences, natural sciences, agricultural sciences, engineering, medicine, and others (multidisciplinary group). Latindex emerged in 1995 in Mexico (Spain and Portugal joined in 1999) with the mission of disseminating, making available and improving the quality of scholarly journals published in those focus regions. Latindex's main contribution lies in the development of a set of 33 editorial quality criteria (available online), which are applicable across regions and have served as a basis for the development of similar lists around the world. A case in point are the criteria developed by the Foundation for Science and Technology [FECYT], the research instrument used in this study and discussed in detail in Sections 3.3 and 4.

ERIH PLUS[2] is the European Reference Index for the Humanities and the Social Sciences. It was developed by the European Science Foundation [ESF] under the co-ordination of its Standing Committee for the Humanities [SCH] with a view to enhancing global visibility of high-quality humanities research published in academic journals in various European languages across Europe. The first ERIH lists, published in 2008, were solely focused on the humanities, but in 2014 a new reference index was created, now with the name of ERIH PLUS, that extended its scope to include the social sciences. The quality criteria for inclusion in ERIH PLUS require journals to comply with six minimum requirements:

---

1   See http://www.latindex.org/latindex/inicio.
2   See https://dbh.nsd.uib.no/publiseringskanaler/erihplus.

1. explicit procedures for external peer review
2. an academic editorial board, with members affiliated with universities or other independent research organisations
3. a valid ISSN code
4. original articles that contain abstracts in English and/or another international language relevant for the field
5. full information on author affiliations and addresses
6. less than two-thirds of the authors published in the journal from the same institution.

Scopus[3] is an interdisciplinary abstract and citation database of peer-reviewed literature that was launched in 2004. It aims at providing global coverage and therefore includes titles (journals, book series, trade journals, conference series and other sources like patents) from all regions worldwide published in any language; non-English titles, however, are required to provide English abstracts along with the articles. To be included in Scopus, journals must meet four minimum criteria at the first stage — that is, peer review, regular publication, relevant content for an international audience, and a publication ethics and malpractice statement. Then they are evaluated by a Content Selection and Advisory Board [CSAB] according to 14 quality criteria in the following five categories:

1. journal policy (for example, type of peer review or diversity in geographical distribution of editors and authors)
2. content (for example, clarity of abstracts and readability of articles)
3. journal standing (for example, 'citedness' of articles in Scopus)
4. publishing regularity (for example, no delays or interruptions)
5. online availability (for example, quality of journal home page or availability of English language home page).

Scopus places a strong focus on the humanities, although they are currently a part of the social sciences cluster. It contains 3538 journals within the subject area 'Arts and Humanities' [A&H], 10% of which (that is, 354 journals) are OA. The area of A&H is a major concern for Scopus, which used, among others, the ERIH lists to initially identify relevant titles for coverage (for this and other details see Scopus Content Coverage Guide, 2016, p. 22) and added around 4200 book titles to signify the diversity of relevant research and provide a better measure of impact in this area.

I turn now to the situation for OA journals perhaps not yet seeking accreditation within these international schemes but still needing to strengthen their credibility for the humanities scholars for whom they provide relevant and accessible publication outlets — the focus of the empirical part of the chapter.

---

3   See https://www.elsevier.com/solutions/scopus.

3. Methodology

3.1. Study aims

The specific goals of the present study are:

1. to support best practices in scholarly publishing by exploring the actual credibility of today's OA emerging journals in the humanities
2. to boost the open access movement by raising confidence in today's OA emerging journals
3. to deter the encroachment of predatory publishing by raising awareness of the existence of good publication practices and proper quality criteria for journals
4. to identify and assess the quality requirements of OA emerging journals in the humanities based on the work carried out in Spain by the FECYT
5. to provide editors and researchers with evidence of good and poor editing practices which may impact the reliability and credibility of an emerging journal.

3.2. Sample journals

The Directory of Open Access Journals [DOAJ] was used to gather the target journals for the sample. DOAJ is an online directory that provides access to over 11 000 journals from 136 countries. It was founded in 2002 as a related project of the BOAI and as one of the outcomes of the first Nordic Conference on Scholarly Communication.

The selection process of the journals in this study followed a number of steps in order to limit the target sample. Given my academic interest and experience with publications in the area of linguistics, I first selected the 'language and literature' subject from the various options available. This yielded 648 journals, after which I narrowed down the search to the area of 'Philology. Linguistics' (282 journals). Then I excluded those journals soliciting author fees because of the association of this feature with predatory practices (1 journal), and selected those which both had a multilingual submission policy and were searchable at article level (172 journals). After this, the keyword 'language studies' helped me to further screen the group, thus arriving at a smaller group of 48 journals. Last, in order to strengthen the relevance of the target sample, I applied various filters. If, for example, it was not clear whether article processing charges [APCs] were applied, I excluded the journal as a suspected or confirmed predatory journal. Likewise, I eliminated from the final group those journals with broken links provided to their websites or those whose websites had not been recently updated. Thus a sample of some 15 journals remained.

The following details apply to the 15 OA emerging humanities journals selected for this study: each journal's ID, its ISSN for both print and online editions, its publisher, its country of publication, and certain subject-related keywords. The identification number [ID] will be used throughout the results and discussion section in this chapter to refer to each journal. Keywords are those contained in the DOAJ and were provided by the publishers when applying for the inclusion of the journal in the directory or when uploading article metadata. All 15 journals are hybrid except for J5, which is electronic only. Titles and other relevant data (such as ISSNs) were collected but are not disclosed here or in Table 6.1 for privacy reasons. The selection in Table 6.1 shows a variety of publishers (10 universities, 4 associations and a joint journal) and countries (mainly European) that contribute to the OA movement with their journals.

ID	Publisher (Country)	Keywords
J1	Aarhus University (Denmark)	Linguistics, technical communication, translation.
J2	University of Bucharest (Romania)	Communication studies, public relations, intercultural research, language, literature.
J3	Nordic Association of English Studies (Sweden)	Linguistics, English literature, English culture.
J4	Slovene Association of ESP teachers (Slovenia)	Linguistics, applied linguistics, Languages for Specific Purposes [LSP], Foreign Language Teaching [FLT].
J5	University of Belgrade and the Serbian Association for the Study of English (Serbia)	English for specific purposes, applied linguistics.
J6	Vilnius University (Lithuania)	Germanic studies, Romance studies, contrastive linguistics, language studies.
J7	Saarland University of Applied Sciences (Germany)	Applied linguistics, language methodology, English Language Teaching [ELT], corpus linguistics, learning techniques.
J8	University of Hawaii (USA)	Language, linguistics, literary studies, education.
J9	Stellenbosch University (South Africa)	Lexicography, dictionaries.
J10	University of Antwerp (Belgium)	Cognitive processes, academic writing, writing.

J11	Roehampton University (United Kingdom)	Translating and interpreting, specialised translation, non-literary translation.
J12	Spanish Association of Applied Linguistics (Spain)	Applied linguistics, descriptive linguistics, quantitative linguistics.
J13	University of Jyväskylä (Finland)	Applied linguistics, language education, multilingualism, language and identity.
J14	University of Southern California (USA)	Communication studies.
J15	The Nordic Network for Intercultural Communication (Sweden)	Cultural studies.

Table 6.1: Sample journals.

3.3. Data collection and research instrument

In order to specifically identify and assess the quality requirements of OA journals in the humanities, I identified a group of quality requirements for journal publishing using, as a basis, the ongoing work on academic publishing carried out by the Spanish Foundation for Science and Technology [FECYT]. I also drew on the FECYT's main publication on this matter (Delgado López-Cózar et al., 2006).

The publication by Delgado López-Cózar et al. (2006) contains the fundamentals, requirements and methodology for the assessment of academic journals. It lists and examines in detail the corresponding quality requirements, so that today it is the main reference for the establishment of journal quality requirements in Spain. These requirements are commonly referred to as the 'FECYT guidelines', 'FECYT criteria' or 'FECYT requirements' among Spanish journal editors and other stakeholders. The FECYT criteria were developed both on the basis of previous work initiated in the 1980s by the Ministry of Education and Science and on other quality guidelines available worldwide. The source for the Spanish criteria were mainly the requirements set by the Institute of Scientific and Technological Documentation [ICYT] and the Institute of Humanities and Social Sciences Documentation [ISOC], delivered in 1984 by the General Subdirection of Documentation and Scientific Information, and then updated and established as a part of the National Plan for Scientific Research and Technological Development 1986; the outcomes of the 1987 UNESCO working group for the dissemination of Spanish scientific journals in international databases; and last, and more recently (2005), the work carried out by the National Commission for the Assessment of Research Activity [CNEAI], which established 14 criteria recognising the 'minimum impact' of any scientific publication (including journals, books and conferences) in any scientific area (not only the humanities). The source for the international criteria, some of which I discussed earlier, were those required by databases and information systems such as Latindex, Index Medicus-Medline[4], SciELO[5], ISI[6], LILACS[7], PsycINFO[8] and ERIC.[9]

In accordance with the FECYT guidelines, a journal must satisfy 56 requirements in order to demonstrate quality and excellence. These are known as mandatory quality requirements [MQRs] and are categorised into four groups:

- Type 1: 14 QRs which are 'fully mandatory' across journals
- Type 2: 22 requirements which are weighted against the total (that is, 'weighted mandatory requirements'), at least 16 of which must be met
- Type 3: 15 less stringent requirements which add to Types 1 and 2 above (that is, 'additional requirements') in order to meet the final 56
- Type 4: 2 or 3 MQRs which are specific to print or electronic editions, respectively.

In this study, the sample journals were examined for compliance with fully mandatory requirements, weighted mandatory requirements and electronic edition requirements — that is, against Types 1, 2 and 4 MQRs above — which make up the core of the quality criteria and set a compliance threshold level. Type 3 additional requirements have not been taken into account as they are considered peripheral and relevant if, and only if, the other 39 core requirements have been met.

4. Results and discussion

This section is organised in terms of the four groups of QRs proposed by the FECYT. Data gathered from websites are shown in tables and discussed according to this proposed classification. In the tables, 'Y' and 'N', standing for 'yes' and 'no' respectively, indicate that a particular journal does or does not meet a particular requirement. The question mark '?' indicates that it is not possible to establish, according to the information supplied on the journal's website, whether a particular journal does or does not satisfy a particular requirement. Finally, when information is not clearly available but can be easily inferred from the relevant date, the journal has been classified accordingly as 'Y' or 'N'.

---

4   See https://www.nlm.nih.gov/bsd/aim.html.
5   See http://www.scielo.org/php/index.php?lang=en.
6   See http://login.webofknowledge.com/.
7   See http://lilacs.bvsalud.org/en/.
8   See http://www.apa.org/pubs/databases/psycinfo/.
9   See https://eric.ed.gov/.

4.1. *The informative quality of the journal as a means of scientific communication*

The informative quality of a journal is demonstrated on the basis of compliance with at least seven requirements that fall within the scope of 'reputed', 'surface' and 'experienced credibility', as discussed in Section 2.

In this particular group of requirements, the degree of compliance has proved to be almost total. Exceptions are J1 and J4, which do not provide style sheets, instructions or guidelines for authors, and which demonstrate a lack of consistencies when it comes to the provision of key words. In addition, the degree of detail provided in the guidelines is extremely variable: all journals, except J1 again, provide detailed style sheets on their websites or via a downloadable document; J4 does provide instructions to authors but these are too broad to comply with this QR. From these requirements it is to be understood that the more details regarding form or presentation, the greater the transparency for potential authors ('surface credibility'). Under MQR 3, all articles must contain an abstract in the language of the article; and MQR 4 requires the provision of an abstract, title and keywords in English regardless of the language of the article itself. MQR 4 is particularly relevant for non-English articles, and favours English as a common language for international communication. Most journals provide abstracts and keywords in English, but do not provide an English title; this practice puts English-only articles at a clear advantage in terms of research dissemination because databases will prioritise their searches.

If the journal is managed by an editorial and/or a scientific board (see Section 4.2.4 for further discussion), their members must be listed clearly (MQR 1). This information will allow prospective authors to identify prestigious scholars within the field at the same time helping to build confidence in the relevance of the publication ('reputed credibility'). In an international advisory board renowned researchers act as supporters for the journal and are an asset because their academic credibility and reputation bring similar credibility and repute to the journal. Also, the names of editorial board members together with their academic backgrounds and achievements respond to the expectations of authors by providing a reliable context for eventual publication — see Section 4.2.4 for further discussion.

MQRs 5 and 6 refer to the ways in which authorship is presented and used. Authors are required to provide their institutional affiliations and contact information so as to show some formal connection with a particular organisation and to prove that they are members of the academic community ('verifiable credibility'). Full affiliation provides additional details about the country of origin and the institution. It may help prospective authors to assess the international reach of the journal and the prestige of the institutions involved, and, hence, the international reach and impact of their own

Table 6.2 (right): Fully mandatory (bold type) and weighted quality requirements pertaining to the informative quality of the journal as a means of scientific communication (Y = Yes; N = No).

MQRs Journal	J1	J2	J3	J4	J5	J6	J7	J8	J9	J10	J11	J12	J13	J14	J15
1. Identification of members of editorial and scientific boards	Y	Y	Y	Y	Y	Y	Y	Y	Y	Y	Y	Y	Y	Y	Y
2. Detailed guidelines for authors	N	Y	Y	N	Y	Y	Y	Y	Y	Y	Y	Y	Y	Y	Y
3. Abstracts included with all articles	Y	Y	Y	Y	Y	Y	Y	Y	Y	Y	Y	Y	Y	Y	Y
4. Article title, abstract, and keywords in English	Y	Y	Y	N	Y	Y	Y	Y	Y	Y	Y	Y	Y	Y	Y
5. Full affiliation of all authors stated (3/4)	Y	Y	Y	N	Y	Y	Y	Y	Y	Y	Y	Y	N	Y	Y
6. Consistent use of authors' names (3/4)	Y	Y	Y	Y	Y	Y	Y	Y	Y	Y	Y	Y	Y	Y	Y
7. Consistent presentation of bibliographical references (3/4)	Y	Y	Y	Y	Y	Y	Y	Y	Y	Y	Y	Y	Y	Y	Y
8. Keywords included with all articles (3/4)	N	Y	Y	N	Y	Y	Y	Y	Y	Y	Y	Y	Y	Y	Y

research if eventually published. In the sample journals, J4 and J13 are not consistent when providing information about the affiliation of authors. Another issue is that authors' names must be consistently provided throughout the whole publication (MQR 6). This means that the same expression must be used to refer to a scholar both in the contents section, editorial note, main text and final list of references — for example, the use of initials or surnames must be consistent throughout the text.

Last, MQR 7 requires bibliographical references to be listed consistently and accurately across all articles in each journal volume ('verifiable credibility'). The analysis showed that all journals in the sample contained detailed instructions about the use of bibliographical references in their own instructions-for-authors sheets, or they refer authors to well-known citation conventions such as those of the APA or Harvard.

4.2. The quality of the editorial process

The FECYT guidelines explore the editorial process from four different perspectives that make up four MQR sub-groups. These are discussed in the next sub-sections.

4.2.1. Publication timeliness

There is one particular requirement (MQR 20) which demands publication regularity and compliance with journal deadlines. MQR 20 embraces two sub-requirements: the time of publication has to be clearly stated and demonstrated accordingly. It seems highly likely that MQR 20 is the most important requirement for building initial confidence among potential authors but, as Table 6.3 shows, seven journals do not fully satisfy the requirement of publication regularity (for example, J1, J7, J11, J12, J13, J14, J15).

It is interesting to note that some journals (J2, J4, J6, J8) state their publication times only in very general terms (for example, 'annually', J2; 'twice a year', J4). It may happen that a journal (such as J7) does not clearly indicate the periodicity at which it is published (and, therefore, fails to comply with this requirement in full); however, from its website it is possible to gather that it does

MQRs	J1	J2	J3	J4	J5	J6	J7	J8	J9	J10	J11	J12	J13	J14	J15
20. Publication regularity is stated and complied with	N	Y	Y	Y	Y	Y	N	Y	Y	Y	N	N	N	N	N

Table 6.3 (right): Fully mandatory quality requirements (bold type) pertaining to the quality of the editorial process: Publication timeliness (Y = Yes; N = No).

in fact publish two volumes on time per year. It may also happen that a journal states a periodicity which, upon perusal of the website, it does not meet. For example, J1 states that issues of the journal are published 'twice a year, summer and winter', but a glance at its website reveals one publication annually. Others like J5 and J9 commit themselves to publication on a particular date (for example, 'in October', J9), thus building more confidence. Finally, a third option (adopted by J3 and J10) is either to offer vague information (for example, 'two to three times a year', J3) or to ensure that subscribers are notified upon publication of each new issue (for example, J10).

Failure to meet MQR 20 works against the 'experienced credibility' of a journal. Journals with a traceable history imply stability of publication, and such stability raises authors' confidence for a potential submission.

4.2.2. Selection of manuscripts and assessment process

This second subgroup of requirements focuses on the ways manuscripts are selected, assessed, and eventually rejected or accepted for publication. Fourteen MQRs are listed in Table 6.4, of which 2 are mandatory and 12 are weighted (at least 9 out of 12 need to be met). MQRs 23, 24, 26, 27, 28, 29, 30, 31 and 33 are directly related to the quality of the assessment process whereas MQRs 25, 32, 34, 35 and 36 are directly related to the editorial management of proposed submissions. All of them as a group help to raise the 'surface', 'experienced' and 'verifiable credibility' of the journal as discussed in Section 2.

This group contains 59% of requirements for which information is not known (that is, 124 instances out of 210 are unknown), and this is due to the scant information that the journals post on their websites. Such a lack of information does not mean that the journals do not in fact proceed in the manner stipulated by the requirements, but that such information is not available online; hence it is not visible to authors. There might be two reasons for this: first, these issues may be regarded as internal procedures and hence the editors do not deem it necessary to disclose them; second, simply, they may be regarded as irrelevant to authors (or of little relevance in terms of prioritising information for the website) and therefore omitted. In the case of those journals which are fully managed electronically, some MQRs (for example, MQR 25) are met because they are automatic actions inherent to the computer software (for example, submissions are automatically acknowledged upon receipt).

The main concern at this stage is to ensure that submissions are subject to some form of scientific assessment and that these submissions are blinded and reviewed by peers. The editorial board plays an important role here, as its members are held responsible for selecting the right reviewers for a particular article and ensuring that both parties (authors and reviewers) are not known to each other. Thus, in this humanities context, double-blind peer reviewing is accepted as the most reliable (and therefore valid) procedure for avoiding bias and selecting higher-value articles.

All the sample journals in this study overtly state that an article has undergone rigorous evaluation (MQR 23) — for example, 'fully-refereed journal' (J8) or 'Articles and review articles are subjected to strict anonymous evaluation by independent academic peers' (J9). Nonetheless, less than half (that is, seven journals) clearly specifiy the implementation of a double-blind peer-review process — for example, 'All submitted papers will be subject to a double-blind review process' (J5). MQR 24 aims at ensuring that proposed submissions and assessment reports remain anonymous and that manuscripts have been assessed by at least two reviewers from a particular field of expertise. J13 is a unique case, in that it proudly displays a 'label for peer-reviewed scholarly publications' on its website, assigned by the corresponding educational authority. Only one journal (J7) openly states that submissions are assessed internally by the editorial board. What follows is a group of weighted requirements focused on the internal editorial process of the submission.

It is important to ensure that authors are notified as soon as their submissions have been received (MQR 25); this simple action builds confidence on the authors' part from the outset of the publication process. Once the submission has been reviewed and accepted, it is advisable that authors should be offered the possibility of revising first proofs and, most importantly,

Table 6.4 (right): Fully mandatory (bold type) and weighted quality requirements pertaining to the quality of the editorial process: Selection of manuscripts and assessment process (Y = Yes; N = No; ? = Unknown).

MQRs / Journal	J1	J2	J3	J4	J5	J6	J7	J8	J9	J10	J11	J12	J13	J14	J15
23. Use of scientific assessment is stated	Y	Y	Y	Y	Y	Y	Y	Y	Y	Y	Y	Y	Y	Y	Y
24. Double-blind peer review is used	?	Y	?	?	Y	Y	N	Y	?	Y	?	Y	Y	?	?
25. Acknowledgement of receipt is made (9/12)	Y	Y	Y	?	?	?	?	?	Y	?	?	Y	Y	Y	?
26. All manuscripts are revised by editors (9/12)	?	Y	?	Y	Y	?	Y	Y	?	Y	?	Y	Y	?	?

Item	J1	J2	J3	J4	J5	J6	J7	J8	J9	J10	J11	J12
27. Assessment by 2 reviewers — 3 in case of disagreement (9/12)	?	?	?	?	?	?	?	Y	?	Y	Y	?
28. Authors may suggest potential reviewers (9/12)	?	?	?	?	Y	?	?	?	Y	?	?	?
29. Methodological reviewers are used (9/12)	?	?	?	?	?	?	?	?	?	?	?	?
30. Journal possesses its own reviewers' database (9/12)	Y	?	?	?	?	?	Y	?	?	?	?	?
31. Assessment instructions and sheets are available (9/12)	Y	Y	?	?	?	?	?	Y	Y	Y	Y	?
32. Editorial decision is well reasoned and communicated (9/12)	?	?	Y	?	Y	?	Y	?	?	Y	Y	?
33. Quality of reviewers' reports is controlled (9/12)	?	?	?	?	?	?	?	Y	?	?	Y	?
34. There is a correspondence section (9/12)	N	N	N	N	N	N	N	N	N	N	N	N
35. English language communication services are used (9/12)	?	?	?	?	?	?	?	Y	Y	?	?	?
36. Revision of first proofs by authors is allowed (9/12)	?	?	?	Y	?	?	?	?	?	?	?	?

that they are aware of that task and are ready to do so (MQR 36). In my sample, J5 is the only journal to make this clear.

A further important component of the assessment process is the assurance, somewhere in the information provided, that all submissions are first revised by the editor (MQR 26). This is in fact a *sine qua non* of the reviewing process, as no reviewing can be carried out until the journal editor examines the submissions. Even so, this is not often explicitly stated. Likewise, it is important for authors to know what happens when two reports disagree. In such cases, authors should be informed that a third reviewer will be sought in order to arrive at a final decision (MQR 27). In this sample, J2, J5, J8 and J13 are particularly clear and detailed in their explanations of the assessment process and the timeframes for a final decision.

Allowing authors to suggest names of potential reviewers appears to be seen as a positive thing and as an enhancement to credibility (MQR 28). The same can be said to be true when a journal has its own reviewer database (MQR 30). Four journals (J2, J8, J10 and J11) state that they do indeed have a database or pool of referees, but list no names on their websites. J10 and 11 also welcome suggestions for potential reviewers.

It is clear that reviewers' reports have to be as self-explanatory and meaningful as possible (MQRs 31, 32 and 33), that websites have to provide as much information as possible about the assessment process, and that the final editorial decision has to be well reasoned and supported by reviewing reports. The duration of the peer-review process, the availability of assessment sheets, and other similar matters, if addressed on journal websites, help to increase the transparency of information and thus the 'surface' and 'presumed credibility' of a journal. J12, for instance, contains a flowchart providing a detailed account of all the stages and steps in the editorial and publishing process. Other journals (for example, J9 and J10) are very specific about what they require authors and reviewers to do. J13, for instance, offers a whole section containing a short guide for reviewers and very detailed instructions on the role of reviewers who write reviews or reports for the editor.

In some cases, the assessment sheet that reviewers are asked to use is available online (for example, J2) and this may well serve to assist and guide authors when preparing their manuscripts. Quality requirements praise the existence of services to assist authors in dealing with the use of the English language (MQR 35). The FECYT has identified a clear need to assist non-anglophone scholars when writing in English for an international audience, and journals should ideally provide the tools for meeting such a need. In this sample, two journals satisfy this requirement: J11 displays the names of 4 people working as 'English editors'; and J10 explains the functions of a group of 10 language editors who will 'ensure the linguistic and stylistic quality of the manuscript', 'formulate recommendations to the authors on how to improve the language of their text (minor shortcomings)' or 'formulate advice to contact a native speaker (major shortcomings)'.

Last, two requirements which might be relevant among the social and natural sciences (MQRs 29 and 34) have no impact in this humanities context. The use of 'methodological reviewers' (MQR 29) refers to the availability of reviewers who specialise in assessing the methodology used in the article. In contravention of the recommendation in MQR 34, no journal contains a 'correspondence section', although J8, which offers a 'discussion forum' for replies to issues raised in any previous article, might be regarded as an exception.

4.2.3. Management of the editorial process

Today, the handling of submissions by anything other than electronic means is no longer acceptable. Journals are required to make use of some kind of automated system that monitors the receipt, revision, acceptance and eventual publication of the submitted manuscripts. This contributes to the control and transparency of the corresponding dates (which must be explicitly and prominently stated in the article) and may help authors to compare turnaround times across journals. Two MQRs specifically target this issue (see Table 6.5).

Email communication, as required by MQR 37, may be enough for handling inbound and outbound article traffic among authors, editorial team, reviewers, style correctors, publishers and so on; however, journals may be assisted by the widely known open source software Open Journal System [OJS] to manage the whole process electronically, from submission to final publication (MQR 38). OJS is a facilitator for journal management and publishing which has gradually been implemented worldwide. Its capabilities help to speed up the editorial process, reduce turnarounds and, at the same time, exert greater control — thus, human error is minimised and the overall journal management quality is improved. MQR 38 is clearly targeted at OJS journals because not only reception or acceptance dates are automatically registered, but also every stage of the refereed publishing process, from online submission to final publication, indexing, email notifications and so on. There are eight OJS journals in this sample.

MQRs	Journal	J1	J2	J3	J4	J5	J6	J7	J8	J9	J10	J11	J12	J13	J14	J15
37. Automatic management of the editorial process		Y	Y	Y	Y	Y	Y	Y	Y	Y	Y	Y	Y	Y	Y	Y
38. Full electronic management of the editorial process		Y	Y	Y	N	N	N	N	N	Y	Y	N	Y	Y	Y	N

Table 6.5 (right): Fully mandatory quality requirements (bold type) pertaining to the quality of the editorial process: Management of the editorial process (Y = Yes; N = No).

4.2.4. Editorial organisation and structure

The quality requirements in this group (listed in Table 6.6) have two purposes:

1. to monitor the existence of both editorial and advisory (also scientific) boards
2. to safeguard the journal from institutional inbreeding, parochialism and a reach that is too local.

From the data gathered for this particular group of QRs, the distinction between editorial and advisory boards is not clear and there seems to be some confusion in the use of the correct terms. A high number of journals (9 out of 15) have no advisory board (alternatively named 'scientific board'). All journals have an editorial board, but a closer examination of the data reveals apparent inconsistencies, contradictions or implausible information. By way of example, J3 has no advisory board but does have an 'editorial team' of 3 people and an 'editorial board' of 20 members from many different universities in the same country or region. It seems probable that the editorial team is in fact the editorial board, and that the editorial board operates as the advisory or scientific board. Somewhat surprisingly, J14 boasts an editorial board of 84 members and no advisory board.

Table 6.6 (right): Fully mandatory quality requirements (bold type) pertaining to the quality of the editorial process: Editorial organisation and structure (Y = Yes; N = No; ? = Unknown).

MQRs / Journal	J1	J2	J3	J4	J5	J6	J7	J8	J9	J10	J11	J12	J13	J14	J15
39. There is an editorial board	Y	Y	Y	Y	Y	Y	Y	Y	Y	Y	Y	Y	Y	Y	Y
40. There is an advisory board	N	Y	N	N	Y	N	N	Y	Y	N	Y	Y	Y	N	N
41. > 1/3 of advisory board = institutions different from publishing body	N	Y	N	N	Y	N	N	N	Y	N	?	Y	N	N	N
42. > 1/3 of editorial board = institutions different from publishing body	N	Y	Y	Y	Y	Y	Y	Y	Y	Y	?	Y	Y	Y	Y
43. > 20% of members of advisory board are foreign	N	Y	N	N	Y	N	N	N	Y	N	?	Y	N	N	N

An editorial board should have direct work duties in relation to the journal and functions such as helping the editor-in-chief with regular publication, filtering articles and desktop-rejecting, proposing advisory board members and reviewers, setting the aims and scope of the journal, developing and refining guidelines for authors, meeting at different times of the year with clear objectives and so on. In addition to the editor-in-chief, an editorial board may be made up of assistant editors, a secretary or administration office, possibly a treasurer, and individuals assigned with specific duties — for example, there is a 'website administrator' for J6; J11 specifically has a 'peer-review manager'; and J10 has a group of 10 'language editors'.

In contrast to an editorial board, a scientific or advisory board is a kind of hallmark for the journal. It is often made up of eminent scholars in the field who will add prestige to the journal and often act as journal representatives outside the editing organisation. An advisory board may also work as a 'feeder' group which provides informed guidance and advice to the journal's editorial board on particular issues. From the authors' point of view, the presence of well-known researchers in a particular field strengthens the reputation of the journal and raises confidence in the reliability of the publication. By listing members of both editorial and advisory boards, particularly when members are those whom a community of scholars might expect or hope to see listed, journals meet the expectations of the academic community and strengthen 'reputed credibility'.

It is with the above-mentioned second purpose in mind (that is, safeguarding the journal from institutional inbreeding, parochialism and a reach that is too local) that no fewer than a third of the members in both editorial (MQR 41) and advisory boards (MQR 42) are required to belong to institutions that are different from those responsible for publishing the journal. More precisely, if the publishing body is a particular university, members of the editorial board should be employed by other universities; if the editing body is an association, such members should not be a part of the association's governing body. Also, 20% or more of the advisory board should contain foreign researchers (MQR 43). It should be noted here that the term 'foreign' refers to researchers from foreign universities, so that a foreign scholar employed by a national university would not qualify as 'foreign'. As shown in Table 6.6, from the information available online it is possible to identify the affiliations and origins of researchers in both boards: only 4 journals meet MQRs 41 and 43, but a higher number (13 journals) meet MQR 42. An exception in this list is J11, which has both editorial and advisory boards but provides no information about member affiliation, and thus its compliance with MQRs 41, 42, 43 and 48 cannot be attested.

4.3. Scientific quality

There are seven requirements related to the scientific quality of journals and under this group, similar to the MQRs in 4.2.4 above, we find the responsibility of safeguarding the journal from institutional inbreeding, parochialism and a reach that is too local.

Scientific quality may be measured via the provision of original findings (MQR 46), the authors' origin (MQRs 47, 48 and 50), journal acceptance rate (MQR 49), article intake (MQR 51) and economic support (MQR 52). As shown in Table 6.7, the requirement demanding the provision of original research results is mandatory (MQR 46), whereas the remaining six requirements are weighted.

MQR 46 monitors whether the publication of original research articles represents the bulk of the journal's content. This requirement is fully satisfied across this journal sample and made clear in the instructions or guidelines for authors as one of the journals' major goals, with statements such as '[o]nly original contributions will be considered for publication' (J9).

Regarding the origin of authors, the data show that, in all cases, over 80% of authors do not serve on the editorial board (MQR 47), and in most cases (11 journals) over 80% of authors are not employed by the publishing organisation (MQR 48). Two journals (J4 and J6) clearly flout this MQR 48, and there is no information on the website to attest compliance in the cases of J11 and J13 — in particular, J11 does not provide the affiliation of editing board members and J13 does not provide full affiliation of all authors; hence, it is not possible to cross-check the corresponding data. Last, most journals (10 in all) have published over 15% of content produced by foreign researchers (MQR 50). Again, in the particular case of J13, authors have not been properly identified and therefore it is not possible to know from the information available online what proportion of them is in fact foreign. As noted before, here the term 'foreign' refers to researchers from foreign universities.

No journal, except for J15, provides information about the acceptance (or, indirectly, rejection) rate of papers (estimated to be lower than 60% or over 40%, respectively). A low acceptance rate is usually interpreted as a sign that there is little chance of getting a paper published, and this may discourage scholars from eventually submitting their manuscripts. Although this certainly explains why some journals do not publish acceptance/rejection rates on their websites, interpreting low rates in this way fails to take into account the many other factors that may contribute to a paper being rejected. The positive side of publishing the acceptance/rejection rates is that some scholars will see submitting a paper to a journal with low acceptance rates as a challenge and as a clear indication of the quality and prestige of the journal. Acceptance/rejection rates are indicators of the journal's trend and of its relevance as a reliable publishing outlet in a particular field ('experienced credibility'). These rates vary every year and should be published only after a certain number of volumes or issues have come out.

Unlike MQRs 46, 47, 48 and 50, it is very unlikely that websites provide data regarding MQRs 51 and 52. In our sample journals, it is clear that five journals satisfy MQR 51. The corresponding information may be guessed from the overall number of

Table 6.7 (right): Fully mandatory (bold type) and weighted quality requirements pertaining to scientific quality (Y = Yes; N = No; ? = Unknown).

MQRs	Journal	J1	J2	J3	J4	J5	J6	J7	J8	J9	J10	J11	J12	J13	J14	J15
46. > 50% of articles communicate original research results		Y	Y	Y	Y	Y	Y	Y	Y	Y	Y	Y	Y	Y	Y	Y
47. > 80% of authors do not serve on the editorial board (4/6)		Y	Y	Y	Y	Y	Y	Y	Y	Y	Y	Y	Y	Y	Y	Y
48. > 80% of authors do not serve on the publishing body (4/6)		Y	Y	Y	N	Y	N	Y	Y	Y	Y	?	Y	?	Y	Y
49. Acceptance rate is ≤ 60% (4/6)		?	?	?	?	?	?	?	?	?	?	?	?	?	?	Y
50. >15% of authors are foreign (4/6)		N	Y	Y	N	Y	N	Y	Y	Y	Y	Y	N	?	Y	Y
51. No. of papers received per year is ≥ 20 (4/6)		?	?	Y	?	?	?	?	?	Y	?	Y	?	Y	Y	?
52. % of papers financed by public/private bodies > 40% (4/6)		?	?	?	?	?	?	?	?	?	?	?	?	?	?	?

papers published per year. Among them, J14 stands out due to its disproportionately high (and low) numbers; they have 84 members on the editorial board, no advisory board, and publish one volume per year containing 156 articles.

Last, MQR 52 requires the acknowledgment of funding for the research carried out but evidence for this requirement (a more common practice in science-related papers) is certainly scarce in these sample journals. Also, instructions or guidelines for authors are not usually specific about the need to state whether the research has been carried out within the framework of a particular research project or program. Rather than a part of the journal policy, funding statements seem to be provided at the authors' discretion and are closely linked to the variability of publication cultures across disciplines. Today, this trend is changing in the humanities, probably because of the influence of usual practices in other areas, mainly health and hard sciences, and the explicit command from research agencies, at least in Spain, which obliges researchers to acknowledge the origin of funds when a publication falls within the scope of a research project and such project has been supported economically.

4.4. Quality of journal dissemination and visibility

The last group contains two requirements (see Table 6.8) and is related to the projection of the journal in terms of online visibility and accessibility (MQR 56) and journal reach (MQR 53).

MQR 56 refers to the existence of a journal website and whether or not this may be accessed (fully or partially) online. This particular requirement relates directly to the 'cost-effort credibility' of the journal (as it may impact the ease with which interested parties can access scholarly information) and indirectly to its 'presumed', 'surface' and 'verifiable credibility'. MQR 53 is measured in terms

Table 6.8 (right): Fully mandatory quality requirements (bold type) pertaining to the quality of dissemination and visibility of the journal (Y = Yes; N = No).

MQRs	Journal	J1	J2	J3	J4	J5	J6	J7	J8	J9	J10	J11	J12	J13	J14	J15
53. Journal is indexed in ISI-WoK or listed in main national and international databases in the research field		N	N	Y	Y	Y	Y	N	N	Y	Y	Y	Y	N	Y	Y
56. Journal has a website		Y	Y	Y	Y	Y	Y	Y	Y	Y	Y	Y	Y	Y	Y	Y

of indexing and abstracting in domestic and foreign sources. Impact factors may come into play here, although the existence of an impact factor is not the only indication of quality attainment. The inclusion of the journal in recognised lists and databases (some of them lacking IFs) attests compliance with this requirement.

4.5. A final note

Results lead to the conclusion that instances of compliance can be said to cluster into three clearly defined groups (see Table 6.9):

1. a low-quality group containing the least credible journals (J1, J4, J6, J7, J15)
2. a medium-quality group (J3, J8, J11, J13, J14)
3. a high-quality group containing the most credible journals in the sample (J2, J5, J9, J10, J12).

ID	Compliance rate (%)	Degree of compliance
J1	15.4	Low
J4	10.2	Low
J6	30.8	Low
J7	25.6	Low
J15	33.3	Low
J3	48.7	Medium
J8	46.1	Medium
J11	46.1	Medium
J13	41.0	Medium
J14	48.7	Medium
J2	64.1	High
J5	64.1	High
J9	64.1	High
J10	64.1	High
J12	61.5	High

Table 6.9: Compliance rate of quality requirements across journals.

Findings point to J2, J5, J9 and J10 as the journals which meet the highest number of MQRs (64.1% of compliance in all cases). On the opposite end, J4 and J1 show the lowest degree of compliance with 10.2% and 15.4% compliance rates, respectively.

The reasons underlying compliance failure vary across the three groups, although they show some consistency among the medium- and high-quality categories. Broadly speaking, low-quality journals show similar scores for all types of requirements and levels (compliance, non-compliance, unknown). In particular, they strikingly fail in meeting fully mandatory requirements, among them some of the most important in view of credibility: publication regularity, peer reviewing or editorial information. Also, information missing in websites prevails among these journals (and therefore there are a higher number of unknown requirements). By way of example, J4, which has been found to be the least credible journal, complies with 15 requirements and does not comply with 11 requirements, while its compliance with 13 requirements is unknown.

The picture for medium- and high-quality journals is different. In general terms, journals in these two categories are consistent in the number and type of requirements that are unknown because of the lack of information on websites. Also, they generally comply with fully mandatory requirements — except for MQR 20 regarding publication regularity in the cases of J11, J13, J14 (medium) and J12 (high) — and show a similar pattern regarding weighted requirements. Thus the main differences among them lie in the number (and not type) of requirements that are and are not complied with. By way of example, let's consider the highest medium-quality journal, J3, and one of the highest high-quality journals, J9. Requirements are broken down as follows: J3 complies with 23 requirements and does not comply with 4 requirements, while its compliance with 12 requirements is unknown; J9 complies with 26 requirements and does not comply with 1 requirement and its compliance with 12 requirements is unknown. It is obvious, therefore, that the bulk of unknown requirements in these two categories prevents the gathering of more realistic compliance/non-compliance percentages.

5. Conclusions and insights gained

The target group of journals in this study has been assessed against a particular set of quality requirements (those put forward by the FECYT in Spain) and the data under study has been gathered from the information available on the journal websites as of late 2015. It has not been my intention to carry out an in-depth quality assessment of OA emerging journals within the humanities. Instead, I have tried to raise awareness of the multiple variables that furnish evidence for information credibility in scholarly publishing, particularly in academic journals.

A close examination of the FECYT criteria for quality journal assessment unveils four relevant findings which, to my understanding, have important and useful implications for humanities journals — not only because of their applicability in other contexts, but also because they open new avenues for reflection on journal quality assurance against an open access scenario for research dissemination:

1. There is more to journal credibility than IFs, and OA journals offer a window of opportunity to ensure good scientific practice and maintain quality assurance standards in scholarly publishing.
2. Three main concerns are the focus of MQRs: strict compliance with publishing schedules (MQRs 20, 37, 38); safeguarding of peer-review assessments (MQRs 23, 24, 27, 28, 30, 31, 32, 33, 34); and prevention of institutional inbreeding (MQRs 1, 5, 39, 40, 41, 42, 43, 47, 48). These three global concerns strengthen the multifaceted reliability of a journal in terms of 'presumed', 'reputed', 'surface', 'experienced', 'verifiable' and 'cost-effort' credibility.
3. Website errors or missing information lead to distrust or, at the very least, to suspicion. They may also be an indication of poor professional commitment. The more visible and transparent the information about the selection of manuscripts and the assessment process or the scientific quality of a journal, the more reliable and credible the journal will be.
4. Some requirements are key for quality, because, whether mandatory or weighted, they are interrelated, and non-compliance with particular MQRs will have an effect on the final outcome which eventually undermines the 'reputed' and 'verifiable credibility' of the journal.

Both editors and researchers can benefit from the findings of the present study. Editors can use them to assess the quality standards of their journals; in this vein, they should be ready to gradually introduce changes and improvements to their websites whilst discarding at the same time erroneous but established practices. By assessing other journals from the MQRs viewpoint, it is possible to learn some lessons and identify potential good practices in journal editing. The FECYT guidelines may be regarded as a baseline for measuring the quality of journal publishing; however, a closer look at target journals will provide editors and publishers with additional features for journal upgrading which may also impact credibility and which are not contained in the MQRs under study. Some examples may be the availability of submission preparation checklists; the inclusion of statements regarding specific actions against plagiarism; adherence to open access policies; copyright and licensing information; clear non-APC statements and so on. This study may also interest researchers who seek to place their research in trustworthy journals. The FECYT guidelines will help them to discriminate between credible and untrustworthy journals, rate most and least reliable journals, and identify appropriate outlets for their work. Last, and not least, research assessment bodies and accreditation agencies might take journal compliance with the FECYT requirements as a reliable quality measure against which to qualify applicants' publications when evaluating promotion or allocating grants and funding.

Today, OA emerging journals are faced with many challenges, particularly in the humanities, and the need for overall credibility is centre stage. However, the introduction of quality control measures such as those discussed in this chapter may help to enhance the validity of OA journal articles and build confidence in the OA model among stakeholders. OA journals can individually exhibit quality standards, and these should be set as main goals, but the whole OA movement needs to move forward to strengthen the alternative models of quality which impact upon the scholarly publishing industry and the accredited merit of researchers. It is only with this view in mind that the *raison d'être* of an OA science will be ensured and protected.

Acknowledgements

I am grateful to the two co-editors of this volume and the editors of two OA humanities journals (Carmen Pérez-Llantada and Nadežda Silaški) for their insightful comments and valuable feedback on the earlier versions of this chapter.

This work is a contribution to national research project FFI2015-68638-R MINECO/FEDER, EU, funded by the Spanish Ministry of Economy and Competitiveness.

References

Budapest Open Access Initiative [BOAI]. (2002). Retrieved 4 December 2015 from http://www.budapestopenaccessinitiative.org/read.

Berlin Declaration on Open Access to Knowledge in the Sciences and Humanities. (2003). Retrieved 4 December 2015 from http://openaccess.mpg.de/Berlin-Declaration.

Bethesda Statement on Open Access Publishing. (2003). Retrieved 4 December 2015 from http://legacy.earlham.edu/~peters/fos/bethesda.htm.

Adema, J., & Ferwerda, E. (2014). Publications practices in motion: The benefits of open access publishing for the humanities. In P. Dávidházi (Ed.), *New publication cultures in the humanities: Exploring the paradigm shift* (pp. 131-146). Amsterdam: Amsterdam University Press.

Bartholomew, R.E. (2014). Science for sale: The rise of predatory journals. *Journal of the Royal Society of Medicine, 107*(10), 384-385.

Beall, J. (2012). Predatory publishers are corrupting open access. *Nature, 489*(7415), 179. Retrieved 8 July 2016 from http://www.nature.com/polopoly_fs/1.11385!/menu/main/topColumns/topLeftColumn/pdf/489179a.pdf.

Bohannon, J. (2013). Who's afraid of peer review? *Science, 342*(6154), 60-65.

Dávidházi, P. (2014). Exploring paradigms and ourselves. In P. Dávidházi (Ed.), *New publication cultures in the humanities: Exploring the paradigm shift* (pp. 9-18). Amsterdam: Amsterdam University Press.

Delgado López-Cózar, E., Ruiz-Pérez, R., & Jiménez-Contreras, E. (2006). *La edición de revistas científicas: Directrices, criterios y modelos de evaluación*. Madrid: FECYT.

European Association of Science Editors [EASE]. (2007). *The EASE statement on inappropriate use of impact factors*. Retrieved 15 January 2016 from http://www.ease.org.uk/sites/default/files/ease_statement_ifs_final.pdf.

Garfield, E. (2005, September 16). The agony and the ecstasy — The history and the meaning of journal impact factor. Paper presented at the *5th International Congress on Peer Review in Biomedical Publication*, Chicago, USA. Retrieved 29 July 2016 from http://garfield.library.upenn.edu/papers/jifchicago2005.pdf?utm_source=false&utm_medium=false&utm_campaign=false.

Gruber, T. (2014). Academic sell-out: How an obsession with metrics and rankings is damaging academia. *Journal of Marketing for Higher Education, 24*(2), 165-177.

Harnad, S. (2008, January 30). The university's mandate to mandate open access [guest blog post, Open Students: Students for Open Access to Research]. Retrieved 15 January 2016 from http://openaccess.eprints.org/index.php?/archives/358-guid.html.

Laakso, M., Welling, P., Bukvova, H., Nyman, L., Björk, B-C., & Hedlund, T. (2011). The development of open access journal publishing from 1993 to 2009. *PLoS ONE 6*(6), e20961. DOI: http://dx.doi.org/10.1371/journal.pone.0020961.

Liu, Z. (2004). Perceptions of credibility of scholarly information on the web. *Information Processing & Management, 40*(6), 1027-1038.

Salager-Meyer, F. (2012). The open access movement or 'edemocracy': Its birth, rise, problems and solutions. *Ibérica, 24*, 55-74.

Salager-Meyer, F. (2015). Peripheral scholarly journals: From locality to globality. *Ibérica, 30*, 15-36.

Scopus content coverage guide. (2016). Amsterdam: Elsevier. Retrieved 30 July 2016 from https://www.elsevier.com/__data/assets/pdf_file/0007/69451/scopus_content_coverage_guide.pdf.

Tseng, S., & Fogg, B.J. (1999). Credibility and computing technology. *Communications of the ACM, 42*(5), 39-44.

Zuccala, A. (2009). The layperson and open access. *Annual Review of Information Science and Technology, 43*, 359-396.

7

Disseminating research internationally:

Intra-subdisciplinary rhetorical structure variation in immunity and allergy research articles

Pedro Martín and Isabel K. León Pérez

1. Introduction

In today's context of disseminating research internationally, the need to publish research papers in English-medium journals has become ever more pressing, not only for those scholars who seek to make their research visible to a wider audience and gain international recognition, but also for those who intend to obtain academic promotion and professional benefits, such as research funding and salary increment (Lillis & Curry, 2010; Moreno, 2010; Hanauer & Englander, 2011; Martín, Rey-Rocha, Burgess & Moreno, 2014). This is particularly the case in disciplinary areas such as the health sciences, where the number of scientific journals published in languages other than English has diminished dramatically over the last few years to almost total extinction.

Aside from geopolitical considerations related to the dominance of English (see, for example, Ammon, 2001, 2012; Ferguson, 2007), it is a fact that the writing up of a research paper generally involves difficulties, especially for inexperienced writers and users of English as an Additional Language [EAL]. In order to get their papers accepted, scholars have to demonstrate to the other members of their particular disciplinary communities, especially the editors and reviewers of international English language journals, that they have mastered the established rhetorical conventions which have been institutionalised in a specific research genre, such as the research article [RA]. In response to this situation, many English for Research Publication Purposes [ERPP] researchers and practitioners have put their energies into providing support to these scholars, including the analysis of the structural organisation of experimental RAs. Many of these studies have revealed that the typical macro-structure of experimental papers adheres to the IMRD [Introduction, Methods, Results and Discussion] pattern, not only across disciplines but also across languages. Other authors, such as Cargill and O'Connor (2013) and Burgess and Cargill (2013), have also noted a slight variation to this prevalent pattern in terms of the order in which these sections appear throughout the paper [IRDM], which consists in presenting the methods section at the end of the RA.

At a micro-structural level, following Swales's (1990, 2004) notion of 'move' and 'step' as a framework for genre-analytic research, many studies have revealed rhetorical variation across disciplines. Examples include Nwogu (1997) in medicine; Posteguillo (1999) in computer science; Young and Allison (2004) in applied linguistics; and Lin and Evans (2012) in several disciplines in the fields of engineering, applied sciences, social sciences and humanities, to cite just a few. Variation has also been reported within subdisciplinary fields. In her analysis of RA introductions from two related subdisciplines of biology, Samraj (2002) found a higher frequency of occurrence of centrality claims to establish the importance of the general topic of the paper in the conservation biology introductions than in the wildlife behaviour ones, indicating that the former fulfil a greater promotional function. Ozturk (2007) also revealed the existence of intradisciplinary move structure variation in his analysis of two closely related subdisciplines of applied linguistics, namely second language acquisition and second language writing research. He explained the variation in terms of established and emerging fields. More recently, in her study of three engineering subdisciplines (civil, software and biomedical), Kanoksilapatham (2015) showed that each subdiscipline is unique in its nature, having a discourse community with its own writing conventions, which are manifested in the selective choice of certain moves and steps.

With the aim of extending the study of levels of specificity, in this chapter we posed the following research questions: Do RAs that belong to a single subdiscipline but are published in different journals share the same textual organisation? If some type of variation is found, could this be conditioned by the broad/narrow scope of the journals, the specialised/generalised nature of the journal's readership and/or certain rhetorical specificities of long-established versus emergent journals?

To answer these questions, we examined the macro-structure and micro-structure (moves/steps) of 30 RAs, published in five high-impact English language journals in the medical subdiscipline of immunology and allergy, a leading research area which is currently generating a growing number of publications. A qualitative analysis of these journals was also conducted in order to identify potential reasons for variation in RA structure.

2. Methods

2.1. Data collection and procedures

For the selection of the journals, we used the Scimago Journal Rank [SJR], a recent approach to the measurement of journals' scientific prestige that ranks scholarly journals based not only on the raw number of citations received by a journal, but also on the importance or influence of journals that issue those citations. These new metrics thus represent scientific impact as a function of both the quantities of citations received and the combination of the quantity and the quality (see González-Pereira, Guerrero-Bote & Moya-Anegón, 2010). Within the broad subject area of medicine, we focused on the specific subject category of immunology and allergy. In order to avoid genre variation, we excluded the journals that publish only review or opinion articles and selected the five top-ranked journals that publish experimental RAs, which are listed in the following order of ranking (SJR, 2015): *Immunity*, *Journal of Experimental Medicine*, *Journal of Allergy and Clinical Immunology*, *Annals of Rheumatic Diseases*, and *Mucosal Immunology*.

We selected at random six RAs from each journal, making a total of 30 recently published papers (see Appendix I), all of which had been issued over the last seven years (2009-15). For the purposes of describing comparatively and quantitatively the prevalent rhetorical practices used by writers in RAs, we analysed the macro-structural sections of the texts and their micro-structure. For the micro-level analysis, we adopted a genre-analytic approach following the work by Swales (1990, 2004), in which he uses the concept of 'move' to refer to functional text elements, as viewed in relation to the rhetorical goal of a text. Moves manifest themselves as text units that occur in typical sequences, and these can be realised by either one or a combination of submoves or 'steps'. In our research, the move analyses of the texts were first carried out independently by each co-researcher and then compared. A high level of agreement (95% inter-rater reliability) was reached after discussion. In those cases in which discrepancies occurred, we resorted to the assistance of a specialist informant in the subdiscipline.

In order to explain possible structural variation, the journals from which the articles were selected were also analysed mainly in terms of their scope, the level of expertise of the potential readership (that is, general versus more specialised), the trajectory of the journals (emergent versus long-established journals), and any explicit indications for structuring the submitted manuscripts in the guidelines for authors. To this purpose, we consulted the official websites of the journals on which this information is provided.

3. Results and discussion

3.1. Journal instructions for authors and quantitative/qualitative findings

On the basis of the quantitative and qualitative findings presented and discussed below, we can distinguish two main subgroups of journals, according to the higher or lower tendency they show to use certain defining '+/- promotional' rhetorical strategies (see Table 7.1). As far as we could observe, the distribution of conventional (neutral) and unexpected (persuasive) rhetorical choices seems to show an inverse correlation. Nevertheless, both subgroups seem to share some common (non-defining) traits. Among these were that the instructions for authors systematically indicated a macro-structural pattern of choice, and that results and methods sections were highly structured (containing subheadings), while introductions and discussions were universally non-structured. Introductions were typically brief and discussions long. It is also worth pointing out that, with the singular exception of *Mucosal Immunology* as the most recently emerged journal, all the journals analysed have released monthly issues with regularity since their founding.

3.1.1 The '+ promotional' subgroup

In general terms, the predominant linguistic traits of the journals sharing the '+ promotional' profile are the use of Macro-structural Pattern 2 (IRDM), the sentence-type title, a non-structured abstract lacking keywords, and the results as the longest section of the article, together with the regular occurrence of acknowledgments and other minor sections. From an extra-linguistic standpoint, this subset is formed by journals that offer a broad-spectrum, wide-ranging scope and are thus addressed to a more generalised readership. *Immunity*, the *Journal of Experimental Medicine* and *Mucosal Immunology* comprise the group meeting these criteria. Their individual characteristics beyond those summarised in Table 7.1, as they manifest in our corpus, can be briefly described as follows.

The journal *Immunity*, published by Elsevier, although specialised and aimed at a scientific readership, has quite a comprehensive scope. Its area of interest is defined far beyond the mere characterisation of immune genes and cells, including any research that may contribute to a better understanding of infection and host defenses. The instructions for authors require articles to contain a graphical abstract as well as the commonly required sections. Authors are allowed to use subheadings in the discussion, which can also be combined with the results in a single section. However, no instances of either feature were found in the current study.

The *Journal of Experimental Medicine* (*J Exp Med*), published by the Rockefeller University Press, releases articles on medical biology. It focuses both on human studies

Table 7.1 (overleaf): Distribution of journal macro-structural traits analysed (√ = generalised tendency, X = never applied, + = instance presenting a trait, − = instance lacking a trait).

and diverse experimental models of human disease which address multiple topics such as genetics, inflammation, immunity, infectious diseases, cancer, vascular biology, metabolic disorders, neuroscience, and stem cell biology. With a broad readership interested in medical biology, the journal expects abstracts to be accessible also to non-specialist readers. This is the only case of this requirement in all the journals of our corpus. The results, which may be also combined with the discussion in a single section, should contain subheadings. Once again, no instances were identified in our study.

As the official journal of the Society of Mucosal Immunology [SMI], *Mucosal Immunology* (*Mucosal Immunol*) covers all aspects of the fields of immunity and inflammation potentially affecting mucosal tissues. It publishes basic, translational and clinical research on a wide range of aspects connected to immunology (gastrointestinal, pulmonary, nasopharyngeal, oral, ocular and genitourinary immunology). It thus addresses scientists who specialise in different human bodily systems. It is the most recent journal and has been edited by the Nature Publishing Group since its founding. Subheadings in the results section are highly complex, of the sentence-type, and may appear either alone or in combination with complex noun phrases [NPs]. Co-ordinated sentences are also used sometimes as subheadings in the results section. A section for supplementary material appears in half of the corpus instances, where a link for visiting the online version of the article is provided. An author contributions section precedes the references, though this may be a publisher decision rather than that of the authors or editorial board.

3.1.2. The '- promotional' subgroup

The '- promotional' subgroup of journals is characterised by the following common linguistic traits: the use of Macro-structural Pattern 1 [IMRD], a marked tendency to the noun-phrase-type title, and a structured abstract with keywords. In extra-linguistic terms, this subset is formed by long-term established journals (in the first half of the 20th century), comprehensively covering an extensive subject range and targeting a specialised, expert readership. The *Journal of Allergy and Clinical Immunology* and *Annals of Rheumatic Diseases* are members of this group. Their particular features beyond those found in Table 7.1, as they became apparent in our corpus, are summarised along the following lines.

The *Journal of Allergy and Clinical Immunology* (*J Allergy Clin Immunol*) was originally created as the *Journal of Allergy* and obtained its current name 42 years later (in 1971). Since then, it has been published by Elsevier. The papers in this periodical are addressed to physicians and researchers interested in allergy and immunology, but they also target dermatology, gastroenterology, and other related areas connecting allergic diseases and clinical immunology. Thus research about asthma, food allergy, allergic rhinitis, atopic dermatitis, primary immune deficiencies, occupational and environmental allergy, and other allergic and immunologic conditions can be reported. As well as a traditional structured abstract, a capsule summary with keywords, particularly addressed

Categories and items for the rhetorical variation analysis		Immunity	J Exp Med	Mucosal Immunol	J Allergy Clin Immunol	Ann Rheum Dis
			'+ promotional' subgroup		'- promotional' subgroup	
RHETORICAL MACRO-STRUCTURE						
Macro-structural Pattern 1: IMRD		X	X	X	√	√
Macro-structural Pattern 2: IRDM		√	√	√	X	X
Macro-structural pattern indicated: Instructions for Authors		√	√	√	√	√
RHETORICAL MICRO-STRUCTURE						
Title type	Noun-phrase (NP-Type), often complex	------	------	-----+	++++--	+++---
	Sentence (S-Type)	++++++	++++++	+++++-	-----++	-----++
Abstract/ Summary	Abstract main heading	++++++	------	------	------	++++++
	Structured abstract (subheadings present)	------	------	------	++++++	++++++
	Keywords present	++++++	------	------	++++++	------
Introduction	Introduction main heading	++++++	++++++	++++++	------	+++++-
Results	Structured Results (subheadings present)	++++++	++++++	++++++	++++++	+++++-
	Results is the longest section of the article	++++++	++++++	++++++	------	-----++

Discussion	Discussion main heading	++++++	++++++	++++++	++++++	++++++
Methods	Supportive/Supplemental info (usu. online)	++++++	+++---	+++---	------	---+++
Other	Acknowledgments (and other minor sections)	++++++	++++++	++++++	------	++++++
	References main heading	++++++	++++++	++++++	++++++	++++++
EXTRALINGUISTIC INFORMATION						
Temporal evolution	Long-established journal (founding year)	X	√ (1896)	X	√ (1929)	√ (1939)
	Emergent journal (founding year)	√ (1994)	X	√ (2008)	X	X
Subject range	Broader scope	√	√	√	X	X
	Narrower scope	X	X	X	√	√
Target audience expertise	More generalised readership	√	√	√	X	X
	More specialised readership	X	X	X	√	√
Publication frequency	Higher: monthly frequency	+	+	-	+	+
	Lower: bi-monthly frequency	-	-	+	-	-

to clinicians (that is, an expert readership), is requested, with the aim of emphasising the most relevant findings and contributions to the literature. This requisite is uniquely found in the current journal.

Annals of Rheumatic Diseases (*Ann Rheum Dis*), published by the BMJ Journals group, includes all aspects of rheumatology, from musculoskeletal conditions through arthritic disease to connective tissue disorders. Of interest in our subcorpus is that keywords (although recommended) are never used.

3.2. Accounting for the prevalent macro-structural pattern

As seen in Table 7.1, two different variations to the IMRD pattern emerged. From this table we can infer that in this subdiscipline the macro-structure of RAs follows two conventions, depending on the journal in which they are published: the traditional IMRD pattern is used in two journals, whereas the variation IRDM (prevalent in three journals) seems to highlight the importance of the results in the research by placing the results section immediately after the introduction (foregrounding) and moving the methods to the last section in the paper (backgrounding). The importance given to the results section is reinforced by the fact that this is typically the longest section in the papers analysed in the cited three journals. We can therefore assume that, by deciding to establish the IRDM pattern, the members of the editorial boards in *Immunology*, *Journal of Experimental Medicine*, and *Mucosal Immunology* have sought to publish in their journals persuasive papers which fulfil a greater promotional function than the papers published in the other two journals in which the results section plays a less prominent, less persuasive role. Conversely, this may indicate that the methodological considerations play a more important role for the discourse communities associated with the *Journal of Allergy and Clinical Immunology* and *Annals of Rheumatic Diseases*.

One possible explanation for the rhetorical difference might lie in the distinction we mentioned in Sections 3.1.1. and 3.1.2. above, in relation to the level of expertise of the potential readership. It seems that in an attempt to attract a more heterogeneous readership, the editorial board of the three journals with a broader scope decided to establish the policy of using the IRDM pattern (as explicitly stated in the guidelines for authors), where the results are given more prominence. We could also account for this difference in terms of emergent versus long-established journals (see journal founding dates displayed in Table 7.1). It may seem that the long-established journals tend to stick to the traditional IMRD pattern, since they are consolidated and prestigious journals which apparently do not need to promote themselves to attract (their already specialised) readership. However, as opposed to this hypothesis, we find the striking case of the *Journal of Experimental Medicine* (founded in 1896), whose papers follow the IRDM pattern.

As regards this particular case, we decided to carry out a chronological analysis to look for a possible macro-structural variation at some point over time. What we found is that the articles published before the year 2005 followed the traditional IMRD pattern, but from that year onwards there was a change to the IRDM macro-structural pattern, as explicitly stated in the journal guidelines. This shows that the editorial board of this journal, probably in an attempt to make the journal more competitive, decided to adopt the general tendency of emergent journals and establish the IRDM pattern in 2005. This particular case reflects how genres may change over time as a consequence of the values and demands of the members of disciplinary communities. This also corroborates Bazerman's (1988) observations about the diminishing rhetorical importance given to the methods section over the last decades in favour of the more central, highly focused role that the results have more recently taken on in the experimental article.

3.3. The rhetorical function of titles and abstracts

It is worth highlighting an additional difference found in the two subgroups of journals in terms of how titles are constructed and the corresponding degree of promotional value that they may confer. As seen in Table 7.1, only 9 (that is, 30%) of the 30 RAs in the corpus analysed were of the noun-phrase [NP] type, whereas 21 (that is, 70%) were sentence-type instances. However, complexity appears to be a common feature for both types. Titles may reach a noticeable level of intricacy in structural terms, as shown in Examples 1-4 below, including various instances of embedding, defining and non-defining explanatory descriptions, co-ordination, subordination and juxtaposition, often used in combination, among other possible complexities.

1. NLRC3, a Member of the NLR Family of Proteins, Is a Negative Regulator of Innate Immune Signaling Induced by the DNA Sensor STING. (Im. 6)
2. Exhaled nitric oxide levels and blood eosinophil counts independently associate with wheeze and asthma events in National Health and Nutrition Examination Survey subjects. (J. All. Cl. Im. 4.)
3. Improvements in productivity at paid work and within the household, and increased participation in daily activities after 24 weeks of certolizumab pegol treatment of patients with psoriatic arthritis: results of a phase 3 double-blind randomised placebo-controlled study. (An. Rhe. Dis. 5.)
4. Regulatory B cells from hilar lymph nodes of tolerant mice in a murine model of allergic airway disease are CD5+, express TGF-β, and co-localise with CD4+Foxp3+ Tcells (Muc. Im. 4.).

In our sample (see Table 7.1), the use of S-Type (sentence-type) titles invariably co-occurs with the use of Macro-structural Pattern 2 (IRDM), showing a higher promotional value achieved by anticipating the results section. Besides, both patterns directly correlate with non-structured abstracts, which are used in 18 of the 30 articles analysed (60% of the corpus). Such a universal tendency allowed us to identify a well-defined correspondence between two different journal profiles and a higher or lower degree of rhetorical promotion. In summary, articles in the more recently emerged periodicals — that is, those with an apparently broader scope, which are addressed to a more heterogeneous readership — exhibit a combination of several rhetorical strategies with a more marked promotional intention. Those strategies are illustrated, in this case, by the occurrence of the S-Type title, the non-structured abstract, and the IRDM model (Pattern 2).

Conversely, the occurrence of structured abstracts, provided with subheadings and key words, in 12 of the 30 articles analysed (40% of the corpus), characterises articles published in the long-established publications, which, addressed to a more homogeneous readership, seem to have a narrower scope. Because of their commitment to a well-established tradition, they conform to the highly influential, conventional IMRD model (Pattern 1) as the preferred standard choice at the macro-structural level. Their use of highly structured abstracts, with a more predictable organisation of the information and a matter-of-fact, though perhaps less persuasive, rhetorical function, signals a more straightforward, neutral, less promotional standing point.

3.4. Analysis of the micro-structure: The general rhetorical structure

At the level of move, we found the same sequence of occurrence of eight moves in all the texts analysed. The general rhetorical scheme is presented in Table 7.2, together with the most prevalent steps identified in each of the moves.

INTRODUCTION
Move 1 — Creation of a research context
1A — Claiming the importance of the research topic (with or without citations)
1B — Expressing what is known about the topic (with or without citations)
1C — Reviewing previous literature
Move 2 — Justification of research
2A — Indicating a knowledge gap
2B — Criticising weak points of specific previous studies
2C — Criticising previous research (generalised reference)
Move 3 — Announcement of present research
3A — Describing main features/aims of the study
3B — Stating hypothesis or research questions
3C — Summarising (and interpreting) main findings
3D — Highlighting the main contribution of the study

METHODS
Move 4 — Description of methodology
4A — Describing data collection and materials (patients, subjects, animals, samples, study design)
4B — Describing experimental procedures
4C — Describing statistical (or data) analysis
RESULTS
Move 5 — Statement of findings
5A — Providing background information (restating procedures)
5B — Announcing where the results or data are located (in graphs, tables)
5C — Making observations on the results
5D — Reporting expected and/or unexpected results
DISCUSSION
Move 6 — Discussion on the meaning of findings
6A — Restating main results
6B — Interpreting findings
6C — Explaining findings
6D — Comparing results with previous research
6E — Drawing conclusions
Move 7 — Evaluation of the significance of findings
7A — Highlighting the meaning of findings
7B — Stating the limitation of findings
Move 8 — Drawing implications of findings
8A — Recommending future research or practice
8B — Reporting future research

Table 7.2: General rhetorical structure of immunology and allergy RAs across the five sets of journals.

Although the eight moves were obligatory in all the texts analysed, at the level of step we found some degree of rhetorical variation. Whereas in the methods, results and discussion sections the frequency of occurrence of steps is similar, we found a marked difference in the frequency of occurrence of some steps in the introduction section: some of these steps occurred occasionally in a few of the papers analysed, and some others were very frequent in some of the journals but very infrequent in others. We therefore investigated this phenomenon more closely.

3.5. Quantitative move-analysis of the introduction section

In the light of the findings discussed above, and in order to establish quantitative differences, we analysed the frequency of use of the steps occurring in the introduction section. The results of this analysis are presented in Table 7.3.

Our findings revealed that for the creation of the research context (Move 1), all the writers used the Steps 1B ('Expressing what is known about the topic') and 1C ('Reviewing previous literature'), as illustrated in Examples 5 and 6 below:

5. Psoriatic arthritis [PsA] is a chronic inflammatory arthritis which affects up to 30% of patients with psoriasis.[1-3] (An. Rhe. Dis. 5)

6. Studies on bacterial pathogens have revealed that some bacteria are cleared from the cytoplasm by autophagy (Andrade et al., 2006; Gutierrez et al., 2004; Ling et al., 2006; Nakagawa et al., 2004; Ogawa et al., 2005; Singh et al., 2006. (Im. 1)

However, for Step 1A ('Claiming the importance of the research topic'), the situation was different. Although it was prevalent in the RAs from the *Journal of Experimental Medicine*, *Immunity*, and *Mucosal Immunology* (the journals following the IRDM pattern), it occurred in only one instance in *Annals of Rheumatic Diseases* and in only two papers (33.3%) of the *Journal of Allergy and Clinical Immunology*, as exemplified in 7-9 below (emphases added):

7. Cell volume regulation is *of prime importance* to the CNS because of the restricted volume of the skull, and current clinical treatment of stroke aims to reduce intracranial pressure by administration of hypertonic solutions (Jain, 2008). (Im. 4)

8. The incidence of asthma and other allergic respiratory diseases has increased *dramatically* worldwide in the last 3 decades. (J. All. Cl. Im. 2)

9. STAT3 *plays a critical role* in signal transduction for many cytokines and receptor-type tyrosine kinases. (J. Ex. Med. 1)

As regards Move 2 ('Justification of research'), the prevalent step for its realisation was 2A ('Indicating a knowledge gap'), although in a few occasions the writers also opted

Table 7.3 (right): Frequency of occurrence of moves/steps across the five sets of RA introductions.

Tendency to '+/− promotional' rhetorical strategies	'− promotional' subgroup			'+ promotional' subgroup		
Journals	An.Rh.Dis.	J.All.Cl.Im.	J.Ex.Med.	Im.	Mu.Imm.
Rhetorical pattern	[IMRD]	[IMRD]	[IRDM]	[IRDM]	[IRDM]
Case number (percentage)	N. (%)	N. (%)	N. (%)	N. (%)	N. (%)
Move 1 — Creation of a research context	6 (100)	6 (100)	6 (100)	6 (100)	6 (100)
1A — Claiming the importance of the research topic	1 (16.6)	2 (33.3)	6 (100)	6 (100)	6 (100)
1B — Expressing what is known about the topic	6 (100)	6 (100)	6 (100)	6 (100)	6 (100)
1C — Reviewing previous literature	6 (100)	6 (100)	6 (100)	6 (100)	6 (100)
Move 2 — Justification of research	6 (100)	6 (100)	6 (100)	6 (100)	6 (100)
2A — Indicating a knowledge gap	6 (100)	6 (100)	6 (100)	6 (100)	6 (100)
2B — Criticising weak points of specific previous studies	None	None	None	1 (16.6)	None
2C — Criticising previous research (generalised reference)	1 (16.6)	1 (16.6)	None	None	None
Move 3 — Announcement of present research	6 (100)	6 (100)	6 (100)	6 (100)	6 (100)
3A — Describing main features/aims of the study	6 (100)	6 (100)	6 (100)	6 (100)	6 (100)
3B — Stating hypothesis or research questions	None	None	1 (16.6)	None	None
3C — Summarising (and interpreting) main findings	None	None	6 (100)	6 (100)	6 (100)
3D — Highlighting the main contribution of the study	None	None	6 (100)	6 (100)	6 (100)

for 'Criticising weak points in specific previous studies' (2B) or 'Criticising previous research' (2C). These three steps are illustrated in 10-12 as follows (emphases added):

10. While there is published evidence on the burden of the disease on work disability in related rheumatic diseases such as rheumatoid arthritis (RA) and ankylosing spondylitis (AS),[10-13] *to date there are few data on* work disability in PsA.9 14. (An. Rhe. Dis. 5)

11. ... *These studies did not directly determine* the anatomical location along the follicular periphery of these interactions, however. (Im. 3)

12. However, the specific pollen taxa implicated *have not been consistent across studies*. (J. All. Cl. Im. 2)

In relation to Move 3 ('Announcement of present research'), the common obligatory step in all papers is 3A ('Describing main features/aims of the study'). On only one occasion, the writers of a paper also used 3B ('Stating hypothesis or research questions'). These steps are exemplified in the following examples (13-14, emphases added).

13. *The objectives of this study were* (1) to identify potential demographic and clinical predictors measured 15 years prior to and potential variables associated with OLD and RLD at time of the spirometry test in patients with inflammatory polyarthritis [IP], *and* (2) *to compare* the prevalence of abnormal lung function in patients with IP and the general population. (An. Rhe. Dis. 1)

14. *We therefore hypothesised that Stm might* evade or prevent rapid activation of a canonical NLRP3 inflammasome, *and that* this evasion *might* contribute to systemic bacterial virulence. (J. Ex. Med. 4)

But what emerged to be a most striking difference is that although Steps 3C ('Summarising — and interpreting — main findings'), and 3D ('Highlighting the main contribution of the study') were obligatory elements in the *Journal of Experimental Medicine, Immunity,* and *Mucosal Immunology,* these were absent in *Annals of Rheumatic Diseases,* and the *Journal of Allergy and Clinical Immunology.* Two examples of each of these steps are illustrated in 15-18 as follows (emphases added):

15. Here, *we showed that* autophagy controlled vesicular stomatitis virus (VSV) replication in both cultured Drosophila cells and adult flies. (Im. 1)

16. *Our data* further *suggest that* sensing of bacterial metabolites may provide an additional level of innate immune recognition, and that regulation of metabolite production by intracellular pathogens represents a pathogen immune evasion strategy. (J. Ex. Med. 4)

17. Here *we present evidence that challenge* [sic] *tenants of the current model* of GC development. (Im. 3)

18. *The results presented in this study detail a novel* biological mechanism in which a Th1 inducing cytokine, IL-12, suppresses Th17 cytokine production through induction of IL-10 and independently from IFN-signaling. (Muc. Im. 2)

What is clear at this point is that, once again, we can see that the papers in the journals following the IRDM model (Pattern 2) fulfil a more promotional role than those published in the journals following the traditional IMRD scheme (Pattern 1).

This is also shown through the prevalent rhetorical practice of including main findings and highlighting the importance of the study in the last part of the RA introductions published in the former journals.

4. Conclusion

This study has explored the degree of variability in the rhetorical structure of research papers published in different high-impact English language journals within a single subdiscipline of medicine: immunology and allergy. The overall results have revealed that in the particular subdiscipline under study, we can find two groups of journals that differ at both the macro-structural and micro-structural levels, showing a more or less promotional rhetorical style. A group of journals emerged as being more promotional in terms of the choice of a particular macro-structural pattern (IRDM) which highlights the importance of results, whereas the methods seem to be secondary in importance, since they appear backgrounded as the last section in the RA. It is worth highlighting the fact that the results section, always highly structured following the recommended guidelines, is typically the longest section in the papers from this group of journals, which also show a clear-cut tendency for the authors to write their titles in the more assertive and persuasive sentence form. Likewise, the more promotional function in this group is also seen at the micro-level through the prevalent use of statements of centrality (Step 1A), and, more significantly, through the two other promotional strategies which allow writers to enhance the contribution of their research by anticipating findings (Step 3C) and by highlighting the value of their research (Step 3D) in the introduction section.

The type of rhetorical variation identified in this study can mainly be explained in terms of three factors: journal scope, readership expertise, and the prevalent rhetorical practices in emergent versus long-established journals and their corresponding communities. We can thus conclude that discourse practices may vary even within RAs published in the same subdiscipline due to the different written conventions established by the members of particular academic communities (editorial boards of specific journals), which seem to be unique. Moreover, from a rhetorical point of view, there seems to be a negative correlation between the long-established, prevalent conventions and the more unusual, innovative possibilities. Their suitability in a particular situation will depend on how much the abovementioned factors may weigh. These findings may thus have pedagogical implications for those scholars working in specific areas of research, provided that they need to meet the expectations of the members of their individual subdisciplinary communities, including the prevalent discourse practices of specific subdisciplinary journals, in order to write readership-relevant papers and get those papers eventually accepted. Finally, this exploratory study has also corroborated the relevance of rhetorical promotion in the increasingly competitive world of academia and identified the need for more effective targeting of future, more extensive studies aimed at further distinguishing the prevalent rhetorical practices and specificities of particular discourse communities.

References

Ammon, U. (Ed.). (2001). *The dominance of English as a language of science: Effects on other languages and language communities.* Berlin: Mouton de Gruyter.

Ammon, U. (2012). Linguistic inequality and its effects on participation in scientific discourse and on global knowledge accumulation — With a closer look at the problems of the second-rank language communities. *Applied Linguistics Review, 3*(2), 333-355.

Bazerman, C. (1988). *Shaping written knowledge: The genre and activity of the experimental article in science.* Madison, WI: University of Wisconsin Press.

Burgess, S., & Cargill, M. (2013). Using genre analysis and corpus linguistics to teach research article writing. In V. Matarese (Ed.), *Supporting research writing: Roles and challenges in multilingual settings* (pp. 55-71). Oxford: Chandos Publishing.

Cargill, M., & O'Connor, P. (2013). *Writing scientific research articles: Strategy and steps* (2nd ed.). Oxford: Wiley-Blackwell.

Ferguson, G. (2007). The global spread of English, scientific communication and ESP: Questions of equity, access and domain loss. *Ibérica, 13*(1), 7-38.

González-Pereira, B., Guerrero-Bote, V., & Moya-Anegón, F. (2010). A new approach to the metric of journals' scientific prestige: The SJR indicator. *Journal of Informetrics, 4*, 379-391.

Hanauer, D.I., & Englander, K. (2011). Quantifying the burden of writing research articles in a second language: Data from Mexican scientists. *Written Communication, 28*(4), 403-416.

Kanoksilapatham, B. (2015). Distinguishing textual features characterizing structural variation in research articles across three engineering sub-discipline corpora. *English for Specific Purposes, 37*, 74-86.

Lin, L., & Evans, S. (2012). Structural patterns in empirical research articles. *English for Specific Purposes, 25*, 282-309.

Lillis, T., & Curry, M.J. (2010). *Academic writing in a global context: The politics and practices of publishing in English.* London: Routledge.

Martín, P., Rey-Rocha, J., Burgess, S., & Moreno, A. (2014). Publishing research in English-language journals: Attitudes, strategies and difficulties of multilingual scholars of medicine. *Journal of English for Academic Purposes, 16*, 57-67.

Moreno, A.I. (2010). Researching into English for research publication purposes from an applied intercultural perspective. In M.F. Ruiz-Garrido, J.C. Palmer-Silveira, & I. Fortanet-Gomez (Eds.), *English for professional and academic purposes* (pp. 57-71). Amsterdam: Rodopi.

Nwogu, K. (1997). The medical research papers: Structure and functions. *English for Specific Purposes, 16*, 119-138.

Ozturk, I. (2007). The textual organisation of research article introductions in applied linguistics: Variability within a single discipline. *English for Specific Purposes, 26*, 25-38.

Posteguillo, S. (1999). The schematic structure of computer science research articles. *English for Specific Purposes, 18*, 139-160.

Samraj, B. (2002). Introductions in research articles: Variations across disciplines. *English for Specific Purposes, 21*, 1-17.

Swales, J.M. (1990). *Genre analysis: English in academic and research settings.* Cambridge: Cambridge University Press.

Swales, J.M. (2004). *Research genres: Explorations and applications.* Cambridge: Cambridge University Press.

Young, R., & Allison, D. (2004). Research articles in applied linguistics: Structures from a functional perspective. *English for Specific Purposes, 23,* 264-279.

Appendix I

Internet localisation [DOIs] of the articles conforming the corpus per journal (SJR, 2015)		
Immunity (Immunity)		
Article No.	Identification Code	Digital Object Identifier
1	Im. 1.	doi:10.1016/j.immuni.2009.02.009
2	Im. 2.	doi:10.1016/j.immuni.2010.04.016
3	Im. 3.	doi:10.1016/j.immuni.2011.03.024
4	Im. 4.	doi:10.1016/j.immuni.2012.06.013
5	Im. 5.	doi:10.1016/j.immuni.2013.09.005
6	Im. 6.	doi:10.1016/j.immuni.2014.01.010
Journal of Experimental Medicine (J Exp Med)		
Article No.	Identification Code	Digital Object Identifier
7	J. Ex. Med. 1.	doi/10.1084/jem.20100799
8	J. Ex. Med. 2.	doi/10.1084/jem.20110645
9	J. Ex. Med. 3.	doi/10.1084/jem.20122508
10	J. Ex. Med. 4.	doi/10.1084/jem.20130627
11	J. Ex. Med. 5.	doi/10.1084/jem.20132308
12	J. Ex. Med. 6.	doi/10.1084/jem.20141091
Journal of Allergy and Clinical Immunology (J Allergy Clin Immunol)		
Article No.	Identification Code	Digital Object Identifier
13	J. All. Cl. Im. 1.	doi:10.1016/j.jaci.2011.08.010
14	J. All. Cl. Im. 2.	doi.org/10.1016/j.jaci.2012.06.020
15	J. All. Cl. Im. 3.	doi:10.1016/j.jaci.2012.05.030
16	J. All. Cl. Im. 4.	doi:10.1016/j.jaci.2013.06.007

17	J. All. Cl. Im. 5.	doi:10.1016/j.jaci.2013.11.025
18	J. All. Cl. Im. 6.	doi:10.1016/j.jaci.2014.10.026
Annals of Rheumatic Diseases (Ann Rheum Dis)		
Article No.	Identification Code	Digital Object Identifier
19	An. Rhe. Dis. 1.	doi:10.1136/annrheumdis-2012-201698
20	An. Rhe. Dis. 2.	doi:10.1136/annrheumdis-2013-205171
21	An. Rhe. Dis. 3.	doi:10.1136/annrheumdis-2011-20030
22	An. Rhe. Dis. 4.	doi:10.1136/annrheumdis-2012-201611
23	An. Rhe. Dis. 5.	doi:10.1136/annrheumdis-2014-205198
24	An. Rhe. Dis. 6.	doi:10.1136/annrheumdis-2015-207326
Mucosal Immunology (Mucosal Immunol)		
Article No.	Identification Code	Digital Object Identifier
25	Muc. Im. 1.	doi:10.1038/mi.2009.139
26	Muc. Im. 2.	doi:10.1038/mi.2010.9
27	Muc. Im. 3.	doi:10.1038/mi.2010.46
28	Muc. Im. 4.	doi:10.1038/mi.2012.42
29	Muc. Im. 5.	doi:10.1038/mi.2012.106
30	Muc. Im. 6.	doi:10.1038/mi.2012.123

Note: Abbreviated names were taken from the NLM [National Library of Medicine] Title Abbreviation list, and from the ISI [Institute of Scientific Information] Journal Title Abbreviations list when necessary. The identification codes (appearing in the central column above and in Table 7.3) given along the present chapter to each illustrating example were only used for their traceability in the corpus articles.

8

Scientists publishing research in English from Indonesia:

Analysing outcomes of a training intervention to inform institutional action

Margaret Cargill, Patrick O'Connor, Rika Raffiudin, Nampiah Sukarno, Berry Juliandi and Iman Rusmana

1. Introduction

Indonesian universities are now facing a mandatory requirement for candidates to publish a paper in English in an international journal before a PhD degree can be awarded (Directorate Generale of Higher Education-Indonesian Ministry of Education [DGHE], 2012). The introduction of this requirement follows a similar action in China, where the bar is set higher at a journal indexed in the Science Citation Index or equivalent for candidates in the sciences (Li, 2006). This new requirement adds considerably to the already strong pressure experienced by Indonesian academic supervisors/advisors to achieve international publications and citations themselves (Sanjaya, Sitawati & Suciani, 2015), especially in the natural and life sciences (Hanauer & Englander, 2013). A factor that can be expected to contribute to the pressure is the limited nature of instruction in English for Academic Purposes [EAP] for both undergraduate and graduate students (Sadtono, 2001), especially as regards academic writing. There is thus a need to investigate how Indonesian academics are adapting to this additional pressure, as well as to test new educational initiatives for strengthening the skills of both mentors and authors in Indonesia when writing for publication in English. Such an initiative is the CIPSE [Collaborative Interdisciplinary Publication Skills Education] training approach. Developed by Cargill and O'Connor for use with early-career science researchers and implemented successfully in a range of Chinese contexts (Cargill, 2011; Cargill & O'Connor, 2012), this approach features the integration of perspectives from science, applied linguistics and education. However, a range of context-specific differences may affect its suitability for use in the Indonesian higher education setting. Overall, little research has been published to date investigating the challenges faced by Indonesian supervisors and their graduate students in this new context, or moves to help address the challenges. Here we contribute to addressing this lack by reporting on an invited intervention (a five-day CIPSE workshop) delivered to a cohort of staff from one faculty of a highly ranked Indonesian university in 2014, and a follow-up study with participants 12 months later.

A strength of the project design was that it built on an existing network based on scientific and educational collaborations over 20 years, which was expected to help overcome the potential pitfall of 'one-shot' professional development programs (Cannon & Hore, 1997). The workshop design and the follow-up study both reflected learning gained from analysis of similar events in Chinese contexts by the two first-named authors of this chapter across the period 2001-14 (Cargill & O'Connor, 2006a, 2006b; Cargill, O'Connor & Li, 2012; Cargill, O'Connor & Matthews, 2014). Questions addressed in the research presented here are as follows:

1. What were the most serious problems in getting published noted by participants before the intervention?
2. To what extent did the confidence of workshop participants to write research articles in English and to mentor their students' article writing change between pre- and immediate post-workshop data collection, and what further changes in confidence were reported 12 months post-workshop?
3. What were the subsequent trajectories of the papers that participants worked on at the workshop?
4. What were participants' perceptions of the usefulness of the workshop immediately post-attendance, and what had they used most 12 months later?
5. How did their suggestions for improvements differ between the two time points?
6. What did they think they most needed 12 months post-intervention in order to contribute to future progress?
7. How did they think their university should provide support to staff and graduate students for publishing in English?

In the light of the data and analysis presented in answering these questions, we discuss implications for moves to embed this kind of educational initiative in the research training and professional development activities of the university, both in the faculty where it was trialled and more broadly. We also compare the perceptions of our workshop participants with those of academics in other comparable countries, with the goal of presenting recommendations grounded both in the literature and in the lived experience of Indonesian scientists.

2. Material and methods

2.1. The 2014 intervention: Five-day CIPSE workshop

The workshop was collaboratively designed by the author team with dual focuses:

1. development of authoring skills and drafts of research articles already in progress
2. development of skills and materials for teaching and mentoring graduate students in writing papers for publication in journals that meet the national requirements.

Participants were selected by team members from the Department of Biology, Bogor Agricultural University [IPB], Indonesia (Raffiudin, Sukarno, Juliandi and Rusmana). In all, 23 people (4 male, 19 female) completed the workshop, of whom 16 were working on their own manuscript as well as learning mentoring skills. Three participants came from other departments of the Faculty of Mathematics and Natural Sciences (Computer Science, Mathematics and Geophysics and Meteorology), at the request of the faculty dean. All participants were provided with a copy of the workshop textbook (Cargill & O'Connor, 2013), and the workshop program (Appendix I) followed the order of materials in the book. Where writing time was built into the program, participants without their own drafts worked in small groups to discuss the applicability of the materials and exercises just presented to their own teaching contexts and to adapt them for enhanced usability. The workshop was presented by the two first-named authors of this chapter, with Cargill (an applied linguist) taking the lead where the material emphasised genre analysis, corpus linguistics and specific aspects of the use of English in science writing, and O'Connor (a scientist and science educator) taking the lead for issues of publication strategy and data presentation. (More detailed discussion of the collaborative and interdisciplinary nature of the CIPSE workshops can be found elsewhere; see Cargill, 2011; Cargill & O'Connor, 2010.)

Participants completed pre- and post-workshop seven-point Likert scale estimations of their confidence for four tasks: writing a paper in English for international publication, dealing with the publishing process in English, mentoring/assisting others to write a paper in English, and mentoring/ assisting others to deal with the publishing process in English (1 = not confident, 7 = very confident). They also provided pre- and post-workshop assessments of the percentage completed of their manuscript, if applicable. Participants also responded to open-ended questions:

- What are the three most serious problems you face in getting published? (pre-workshop)
- What were the most useful things in this workshop for you? (post-workshop)

- How could this workshop be improved to make it more useful for Indonesian researchers? (post-workshop)

The workshop was conducted, and questionnaires were written, in English, with translation into Bahasa Indonesia available on request at all times. Questionnaires were identified by participants' dates of birth to allow matching of pre- and post-workshop responses. Paired sample *t*-tests were used to test for significant differences.

2.2. The 2015 follow-up study

Twenty of the original 23 participants were able to be contacted 12 months after the 2014 workshop and agreed to meet with the first-named author of this chapter, Cargill. Each participant was asked if they preferred the interview to be conducted in Bahasa Indonesia, with translation assistance provided by one of the IPB team members, or in English. All but one opted for English. Participants were first asked to complete the same four post-workshop Likert-scale questions they had answered immediately after the original workshop in 2014. The remainder of the interviews were semi-structured, and response notes were constructed in consultation between the interviewer and the interviewee. Text in quotation marks in the following sections presents representative quotations from these notes, or from participants' questionnaire responses; quotes are identified with a participant number and year — for example, P21, 2014. Questions that guided the interviews were as follows:

1. Looking back, what are the things from the 2014 workshop that you have used most in the last 12 months?
2. From the perspective of 12 months' experience, how could the workshop you attended in 2014 be improved to make it more useful for Indonesian researchers?
3. What is the subsequent history of the manuscript you worked on in the 2014 workshop?
4. What is the most important thing you need now to help you write and submit publishable papers on your research?
5. In your opinion, how should IPB provide training or support in journal article writing for staff and PhD students?
6. Do you have any additional comments for us about your experience of trying to publish your research in international journals?

3. Findings and analysis

3.1. The most serious problems faced in getting published: Pre-intervention assessment

Before the training commenced, participants were asked to list the three most serious problems they faced in getting published. Responses clustered in three main areas: issues to do with obtaining suitable data, including analysis, infrastructure and facilities;

English grammar; and writing effectively in English, including constructing a well-argued story within the conventional article sections (Table 8.1). Lower numbers of responses highlighted lack of publication experience, especially journal selection; time; access to and use of appropriate literature; dealing with the publication process; and funding for research activities and publishing fees.

Issues related to English rated highest overall when the two subcategories are combined, and it is of interest that these scientists made clear distinctions in these initial responses between the more mechanical, sentence-level issues (grammar) and those relating to the production of a convincing argument or story. This level of sophistication boded well for their ability to engage effectively with the workshop approach.

Problem category	Number of instances
Data issues, analysis, research quality, technology	21
English — grammar	14
English — argument, story, article sections	12
Lack of publication experience/choosing journals	6
Time	5
Literature access and use	3
Dealing with review process	3
Funding	3

Table 8.1: The most serious problems in getting published faced by Indonesian scientists (n = 23, up to 3 items per respondent). This analysis of written responses was collected at the start of the 2014 CIPSE workshop.

3.2. Confidence to write and mentor writing of research articles in English for international publication

Participants' mean self-reported confidence increased by more than one point on the seven-point scale (p<0.001) measured immediately pre- and post-workshop for all four competencies targeted in the 2014 workshop: writing articles in English for international publication, mentoring/assisting others to write such articles, dealing with the publishing process in English, and mentoring/assisting others to deal with it (Table 8.2). In a realistic response, as also seen in other training contexts, some participants reported a decrease in confidence on gaining a better understanding of the challenges involved: 'I don't have enough of confidence because I need more time to learn how to make manuscript especially in English' (P21, 2014).

Task	Pre-workshop (n = 23)	Immediately post-workshop (n = 23)	12 months post-workshop (n = 20)
Write a research article in English	3.5	4.9	5.1
Mentor/assist others to write a research article in English	3.3	4.7	4.9
Deal with the publishing process in English	3.3	4.5	5.0
Mentor/assist others to deal with the publishing process in English	3.1	4.5	4.9

Table 8.2: The mean self-reported confidence of workshop participants for four tasks at three time points. Confidence was assessed on a seven-point Likert scale (1 = not confident, 7 = very confident).

The increases in mean confidence were maintained and further increased after 12 months (Table 8.2), but the further increases were again not completely uniform across the workshop cohort, with 3 to 5 participants reporting a decrease in confidence for these competencies 12 months post-workshop (Table 8.3). These findings highlight the range of levels of experience and skill among the participant cohort, and emphasise the challenges inherent in providing professional development for them.

Task	Increase in confidence	No change in confidence	Decrease in confidence
Write a research article in English	7	10	3
Mentor/assist others to write a research article in English	7	8	5
Deal with the publishing process in English	9	7	4
Mentor/assist others to deal with the publishing process in English	5	12	3

Table 8.3: The number of participants (n = 20) who reported an increase, a decrease or no change in self-assessed confidence for four tasks between immediately post-workshop data collection and 12 months post-workshop.

3.3. Most used things from the 2014 workshop

All 2015 interviewees reported content from the 2014 workshop that had been frequently useful and used in the subsequent 12 months. Commonly mentioned was the process taught for article construction: starting with results visuals plus dot-points under each one and identifying take-home message/s. Several respondents mentioned that students often were not comfortable with this approach when it was first introduced because they expected to start with the introduction, but that it gave good results. This process was linked to the importance of identifying a suitable target journal early in the process: 'The crucial problem in publishing scientific paper is to find the right targeted journals' (P8, 2015). Participants reported that the whole *Writing Scientific Research Articles* [WSRA] package (Cargill & O'Connor, 2013) had been used in teaching undergraduate and master's students and in their own research groups, as well as for correcting drafts and reviewing for Indonesian journals:

> Almost all because they are in one package — how to design experiments to get publishable data which also drives discussion. Opens minds of students that they need to read a lot to choose topic, which increases logic and critical thinking, analytical thinking — workshop materials do that in a comprehensive way, by demonstration. (P3, 2015)

One respondent reported that the training workshop slides had been incorporated unchanged into materials for a research methodology course he taught to 100 students. Specific aspects of English grammar and usage were also frequently mentioned as most used, especially verb tense. The freeware concordancing software the Adelaide Text Analysis Tool [AdTAT] (Hall, 2007) had been introduced to students by many participants, including in the department's journal club, for identifying key vocabulary and checking issues such as preposition usage. Thus it is clear that the workshop content, textbook and approach had met real needs for the participants and provided a raft of material for ongoing use.

All the mentioned elements had also been present in the responses to the 2014 post-workshop question: 'What were the most useful things in the workshop for you?', but in less specific forms overall. In those data there was an emphasis on increased confidence, on strategies for getting published, on the process of starting from the results when writing, and on improved English language skills, but with a focus on articles, 'right words' and writing sentences rather than on tenses, which was the stand-out feature 12 months later. The AdTAT program was mentioned several times, indicating that its usefulness was recognised right from its first introduction.

3.4. Subsequent trajectories of workshop manuscripts

Self-reported level of manuscript completion reached a mean of 60% subsequent to the 2014 workshop, increasing over the five days by a maximum of 60% (mean 28%), with five participants having begun with no text written (data not shown). Of the 16 papers that were being worked on during the workshop, 7 were submitted in the following 12-month period: 3 published in Scopus-listed journals, including 1 in the highly regarded *Nature Communications*; and 4 submitted to non-Scopus-listed journals. Interestingly, however, 18 subsequent papers had been published, 5 in Scopus-listed journals, and another 9 submitted (3 to Scopus-listed journals), most of which had been co-authored with master's students. These figures point towards a factor likely to be highly relevant to the modest numbers of workshop papers submitted or published — the high number of master's students for whom these staff members serve as supervisors, and who must also publish their results in academic journals, although the international journal requirement does not apply for master's-level candidates. Members of the biology department supervise on average six master's students, although not all of these proceed to undertake PhD degrees at IPB, some preferring to seek to study overseas. This high number of master's students is due to the high number of applicants to the study programs in the Department of Biology, but it seems to militate against increasing staff publication rates: 'Student deadlines push my own further distant' was an interview comment made (P7, 2015).

3.5. *The most important things needed now to enhance progress (n = 19): 2015 views*

The cluster of factors covered by 'facilities, infrastructure and funding' was the most prevalently cited overall as important for future progress at the time of the interviews. These issues were held responsible for limiting the level of journal that would accept papers, as reflected in these comments: 'not very high level journal because of infrastructure limitations' (P5, 2015); and 'rejected due to quality of the photomicrographs' (P20, 2015). Funding was specifically requested to cover open access article processing charges. Time was the most frequently mentioned single factor (6 mentions), with heavy teaching and administrative workloads often being responsible; these are in most cases increased for staff who have just finished higher degrees. Five participants indicated a need for a consultant or mentor to work with them on their article writing when they were ready for assistance; another 3 specifically focused on the need for assistance with English. Taken together, these suggest that language-related support is commonly felt to be an important need, but the number of mentions is much lower than that before the intervention (Table 8.1). This change suggests that the relative importance of infrastructure and facilities had become greater for the participants after 12 months of working with the techniques and strategies introduced in the workshop. One interviewee cited 'good quality students' (P17, 2015) as one of their most important needs, an issue that had not been mentioned previously.

3.6. Suggestions for workshop improvement

Participants were asked both immediately after the completion of the workshop and 12 months later how the workshop could be improved to make it more useful for Indonesian researchers. There were three main differences between the two sets of answers. Twelve months post-workshop there was a much-increased recognition that participant preparation was a key to obtaining best benefit from the workshop, and that the most important improvements needed to take place before the workshop was delivered: the English writing ability of participants needed to be stronger, and all participants needed an advanced draft manuscript so they could take better advantage of the presenters' expertise. One participant stated:

> We have to have a good ability in making sentences — otherwise we get stuck ... I have trouble helping my students with that. Participants, including staff need prior help at this level before your workshop. (P20, 2015)

Second, there was an ongoing emphasis on how the workshop should be presented but no single agreed position, although scheduling the workshop in the exam period to allow good access for staff was a common thread. One cluster of respondents thought five days was sufficient but wanted a less intensive format with more discussion. A larger grouping of responses recommended doubling the workshop duration to two weeks but halving the contact time to half-days only, so participants had plenty of writing time to apply the teaching to their drafts. Both groups requested more individual support with their writing, including editing assistance, and suggested ongoing support by email after the presenter/s returned home.

Immediately post-workshop, there had been a strong emphasis in responses to the question of extending the reach of the training to more Indonesian researchers and to postgraduate students. Twelve months later, this issue was taken up in a separate question on recommendations to the institution.

3.7. Views on the institutional provision of support for article writing

The question posed was this: 'In your opinion, how should IPB provide training or support in journal article writing for staff and PhD students?' Provision of support was seen as a priority: 'Strongly needed ... ' (P23, 2015). There was a clear consensus that the university should integrate the training into its regular programs. One participant described the developing situation this way:

> When you came here I think it opened many staff minds that writing papers needs a certain capacity ... IPB should integrate training into the regular program. (P20, 2015)

For students, a credit-bearing course was commonly suggested, often integrated with research methodology, which is already taught. One respondent recommended: '[W]orkshops better than courses for students — interactive, not boring' (P1, 2015). It was also suggested by many respondents that the workshop text (Cargill & O'Connor, 2013) should be translated into Indonesian and disseminated widely. (One suggestion along these lines had been received immediately post-workshop in 2014, and a team had already been established to progress the proposal by the time of the follow-up research visit 12 months later.)

For staff, suggestions featured workshops like that run in 2014 or run by those trained in the Adelaide-run workshops, annually for two weeks in the exam period. Mentor training was a common priority but not seen as a total solution: 'Invite experts like you to teach us to be mentors so IPB has more mentors — we need about 1:5. But still need more help from international experts every one or two years' (P5, 2015). One respondent reported that a five-day workshop was not enough, and recommended sessions once a month taught by train-the-trainer graduates from the 2014 workshop: 'Regular meetings are necessary to reinforce and remind' (P13, 2015). Another focused on the language of training presentations, saying she needed training by Indonesian staff: 'Although native English speakers give good material, I sometimes miss the points — if it is an Indonesian I can ask easily' (P11, 2015). Whatever the format, the recommendation was that training should happen at an institution-wide level, not just in some departments, and in a discipline-specific way: 'IPB should make training that is more private/personal — smaller groups, similar disciplines, not half or one day general training' (P7, 2015).

The need to build in higher English proficiency in reading and writing for students and staff was also clearly recognised. For students, this set of recommendations is representative: 'Get better Master students — use English as a selection criterion and restrict numbers. Give more English teaching using trained ERPP [English for Research Publication Purposes] teachers' (P5, 2015). This last comment refers to an additional training initiative that was undertaken by Dr Kate Cadman, from the School of Social Sciences at the University of Adelaide, at the same time as the research visit, with input from the first author. This initiative involved a full-day workshop for the public and invited guests, plus a train-the-trainer workshop for IPB English language teachers; it introduced the teaching and research specialty field of ERPP (Cargill & Burgess, 2008). This next response reflects the experience of one participant, highlighting the need for an integrated approach: 'Focus on both story/structure AND English grammar; workshops just like 2014; because we got a paper translated by the English service translator, but they have limitation in biology terms, therefore we had to modify it to correct one' (P15, 2015). One participant had specific suggestions about working with ERPP-trained staff for both student and staff training: 'Divide but teach both types in teams of scientist with trained ERPP staff: grammar stuff 30/70; scientific writing 70/30' (P19, 2015). Another respondent said: 'Staff English — make a ERPP course for them, but timing is an issue' (P6, 2015). Thus our workshop participants had both recognised the importance of addressing issues of English proficiency in discipline-specific ways, and developed ideas about how this could effectively be done in their institutional context.

4. Discussion

The 12-month gap between the 2014 delivery of our workshop and its re-evaluation by the participants in 2015 has allowed a fresh and informative perspective from which to view the effectiveness of this invited intervention. The picture we have been able to build falls between those that can be painted immediately after training interventions (for example, Cargill & O'Connor, 2012) and those developed from respondents' views gathered in the absence of a focus on any specific training (for example, Hanauer & Englander, 2013; Lillis & Curry, 2010). All three types can contribute to the search for understanding of the issues and challenges facing scholars seeking to publish their research in the context of the dominance of English, and comparing these types of study can add richness to the overall picture.

The workshop participants in 2014 reported significant gains in self-assessed confidence immediately post-workshop (means of 1.2-1.4 points on a seven-point Likert scale) for four competencies: writing a research article in English, mentoring others to write a research article in English, dealing with the publishing process in English, and mentoring others to deal with it. These gains are similar to those typically recorded after CIPSE workshops in China (Cargill & O'Connor, 2012). Of particular interest here is the finding that these gains appear to have been sustained over 12 months for the 20 participants (of 23) who were available in 2015, with modest further increases reported by most participants. The interview study was able to provide details of how participants' efforts to apply the training in their everyday academic working lives may have contributed to this sustained general increase in confidence.

We asked about the subsequent trajectories of the article drafts the participants had been working on in the 2014 workshop. (Not all participants had worked on a paper of their own — some enrolled specifically to gain skills in mentoring: the train-the-trainer cohort.) Of the 16 papers that were worked on, 3 had been published and 4 submitted in the subsequent 12 months — but 18 subsequent papers had been published in English language journals and 9 submitted (8 of the 27 in Scopus-listed journals). A large majority of these papers were with master's students, who are also required to publish their results, although not in Scopus-listed journals. The workload associated with supervising this large number of master's-level papers was identified as a factor leading to the lower productivity of their own first-authored papers for many participants, along with high teaching and administrative workloads. Suggestions for improving productivity included getting better master's students, increasing the English proficiency selection criterion, and introducing more English teaching with ERPP-trained teachers. The workshop materials and strategies had clearly been seen as useful, and used extensively, by the participants in their work with their master's students over the 12 months since the workshop delivery. This included in teaching various courses, in providing advice and mentoring in article preparation, and in correcting drafts. However, it was unclear whether the assistance provided by the workshop training was likely to free up sufficient time to have an impact on staff article productivity. It is well known that writing articles in English as an additional language [EAL] imposes extra burdens on scholars, and in particular that of the extra time taken to write and edit (Ferguson, Perez-Llantada & Plo, 2011; Flowerdew, 1999). Hanauer and Englander (2013) found that the extra burden experienced by scientist authors writing in English as a second language was greater for those working in a teaching institution, such as the one studied here, than in a research institute. Time was the top-rating single thing identified by our participants as most needed now for progress.

The cluster of factors covered by the terms 'facilities', 'infrastructure' and 'funding' was also commonly cited as most needed now for progress by our participants. There was a clear recognition that the limitations experienced in these areas were affecting the research being conducted and its suitability for publication in the level of journal being targeted by the university as a result of the national policy.

These findings further validate the choice taken early in the development of the CIPSE approach to use confidence as a surrogate measure for outcomes of the workshops (Cargill & O'Connor, 2006a, p. 212). They provide concrete examples of the kinds of factors that can and do intervene between training, however well conceived and presented, and outcomes in the form of published papers. This point is implicit in the strong focus on ethnographic research and text histories in the recent literature in the field of academic publishing (Hanauer & Englander, 2013; Lillis & Curry, 2010).

Participants' reports of what they had used most from the training in the following 12 months featured a strong emphasis on 'the whole package', and indeed the workshop slides, made available to participants in full, had been incorporated into materials used in their own teaching in various ways. Participants had used, in both classroom teaching and individual mentoring contexts, the recommended process for preparing an article, starting with results and the identification of a target journal that matches the type and level of the take-home message (Cargill & O'Connor, 2013, p. 109). It was reported that the effects of using the materials extended to encouraging and informing students' reading, itself important in the development of writing skills (Bazerman, 2007). This suggests that the CIPSE approach can contribute effectively to two of the types of educational intervention posited as useful by Hanauer and Englander (2013): explicit teaching and mentoring programs. The role of the thesis supervisor as mentor is clearly important in supporting first publication efforts by research students in the sciences (Lei & Hu, 2015). Recommendations to the institution by our participants included continuing the training of mentors using workshops like the one run in 2014 until a ratio of 1:5 is reached.

Specific elements of English grammar and usage were also frequently mentioned as most used. Twelve months post-workshop, the most commonly cited issue was verb tense — unsurprisingly, given the important role of tense in differentiating reference to past studies and current work, and in marking the author's stance and strength of claim (Swales & Feak, 1994), and the differences between English and Bahasa Indonesia in the marking of tense. This prominence contrasted with a more general usefulness of English grammar identified immediately post-workshop, and suggests that a reason for the shift may have been the relevance of tense to effective storytelling about results, related to the article-writing process focus mentioned previously. The concordancing software introduced and provided in the workshop, AdTAT (Hall, 2007), had been frequently used and introduced to students in a range of contexts, further validating the effectiveness of combining genre-analytic and corpus linguistics approaches for teaching and mentoring article writing (Burgess & Cargill, 2013).

However, issues with the linguistic aspects of article writing clearly remained a strong concern for our participants. The variability of the English abilities of research students, especially master's students, added to their mentoring workload to a large extent. Their recommendations for institutional support for article writing included improving the recruitment of students to increase the English proficiency level used as a criterion, and the introduction of more instruction in discipline-specific English by appropriately trained ERPP teachers. These recommendations echo those of Hanauer and Englander (2013), working in a Mexican university science context. They suggest (in their Figure 8.5, p. 157) commencing explicit instruction and mentoring in scientific writing (and reading) at the bachelor level, in both students' first language and English, and then adding to the types of support provided as students proceed through the master's and PhD levels to become professional scientists/academic staff. The funding implications of such a change in the IPB context would be significant, but without it, efforts to increase publication outputs in line with the university's policy goals are likely to be severely handicapped. Improved participant preparation, including in English, was recognised as the most important improvement that could be made to the workshop, from the perspective of 12 months' experience. The institution's ability to provide the sort of instruction and mentoring recommended by our participants will depend on building a skilled cohort of ERPP-trained staff. The move from general English teaching for passing a TOEFL-type examination to ERPP would require ongoing specialist training. This could build on the foundation laid in 2015, which identified a core of interested staff.

Additional support is also recommended for academic staff by our participants, in terms both of a course to raise English writing skills for those who need it, and of a consultant available to work on drafts with authors in the ways demonstrated during the 2014 workshop. This recommendation echoes the situation in other comparable countries where English is an additional language. Even in Iceland, a country where exposure to English is high and general English proficiency is good but much university education is delivered in Icelandic, almost two-thirds of 238 academics surveyed reported that they needed assistance in writing papers in English (Ingvarsdóttir &

Arnbjörnsdóttir, 2013). A similar situation has been reported from Spain (Moreno, Rey-Rocha, Burgess, López-Navarro & Sachdev, 2012).

Thus the recommendations made by our participants 12 months after the training intervention echoed to a notable degree the seven principles identified by Hanauer and Englander (2013, pp. 166-7) as parameters for institutional decision making:

- long-term commitment to writing education
- differential needs and diversified educational interventions
- multilayered understanding of the research article
- provision of expert support for science and writing
- personalised, continual and immediate support for research article writing
- demystification of the structures and processes of scientific publication
- broad administrative, institutional and financial support.

5. Conclusions

In summary, CIPSE workshop participants reported significantly increased confidence to write articles and deal with the publishing process in English and to mentor others in both areas, and the increases were sustained 12 months later. Their recommendations from the 12-month perspective emphasised the importance of institutional-level support for journal article writing delivered in discipline-specific ways. For master's-level students, credit-bearing courses were preferred, combining materials from the 2014 workshop with the research methodology courses already offered in the various faculties and departments. To facilitate this, there was a desire to see the workshop textbook (Cargill & O'Connor, 2013) translated into Indonesian. (Notification has recently been received of the signing of an agreement with the publisher for this to occur, with full funding support provided by IPB.)

However, parallel recommendations concerned strengthening the master's student recruitment process by increasing the English proficiency criterion, and improving instruction in English scientific writing using staff trained in ERPP, including genre-analytic and corpus linguistics methods. These changes are expected to help alleviate the workload pressure that is currently affecting the conversion of a highly positive training experience into published papers at the level desired by the Indonesian higher education sector. For staff, repeated CIPSE workshops were recommended, during the exam period, to increase the ratio of trained mentors to students to 1:5. The strongest recommendation to improve the workshops was better participant preparation beforehand, both in terms of English language ability and prior preparation of an advanced draft manuscript. Expert feedback on drafts was seen as a strong ongoing need, as was improved funding for infrastructure and facilities to address issues with the type and quality of research data that often led to rejection.

This interrelated set of recommendations represents a synthesis of the immediate post-workshop evaluations of participants with their views after 12 months of applying the workshop materials and strategies in the workplace, providing a more nuanced picture of their situation. It reflects similarities with findings from other comparable resource-limited contexts where scientists are facing increased pressure to publish their research in journals written in English but where English is an additional language. What can be claimed on the basis of this analysis, however, is that the CIPSE training approach has provided these Indonesian workshop participants with effective conceptual and practical tools to help manage the pressures they face.

Acknowledgements

We thank the Department of Biology, IPB, and The Crawford Fund, South Australia for supporting the 2014 workshop (Project ID: SA-641-2014), as well as Dr Sukendra Mahalaya for valuable translation assistance in the workshop. *The University of Adelaide Priority Partner Grant 2015 — Bogor Agricultural University [IPB]* and the Directorate of Research and Innovation IPB supported the 2015 follow-up research visit.

References

Bazerman, C. (Ed.). (2007). *Handbook of research on writing.* New York: Routledge.

Burgess, S., & Cargill, M. (2013). Using genre analysis and corpus linguistics to teach research article writing. In V. Matarese (Ed.), *Supporting research writing: Roles and challenges in multilingual settings* (pp. 55-71). Cambridge: Woodhead Publishing.

Cannon, R., & Hore, T. (1997). The long-term effects of 'one-shot' professional development courses: An Indonesian case study. *International Journal for Academic Development, 2*(1), 35-42. DOI: http://dx.doi.org/10.1080/1360144970020104.

Cargill, M. (2011). *Collaborative interdisciplinary publication skills education: Implementation and implications in international science research contexts* (Doctor of Education thesis, The University of Adelaide). Retrieved 8 February 2017 from http://digital.library.adelaide.edu.au/dspace/handle/2440/72719.

Cargill, M., & Burgess, S. (2008). Introduction to the special issue: English for Research Publication Purposes. *Journal of English for Academic Purposes, 7*(2), 75-76.

Cargill, M., & O'Connor, P. (2006a). Developing Chinese scientists' skills for publishing in English: Evaluating collaborating-colleague workshops based on genre analysis. *Journal of English for Academic Purposes, 5*(3), 207-221.

Cargill, M., & O'Connor, P. (2006b). Getting research published in English: Towards a curriculum design model for developing skills and enhancing outcomes. *Revista Canaria de Estudios Ingleses, 53*, 79-94.

Cargill, M., & O'Connor, P. (2010). Structuring interdisciplinary collaboration to develop research students' skills for publishing research internationally: Lessons from implementation.

In M. Davies, M. Devlin, & M. Tight (Eds.), *International perspectives on higher education research series: Vol. 5. Interdisciplinary higher education: Perspectives and practicalities* (pp. 279-292). Bingley, UK: Emerald Group Publishing Ltd.

Cargill, M., & O'Connor, P. (2012). Identifying and addressing challenges to international publication success for EFL science researchers: Implementing an integrated training package in China. In R. Tang (Ed.), *Academic writing in a second or foreign language: Issues and challenges facing ESL/EFL academic writers in higher education contexts* (pp. 21-44). London: Continuum.

Cargill, M., & O'Connor, P. (2013). *Writing scientific research articles: Strategy and steps* (2nd ed.). Oxford: Wiley-Blackwell.

Cargill, M., O'Connor, P., & Li, Y. (2012). Educating Chinese scientists to write for international journals: Addressing the divide between science and technology education and English language teaching. *English for Specific Purposes, 31*, 60-69. DOI: http://dx.doi.org/10.1016/j.esp.2011.05.03.

Cargill, M., O'Connor, P., & Matthews, R. (2014). Publication skills development in the sciences: Decision support for effective program design. *Revista Canaria de Estudios Ingleses, 69*, 101-114.

Directorate Generale of Higher Education-Indonesian Ministry of Education. (2012). Surat Edaran No. 152/E/T/2012 tentang Publikasi Karya Ilmiah. Indonesia: Indonesian Ministry of Education.

Ferguson, G., Perez-Llantada, C., & Plo, R. (2011). English as an international language of scientific publication: A study of attitudes. *World Englishes, 30*(1), 41-59.

Flowerdew, J. (1999). Problems in writing for scholarly publication in English: The case of Hong Kong. *Journal of Second Language Writing, 8*(3), 243-264.

Hall, A. (2007). Adelaide Text Analysis Tool (Version 1.5) [Concordancer]. Adelaide: University of Adelaide. Retrieved 8 February 2017 from https://www.adelaide.edu.au/carst/resources-tools/adtat.

Hanauer, D.I., & Englander, K. (2013). *Scientific writing in a second language*. Anderson, SC, USA: Parlor Press.

Ingvarsdóttir, H., & Arnbjörnsdóttir, B. (2013). ELF and academic writing: A perspective from the expanding circle. *Journal of English as a Lingua Franca, 2*(1), 123-145.

Lei, J., & Hu, G. (2015). Apprenticeship in scholarly publishing: A student perspective on doctoral supervisors' roles. *Publications, 3*, 27-42. DOI: http://dx.doi.org/10.3390/publications3010027.

Li, Y. (2006). *Writing for international publication: The case of Chinese doctoral science students* (doctoral thesis, City University of Hong Kong, Hong Kong).

Li, Y., & Flowerdew, J. (2007). Shaping Chinese novice scientists' manuscripts for publication. *Journal of Second Language Writing, 16*(2), 100-117.

Lillis, T., & Curry, M.J. (2010). *Academic writing in a global context: The politics and practices of publishing in English*. London: Routledge.

Moreno, A.I., Rey-Rocha, J., Burgess, S., López-Navarro, I., & Sachdev, I. (2012). Spanish researchers' perceived difficulty writing research articles for English medium journals: The impact of proficiency in English versus publication experience. *Ibérica, 24*, 157-184.

Sadtono, E. (2001). Fighting a losing battle : English for Academic Purposes in Indonesia. *NUCB journal of language culture and communication, 3*(1), 45-58.

Sanjaya, I.N.S., Sitawati, A.A.R., & Suciani, N.K. (2015). Comparing hedges used by English and Indonesian scholars in published research articles: A corpus-based study. *TEFLIN Journal, 26*(2), 209-227. DOI: http://dx.doi.org/10.15639/teflinjournal.v26i2/209-227.

Swales, J.M., & Feak, C.B. (1994). *Academic writing for graduate students: A course for nonnative speakers of English*. Ann Arbor: University of Michigan Press.

Appendix I

CIPSE Workshop Outline: IPB, Sep.-Oct. 2014[1]

M. Cargill, P. O'Connor and S. Mahalaya

Day 1

1. Introductions, questionnaires; workshop goals and methodology; results take-home messages and journal choice issues; article structures and referee criteria; presentation of participants' journal choices
2. English development issues: concordancing and the New Phytologist corpus; sentence templates
3. Results as article 'driver'; data presentation and refining figures and tables; writing results sentences
4. Revision of Results drafts (continued for homework)

Day 2

1. Q&A on results revisions
2. Methods input and revision of prepared methods sections
3. Introductions (genre analysis of examples) and flow/readability issues
4. Drafting/revising Introduction sections (continued for homework)

Day 3

1. Q&A on Introduction sections
2. Discussion/conclusion sections and strength of claim issues
3. Drafting/revising Discussion and Conclusions (continued for homework)

Day 4

1. Abstracts/summaries; drafting of abstracts
2. Titles and keywords; revision of titles/keywords
3. Process recap and editing procedures
4. Revision/redrafting with input from presenters

---

1 This outline is extracted from the (unpublished) Powerpoint slides used for the workshop given by Cargill, O'Connor and Mahalaya in 2014.

Day 5
1. Submitting and covering letters
2. Responding to reviewers' and editors' comments
3. Final revisions with input from presenters
4. Discussion of pedagogic options for the Department
5. Final questionnaires and evaluation

9

'The one who is out of the ordinary shall win':

Research supervision towards publication in a Chinese hospital

Yongyan Li

1. Introduction

Research supervision and research education success have been issues of extensive interest for educators at the tertiary level. Much attention is being paid to what happens in the university setting (for example, Casanave & Li, 2008; McCallin & Nayar, 2011). At the same time, research mentoring in medical contexts, which involves senior clinician researchers and medical students or junior clinician researchers, has also been an issue of long-standing interest in academic medicine (for example, DeCastro, Sambuco, Ubel, Stewart & Jagsi, 2013). Yet although there seems to be some consensus on what characterises a good mentor and what an effective mentoring relationship might be like (Casanave & Li, 2008; Zerzan, Hess, Schur, Phillips & Rigotti, 2009), surprisingly little is known as to how research supervision and mentoring actually unfolds in its natural settings, especially as to how it is manifested through the mentor's verbal communication. In Asia and elsewhere in the world, given the widespread requirement for research students to publish — especially at the doctoral level across the disciplines of science and medicine — including in English-medium international journals (for example, Barbero, 2008; Huang, 2010; Li, 2016), understanding the process of research supervisory communication will have theoretical and pedagogical implications. The present chapter aims to make a contribution in this direction by reporting a study on how the director of the Orthopedics Department at a major Chinese hospital mentors his students through verbal communication to push the novices to work hard in scientific research and publication.

I will first give a brief overview of the potential benefits for medical students of engaging in research and the challenge that their supervision poses in Chinese hospitals. I will then outline the theoretical background of the study, based as it is on some tenets drawn from cultural-historical activity theory [CHAT] (Engeström, 1987, 2000, 2001, 2009; Engeström, Miettinen & Punamäki, 1999).

1.1. Medical students as researchers and the publication requirement for Chinese medical students

Literature in medical education suggests that it is professionally significant for medical students to engage in research and publishing. It has been acknowledged that research prepares medical students for the practice of medicine, for 'the ability to understand and integrate new knowledge into clinical practice is a necessary quality of good physicians' (Parsonnet, Gruppuso, Kanter & Boninger, 2010, p. 405). Research also develops the students' critical skills in reading the literature, analysing the data and writing for publication, and cultivates positive attitudes towards future research (Dyrbye, Thomas, Papp & Durning, 2008; van Eyk et al., 2010). Furthermore, medical students can contribute to the research productivity of a host institution, and, in a more instrumental light, research-based publishing will both give the students advantage in a competitive job market and facilitate their career path selection (Griffin & Hindocha, 2011).

Chinese postgraduate medical students attached to major teaching hospitals are generally under the dual pressures of their university's requirement for them to publish ('publish or no degree') and to participate in a clinical internship. To meet their graduation requirement, a master's student is usually expected to publish one Chinese article in an indexed national journal, while a doctoral student should publish two English-medium articles in international SCI [Science Citation Index] journals, or one such article plus two domestically indexed papers (Li, 2014a). From the point of view of supervision, the great number of postgraduate medical students attached to the country's teaching hospitals poses a major challenge for their full-time clinical supervisors in terms of providing quality research supervision, as these doctors generally have busy clinical schedules (Li, 2014b) and their research experience and level of commitment to research vary widely (Liang & Chen, 2009). In this situation, the strong leadership of a research-minded senior supervisor would seem to be crucial for potential research productivity.

1.2. Theoretical background

As a collective human activity, research supervision can be usefully examined by drawing upon cultural-historical activity theory [CHAT], or activity theory (Engeström, 1987; Engeström et al., 1999; Leont'ev, 1978; Vygotsky, 1978). Under activity theory, collective human activity is the basic unit of analysis and an activity system can be represented in a dynamic triangular structure (as seen in Figure 9.1, to be described in detail in Section 2.1), which sets up dialectal relationships between a number of nodes. In the upper part, there are the *subject* (the actor whose point of view is adopted in the analysis); the *object* (the problem space), which is continuously being transformed into the *outcome*; and the *tools* (material or symbolic artifacts mediating the object-directed activity). In the lower part of the structure, there are the *rules* (the explicit and implicit norms/values that govern the activity), the *community* (the socio-historical environment of the activity), and the *division of labour* (the different roles of the participants and their power relationship). Contemporary activity theory places an emphasis upon studying the interacting relationships between activity systems (Engeström, 2001). Such interacting relationships may take a variety of forms. For example, two activities may have a partially shared object (Engeström, 2001), or there may be two interwoven activity systems, with each being altered somewhat as a result (Li, 2014b; Prior & Shipka, 2003). Alternatively, there may be a 'flow' of elements (which occupy the nodes of the triangular structure described above) between activity systems (Barab, Barnett, Yamagata-Lynch, Squire & Keating, 2002; Engeström, 2009).

In addition, a hierarchical view of activity posits that object-directed activity comprises sequences of goal-oriented *actions* (Engeström, 2000; Leont'ev, 1978). The literature has addressed both academic and professional contexts in illustrating (Engeström, 2000) or applying (Li, 2013, 2014b; Barab et al., 2002) the hierarchical view of activity. Previous research has mostly focused on physical actions as being constitutive of an activity — for example, actions taken by a student in fulfilling a written assignment, or by a group of students in fulfilling a classroom task, or by a doctor in diagnosing a patient (Li, 2013, 2014b; Barab et al., 2002; Engeström, 2000). However, it may also be possible to apply the hierarchical view of activity to studying rhetorical actions. As Bazerman (1997) pointed out, the structure of an academic text reflects 'the goal of many of the supporting actions' (p. 297). Similarly, a supervisor's commentary during a student's oral presentation at a research meeting represents a form of structured oral discourse comprising sequences or strings of goal-oriented rhetorical actions, such as asking the student a question, giving a suggestion on data interpretation, or pointing out a major problem in the student's research design. What gives coherence to these actions is the macro-level motive-carrying object (Engeström, 2000) — for example, progress in research and quality work.

2. The study

In exploring a supervisor's verbal communication in the activity of research supervision at a Chinese hospital, I was guided in my study for this chapter by two research questions:

1. What neighbouring activity systems provide the main sources of reference in the supervisor's mentoring of his student supervisees? (That is, what neighbouring activity systems does the research supervision activity interact with?)

2. What rhetorical actions constitute the supervisor's commentaries during his students' presentations at research meetings?

The study was part of a larger project that I conducted during April through to December 2012 at the Orthopedics Department of a major Chinese hospital located in east China, in order to investigate how research takes place in the department (Li, 2014a, 2014b). Convenience facilitated by a personal contact and the fact that the department was reputable clinically and research-wise had led to my selection of the research site. Thus the research site has the quality of being 'intrinsically interesting' so that it merits study in its own right (Denscomb, 2007, p. 41).

The department consists of four specialist sections, each headed by a chief doctor and the largest by the department director. In the following section, based on the data gathered in the larger project (see Li, 2014a, 2014b), I will briefly examine the research supervision activity in the section headed by the department director through the lens of CHAT, before describing the data collection and data analysis procedures adopted for the study.

2.1. *The department director and the research supervision activity in his specialist section*

The director was in his mid-50s and was a reputable surgeon in his specialist field in the country. After a decade of clinical experience, and upon obtaining a higher medical degree in the early 1990s, he went overseas and accumulated many years of clinical experience before joining the present hospital in the early 2000s. Under his strong leadership, his department, and in particular his specialist section, had earned a strong reputation in research. At the time of the study, the section had an attachment of 17 postgraduate students (all male, in their 20s), about two-thirds being master's students and the rest doctoral students. The director was referred to by the students as 'the big boss', and his doctorate-holder research-active colleagues in the section, for whom there was also an English publication requirement of two SCI papers every three years (Li, 2014a), were known as 'the second-tier bosses [supervisors]'. These latter numbered about seven at the time of the study: all were male, and all but one, who was in his 40s, were in their 30s. Adopting the triangular structure of activity system depicted in the literature (Engeström, 1987; Engeström et al., 1999), Figure 9.1 presents the activity system of research supervision in the director's specialist section, from the point of view of the director.

The *object* in Figure 9.1 is portrayed as quality research and efficient publication. 'Quality' here pertains to publishing in high-ranking international and national journals; and efficiency applies to both the students and the second-tier supervisors when meeting the publication requirements. Both quality and efficiency contribute to the credentials of the section and the department. Publication requirements and data collection protocols constitute salient *rules*; while the *community* covers the specialist section led

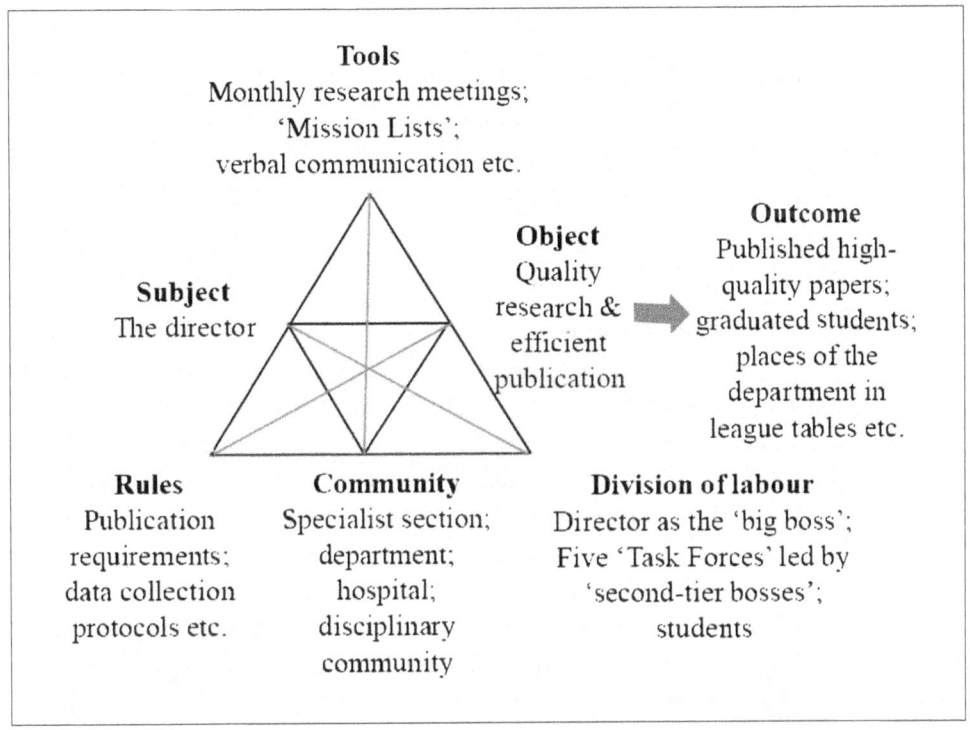

Figure 9.1: The activity system of research supervision in the director's specialist section.

by the director, the department, the hospital and the wider disciplinary community. The *division of labour* reflects the section's multigenerational supervisory system (Rose, Rukstalis & Schuckit, 2005), with a set-up of five 'Task Forces' (as they were called in the section), each focusing on a research direction led by a second-tier supervisor and including a group of medical students at master's and doctoral levels. Monthly research meetings, 'Mission Lists' (the original English title used for the documents), and verbal communication are listed under the *tools*. As stipulated by the director, the second-tier supervisors and the students in the section, each has a Mission List which lays out their research topics by 'basic research' and 'clinical research', with progress on each topic indicated and updated before each meeting. (Progress may be delineated, for example, in the following ways: protocol 70%, data collection 50%, measurement 30%, draft 10%, under review with an indicated journal, and so on). The verbal communication of the director — that is, what he says to the second-tier supervisors and the students, on a daily basis but in particular at monthly research meetings — is also listed as an important mediational tool in Figure 9.1. The director's verbal remarks targeted at the medical students attached to his specialist section constituted the focus of the study presented below.

2.2. Data collection and data analysis

The data of a number of sources formed the basis of this study:

1. one particular item in a questionnaire responded to by the 17 students attached to the director's section
2. interviews with 14 of the students who were available for interview
3. my observations at the section's monthly research meetings on three dates in April and June 2012.

The short Chinese-medium questionnaire used in the first source was designed to obtain preliminary information on the students' research activities; one item in the questionnaire invited them to write down three of the director's remarks which impressed them, as well as their understanding of the director's intentions in making these remarks. The interviews with the students which made up the second source were conducted in Mandarin Chinese, aimed to better understand their research activities and their views of the director's verbal remarks; the interviewees were accessed with the help of a student representative, a second-year doctoral student referred to as 'monitor' in the director's section. With regards to the meetings that were used as the third source for this study, two consecutive meetings were held one day apart in June, with the second convened to carry on the agenda of presentations which had not been completed in the first meeting. Such research meetings typically lasted between 4 to 6 hours each time and my attendance at the meetings on the three dates in April and June 2012 was 3.5 hours, 5.5 hours and 2 hours respectively. In the first meeting that I attended, I took observational notes; I conducted audio-recording at the latter two meetings in addition to note-taking. The relevant parts in the interviews and research meetings were later transcribed for analysis.

For data analysis, following initial familiarisation with the data and summary of the relevant questionnaire data in a tabular form, these summaries, the interview and research meeting transcripts, and my observational notes at the meetings were then coded in order in NVivo (a qualitative data analysis software program[1]). To answer the first research question outlined in Section 2, I first put the director's remarks into an array of different subgroups, each represented by a representative remark (see the second column in Table 9.1); these subgroups (of codes) are then subsumed under four broader categories (see the first column in Table 9.1) to indicate the meanings conveyed (that is, 'Go beyond the minimum requirement to aim high', 'Dedicate to research and adopt a high standard', 'Work hard to move up the social ladder', and 'Achieve success to uphold family honour'). While mapping out such a 'typology' (Bryman & Burgess, 1994) of verbal communication *tools*, I also made notes on the underlying moral messages; these underlying messages were found to constitute *rules* in a range of five neighbouring source

---

1 See http://www.qsrinternational.com/.

activity systems in which the novices were also participants. In other words, I recognised that there was a 'flow' (Engeström, 2009) of *rules* from some neighbouring activity systems which helped construct the *tools* in the central activity of research supervision.

For answering the second research question, the focus of analysis was on the supervisor's commentaries at research meetings during the individual students' presentations on their projects. NVivo-based and manual analyses were conducted simultaneously, combining categorising and connecting strategies (Maxwell & Miller, 2008) in order both to look for regularities in the supervisor's rhetorical actions and to examine how they formed sequences in context. As shown in Table 9.2, the supervisor's rhetorical actions were found to fall into three categories.

The following section will elaborate on the hierarchical classification systems (Patton, 1990) constructed during the process of data analysis, in order to answer the two research questions specified in Section 2 respectively. I refer to the director as 'the supervisor', in order to clarify his role in relation to his students.

3. Findings

3.1. Rules *in neighbouring activity systems underlying the supervisor's verbal communication* tools *in the research supervision activity*

Table 9.1 (with the Chinese *pinyin* of a few figurative expressions provided in italics) indicates that rules from five neighbouring activity systems — those of evaluation, publishing world, scientific research world, competitive society-at-large, and Chinese culture — were drawn upon by the students' 'big boss' supervisor, or the director of the department in this case, to construct the tools in the central activity of research supervision.

The connections between the supervisor's categories of verbal communication tools and the five source activity systems, as captured in Table 9.1, are reflected in the headings of the sections below. His words are indicated by the use of inverted commas.

3.1.1. *Going beyond the minimum requirement to aim high to accommodate evaluation and the publishing world*

The supervisor expected the students attached to his section to go beyond the minimum requirement of publication stipulated by their universities and to aim to do the best they could in their publication goal. There was thus a concern for both quantity (fulfilling the number required) and quality (achieving excellence, typically through publishing English papers in SCI international journals), which together accommodated rules in the evaluation system and the publishing world.

As each student had a collection of 'basic' and 'clinical' research topics (linked to their second-tier supervisor's projects in a 'Task Force' group) as indicated in their

Mission List, the idea was that they were expected to move ahead by working on multiple topics and multiple papers at the same time. To the supervisor, some papers would be relatively easy to write up, and these should be dealt with first as *duan ping kuan* (short, plain and fast) types. Furthermore, publications were of different levels — 'diamond', 'gold', 'silver' and 'bronze', in the words of the supervisor. Higher-grade publications or papers published in prestigious journals would be looked up in the publishing world while bringing extra credits in evaluation, and therefore they should be earnestly pursued. The supervisor would say to the students, 'Hurry up on these gold-standard papers!' or, 'You don't have a gold-standard paper in hand yet!'

Papers published in overseas, English-medium, indexed journals were of a higher grade in the supervisor's eyes than those published in Chinese-language journals. He referred to English as '*yangwen*', an archaic expression in Chinese for 'foreign tongue', rather than as *yingwen* or *yingyu*, the contemporary expressions for 'English', in order to figuratively highlight the power of the English language and the relative lack of power of Chinese-speaking authors in this situation. ('*Yangwen a yangwen!*' he would say, meaning, 'English, o English!'). He advised: 'Produce Chinese publications first to *baodi* (meet the minimum requirement) and then *siqiu* (fight to death for) *yangwen* papers!'

3.1.2. Dedication and a high standard are expected in the research world

One student said in an interview: 'When I first entered the department, the director kept telling us: being a doctor you can't just know how to do surgeries, you should also collect data for research,

The director's verbal communication tools		Rules called upon in the source activity systems	Source activity systems
Categories	Representative remarks		
Go beyond the minimum requirement to aim high	• '*Duan ping kuan* (short, plain and fast) papers' (can be produced first). • 'You don't have a gold-standard paper in hand yet!'	• The number of publications counts. • Speed counts in publishing. • Publications are of different levels. • Prestigious publications bring pride.	• Evaluation • Publishing world

Table 9.1: The supervisor drawing upon *rules* from source activity systems to create verbal communication *tools* in research supervision.

Publishing Research in English as an Additional Language · 195

Dedicate to research and adopt a high standard	• 'Produce Chinese publications first to *baodi* [meet the minimum requirement] and then *siqiu* [fight to death for] *yangwen* [English] papers!'	• Meet the publication requirement first. English publication is privileged and should be the more important goal.	• Scientific research world
	• 'This matter I will get done well without eating or drinking.'	• Research is a priority and dedication is required.	
	• 'Scientific thinking is important.'	• Scientific thinking is a basic requirement in doing research.	
	• 'Does it *jiegui* [connect] with the international?'	• An 'international' standard should be adopted in research and writing.	
Work hard to move up the social ladder	• 'five mountains'	• The realities are tough and one can only tackle them by working hard.	• Competitive society-at-large
	• 'the three secrets of success'	• Be different.	
	• 'Be prepared to *po fu cheng zhou* [break the caldrons and sink the boats or cut off all means of retreat].'	• Determination is required for success.	
	• 'Have you positioned yourself?'	• Know your direction and work hard from the beginning.	
Achieve success to uphold family honour	• 'You have three years to change fate.'	• Change your humble background by working hard.	• Chinese culture
	• 'Your family places high hopes on you.'	• Fulfilling parents' expectations is virtuous.	
	• 'You should earn some honour for your family.'	• Bringing honour to family is laudable.	

develop understanding of issues and write papers'. For research, the supervisor stressed dedication, rigour and an 'international' standard, all of which are supposedly *rules* that participants in the scientific research world are expected to abide by.

Many students were particularly impressed by one remark that the supervisor urged them to say to themselves: 'This matter I will get done well without eating or drinking'. This meant that students should approach research with determination and strong willpower, and be prepared to prioritise it even at the cost of physical suffering. In sharpening one's 'scientific thinking', the director emphasised, students should be 'quick-minded' and sensitive to valuable patient-cases during data collection; they should also 'attend to details', since 'details determine the result'; and they should 'double-check' results. Importantly, both research and writing should 'connect with' (*jiegui*) the 'international' standard. At research meetings, the director would ask from time to time: 'Does the protocol connect well with the international?' 'Does the title connect well with the international?' He was blunt in pointing out that the standard he expected of his students was not the same as that which might be more commonly found in other Chinese hospitals: 'Not many do research in our way'. By this, the supervisor seemed to urge the students to draw a line between themselves and lower standards. He took pride in the high standard that he expected of his section's research, pointing out that the section had a 'more demanding' requirement than that at a corresponding department of a university outside mainland China with whom they had a joint doctoral program.

3.1.3. Working hard to move up the social ladder is the way to go in a competitive society

The competitive society-at-large is run by many rules for survival and success. The supervisor evoked these rules in characterising the kinds of challenges faced by the students and in proposing ways to 'march forward with the tide of time'.

He talked of 'five mountains' faced by the students: getting into the doctoral program (given an examination-based and highly competitive selection process); graduation (given the 'publish or no degree' policy); finding a job (in an acutely competitive job market); buying a house (possession of a great sum of money being a precondition); and finding a spouse (for which both financial and job security were needed). As seen in the questionnaire and interviews, the students held very similar views on the best way to scale the 'five mountains': they aimed to prioritise study at present and work hard to excel, believing that the rest would be resolved naturally. Apparently, the supervisor's teaching on a daily basis had gone down well.

The supervisor also spoke of 'the three secrets of success': 'Knowledge shall change fate'; 'English shall change the employment'; and 'The one who is out of the ordinary shall win'. The last of the three aphorisms (Chinese *pinyin*: '*yu zhong bu tong zhe sheng*') became a phrase often cited by the students among themselves over time. Merely meeting the minimum requirement of publication, which would also be achieved by others, 'guarantees a degree certificate but does not guarantee a job', the supervisor warned.

The supervisor capitalised on Chinese idioms and referred to the story of one particular student as exemplifying a case of *po fu cheng zhou* ('breaking the caldrons and sinking the boats, or cutting off all means of retreat)'. This student, having failed to be admitted into the doctoral program headed by the supervisor in a previous attempt, decided to give it a second try instead of looking for a job, despite the fact that he would be financially pressurised during the year of preparing for the next round of entry examinations. One should be prepared to *po fu cheng zhou* in pursuing dreams, the supervisor emphasised. How can one afford not to know the direction one must go in and work hard towards it from the very beginning? He questioned new students: 'Have you positioned yourself?' Alternatively, he simply chided: 'You have not positioned yourself yet!' or 'You have not entered your role yet!'

3.1.4. Achieving success to uphold family honour is a virtue in the Chinese culture

For many university students in China, who come from less well-off regions of the country, being able to go to a big city for university and find a job thereafter in a major city is a dream coming true. The achievement is also considered immensely glorious, by changing one's destiny and bringing honour to family. The supervisor tapped into these values in the Chinese culture in his exhortations to the novices.

He conveyed a message of urgency in saying to the students that they could turn their lives around by working hard: 'You have three years of a golden opportunity to change your fate'.[2] He would pick on students' names and point out that they should live up to their parents' expectations. One student's name contained a character composed of three 金.[3] The mentor remarked: 'Three gold — your family places high hopes on you: making a huge amount of money', implying that the student should work hard. Two students' names contained the character 龙.[4] The director said to them: 'You should earn some honour for your family'. One student's name (consisting of two characters) was homophonous with the Chinese equivalent of 'marshal general' (also two characters); so the director asserted, while commenting on the student's presentation at a research meeting, that he should act like a marshal general. The first name of another student

---

2   In China, the normative candidature for a master's degree and for doctoral study lasts three years in each case.

3   The character made of three 金 (*jin* [gold]) is 鑫 (*xin*). When used in (male) names, the latter character means 'rich and prosperous'. Chinese parents give their children names composed of characters which have positive meanings and which sometimes imply their expectations for their children's future. Simplified Chinese characters used in mainland China are adopted in the present chapter.

4   The Chinese character 龙 (*long* [dragon]), when used in (male) names, implies nobility and success.

198 · Publishing Research in English as an Additional Language

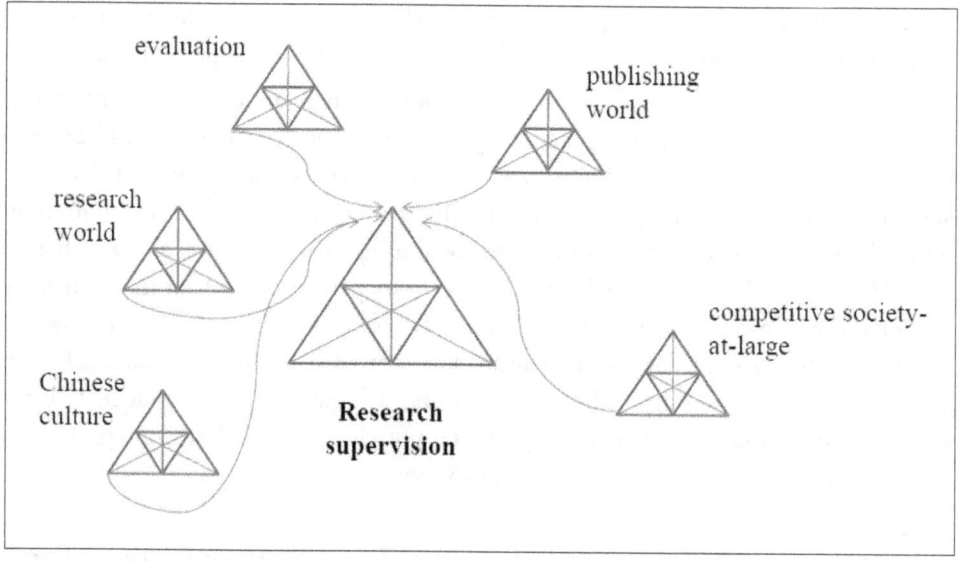

Figure 9.2: The 'flow' of rules from neighbouring activity systems to the node of *tools* in the activity of research supervision.

consisted of two characters that literally meant 'overtaking tigers' — needless to say, the supervisor picked on that to suggest that the student should live up to his name and fulfill his parents' wishes!

As a summary, Figure 9.2 depicts the flow of *rules* from the five neighbouring activity systems to the node of *tools* in the central activity of research supervision.

3.2. The supervisor's rhetorical actions at research meetings

The section-level monthly research meetings were the central venue in which the supervisor advised on projects and papers. Table 9.2 summarises the supervisor's rhetorical actions into three categories: 'Advising on the research process', 'Advising on paper strategies', and 'Criticising/warning/reminding', each with a range of subcategories.

In the following sections, the three categories are elaborated separately, with details that illustrate the subcategories shown in Table 9.2.

Categories	Subcategories
Advising on the research process	• data collection • data analysis • project planning • time management • use of resources

Advising on paper strategies	• suggesting the topic/content/scope of a paper • strategic planning on Chinese vs. English papers • target journal selection and paper submission
Criticising/warning/reminding	• warning on slow progress/not to meet the graduation requirement • urging attentive listening and note-taking • holding the second-tier supervisor responsible • reminding the monitor to take notes for the student presenter

Table 9.2: The supervisor's rhetorical actions at research meetings.

3.2.1. Advising on the research process

The supervisor gave plenty of comments and reminders concerning the research process. Advice was given on

1. data collection (for example, that the patient-cases at both the wards and the outpatient clinic [OPC] should be collected, and that patient films of the post-operation check should also be gathered)
2. data analysis (for example, the supervisor might say, 'Measure [the data] as you collect them', or he might point out that that a student's work had 'fatal flaws' in its measurement method)
3. project planning (for example, the supervisor might say, 'You should have back-up [clinical] projects when doing basic research', since basic research tends to be slow in producing results; or, 'Hurry up on research that will lead to gold-standard papers')
4. time management (for example, 'Measurement is a humanly controllable stage, so speed up on it to leave more time for drafting the paper'; or, 'Write it up by the end of the year'; or, 'Submit it soon')
5. use of resources, which could include:
   a. encouraging internal mutual support (for example, 'Has XXX [another student] used the method before? Go talk to XXX about it', and 'Can you co-author the paper?')
   b. suggesting utilisable external resources (for example, 'Go and communicate with the Department of Anesthesiology'; or, 'Discuss with our collaborators in [a region outside mainland China]')
   c. assuring financial support (for example, 'Adopt an international standard; don't worry about the money'; or, 'The expenses on phone cards can be claimed').

3.2.2. Advising on paper strategies

Given that 'published high-quality papers' makes up part of the outcome of the research supervision activity (see Figure 9.1), it is not surprising that the director also constantly made suggestions on paper strategies. Referring to the paper topics proposed by a student (usually in consultation with his second-tier supervisor) in his Mission List or on a PowerPoint slide, or in the middle of discussing certain topics, the supervisor might suggest a related topic for an additional paper, with suggestions on its scope and content. An indicative remark might be: 'It can be broken down to several papers, definitely not just one. You may include a Chinese paper'.

The 'Task Forces' (research groups) in the supervisor's specialist section aimed to publish both Chinese and English papers, with the latter considered more prestigious, as indicated earlier. To the supervisor, in general, for each project there should be a few 'decent Chinese papers'; and some work might be good for a Chinese version only, when 'the data are important but have no reference value for foreigners' and 'an English version would be incomprehensible to those Chinese readers who might be interested'. For Chinese papers (which are relatively short), students should normally 'just ensure there is no error or no self-contradiction'. By contrast, in putting together an English paper, which is worth 'fighting to death for' when there is a 'diamond-/gold-standard paper', one might consider 'combining the best results in these several Chinese papers', or 'adding additional validation procedures'.

Paper-related strategies also included deliberating over the selection of target journals and submission strategies. That is, when not too sure of a target journal, a student might try and submit to a journal to 'pique its interest', the supervisor advised; and when the work crossed over several specialist areas, it might be a good idea to 'try an on-the-border, not highly-specialised journal'. There was also a timing issue in paper submission: 'For those who need to graduate next year, submit in July or August at the latest!'

3.2.3. Criticising/warning/reminding

With reference to the graduation time and the need to meet the publication requirement, the supervisor might say to a student who was not making satisfactory progress: 'You should graduate next year; how can you graduate?' With the warning he might then outline a course of action for the student. He might also criticise a student for falling behind schedule, for not concentrating on research enough, or for failing to present an interim report at an earlier point so that a 'fatal flaw' in research design was not detected earlier. In addition, a second-tier supervisor might be criticised for failing to keep an eye on a student's progress.

As he gave concrete suggestions to a student on either the research itself or on timeline, he expected the student, and sometimes the relevant second-tier supervisor as well, to take notes. He might give a student a heads-up: 'Your boss (the second-tier supervisor) is taking notes; you are not!' The monitor (a second-year doctoral student) was also expected to take notes, for a quick sharing with the student concerned afterwards. Thus the supervisor might ask the monitor at junctures of his commentaries: 'Have you noted this down for him?'

3.2.4. The supervisor's goal-oriented rhetorical actions occurring in sequence

The supervisor's three types of rhetorical actions at research meetings — that is, 'Advising on the research process', 'Advising on paper strategies' and 'Criticising/warning/reminding' — occurred in sequence, as will be illustrated in context briefly in this section.

In the following advisory episode, the supervisor was pointing out that the student should factor in the unpredictability of laboratory research and proactively utilise existing internal and external resources to push a project ahead. In terms of the rhetorical actions, the supervisor both advised on the research process and sent warnings. In this extract, the student presenter has just talked about a slide on the in-vitro culturing of osteoclast [bone-resorbing cells].

> *Director*: You should prepare for the worst. What if the in-vitro culturing of osteoclast [fails] — what's the weight of this step in the whole study? According to what you said just now, this step is optional.
>
> *Student*: This hasn't been done [here] before.
>
> *Director*: But you want to graduate. In extreme circumstances, you will fail [in culturing the cells], as it's hard to do. Anyone else who has done this before? Any place in China?
>
> *Student*: [giving the name of a hospital in Beijing]
>
> *Director*: Why didn't you go and visit them? Contact them. If there's any difficulty, we can help. Why didn't you think of that? Visit them, save your time. Did you communicate with WWW [a doctor in the section who was on a secondment to a hospital in Europe at the time and was not the student's second-tier supervisor]? He is an expert in cultivating tumour cells. You should graduate in 2014 — how can you graduate? (Research meeting, 3 June 2012)

To give further illustration, Table 9.3 presents another extract, with the supervisor's goal-oriented rhetorical actions, in terms of the subcategories shown in Table 9.2, indicated on the right-hand side.[5]

---

5   The director addressed both the students and second-tier supervisors by their full names, which also indicated his top position in his section's status hierarchy.

(The student presenter, XXX, showed a Table of Results on a PowerPoint Slide)		Supervisor's rhetorical actions
Supervisor:	Which is nearer the normal? Which is better? Is it the larger the better, or otherwise?	• data analysis
XXX:	Maybe hard to say.	
Supervisor:	Hard to say? Can you check with the Cardiograph Department? … — there's a normal range but is it the bigger the better? Or is it OK if within a certain range as with red cells? Which kind is it? Who is revising the paper?	• use of resources • data analysis • holding the second-tier supervisor responsible
YYY (The student's second-tier supervisor):	It's not yet submitted to me.	
Supervisor (to XXX):	You need to re-think. You should have done an interim report, before you started drafting. Otherwise you waste time in writing. Why haven't you presented a report? YYY, have you asked about it?	• project planning • holding the second-tier supervisor responsible
YYY:	…	
Supervisor (to XXX):	… What's your conclusion? Your conclusion just now is not logical. [Reading the slide] You shouldn't say [this]; it should be [this] … Now that you've written this, I think you can also include analysis of the data of adult patients … Take another group to compare whether there is difference. If there is no difference, then in your conclusion, you may say [that] during adolescence the heart function is not influenced by [this] … If there is a difference, when you discuss [it], you can *say maybe* there is an effect for patients above 40 or 45 years of age. Who is the second-tier boss? Note it down; don't appear to be in a daze!	• data analysis • data analysis • data analysis • suggesting content of paper • holding the second-tier supervisor responsible • urging attentive listening and note-taking
YYY:	I am writing. (With a smile)	

Supervisor:	The mind is not quick at all! ZZZ [the monitor), note it down for him — add: 'adolescent patients, possible influence on heart function' [etc.] ... 'Adult patients versus adolescent patients'. [To the student presenter] Your supervisor is taking notes; you are not — XXX, you have not entered your role yet!	• reminding the monitor to take notes for the student presenter • urging attentive listening and note-taking • warning on slow progress

Table 9.3: The supervisor's rhetorical actions during a student presentation (Research meeting, 3 June 2012).

The sequence of actions as laid out in Table 9.3 was given coherence by the macro-level object (Engeström, 2000) of 'quality research and efficient publication' (as shown in Figure 9.1), which provided the motive for all the actions. Examining the actions in sequence lends insights into how the different types of rhetorical actions as shown in Table 9.2 might interweave to achieve the effect of advising desired by the supervisor. Clearly, the actions also demonstrated the supervisor's absolute authority in the supervision activity (that is, illustrating the *division of labour* in Figure 9.1). However, it should be noted that although he seemed to chide the students and even the second-tier supervisors freely in issuing his directives, he did not do so with a stern look or a harsh tone. A second-tier supervisor's responding to the director's chide with a smile, as shown in Table 9.3 (towards the end of the excerpt), would indicate that the atmosphere was down-to-earth and respectful but not unnervingly tense.

4. Discussion, implications and conclusion

Drawing upon the theoretical perspective provided by cultural-historical activity theory [CHAT] (for example, Engeström, 1987; Engeström et al., 1999), the study in this chapter investigated a 'big boss' supervisor's verbal communication in research supervision at the Orthopedics Department of a major Chinese hospital. The study was guided by a two-fold aim: to find out with what neighbouring activity systems the research supervision activity interacted and how, and to describe the supervisor's rhetorical actions when providing commentaries during his students' presentations at research meetings. It was found that the supervisor evoked rules in five surrounding activity systems to feed into the tools in his supervision activity: those of the evaluation, publishing world, scientific research world, competitive society-at-large, and Chinese culture. It was also revealed that the rhetorical actions implemented by the supervisor at research meetings fell into three groups — advising on the research process, advising on paper strategies, and criticising/warning/reminding; the actions interwove and occurred in sequence in the supervisor's commentaries during the students' presentations, consistently motivated by the object of the supervision activity — that is, quality research and efficient publication. The study both echoes and adds something new to the literature, with theoretical and pedagogical implications and implications for future research, as elaborated below.

4.1. Towards a holistic perspective upon research supervision

The study reported in this chapter, in describing the involvement of five surrounding activity systems with the central activity, highlights the value of taking a holistic perspective on research supervision. Previous research on academic supervision has discussed the influence of societal and policy-level practicalities (Li, 2016; McCallin & Nayar, 2011); the present study extends this proposition to a wider perspective. That is, other than the impact of the competitive society-at-large and of the evaluation system at the policy level, the study also demonstrates a role for the research world, publishing world, and Chinese culture in the process of research supervision in the case under examination.

The employment of CHAT or activity theory in the study has allowed me to conceptualise the resources drawn upon by the featured supervisor as resulting from interactions between a central activity and a series of neighbouring source activity systems. The literature has shown that the *outcome* of one activity system can 'flow' into a neighbouring activity system to become either a *rule*, indicating a power-imbalance relationship between the two activity systems (Engeström, 2009), or a *tool*, indicating a 'nesting' relationship between activity systems (Li, 2013; Barab et al., 2002; Engeström, 2000). The present chapter has reported another type of 'flow': that of *rules* from neighbouring activity systems into the *tools* of the central activity. Future research can continue to explore the interacting relationships between activity systems in terms of varied, dynamic interconnections between the nodes of the systems.

In drawing upon the hierarchical view of activity, which posits that object-directed activity comprises sequences of goal-oriented actions (Engeström, 2000; Leont'ev, 1978), the study also examined the supervisor's rhetorical actions using both categorising and connecting strategies (Maxwell & Miller, 2008). Previous applications of the hierarchical view of activity tended to focus on sequences of physical actions (for example, Li, 2013, 2014b; Barab et al., 2002; Engeström, 2000). The potential productiveness of employing the hierarchical view of activity to examine rhetorical actions and their sequences has only been sporadically discussed in the literature, by reference to academic written texts (Bazerman, 1997; Peters, 2011). The present chapter has exemplified adopting the hierarchical view of activity in studying spoken discourse. It can be suggested that, at a broader level, research supervision such as that in a hospital setting, which necessarily involves both spoken and written communication, is made up of many such goal-oriented sequences of physical and rhetorical actions, which are implemented across space and time.

4.2. A 'power over' supervisory relationship may be productive in a particular context

The literature on research education (Casanave & Li, 2008), situated learning in scientific writing (Blakeslee, 1997), and mentoring in medical settings (Souba, 1999) has revealed that effective mentoring is characteristically based on a kind of 'power with', rather than 'power over', relationship (Heinrich, 1995; Luebs, Fredrickson, Hyon & Samraj, 1998). Instead of having a mentor dominating as an authoritative, bossy figure, it has been suggested that in successful mentorship we tend to find 'guidance, interaction, and a refreshing balance of negotiating strategies and decision-making' (Casanave & Li, 2008, p. 8). The supervisor described in the present study, by contrast, clearly tipped over to a more traditional role, by maintaining a strongly authoritative stance, echoing the previous characterisation of Chinese research supervision as being 'paternal' and 'highly directed' (McClure, 2005, p. 10). This dominance of expert authority on the part of the supervisor contrasts with a view of bi-directionality of learning between expert and novice (for example, Jacoby & Gonzales, 1991). Yet despite evidence of expert dominance and novice deferral not leading to productive learning (Blakeslee, 1997), including in the Chinese context (Li, 2012), it may be reasonable to suggest that in a particular local context, an apparently 'power over' supervisory relationship may actually be both natural and potentially productive.

In postgraduate students' research supervision in a Chinese hospital setting, the existence of those neighbouring activity systems as described in the present chapter is probably more likely to facilitate a 'power over' rather than a 'power with' kind of mentoring relationship. In other words, it may be relatively straightforward for the supervisor (if he or she is willing to do so) to draw upon the power inherent in the neighbouring activity systems and to wield it in supervision. The inclination towards a 'power over' approach can be reinforced, first, by the often strictly hierarchical relationships institutionalised in the hospital setting (a scenario which may likewise be seen in hospitals elsewhere in the world) and, second, by the ethos of 'respecting the teacher' underlying Chinese culture. In addition, although the study reported in this chapter did not gather longitudinal evidence to show how the supervisor's teaching might have a long-term positive effect on his disciples, the unanimously positive and admiring outlook that the students displayed upon the supervisor's teaching during the interviews, together with their section's publication achievements over the years to which the students had crucially contributed, did suggest that the supervisor's 'power over' approach seemed to have had a positive effect on the students' learning in the local setting. This was apparently because, in contrast to the case in previous research (Li, 2012; Blakeslee, 1997), the students were made to be fully engaged in a network of activity systems revolving around research and publication (see, for example, Li, 2014b), a perspective that should point to a future line of research.

Still it may be difficult to recommend the same supervisory strategies to other research supervisors, for, after all, supervision takes place within particular contexts. Whatever supervisors and students themselves bring to their local context, including their personalities and life histories, and their relationships formed over time, will become part of the context and will help to shape productive communication strategies for research supervision. Nevertheless, the featured supervisor's approach of drawing upon resources from a range of activity systems in which the students were also participants, and weaving together a variety of rhetorical actions in advising students during research meetings, might provide perspectives for reference in alternative contexts. For this reason, the study reported in this chapter will have implications for understanding research supervision in different cultures and, in particular, in non-anglophone academic environments where English publication has become a high priority. It can also inform programs that train supervisors to mentor their students for successful research publication.

Future research that is conducted in varied academic, professional and national contexts will continue to build our understanding of effective research supervision. It is hoped that the present chapter has reported findings that will serve as a baseline for comparison for future research. Having tied the findings to the use of cultural-historical activity theory [CHAT] in my study, I hope that the study has also demonstrated the value of this theory in throwing light on the complex, collective activity of research supervision.

References

Barab, S.A., Barnett, M., Yamagata-Lynch, L., Squire, K., & Keating, T. (2002). Using activity theory to understand the systemic tensions characterizing a technology-rich introductory astronomy course. *Mind, Culture, and Activity, 9*(2), 76-107.

Barbero, E.J. (2008). Journal paper requirement for PhD graduation. *Latin American and Caribbean Journal of Engineering Education, 2*(2), 51-53.

Bazerman, C. (1997). Discursively structured activities. *Mind, Culture, and Activity, 4*, 296-308.

Blakeslee, A.M. (1997). Activity, context, interaction, and authority: Learning to write scientific papers in situ. *Journal of Business and Technical Communication, 11*(2), 125-169.

Bryman, A., & Burgess, R.G. (1994). Developments in qualitative data analysis: An introduction. In A. Bryman & R.G. Burgess (Eds.), *Analyzing qualitative data* (pp. 1-17). London: Routledge.

Casanave, C.P., & Li, X. (Eds.). (2008). *Learning the literacy practices of graduate schools: Insiders' reflections on academic enculturation.* Ann Arbor: The University of Michigan Press.

DeCastro, R., Sambuco, D., Ubel, P.A., Stewart, A., & Jagsi, R. (2013). Mentor networks in academic medicine: Moving beyond a dyadic conception of mentoring for junior faculty researchers. *Academic Medicine, 88*(4), 488-496.

Denscombe, M. (2007). *Good research guide.* Buckingham, UK: Open University Press.

Dyrbye, L.N., Thomas, M.R., Papp, K.K., & Durning, S.J. (2008). Clinician educators' experiences with institutional review boards: Results of a national survey. *Academic Medicine, 83*(6), 590-595.

Engeström, Y. (1987). *Learning by expanding: An activity theoretical approach to developmental research.* Helsinki: Orienta-Konsultit.

Engeström, Y. (2000). Activity theory as a framework for analyzing and redesigning work. *Ergonomics, 43*(7), 960-974.

Engeström, Y. (2001). Expansive learning at work: Toward an activity theoretical reconceptualization. *Journal of Education and Work, 14*(1), 133-156.

Engeström, Y. (2009). The future of activity theory: A rough draft. In A. Sannino, H. Daniels, & K.D. Gutiérrez (Eds.), *Learning and expanding with activity theory* (pp. 303-328). Cambridge: Cambridge University Press.

Engeström, Y., Miettinen, R., & Punamäki, R.-L. (Eds.). (1999). *Perspectives on activity theory.* New York: Cambridge University Press.

Griffin, M.F., & Hindocha, S. (2011). Publication practices of medical students at British medical schools: Experience, attitudes and barriers to publish. *Medical Teacher, 33*(1), e1-e8.

Heinrich, K.T. (1995). Doctoral advisement relationships between women: On friendship and betrayal. *Journal of Higher Education, 66*(4), 447-469.

Huang, J.C. (2010). Publishing and learning writing for publication in English: Perspectives of NNES PhD students in science. *Journal of English for Academic Purposes, 9*(1), 33-44.

Jacoby, S., & Gonzales, P. (1991). The constitution of expert-novice in scientific discourse. *Issues in Applied Linguistics, 2*(2), 149-181.

Leont'ev, A.N. (1978). *Activity, consciousness, and personality.* Englewood Cliffs, NJ: Prentice-Hall.

Li, Y. (2012). 'I have no time to find out where the sentences came from; I just rebuild them': A biochemistry professor eliminating novices' textual borrowing. *Journal of Second Language Writing, 21,* 59-70.

Li, Y. (2013). Three ESL students writing a policy paper assignment: An activity-analytic perspective. *Journal of English for Academic Purposes, 12,* 73-86.

Li, Y. (2014a). Chinese medical doctors negotiating the pressure of the publication requirement. *Ibérica, 28,* 107-128.

Li, Y. (2014b). Boundary crossing: Chinese orthopedic surgeons as researchers. *Journal of Technical Writing and Communication, 44*(4), 423-449.

Li, Y. (2016). 'Publish SCI papers or no degree': Practices of Chinese doctoral supervisors in response to the publication pressure on science students. *Asia Pacific Journal of Education, 36*(4), 545-558. DOI: http://dx.doi.org/10.1080/02188791.2015.1005050.

Liang, S., & Chen, J. (2009). Linchuang fushu yiyuan boshi yanjiusheng SCI lunwen chanchu yu daoshi qingkuang de xiangguanxing yanjiu [The correlation between the SCI productivity of the PhD students at clinical affiliated hospitals and the characteristics of their supervisors]. *Huaxi Yixue, 24*(10), 2665-2668.

Luebs, M., Fredrickson, K.M., Hyon, S., & Samraj, B. (1998). John Swales as mentor: The view from the doctoral group. *English for Specific Purposes, 17*(1), 67-85.

Maxwell, J.A., & Miller, B.A. (2008). Categorizing and connecting strategies in qualitative data analysis. In P. Leavy, & S. Hesse-Biber (Eds.), *Handbook of emergent methods* (pp. 461-477). New York: Guilford Press.

McCallin, A., & Nayar, S. (2011). Postgraduate research supervision: A critical review of current practice. *Teaching in Higher Education, 17*(1), 63-74.

McClure, J.W. (2005). Preparing a laboratory-based thesis: Chinese international research students' experiences of supervision. *Teaching in Higher Education, 10*(1), 3-16.

Parsonnet, J., Gruppuso, P.A., Kanter, S.L., & Boninger, M. (2010). Required vs. elective research and in-depth scholarship programs in the medical student curriculum. *Academic Medicine, 85*(3), 405-408.

Patton, M.Q. (1990). *Qualitative evaluation and research methods* (2nd ed.). Newbury Park, CA: Sage.

Peters, S. (2011). Asserting or deflecting expertise? Exploring the rhetorical practices of master's theses in the philosophy of education. *English for Specific Purposes, 30*(3), 176-185.

Prior, P., & Shipka, J. (2003). Chronotopic lamination: Tracing the contours of literate activity. In C. Bazerman, & P. Prior (Eds.), *Writing selves/writing societies: Research from activity perspectives* (pp. 180-238). Fort Collins, CO: The WAC Clearinghouse and Mind, Culture, and Activity.

Rose, G.L., Rukstalis, M.R., & Schuckit, M.A. (2005). Informal mentoring between faculty and medical students. *Academic Medicine, 80*(4), 344-348.

Souba, W.W. (1999). Mentoring young academic surgeons, our most precious asset. *Journal of Surgical Research, 82*(2), 113-120.

van Eyk, H.J., Hooiveld, M.H.W., Van Leeuwen, T.N., Van der wurff, B.L.J., De Craen, A.J.M., & Dekker, F.W. (2010). Scientific output of Dutch medical students. *Medical Teacher, 32*(3), 231-235.

Vygotsky, L.S. (1978). *Mind in society: The development of higher psychological processes*. Cambridge, MA: Harvard University Press.

Zerzan, J.T., Hess, R., Schur, E., Phillips, R.S., & Rigotti, N. (2009). Making the most of mentors: A guide for mentees. *Academic Medicine, 84*(1), 140-144.

10

The geopolitics of academic plagiarism[17]

Karen Bennett

1. Just how serious an offence is academic plagiarism?[1]

Judging by the ominous warnings issued to students by universities in the Anglo-Saxon world (Abasi & Graves, 2008) and the sense of moral outrage with which transgressors are pursued (Pennycook, 1996; Martin, 1994), the answer to that question would seem to be 'very serious indeed'. In fact, the University of Oxford's website (n.d.) is unequivocal on the matter:

> It would be wrong to describe plagiarism as only a minor form of cheating, or as merely a matter of academic etiquette. On the contrary, it is important to understand that plagiarism is a breach of academic integrity.

Consequently, those found guilty of 'committing' plagiarism (the collocation is significant) face the most severe penalties that academia can muster: expulsion, disgrace and, in extreme cases, even prosecution under the Copyright Act.

Yet in many other countries of the world, plagiarism, like other forms of academic corruption, is not viewed with quite the same degree of opprobrium. Gadpaille (2004, p. 57) reports that, in the unspecified Central European country where she worked, not only was cheating endemic in the culture, no shame seemed to accrue to the practice; instead, 'information is widely viewed as common property; honour lies in sharing rather than monopolizing, and competition for grades is minimal'. Similarly, Sherman (1992, p. 191) found that first-year students in an Italian university gave verbatim answers

---

1 This article was first published in 2011 under the title '*Gemeinschaft* and *Gesellschaft*: The geopolitics of academic plagiarism' in the volume *Plagiate — Gefahr für die Wissenschaft?* (pp. 53-69), edited by Thomas Rommel (Berlin: Lit Verlag). Reproduced with the kind permission of the publishers.

without any kind of analysis or sourcing, clearly viewing this as 'not only legitimate but correct and proper'; while Deckert (1993) claimed that the Chinese students in his study routinely engaged in a form of 'learned plagiarism' (p. 95), which involved, amongst other things, rote memorising and recycling (p. 140).

Clearly, then, there is a cultural dimension to plagiarism that urgently needs to be addressed in the increasingly globalised world of modern academia.

Attitudes towards authorship, originality and intellectual property have not always been what they are today (Randall, 2001; Kewes, 2003; Love, 2003). In mediaeval Scholasticism, the term 'author' (auctor) was reserved for those ancient authorities that had produced great truths in accordance with Christian doctrine, and contemporary writers, considered mere *scriptores*, *compilatores* or *commentators*[2], were expected to copy them as faithfully as possible for the purpose of dissemination. In fact, decontextualised fragments of text from ancient sources (*sententiae*) circulated freely at this time with no reference to the original author at all. Similarly, in Humanism, imitation (*imitatio*) had an important part to play in the learning process, and students would copy tropes and phrases of the masters into commonplace books for incorporation into their own work (Randall, 2001; Kewes, 2003). Indeed, the notion that words/ideas can be owned only really developed in the 16th/17th centuries, when the emergence of a market for print meant that people could now earn a living by publication.[3]

In this article, therefore, I consider plagiarism not as a universal or unequivocal evil, but as one component of a particular ethical system that took hold within a specific historical and social context, roughly contemporary with the European Enlightenment (Scollon, 1995; Pennycook, 1996). Today, that ethical framework is so deeply entrenched in the power structures of the modern world that its values go largely unquestioned in countries at the centre of the world economic system. However, as we move away from the centre towards the semi-periphery and the periphery, we find that those values become weaker, and may enter into conflict with another moral code, which is usually more traditional in nature, though no less coherent. Indeed, in some parts of the world, those traditional values actually hold sway in local universities (Canagarajah, 2002), thus raising serious problems for academic mobility and the internationalisation of knowledge.

There has been a certain amount of cross-cultural research into attitudes to plagiarism, with most of the early work (for example, Matalene, 1985; Myer, 1998; Sherman, 1992; Bloch & Chi, 1995; Deckert, 1993) stressing the influence of home

---

2   Even Chaucer considered himself to be no more than a compiler or 'rehearser' of others' stories (Randall, 2001, pp. 35, 197-205).

3   Other important influences were the advance of technology (particularly the printing press), capitalism, and the development of modern science, which discredited the emulation of textual authorities, placing the emphasis firmly upon observation and experimentation (Johns, 1998, pp. 445-62).

culture norms upon foreign student production in English. Much of this is very culture-specific. For example, Gadpaille (2004) describes how communism is often blamed for the lack of respect for individual intellectual property in eastern European countries, while Harris (as cited in Pennycook, 1996) suggests that Confucianism may have conditioned Chinese students' attitudes to textual authority. In this chapter, however, I would like to put forward a more wide-ranging explanation based upon Tönnies's 1887 model of *Gemeinschaft und Gesellschaft*, which, I believe, can account not only for present-day disparities in attitudes to plagiarism, but also for changes in those attitudes over time. What is more, this model also offers a much-needed critical perspective on the values that centre scholars take so much for granted, providing a sympathetic view of the mechanisms generating plagiarism and other forms of academic 'corruption' amongst non-centre scholars.

2. What is academic plagiarism?

Before launching into our geopolitical exploration of academic cultures, let us begin by establishing exactly what is meant by plagiarism today. Modern dictionaries tend to be laconic on the matter, defining it as the 'appropriation of the writings or ideas of another' or as 'literary theft'. However, in practice the word is used to cover a wide range of related offences. The Oxford University website (n.d.) includes not only 'the verbatim quotation of other people's work without acknowledgement', but also 'paraphrasing with only minor alterations', 'collusion', 'inaccurate citation', 'failure to acknowledge all assistance', recourse to 'professional agencies' and 'self-plagiarism'.

Moreover, the meta-discourse surrounding the subject of plagiarism is confusingly ambivalent. Despite the fact that it is not in itself a legal offence (Goldstein, 2003/1994), it is often presented as a form of 'stealing' — that is to say, a crime against the inalienable property rights of the individual (Pennycook, 1996) — though as Bjørnstad (2008) points out, it is difficult to see just what has been stolen, since the author does not have fewer words after the theft. Others prefer to cast it as 'fraud'[4], thereby emphasising the dimension of deceit and illicit gain. Yet others adopt a quasi-religious moralistic tone, rather than a legalistic one, seeking to shame potential perpetrators into obeisance with references to 'dishonesty' and 'integrity' (Abasi & Graves, 2008, pp. 228-9) or 'sin' (Martin, 1994, p. 36; Sutherland-Smith, 2005, p. 90). Hence, although there is a general consensus amongst centre institutions and commentators that it is wrongful, not everyone agrees as to why exactly it is, with plagiarised authors and educators tending to mobilise quite different arguments in their own defence.

What all of these discursive strands have in common, however, is that they are all tightly enmeshed in the network of Enlightenment values and beliefs underpinning

---

4   For example, St Onge (1988, p. 62) describes it as 'verbal fraud', involving 'illicit gains by illicit methods'.

modern society. This ideology not only conceives the individual author as sovereign, rational and autonomous, and in full conscious possession of his words (Scollon, 1995), but has also elevated the pursuit of material gain into a fundamental principle, holding private property sacrosanct and fostering competition as an incentive to productivity and excellence. Hence all practices that undermine these basic market principles are viewed with great distrust, both because they are unfair on 'honest' competitors, and because they threaten the very infrastructure of the whole economic game.

Modern academic transactions, like other marketplace operations, are governed by relationships of *contract*, which presuppose a need for transparency and respect for certain fundamental rights (such as the right to property, the fruits of one's labour, and so on). Whether plagiarism is framed as theft, fraud or simple dishonesty, it therefore constitutes a breach of contract, which inevitably injures other parties — authors, teachers, examiners, fellow students, the academic institution (the name of which may be tarnished), future employers or, in some high-profile cases, the public at large. A British study into students' perceptions of cheating and plagiarism in academic work and assessment (Ashworth, Bannister & Thorne, 1997) showed that students who had been raised in that culture clearly shared these basic principles. For example, one student commented about cheating: 'It's not fair on other students, because I think we are all in competition with each other for the 1st, 2i's and 2ii's' (as cited in Ashworth et al., p. 190). Another believed that 'pressing tutors for help with assignments is a bit wrong because that information should be shared to the whole class' (p. 191). Similarly, the respondents who actually justified cheating and plagiarism did so on the grounds that the university assessment systems and teaching methods were flawed, thereby drawing on the same fundamental argument of 'fair play'.

However, we cannot take it for granted that members of non-centre countries have all internalised these principles quite so fully. As has already been mentioned, early studies into attitudes to plagiarism amongst EFL students (Matalene, 1985; Myer, 1998; Sherman, 1992; Bloch & Chi, 1995, Deckert, 1993) suggested that they were operating according to norms imported from their own cultures and were often shocked to find that these were incompatible with the requirements stipulated by universities in the host country. Consequently, authors such as Scollon (1995) and Pennycook (1996) have called for a more relativistic view of such practices:

> ... [W]hereas we can see how the notion of plagiarism needs to be understood within the particular cultural and historical context of its development, it also needs to be understood relative to alternative cultural practices. (Pennycook, 1996, p. 218)

It is in this light that Tönnies's model of Gemeinschaft and Gesellschaft seems particularly relevant, as it offers an explanation of not only the dynamics operating in different cultural situations today, but also the way in which these change over time.

3. Gemeinschaft and Gesellschaft

Ferdinand Tönnies's influential work *Gemeinschaft und Gesellschaft* was first published in 1887 at a time when the traditional peasant lifestyle in Germany was being irrevocably transformed by the rationalistic forces of mechanisation and commercialisation. Having been brought up in an affluent peasant family, Tönnies naturally viewed these changes with some alarm (Loomis & McKinney, 2002/1957), a personal perspective which undoubtedly coloured his judgement about the relative merits of the two social systems in question. Despite this bias, however, his model has proved to be very influential, offering, amongst other things, a useful counterpoint to Spencer's evolutionary model that was dominant at the time.

In Tönnies's work, the everyday German words *Gemeinschaft* and *Gesellschaft* (literally 'community' and 'society') acquire the force of technical terms within a coherent sociological theory. The former is understood as an organic community, bound by a common *geist*, whose members share bonds of kinship and land, with common ownership and a strong sense of intra-group co-operation. The latter, in contrast, is an artificial aggregate of individuals linked only by the rational ties of contract, where notions of individual ownership prevail over the communal.[5] In this context, competition is strongly encouraged as a way of generating wealth and expertise; hence, failure to abide by the rules is perceived as an affront to the whole notion of citizenship and fair play.

Crucial for our understanding of plagiarism and other forms of 'corruption' in premodern societies is the fact that, in the Gemeinschaft, members of the group co-operate with each other against the 'Other', whether this be a foreign tribe or the organisms and representatives of the modern state. What the Gesellschaft views as despicable cheating is a normal, even honourable, mode of being in the Gemeinschaft, to the extent that, if a 'friend' requests help in drafting a text, passing an examination or acquiring a position or privilege, it would be extremely impolite to refuse. That is to say, loyalty to the immediate group is privileged over and above abstract notions of state or citizenship.

Similarly this notion of 'commonality' that pervades human relations in the Gemeinschaft[6] also extends to property, with obvious repercussions upon the issue of plagiarism. Canagarajah (2002, p. 131), in his seminal work *The Geopolitics of Academic Writing*, explains that, in peripheral academic cultures, such as his own home country of Sri Lanka, 'the idea of intellectual property is less clear-cut' than in centre universities:

---

5   There have been other designations for the same phenomena. Marxist discourse speaks of feudal versus capitalist economies, while contemporary sociologists such as Giddens (1990) and Bauman (2000) refer to 'premodern' versus 'modern' societies.

6   'Common goods — common evils; common friends — common enemies' (Tönnies, 2002, p. 50).

> Borrowing from other texts, like borrowing freely from others' words in the communal stock of oral knowledge, is unrestricted. The ownership of knowledge is fluid, just as copyright laws are hardly in operation. Local scholars see themselves as freely borrowing from and contributing to the pool of available knowledge.

This implies that plagiarism is scarcely recognised as an issue in such environments, much less a reason for expulsion or disgrace.

The question of authority is also of interest here, as it reflects directly upon the notion of 'originality', so highly prized by the modern university (Pennycook, 1996). Tönnies (2002, p. 41) distinguishes three forms of authority in the Gemeinschaft — 'the authority of age, authority of force, and authority of wisdom or spirit', all of which are united in the figure of the father, 'who is engaged in protecting, assisting, and guiding his family'. This paternalistic prototype is reproduced in the master/disciple relationship (Tönnies, 2002) found in institutions such as craft guilds, professional corporations and, by extension, the university. It is significant that originality, in the modern sense, has little role to play in the disciple's training. Instead, the dominant attitude is one of acquiescence, passive reproduction of authoritative models, and absorption of the master's skills and knowledge, in exchange for protection and promotion.

The master/disciple unit is also the building block of the whole system of patronage that is central to social relations in the Gemeinschaft. Unlike the modern university, where there is stringent competition at all stages of the academic career, the Gemeinschaft university is viewed more as a traditional Alma Mater that nurtures its offspring and encourages their trajectory through the system. Hence, in such cultures, mobility tends to be *vertical* rather than *horizontal* (Canagarajah, 2002, p. 197), as teachers are typically recruited from the student body and propelled through the various stages of the academic career fairly automatically (p. 190). As a result, there may be no real competition for jobs; instead, junior staff enjoy the support of more senior professors, who operate 'minifiefdoms' (p. 195), promoting their protégés and cultivating extensive circles of influence in the process. Moreover, as career progression depends more upon interpersonal connections than upon academic production, the 'publish or perish' ethos that dominates in the Gesellschaft also tends to be absent from the Gemeinschaft (pp. 14, 190), and publications, where they occur, are not usually peer-reviewed. Once more, originality is not at a premium. Instead what counts, in editorial decisions, is ensuring that local authorities are properly represented and that due respect is paid.

Given the *magister dixit* ethos that prevails in the Gemeinschaft, students are not encouraged to challenge or dispute authority. In lectures, they are expected to take down the professor's words and to reproduce them verbatim in examinations. Consequently, their intervention in class will be minimal, couched, when it occurs, in highly respectful language. It is hardly surprising, then, that students from Gemeinschaft cultures have difficulty coping with the demands for originality that are made of them in Gesellschaft universities. Indeed, the very concept of student originality must appear to them as deeply at odds with their whole notion of what education entails.

4. The limitations of the model

Despite its usefulness for explaining some of the discrepancies between different academic cultures, the Gemeinschaft/Gesellschaft model does, however, have limitations, as pointed out by Loomis and McKinney in their introduction to the English edition of Tönnies's work (2002/1957, p. 7). In particular, it should be remembered that the two categories are ideal types that are rarely found in a pure form today. So, although Canagarajah's (2002) description of the 'peripheral' academic community has much in common with Tönnies's notion of the Gemeinschaft, such cultures are nevertheless subject to a centripetal force that puts pressure upon them to adapt to centre values (Canagarajah, 2002, p. 41). In such environments, we find modern science existing alongside indigenous forms of scholarship (pp. 50-4), and old-style professors whose social status is 'ascribed' by the traditional hierarchy (p. 226) sharing departments with young socially mobile researchers who have been trained abroad. This conflict of values is particularly evident amongst countries of the 'semi-periphery'[7], which, for geographical and economic reasons, have strong incentives to assimilate to the centre, in some cases becoming more precious about centre values than the centre countries themselves.[8]

Conversely, within the most 'developed' Gesellschaft societies, there are inevitably pockets of Gemeinschaft culture which prove resistant to modern market values. For example, the Universities of Oxford and Cambridge have often been accused of non-meritocratic practices, such as favouring students from certain independent schools (with which they have traditional ties) above brighter students from state institutions, and awarding degrees to undeserving candidates on the basis of social status or family connections. And even the more progressive universities are not always single-minded about the role ascribed to them by neoliberal governments (a role which usually involves training highly specialised personnel to supply the organs of industry and capitalism) or about the fact that they are now expected to function almost as bureaucratic corporations committed to the pursuit of 'excellence'. These uncertainties generate tensions that may filter down and affect university practices in the most unexpected ways.

---

7 The term 'semi-periphery' was coined by Wallerstein (1984) and refers to those countries that are positioned, geographically and economically, between the core and the periphery of the world system and have characteristics of each.

8 This centripetal pressure may explain why Abasi and Graves's (2008) more recent survey of foreign students' attitudes to plagiarism in a Canadian university presented different results to the earlier studies described above. Rather than expressing bewilderment at the whole notion that copying might be wrong, these students now seemed to share the same basic moral framework as the host culture, but claimed that, in their home countries, the offence was treated as less serious and not subject to the same harsh sanctions.

Despite the fact that most people brought up in centre countries tend to subscribe unequivocally to the Enlightenment values of fair play and transparency, the whole issue of plagiarism is rife with contradictions. Take the question of originality. As Pennycook (1996) has pointed out, at undergraduate level, students are usually engaged in acquiring a fixed canon of knowledge and terminology (not so different, in fact, from Gemeinschaft apprentices learning the tools of the trade); they are often encouraged to imitate published models in order to acquire agility in the disciplinary discourse.[9] In the light of this, exhortations to be original seem rather misplaced, for until one has firmly mastered the discourse norms, reformulation is a risky business. As one Taiwanese student pointed out, if she didn't stick closely to the terms used in the book, she would never learn to use them effectively (as cited in Currie, 1998, p. 11).

Then there is the question of authority. The very fact that this is a more fluid notion in the Gesellschaft than in the Gemeinschaft brings its own problems. Students learn that they are expected to quote authorities in the field to demonstrate their breadth of reading and knowledge of the state of the art. But just who or what should be quoted? Is the professor that provides a potted overview in a lecture a worthy source? What about the introductory textbook? And just how much basic knowledge is required before one is even in a position to approach those authorities critically?

There is also a hierarchical dimension to plagiarism that is at odds with the Gesellschaft's view of itself as eminently meritocratic. That is to say, students that fail to acknowledge their sources are open to charges of plagiarism, while established academics are rarely considered to be committing the same offence when they 'borrow' ideas from their students or juniors. Indeed, in the sciences, where teams of researchers habitually collaborate on papers, it is often a junior that writes up the article while the senior researcher (who may have played a minimal role in practice) receives the credit. As Pennycook (1996, p. 213) points out, 'much of what gets claimed as the result of original academic work actually draws heavily on the work of silent others — women, graduate students, research assistants and so on'.[10] Ironically, the justification given is that the junior in question is a 'novice' or 'trainee' who is operating under the supervision of someone more experienced — which suggests that the power balance involved is remarkably similar to that operating in the traditional Gemeinschaft relationship of master/disciple.

Finally, the question of plagiarism is also underpinned by the gritty philosophical problem of the relationship between words and things. Modern science is predicated upon a philosophy of linguistic realism, which posits the ultimate separability of form

---

9 Indeed, many of the books used for the teaching of Academic English today employ techniques of *imitatio* not so different from those used in the Early Modern period within the Humanist rhetorical tradition.

10 Martin (1994) has dubbed the socially acceptable practice of plagiarising the work of subordinates 'institutionalised plagiarism'.

and content; enjoinders to reformulate, paraphrase and summarise therefore presuppose that 'reality' is prior to language and has an objective existence independent of perception or the forms that are used to encode it. Yet this philosophical viewpoint is by no means shared by all intellectual cultures (Pennycook, 1996), nor is it internally coherent. For if science does indeed lift the veil on some pre-existing objective reality, then where does authorship come in? How can such 'truth' be referenced?

Of course, the answer to this is that the 'facts' that science purports to reveal are merely claims that have been sanctioned by the discourse community:

> The construction of academic facts is a social process, with the cachet of acceptance only bestowed on a claim after negotiation with editors, expert reviewers and journal readers, the final ratification granted, of course, with the citation of the claim by others and, eventually, the disappearance of all acknowledgment as it is incorporated into the literature of the discipline. (Hyland, 1999, p. 342)

However, there is clearly a discrepancy between the constructed nature of scientific knowledge and its meta-discourse of transcendent truth, and this possibly raises the most complex challenge to the whole issue of plagiarism. Traditional science textbooks, at undergraduate as well as high-school level, tend to present accepted knowledge as incontrovertible fact, using grammatical structures such as nominalisations, impersonal verb forms and cause-and-effect linkers (Veel, 1998; Halliday & Martin, 1993) to build a picture of an objectively existing world from which all human agency is removed. It is therefore not surprising if students are perplexed when they are faced with all the messiness and uncertainties of 'science in the making' (Latour & Woolgar, 1979; Knorr-Cetina, 1981). As Scollon (1994) has pointed out, it takes considerable expertise to know just when a claim has achieved the sort of consensual recognition that allows referencing to be dispensed with — that is to say, when it is no longer considered to be merely some scientist's theory and has passed into the exalted realm of 'fact'.

The issue of plagiarism is therefore something of a minefield that one has to be very adept to negotiate. No wonder, then, that so many students, foreign and domestic, take the 'safe path' of constructing their texts as 'patchworks' or 'mosaics' of referenced citations from different sources, in which their own input is limited to linking those sources together (Abasi & Graves, 2008; Currie, 1998; Ashworth et al., 1997). In the current climate of persecution, this is at least one way of 'staying out of trouble' (Currie, 1998).

5. Conclusion

In this article, I have argued that the concept of plagiarism is deeply embedded in the web of values and beliefs that sustains modern society, and as such, may be a source of (understandable) confusion for students and scholars raised in Gemeinschaft cultures, where a whole different ethos may prevail with regard to property, knowledge and authorship. What is more, the concept itself is also full of inherent contradictions, caused, at least in part, by historical tensions generated by the passage from one kind of society to the other. Vestiges of the Gemeinschaft continue to penetrate all aspects of modern university culture, ranging from teaching practices (the persistence of *imitatio* in academic writing courses) and hierarchical relations (the power balance inherent in the tutor/student dynamic) to the very philosophy of knowledge underlying modern science (where the rhetorical implications of the citation procedure sit uncomfortably alongside a meta-discourse of transcendental truth).

I have not even mentioned here the wide-ranging critiques of modernity brought by the poststructuralists, despite their profound implications for the subject of plagiarism, as they have been amply treated elsewhere (Randall, 2001; Pennycook, 1996; Thompson & Pennycook, 2008; Scollon, 1995). However, what links Barthes's 'Death of the author' (1968), Foucault's 'What is an author?' (1969), Derrida's 'différance' (1972), Bakhtin's 'dialogism' (1975) and Kristeva's 'intertextuality' (1966) is the belief that all knowledge is mediated by language, which is culturally constructed, and therefore partial and value-ridden. Not only does this makes a mockery of the whole notion of originality (since we learn about the world through the categories set up by our discourses), it also undermines any attempt to claim ownership of words, which are common property and resist appropriation.

At the end of the last century, when poststructuralism was at its height, it seemed as if we might be returning to a Gemeinschaft notion of intellectual property; indeed, a number of alternative academic discourses sprouted up at that time[11], some of which self-consciously employed (unacknowledged) fragments of other discourses, creating deliberate echoes and patchwork effects. However, this tide seems to have receded. Instead, the forces of capitalism, industry and technology which govern our world have tightened the rules of the game, pushing universities into ever-closer partnerships with business, as public sector funding recedes. In a world dominated by patents and copyrights, the plagiarism police are, if anything, becoming even more relentless.

It is curious that the first person to use the term *plagium* in its present-day sense, the Roman poet Martial[12], did not deem it very serious at all. In fact, he rated it on a par with 'old women wearing dentures, or unattractive women wearing makeup or bald men wearing wigs!' (Orgel, pp. 63-4). Today, however, the rewards for youth and beauty are so high that many are turning to drastic forms of plastic surgery to achieve that goal. Instead of persecuting these imposters, perhaps we should first question the social pressures operating upon them and the dominance of a value system that prompts them to act in this particular way.

---

11   These include the various experimental discourses of qualitative research, the emancipatory 'écritures' of feminism and postcolonialism, and the dense interventionist prose of Critical Theory.

12   In his Epigram I.72, Martial applied the Latin word *plagium* (literally 'kidnapping', usually of a slave or child) to the practice of passing off someone else's literary work as one's own (see Orgel, 2003; Randall, 2001; Goldstein, 2003/1994).

References

Abasi, A.E., & Graves, B. (2008). Academic literacy and plagiarism: Conversations with international graduate students and disciplinary professors. *Journal of English for Academic Purposes, 7*(4), 221-233.

Ashworth, P., Bannister, P., & Thorne, P. (1997). Guilty in whose eyes? University students' perceptions of cheating and plagiarism in academic work and assessment. *Studies in Higher Education, 22*(2), 187-203.

Bauman, Z. (2000). *Liquid modernity.* Cambridge: Polity Press.

Bjørnstad, H. (2008). *Borrowed feathers: Plagiarism and the limits of imitation in early modern Europe.* Oslo: Unipub.

Bloch, J., & Chi, L. (1995). A comparison of the use of citations in Chinese and English academic discourse. In. D. Belcher, & G. Braine (Eds.), *Academic writing in a second language: Essays on research and pedagogy* (pp. 231-274). Norwood, NJ: Ablex.

Canagarajah, A.S. (2002). *A geopolitics of academic writing.* Pittsburgh, PA: Pittsburgh University Press.

Currie, P. (1998). Staying out of trouble: Apparent plagiarism and academic survival. *Journal of Second Language Writing, 7*(1), 1-18.

Deckert, G.D. (1993). A pedagogical response to learned plagiarism among tertiary-level ESL students. *Journal of Second Language Writing, 2,* 94-104.

Gadpaille, M. (2004). Academic integrity in a European context. *The English European Messenger, XIII*(1), 57-59.

Giddens, A. (1990). *The consequences of modernity.* Stanford, CA: Stanford University Press.

Goldstein, P. (2003/1994). *Copyright's highway: From Gutenberg to the celestial jukebox.* Stanford, CA: Stanford University Press.

Halliday, M.A.K., & Martin, J. (1993). *Writing science: Literacy and discursive power.* Pittsburgh, PA: University of Pittsburgh Press.

Haviland C.P., & Mullins, J. (Eds.). (2009). *Who owns this text? Plagiarism, authorship and disciplinary cultures.* Logan, UT: Utah State University Press.

Hyland, K. (1999). Academic attribution: Citation and the construction of disciplinary knowledge. *Applied Linguistics, 20*(3), 341-367.

Johns, A. (1998). *The nature of the book: Print and knowledge in the making.* Chicago & London: University of Chicago Press.

Kewes, P. (2003). Historicizing plagiarism. In P. Kewes (Ed.), *Plagiarism in early modern England* (pp. 1-18). Basingstoke, UK: Palgrave Macmillan.

Kewes, P. (Ed.) (2003). *Plagiarism in early modern England.* Basingstoke, UK: Palgrave Macmillan.

Knorr-Cetina, K. (1981). *The manufacture of knowledge.* Oxford: Pergamon.

Latour, B., & Woolgar, S. (1979). *Laboratory life: The social construction of scientific facts.* Los Angeles: Sage.

Loomis, C., & McKinney, J.C. (2002/1957). Introduction to F. Tönnies, *Community and society* (pp. 1-29). New York: Dover Publications.

Love, H. (2003). Originality and the Puritan sermon. In P. Kewes (Ed.), *Plagiarism in early modern England* (pp. 149-165). Basingstoke, UK: Palgrave Macmillan.

Martin, B. (1994). Plagiarism: A misplaced emphasis. *Journal of Information Ethics, 3*(2), 36-47.

Matalene, C. (1985). Contrastive rhetoric: An American writing teacher in China. *College English*, *47*(8), 789-808.

Myers, S. (1998). Questioning author(ity): ESL/EFL, science and teaching about plagiarism. *Teaching English as a Second or Foreign Language*, *3*(2), 1-21.

Orgel, S. (2003). Plagiarism and Original Sin. In P. Kewes (Ed.), *Plagiarism in early modern England* (pp. 56-73). Basingstoke, UK: Palgrave Macmillan.

Pennycook, A. (1996). Borrowing others' words: Text, ownership, memory, and plagiarism. *TESOL Quarterly*, *30*(2), 201-230.

Randall, M. (2001). *Pragmatic plagiarism: Authorship, profit and power*. Toronto: University of Toronto Press.

Scollon, R. (1994). As a matter of fact: The changing ideology of authorship and responsibility in discourse. *World Englishes*, *13*(1), 33-46.

Scollon, R. (1995). Plagiarism and ideology: Identity in intercultural discourse. *Language in Society*, *24*(1), 1-28.

Sherman, J. (1992). Your own thoughts in your own words. *ELT Journal*, *46*(3), 190-198.

St Onge, K.R. (1988). *The melancholy anatomy of plagiarism*. Lanham, MD: University Press of America.

Sutherland-Smith, W. (2005). Pandora's box: Academic perceptions of student plagiarism in writing. *Journal of English for Academic Purposes*, *4*(1), 83-95.

Thompson, C., & Pennycook, A. (2008). Intertextuality in the transcultural contact zone. In R.M. Howard, & A.E. Robillard (Eds.), *Pluralizing plagiarism: Identities, contexts, pedagogies* (pp. 124-139.) Portsmouth, NH: Boynton/Cook.

Tönnies, F. (2002/1887). *Community and society* (C. Loomis, Trans.). New York: Dover Publications.

University of Oxford. (n.d.). Plagiarism. Retrieved 15 February 2017 from http://www.admin.ox.ac.uk.

Veel, R. (1998). The greening of school science: Ecogenesis in school classrooms. In J.R. Martin, & R. Veel (Eds.), *Reading science: Critical and functional perspectives on discourses of science* (pp. 113-151). London & New York: Routledge..

Wallerstein, I. (1984). *The politics of the world-economy: The states, the movements and the civilizations*. Cambridge: Cambridge University Press.

11

Training 'clerks of the [global] empire' for 21ˢᵗ-century Asia?

English for Research Purposes [ERP] in Vietnam

Thuc Anh Cao Xuan and Kate Cadman

1. Introductory background

Recent global escalation of English language [EL] teaching has led to increasing concern, especially in Asia, about the most appropriate ways to teach English and to conduct and publish anglophone research in Asian contexts. Established Western assumptions about the huge benefits of international research are now spreading globally at an accelerating rate: 'the research carried out in universities, in industry, in government laboratories, and in independent research organizations touches the lives of almost every one of the world's billions of people' (Kulakowski & Chronister, 2008, p. 3). As a consequence, government policy reforms in many Asian countries now demand that academics and research students carry out globally acceptable research in order to advance their own country's capacity to access and contribute to international knowledge repertoires.

1.1. Development of ELT and research training in Vietnam

This political trend towards the prioritising of research has been notably evident in Vietnam with accelerating emphasis since the innovations of the reform period of the 1990s. During the periods of warfare in Vietnam in the late 1940s and 1950s, Vietnam's education system was influenced by conflicting models, one of which followed the philosophies of other Socialist countries while the other was under the control of the

Southern government and reflected Western values when the first prime minister of the south put its education 'in a faithful translation of the French education program' (London, 2011, p. 14). After the end of the war, North and South Vietnam reunited and, in 1986, the new government led the nation through a period called *Đổi Mới* or 'Renovation'. Nguyen (2014) shows that marked changes in educational priorities started during the *Đổi Mới* period, in which the Vietnamese Ministry of Education and Training [MOET] actively opened up opportunities for innovation, asking for capital from many sectors, even from foreign countries, and strategically sending educators abroad to learn about international trends in education.

These developments were especially significant in the field of English language teaching [ELT]. Prior to *Đổi Mới*, French and Russian had been the dominant foreign languages in Vietnam, but as a result of the rapid globalisation of English, English has taken over to become the required and most sought-after language right across primary, secondary and tertiary levels (Tran et al., 2014). Significantly, changes in teaching approaches have accompanied these policy movements. Learners in the mid- and late 20th century in Vietnam rarely practised English communication and there was very little language interaction among both students and teachers, as English was primarily learned through grammar-translation tasks. Since Renovation, however, the Vietnamese government has gradually put stronger focus on making English more interactive and 'usable' in communicative contexts. It is now felt that young people have to know how to communicate in English in order to work effectively with scholars and capitalise on flowing investments from foreign trade. Nevertheless, without targeted research to better understand the characteristics, constraints and opportunities relevant to specific Vietnamese contexts of learning, it is still not clearly apparent exactly how these goals may best be achieved.

Intertwined with this new focus on EL communication is the Vietnamese government's recognition of the need to expand the country's research capacity. The fundamental role of research in developing educational practice is generally recognised: 'No one would think of getting to the Moon or of wiping out a disease without research. Likewise, one cannot expect reform efforts in education to have significant effects without research-based knowledge to guide them' (Shavelson & Towne, as cited in Phye et al. (p. 68), 2005). Consequently, research methods are increasingly being taught to students at both undergraduate and postgraduate level. In Vietnam, according to Nguyen (2014, p. 3), government policy is now beginning to recognise that 'emphasis should be placed on expanding the role of research in universities' as a crucial step in implementing its reform goals. However, an in-depth study by Tran and Marginson (2014) reveals that, compared to other countries in the region, training in English language research skills and writing in Vietnamese tertiary contexts is only developing slowly. Pham (2006) provides a range of local, institutional reasons for this, including a lack of effective English language research training opportunities.

1.2. Dilemmas in teaching English for Research Purposes [ERP]

The on going dilemmas facing research training and English for Research Purposes [ERP] in Vietnam are rooted in Vietnamese traditional approaches to education. The first and perhaps the most challenging issue lies, as in many contexts in Asia, in the appropriateness of student-centred pedagogy for the diverse contexts that Asia represents. Recurring questions centre on how far, and how, a research skills teacher should *direct* a learner towards appropriate decisions on research topics, methods, analysis techniques and language — or, alternatively, whether the teacher should rather stimulate learners to experiment creatively and critically evaluate their own work, while s/he *facilitates and guides* the process.

In Western contexts, tertiary teachers tend to emphasise the importance of helping their students to be independent learners (Hunt & Chalmers, 2013). Chalmers and Fuller (2012, p. 3) cite Dawkins to argue strongly that universities should 'increase individuals' capacity to learn, [and] provide them with a framework with which to analyse problems and to increase their capacity to deal with new information' , rather than simply providing them with new content material. Undergraduate students are now perceived as being able to develop their own critical minds without the need for a teacher to hold their hands and show them how things should be done. Nevertheless, this approach has been described as historically very common in Asia, where educational change is gradually taking place at a slow pace (Law & Miura, 2015). In Vietnam specifically, Doan (2004, p. 146) identifies the 'widespread practice of "learning" by memorizing a lesson sample that closely resembles the final exam, so as to maximize student score'. In our experience, and that of our teacher-practitioner students, this practice is still often observed across Vietnam, even where critical, communicative goals are explicitly sought. Thus, with diverse social and institutional pressures like these, teachers easily find themselves struggling to define their own roles. This may especially be the case for ERP courses in which students need to be instructed in unfamiliar research techniques, while simultaneously being guided in the process of designing and implementing an original research project for assessment (as advocated by Pfeffer & Rogalin, 2012).

A further, related obstacle to effective ERP provision may be seen in the experience and qualifications of the academic staff responsible. Even though English language lecturers in Vietnam are required by MOET to conduct and publish their own research — that is, to develop appropriate research skills themselves (Gorsuch, 2006) — it is questionable how many have fulfilled this requirement today. Pham's (2006) detailed study of ELT lecturers' research output shows that in the early 2000s such research was not happening for a variety of endemic reasons. In respect to ERP, this obviously means that teachers are very often not practising researchers themselves, and may thus be unclear about the dominant research and writing procedures of the global academy. Today, there is little Vietnamese scholarship for novices to draw on and thus they have many questions left unanswered about how to research and write their discipline, or how to teach ERP skills as part of an advanced EL curriculum.

For all these reasons, formal education in Vietnam has been described as a system 'at a crossroads' (London, 2011). Teachers are being explicitly encouraged to try new teaching methods which in some places are being effectively implemented, yet teacher instruction and unquestioned obedience are still widely in evidence. Today the conflict between the old ways and the newer philosophy, when 'aspirations and constraints collide' (p. 3), seems to be found in many developing countries, and Vietnam, as an illuminating example, is clearly experiencing it. For those of us invested in the future of ERP, as Wagner et al. (2011, p. 83) have demonstrated, 'There is a pressing need for widespread debate, informed by pedagogical research, around what makes successful research methods teachers'. Under the pressure of globalisation, it is especiallly important to investigate the diverse educational practices of our own contexts.

1.3. 'Glocal' research questions

Others have also recognised the importance today of exploring both the reach and the implications of global trends in local non-anglophone settings. Roudometof (2016) has recently described these wider impacts of globalisation as involving

> waves that pass through the local in a way similar to that of light passing through glass. The result is not only a reflection of its qualities back onto the world stage but also refraction through the local. Glocalization is therefore defined as the refraction of globalization through the local. The result is glocality — a blend of the local and the global. (p. 13)

In fact, as Zielonka (2015, p. 2) has said, today global research needs to probe these 'glocal' forces in their own contexts, since it is 'local culture that assigns meaning to global and regional influences'.

As the authors of this chapter, we are immersed in these 'glocal' investigations in different ways. One of us is the primary researcher for this study: a young Vietnamese English language teacher with a great aspiration to develop broader and more rigorous research skills, as well as to develop effective ways to teach them to ERP learners; she wants, above all, to understand better what is going on in her own country. The other is an experienced researcher and research facilitator who has spent many years teaching and learning in the EL teaching culture of Vietnam and who wants to throw light on her own role in spreading Western epistemologies and rhetorical logics into Asian research contexts. As a team, we found we shared certain values and interests which gave rise to some key questions for us about the implications of teaching Western research methods in Vietnam, and about teaching ERP writing in contexts that are in many ways alien to its history and value systems. We worked together, then, to probe some of the philosophical and practical issues we were meeting in our different teaching situations: Is student-centred learning seen as an appropriate approach for this Vietnamese ERP context? If we follow guidebooks such as that by Burton (2000) in targeting established 'research skills that help students collect, process and analyse data' (p. 1), are we in fact restricting the next generation of Asian researchers to conform to Western procedures, and limiting them to being 'clerks' of the global academic 'empire' (Giroux, 1994; Kim, 2011)? Finally, our personal experiences of both studying and teaching ERP courses prompted us to dig deeper into these issues to answer the question: How is ERP understood, and taught, in practice in Vietnam today?

With that overarching aim in mind, we focused on a specific course on 'English Research Skills and Writing' [ERSW] conducted by what we call in this chapter the City University of Vietnam [CUV], in order to answer the following questions:

- How do teachers perceive their multiple roles in the research skill course in the English Department of CUV?
- How do these teachers carry out their teaching practice and engage in their students' projects?
- How do students respond to their interactions with their teachers and to the ways teachers are engaged in the process of teaching them and facilitating their projects?

2. Methodology and methods

2.1. Critical pedagogic framing

As we have mentioned, we approached the design of this study in light of recent theoretical scholarship, which stresses the potentially destructive impacts of adopting anglophone norms in research and pedagogy for local-periphery contexts in both Europe and Asia (see, for example, Alastrué & Pérez-Llantada, 2015; Cadman, 2014). Thus we were conscious of Western critical values in both teaching and research as we sought to understand how Vietnamese ERP teachers and students saw and enacted their roles in research education. One of the most highly revered leaders in this pursuit is Paolo Freire, as Giroux (1992, p. 1) early pointed out: 'Increasingly, Freire's work has become the standard reference for engaging in what is often referred to as teaching for critical thinking, dialogical pedagogy, or critical literacy' ; many others have very recently endorsed a 'return to Freirean thinking' (O'Shea & O'Brien, 2011). Thus, we adopted a Freirean (1970) framework to inform our investigation and, while we acknowledge that our engagement with Freire's work is primarily pedagogic rather than political, we welcome its yoking of pedagogy, oppression and transformation for our considerations of 'glocal' ERP in Vietnam today.

2.2. Freire's 'banking' and transformation approaches in teaching

Identifying two distinct sets of goals and procedures in formal education, Freire's 1970 study has been seen to offer a yardstick. Here he describes one approach which he suggests prioritises procedures of educational 'banking' and effectively places the teacher at the centre of the educational process as a 'narrating subject' with the students as 'listening objects' (p. 71). For Freire, such a process holds back the development of students, in that even the knowledge itself at the heart of the learning is conceptualised as 'motionless facts' (p. 71) which teachers hand over directly to their students. The student's primary role is to receive that knowledge, thus exercising minimal creativity in their learning. Whether feeling fulfilled or uncomfortable in this process, students are not required to demonstrate autonomy; to become 'good' students requires them basically to follow instructions, learn the given material and question little.

In contrast, Freire's (1970) 'transformation' approach is seen as promoting learners' creativity and freedom. In learning activities, they are encouraged to raise their voices and share their perspectives, which, in Freire's eyes, engages their humanity and transforms them into beings who have their own ways of thinking and interpreting experience. Such a teaching approach has been especially acclaimed as opening dialogic relations between teachers and students for classroom learning (see Young, 1992). In presenting strong arguments against 'banking' procedures, Kim (2011) shows how questions can be raised to show diverse perspectives on field materials, even those usually defined as established 'facts'. He argues that teachers engaged in 'banking' pedagogies often ignore opportunities for analysis and debate; they present 'knowledge as absolute and irrefutable and demand that students believe and accept it without questioning' (p. 55). This is Freire's (1970, p. 74) 'dehumanizing' process, which is seen to reduce learners to 'passive robots who do not have feeling and autonomy' (Shim, 2008, p. 527). A resulting and circular complication may then occur if teachers themselves want to go a different way; it may be that students are not happy with the new freedoms they are given. A striking example of this is shown in McNiff's (2012) analysis of teaching in Ireland and South Africa, where in both contexts the students considered the teacher as 'The One Who Knows' (p. 135) with the responsibility to hand over designated material, and they resisted their teachers' attempts to act differently. As Freire (1970) argues strongly, learners' naturally transformative curiosities can thus be distorted by non-dialogic teaching styles when they are deeply embedded in social customs. It thus became our goal to understand how students may be positioning themselves in ERP in Vietnam.

2.3. 'Banking' and transformative educational approaches in Asia and Vietnam

In Asia, these old-style teaching methods, which involve teachers in transmitting knowledge and students in passively receiving it, have become so deep-rooted that they may not easily be reshaped. A 2015 study by UNESCO on *Transforming Teaching and Learning in Asia and the Pacific* clearly describes the historical conditions of learning in Asia:

> [T]he conventional approach to teaching and learning ... puts an emphasis on uniformity of learning objectives, contents, activities and assessment formats, regardless of the interests and needs of children. This approach is linked with the reproduction model of knowledge transmission, which was considered the key to producing a workforce for the industrial sector. (Law & Miura, 2015, p. 3)

Today, however, significant shifts in pedagogical priorities are being witnessed, towards an approach which 'recognizes that children have diverse learning needs and which engages learners in a series of problem- or issue-based learning experiences to enable them to gain the skills and values required for lifelong learning' (p. 3).

One key to the implementation of these crucial pedagogic changes lies in informed policy development. In recent years, in order to sustain a competitive position in the globalising marketplace, many Asian governments have made significant policy innovations to foster educational change, and these have been well documented in countries such as 'Hong Kong, Singapore, Taiwan, South Korea, Japan, and mainland China' (Mok, 2006, p. 2). Further, in Japan, Yoneyama (2012, p. 228) has shown how, with the goal of producing more creative and critical citizens, the government now offers 'maximum liberty for teachers to be innovative and creative, and encourages students to think outside the textbook'. For Yoneyama, this is a very positive step in the quest for a characteristically Asian model of 'critical thinking' involving 'empathy and respect for the person with whom one holds a critical dialogue' (p. 230). In other words, Asian teachers are here exhorted to listen to students' opinions and try to understand their arguments in respectful critical dialogic interaction.

As we have noted, however, in our experience the wave of pedagogic change is not yet very big in Vietnam. Because the country is 'at a crossroads' (London, 2011), slow progress is inevitable: the old trend still demonstrably wants to keep its important position in the country's education (Doan, 2004), while the new is struggling to be seen and recognised. Nevertheless, thanks to government incentives, not all teachers wish their students to be passive, especially in tertiary institutions, and many students do not enjoy following exactly what they are told to do. As a result, Freire's (1970) theoretical concepts from four decades ago represent a very useful framework for analysing Vietnam's educational practices today, and this is especially true in ERP contexts.

2.4. Research design and method

Since this research aims to offer personal and subjective perspectives, both from the researchers and the participants, a constructivist paradigm and qualitative methodology were chosen. In this paradigm it is understood that human beings are complex and multifocal in their opinions; researching with them means we recognise that 'inner states are not directly observable, so qualitative researchers must rely on subjective judgments to bring them to light' (Hatch, 2010, p. 9). This kind of subjective approach does not aim to establish 'truth', nor to be qualitatively 'managed' in a set of strategic procedures, but rather to draw on Heshusius's (1994) foundational idea of 'participatory consciousness' so as to develop the trustworthy reflexive perspectives of ourselves as situated educational researchers (see Gallagher, 2015).

2.4.1. Setting

Our immediate context here is an ERP workplace that has emerged as a result of the Vietnamese government's demand for, and encouragement of, research both in and out of universities. With the focus on improving both the quantity and quality of research outcomes, research training programs have started to appear in major universities in big cities of Vietnam at both undergraduate and post-graduate levels. This small-scale study aimed to investigate the current goals and practices of undergraduate research training at a well-respected Vietnamese urban university, here referred to as the City University of Vietnam [CUV].

In many undergraduate contexts in Vietnam, research training is conducted under the umbrella of the English department, as a special course which falls under the designated skill of English language writing. Consequently, this target research and writing skills program was located in CUV's English department. Research writing courses were delivered over two years by the department, with the Primary Research Skills and Writing [PRSW] course occurring in the second year. For the purposes of this study, this course is categorised into three phases:

- *Phase 1: Learning the theory.* In this phase, students are introduced to the criteria for research writing for the first time. They have to select a topic, develop research questions, and find references for their own research study.
- *Phase 2: Putting the theory into practice.* Students learn about designing a questionnaire and using it for a survey to gather data. Undergraduates in CUV's English department are advised to use quantitative methodology for its 'objectivity'. They are technically permitted to use qualitative methodologies, but these seem to be unpopular among both teachers and students.
- *Phase 3: Data analysis and writing.* Students use the data gathered in Phase 2 to write an analysis and then produce a final research report.

2.4.2. Participants

The research participants were all teachers and second-year students in this department.[1] Two teachers (T1 and T2) were currently teaching the first two phases of the 2015 course, and the third (T3), had taught the third phase in 2014. The teachers in the project not only taught theoretical material but also supervised their students' work. Each teacher was in charge of one class of approximately 25 second-year students, which

---

1 All participants are referred to by coding labels to protect anonymity.

was further divided into 12 pairs who conducted joint research projects. Though the purpose of this structure was to help reduce the amount of work for teachers, with about 12 research projects to supervise in one semester, teachers had historically met a number of problems.

The student participants (S1-9) were third-year and second-year students who were undergoing Phases 1 and 2 or had recently completed Phase 3 of the PRSW course. Before enrolling in this course, students had no experience of research, so they, too, could meet unexpected problems.

2.4.3. Data collection and analysis

To secure rigour in the qualitative process and ensure that 'the themes emerge from the data and are not imposed upon it by the researchers' (Dawson, 2002, p. 115), data were collected and triangulated from three sources: classroom observation notes, teacher interviews, and student interviews (Pine, 2008). Four classroom observations were carried out, in order to capitalise on a method which can 'be employed in "natural" settings, rather than those set up for research purposes' (Walshe, Ewing & Griffiths, 2012, p. 1049). Teachers T1 and T2 were interviewed during each of the first two phases of the course, and T3 was interviewed after having recently completed the teaching of Phase 3. Also, a total of 15 interviews was conducted with students from all three phases of the course. The teacher interviews were carried out in English, while the student interviews were in Vietnamese because the students found it easier to express their ideas and thoughts in their mother tongue. The passages of response in Vietnamese were translated into English by the bilingual researcher of this chapter, with the aim of representing the students' meanings as faithfully as possible.

Thematic analysis was then conducted, following the well-endorsed guidelines set down by Braun and Clarke (2006), coding the data into different themes that showed 'some level of patterned response or meaning within the data set' (p. 82). Investigating the data initially through the lens offered by Freire's (1970) fundamental pedagogic 'transmission' and 'transformation' approaches described above allowed for the generation of subthemes reflecting how the teachers were conceptualising the PRSW course and working within it, as well as the students' perspectives on the roles that the teachers were playing.

3. Results and discussion

As we focused directly on the ways in which the three participant teachers were engaging 'transmission' or 'transformation' strategies, as Freire (1970) defines them, the categories that emerged from the thematic analysis became 'Classroom atmosphere', 'Teachers' explained goals' and 'Teachers' situated practice'. In this ERP exploration, we felt it was important not only to learn the teachers' views but also to integrate students' perspectives.

Teachers in this context who trust knowledge transfer activities often feel constrained by Vietnamese institutional requirements, and with similar instrumental motivation, some students prioritise what they should do to succeed in the course by pleasing their teachers, following instructions and avoiding disapproval. Other teachers and students may want to go a different way — that is, they may want to use the teaching/learning context to demonstrate independence and creativity. However, there is no simple binary here; students may indeed want to get approval and good results but they may prefer to stand out, and their teachers may well be impressed by their originality.

Importantly for the 'glocal' framing of this research, it was not appropriate for us to observe through only one 'lens'. First, we had to see the teaching and learning through Freire's (1970) validated conceptual framework. However, it was also crucial for us to stand at 'the crossroads' — that is, to look from a locally situated view, at education in a country which is undergoing a period of refreshing its own education system yet still struggling between old traditions and new aspirations.

3.1. Classroom atmosphere

Through both the observations and interviews, it became clear that the content structure of the lessons given by T1, T2 and T3 in part represented the 'banking' approach. As a matter of fact, it was not that all of the lessons given by the three teachers reduced students' autonomy in the classroom, but clearly the teachers often unconsciously made it happen. This was shown in the initial classroom atmosphere of both classes C1 and C2. In Class C1, Teacher T1 was information-focused right from the beginning of the course. She headed the whole class towards a relationship in which she was the 'giver' and her students the 'receivers'. As we observed, this sometimes led to students' distraction because they could not do much but sit still and listen: 'They did not look very active, with their eyes looking out of the window or their hands playing with pens, lost in their own thoughts'. This was the first experience of learning the expectations of research writing for these students, so perhaps Teacher T1 wanted them only to pay attention to the content of her lecture. However, it seemed to discourage her class, as students S2 and S3 described: 'We sat there looking at the task for half of the given time. It was not until the teacher reminded us that our time had almost ended that we started to rush'. T1, however, had her own explanation for her 'banking' approach: 'In this class, the students are quiet. It is not because they are low level students but that seems to be their characteristic'. Feeling she had a class with a tendency to be quiet, she wanted to make sure they had no problem understanding what she said, so she bent her original intention of following a more transformational approach. The principal researcher's observations noted that there were moments when 'the atmosphere was dominated by discipline and conformity' and the teacher's 'authoritarian manner'. She was heard to say, 'I cannot let you leave early because if I do, you will not be able to complete your research. I cannot assure that you will get high marks, because the mark does not depend on me. It depends on you'. In this atmosphere, students were aware of the fact that they were 'recipients' but notably, they did not remain unhappy with these teaching methods. They often engaged consciously, seemingly not with empty minds but with judgment, and were largely quite willing to follow her orders.

By contrast, there were times when teachers deliberately encouraged their class's autonomy. For example, even in the atmosphere described above, T1 gave extra marks to those who raised their voices to interrupt the routine process of 'listen, receive and repeat'. More significantly, for Teacher T2 there were clearly dialogic outcomes from the way she physically organised the classroom. The classroom observation notes show that, in her class, 'students are sitting in groups of four and each group consists of two pairs. The two members of a pair are to work with each other in one research paper'. Tables and chairs were arranged with a path between them so that T2 could easily walk to any pairs who asked for help. This method seemed to have a good influence on the self-management of the whole class, as they did groupwork most of the time and almost no-one was seen to be distracted away from the task given. They looked quite relaxed and as though they were in dialogue with, rather than intimidated by, their teacher.

3.2. Teachers' explained goals

In the interviews, these teachers expressed their desire to follow a transformation-type approach. When asked, all three teachers expressed that they were avoiding methods which relied on students' passive receptivity because making students confident in themselves as researchers was what they wanted. Teacher T1 declared that her goal was to 'help them, not do it for them'. She did not hide her frustration at Class C1's silence when she varied her method in order to teach in a way that was 'different from their learning preferences'. At that time our classroom observations noted that 'the co-operation between the teacher and the students was not that good'. She thought that asking questions would be a good way to prompt them to come up with new ideas, but Class C1 did not understand that she was giving them encouragement. Similarly, Teacher T2 wanted to focus on and nurture her students' interest in research by helping them see 'what they like and what they want to know because being a researcher is to know what there is in life'. T2 set the goal for herself to move students from pragmatism to passion. She 'was ardent' about research writing and thus wanted to spread the spirit so that her students could also be 'passionate about their topic' and participate with joy. Interestingly, both teachers said they wanted their students to understand themselves, and they planned to organise lessons with students at the centre. This clearly reflects Freire's (1970, p. 75) 'quest for mutual humanisation', which involves teachers having 'a profound trust in people and their creative power … [T]hey must be partners of the students in their relations with them'. Both T1 and T2 expressed the desire for this kind of relationship with students.

In contrast, in certain comments, the teachers did not hide their natural tendency to control the class. Teacher T1 thought students 'need the teacher's guidance because as they go, questions arise and I'm there to answer the questions'. She saw her role as central in the classroom, and this was of great importance to her. For T2, her biggest task was to make 'even the weakest student in the class understand what to do'. She did not want her students to 'struggle' on their own, as she felt they might misunderstand her instructions and thus do their research faultily. In fact, teachers acting in the manner of 'clerks' was not seen as negative when what students needed was precise information. Similarly, Teacher T3 explained, that in each of her research courses, she gave her class, C3, a check-list of what to include in their data analysis writing. Dictatorial as this may sound, this 'deposit' method was perceived to actually help C3 avoid unnecessary arguments and digressions in their research. Teacher T3 also made it compulsory for Class C3 to do extra grammar and vocabulary homework to strengthen their academic writing ability. In her view, leaving students to do this voluntarily meant that most of them would avoid it and produce poorly written research. As a result, the so-called 'banking' approach that all three teachers headed towards was seen by us to have not only weaknesses but also strengths in this context.

3.3. Teachers' situated practice

As teachers, it would be ideal for us all if we were consistently able to follow our own best plans. However, when it comes to real-life teaching situations, institutional requirements and student relationships may prevent us.

3.3.1. The 'banking' approach in action

Unsurprisingly, the teachers in this research often acted differently from their own aspirations and found that it was not possible for them to consistently follow their own transformative goals. In practice, all three fundamentally relied on a knowledge transfer approach. For Teachers T1 and T2, this was seen first in the way they organised the content of the course. Being the head of the writing skill division in this department, T1 had built the course and had been invested in improving its quality, as she said, 'for at least five years and it has been quite a success'. Similarly, having taught this subject for several years, T2 knew 'the difficulties, the obstacles and the challenges to help you write a research successfully'. Both these teachers had much experience with the obstacles students often meet, and knew how to deal with them. Consequently, they viewed it as actually legitimate and less time-consuming for students to be following their instructions.

Timeframe was another element that was not negotiable for students, as it was already set by teaching staff. Though very few students challenged course content, some of them complained about the schedule. Student S3 of Class C1 strongly wished she did not have to 'wait another week to see my teacher face to face and receive the comments', because she wanted to carry out the project quickly while her ideas were still fresh. In Class C2, Teacher T2 was relatively more flexible, but she still required time between lessons for her students to think of questions that might have come up, as 'asking the right question … is an art and it is not easy to teach an art', especially in a tight timeframe.

Within such constraints, there was diverse feedback from students of both classes. Student S3 described Teacher T1's suggestion that she change her research topic, saying 'we had to change' in a way that conveyed she was not happy with the decision. She confessed that both she and her partner were 'very fond of the topic', yet she agreed it was appropriate to change the research question for the time-pressure reasons given by the teacher. Similarly, when Student S4 of Class C2 first recalled the time that T2 crossed out half of her questionnaire draft because the questions were irrelevant to the study, her tone was resentful because, in her view, the questions were interesting and relevant enough. Nevertheless, after discussion, both S3 and S4 came to value the advice, as 'only the teacher knew all the details in the study and [our colleagues] did not'. Finally, this pair came up with a way to design new questions, and both they and T2 were content. In these cases, student creativity was nurtured by what first appeared to be teacher dominance, though significantly without any 'depositing' of ideas.

In Class C3, however, a more clearly 'dehumanizing' situation occurred when Teacher T3 gave the students the task of pointing out mistakes made in a previous research paper. After a long time waiting for suggested answers, she said she finally 'had to tell my students, because it is easier for me to see the mistake. They did not have any experience of doing data analysis'. She perceived that, after listening to her, 'they immediately understood' — in other words, when allowed autonomy, Class C3 failed to do the given task. In this activity, they seemed to learn more effectively when T3's role as 'narrating subject' (Freire, 1970, p. 71) was fulfilled.

3.3.2. Practices of educational 'transformation'

When the three teachers announced that they would try to increase their students' creativity in the classroom, they all partly achieved their goal. Through the observations and the interview stories, it was clear that course materials were designed to engage students' autonomy. For students' selection of research topics, for example, T2 tried to reduce their experience of being 'listening objects' (Freire, 1970, p. 71) by giving them a set of personal questions to answer. From this activity, they could narrow down their area of interest and gradually come up with a topic which stimulated them. This enacts Freire's (1970, p. 60) description of the role of a transformational teacher, when he says, 'They must abandon the educational goal of deposit-making and replace it with the posing of the problems of human beings in their relations with the world'. In Class C1, T1 practised this by giving students a questionnaire and asking them to discuss and point out its faults. Student S1 complimented this method as vitally helping her understand 'questions that are not objective, which means we impose our own viewpoint on those questions'. Also using materials to encourage students' dialogic input, Teacher T3 gave handouts about research writing theory as homework for students to do in discussion groups. When they read and talked together at home, they improved their critical perspectives on how to write good research.

It was not only in materials but also in the encouragement of independent critical thinking that the teachers aimed to increase students' autonomy. T1 tried to trigger Class C1's 'critical consciousness' by consistently requiring them to discuss with her their own ideas for topics of research. Freire (1970) explains this in the following way: 'The teacher cannot think for her students, nor can she impose her thought on them. Authentic thinking, thinking that is concerned about *reality*, does not take place in ivory tower isolation, but only in communication' (p. 58, emphasis in the original). Clearly, some students understood the value of such tasks. Students S4 and S5 of Class C2 confidently explained: '[A]t the very beginning, if we had not had a topic, how could the teacher help any of us?', and: 'She can only give comments on our work when there is work for her to do it on'. This also happened in Class C3 when one pair wanted to change their topic too late in the course. At first T3 tried to persuade them to keep the old topic but finally she gave them the choice to act against her specific advice: 'If they wanted to continue, I could still see a way to get them out of the mess. But after giving guidance, they still insisted in changing the topic, so I had to let them change. And then they came up with a wonderful topic'. This pair then spent double the effort and time to catch up with the others, and so, in this case, by transferring the responsibility for learning to the students, T3 not only encouraged their Freirean 'critical consciousness' but also raised their enthusiasm and inspiration.

Conversely, some other students felt discouraged when pressure was placed on their creativity and self-learning ability. Conflict could easily arise in what Freire (1970, p. 79) describes as 'the teacher-student contradiction' which can only 'be resolved [through] dialogical relations'. For Students S8 and S9, a disagreement occurred in the number of surveys they would hand out. After being advised to distribute 50, they thought: '[T]he more questionnaires we hand out, the more reliable our result is', and so they went with 150. They were then given a 'yes' when they consulted T3, who allowed them to follow their own plan. Later, the students realised that the number was too big to work with and were critical of T3 for not stopping them from making that decision. Others also looked for more direction. Student S7 hoped that T3 'could give me more guidance and comments so we can go the right way and then be creative'. Class C3 wished that T3 had given them more structured tutorial sessions, since they 'might not have thought of a question to ask and it was not until I was in the tutorial that I had an idea'. The classroom atmosphere at that time, as S9 recalled, was messy, as the students were all having problems and did not know where to start when they had no chance to discuss anything with the teacher. The explanation from T3 was: 'If I identify the problem for you and then tell you directly how to fix it, then it is no longer your research but it is mine' (S9). For these students, clear initial teacher direction was sought, which raises questions about the applicability of Freire's (1970) arguments in all situations.

4. Conclusion: A view from the crossroads

It is clear, as discussed, that Freire's (1970) strong views on the oppressive outcomes of education based on a fundamental transfer of knowledge approach have been developed and endorsed by many Western scholars. Perhaps such educational leaders would look at the three classrooms in this study and see signs of student oppression, or, at the least, neglect. Especially in a context of research development and ERP, it may be possible to see these students as reprobated 'listening objects', or worse, 'lifeless machines' who are not given enough opportunity to raise their voices and develop their critical faculties. However, as seen in these observations and interviews, the students did not present much resistance or negative feedback about the mixed teaching approaches they experienced; even when teachers gave their students more chance to be creative, self-reliant or innovative, the students did not always value those chances. They often felt they needed guidance from a trusted source, and in this case the trusted source is the teacher. Years of following the old education system still leave their effects on social customs and on students. In fact, in a Vietnamese context, if students sit in the classroom listening to the teacher's presentation of useful information, and complete the tasks required, many today would say it is a healthy educational environment providing appropriate advantages. Thus, even while there are many signs of 'transformational' goals and methods being integrated into these ERP courses, if that old teaching approach is proving itself to be useful for students, it may not be effective for Vietnamese teachers to jump right over from their conventional 'banking' approach and prioritise critical, dialogic strategies.

Thus it seems that changes to accommodate globalisation appropriately take different forms and there is no perfect or homogeneous way of teaching ERP for the whole world. While it is evident that many Asian countries like Vietnam are stepping on the route drawn by Western anglophone research, critics like Hamilton (2008, p. 14) have argued that globalisation's effects may 'overtake a country's traditional identity' and contribute to the 'Westernization or Americanization of the world'. However, as Roudometof (2016, p. 65) points out above, what prevents this is 'glocality', or 'the refraction of globalization through the local'. The Vietnamese teachers here are rewriting their own story with the ideas given by Western scholars, but they do not see uncritically mimicking the West as the best path to take.

In this case, in response to the question of whether we are acting as, and training, 'clerks of the global empire' (Giroux, 1994), it seems we are not. Those of us who are Vietnamese EL teachers clearly value our identities as educators who are open to Western developments, yet we still respond judiciously to the demands of our own classrooms. We aim towards Western theories while we continue to negotiate what will be appreciated by our students, by parents, and by ourselves as situated professionals. We strategically put ourselves in a 'salad bowl' rather than a 'melting pot'. The teaching approaches employed in the three classrooms here might not be flawless, but their significant strengths lie in their synchronicity with the real teaching and learning situations involved.

References

Alastrué, R.P., & Pérez-Llantada, C. (2015). *English as a scientific and research language: Debates and discourses. Vol. 2: English in Europe*. Berlin: de Gruyter.

Bodewig, C., & Badiani-Magnusson, R. (2014). *Skilling up Vietnam: Preparing the workforce for a modern market economy*. Washington, DC: World Bank.

Braun, V., & Clarke, V. (2006). Using thematic analysis in psychology. *Qualitative Research in Psychology, 3*(2), 77-101.

Burton, D. (Ed). (2000). *Research training for social scientists: A handbook for postgraduate researchers*. London: SAGE.

Cadman, K. (2014). Of house and home: Reflections on knowing and writing for a 'southern' postgraduate pedagogy. In L. Thesen & L. Cooper (Eds.), *Risk in academic writing: Postgraduate students, their teachers and the making of knowledge* (pp. 166-200). Bristol: Multilingual Matters.

Chalmers, D., & Fuller, R. (2012). *Teaching for learning at university*. Oxford: Routledge.

Dawson, C. (2002). *Practical research methods: A user-friendly guide to mastering research techniques and projects*. Oxford: How To Books.

Doan, H.D. (2004). Centralism — The dilemma of educational reforms in Vietnam. In D. McCargo (Ed), *Rethinking Vietnam* (pp. 143-152). London: Routledge Curzon.

Freire, P. (1970). *Pedagogy of the oppressed*. New York: Herder and Herder.

Gallagher, D. (2015). The illusion of our separativeness: Exploring Heshusius's concept of participatory consciousness in disability research and inclusive education. In P. Jones, & F. Danforth (Eds.), *Foundations of inclusive education research* (pp. 205-222). Bingley, UK: Emerald.

Giroux, H.A. (1992). Paolo Freire and the politics of postcolonialism. In A. Kempf (Ed.), *Breaching the colonial contract: Anti-colonialism* (pp. 79-90). New York: Springer. Retrieved 10 May 2016 from https://www.henryagiroux.com/online_articles/Paulo_friere.htm.

Giroux, H.A. (1994). Teachers, public life, and curriculum reform. *Peabody Journal of Education, 69*(3), 35-47.

Gorsuch, G. (2006). Doing language education research in a developing country. *TESL-EJ, 10*(2), 1-7.

Hamilton, S.M. (2008). *Globalization*. Minnesota: ABDO.

Hatch, J.A. (2010). *Doing qualitative research in education settings*. New York: SUNY Press.

Heshusius, L. (1994). Freeing ourselves from objectivity: Managing subjectivity or turning toward a participatory mode of consciousness? *Educational Researcher, 23*(3), 15-22.

Hunt, L., & Chalmers, D. (2013). *University teaching in focus: A learning-centred approach*. New York: Routledge.

Kim, Y. (2011). The case against teaching as delivery of the curriculum. *Phi Delta Kappan, 92*(7), 54-56.

Kulakowski, E.C., & Chronister, L.U. (2008). *Research administration and management*. Sudbury, ON: Jones and Bartlett Canada.

Law, E.H-F., & Miura, U. (2015). *Transforming teaching and learning in Asia and the Pacific*. Paris & Bangkok: UNESCO.

London, J.D. (2011). Education in Vietnam: Historical roots, recent trends. In J.D. London (Ed.), *Education in Vietnam* (pp. 1-56). Singapore: Institute of Southeast Asian Study.

McNiff, J. (2012). Travels around identity: Transforming cultures of learned colonization. *Educational Action Research, 20*(1), 129-146.

Mok, K. (2006). *Education reform and education policy in East Asia*. Oxon, UK: Routledge.

Nguyen, T.T. (2014). *The challenge of science, technology and innovation in Vietnamese Higher Education*. Report for the Vietnam Ministry of Education and Training. Melbourne: LH Martin Institute. Retrieved 14 April 2016 from http://www.lhmartininstitute.edu.au/userfiles/files/2014%20Events/ThuyNguyen_STI%20policy.pdf.

O'Shea, A., & O'Brien, M. (Eds.). (2011). *Pedagogy, oppression and transformation in a post-critical climate: The return to Freirean thinking*. London: Continuum.

Pfeffer, C., & Rogalin, C. (2012). Three strategies for teaching research methods: A case study. *Teaching Sociology, 40*(4), 368-376.

Pham, H.H. (2006). Researching the research culture in English language education in Vietnam. *TESL-EJ, 10*(2), 1-20.

Phye, G.D., Robinson, D.H., & Levin, J. (2005). *Empirical methods for evaluating educational interventions*. San Diego, CA: Elsevier Academic Press.

Pine, G.J. (2008). *Teacher action research: Building knowledge democracies*. Thousand Oaks, CA: Sage.

Roudometof, V. (2016). *Glocalization: A critical introducition*. New York: Routledge.

Sheppard, M. (2004). *Appraising and using social research in the human services*. London: Jessica Kingsley.

Shim, S.H. (2008). A philosophical investigation of the role of teachers: A synthesis of Plato, Confucius, Buber and Freire. *Teaching and Teacher Education, 24*(3), 515-535.

Tran, L.T., & Marginson, S. (2014). Education for flexibility, practicality and mobility. In L.T. Tran, S. Marginson, H.M. Do, Q.T.N. Do, T.T.T. Le, N.T. Nguyen … & H.T.L. Nguyen (Eds.), *Higher education in Vietnam: Flexibility, mobility and practicality in the global knowledge economy* (pp. 3-28). New York: Palgrave Macmillan.

Tran, L.T., Marginson, S., Do, H.M., Do, Q.T.N., Le, T.T.T., Nguyen, N.T. … & Nguyen, H.T.L. (Eds.). (2014). *Higher education in Vietnam: Flexibility, mobility and practicality in the global knowledge economy*. New York: Palgrave Macmillan.

Wagner, C., Garner, M., & Kawulich, B. (2011). The state of the art of teaching research methods in the social sciences: Towards a pedagogical culture. *Studies in Higher Education, 36*(1), 75-88.

Walshe, C., Ewing, G., & Griffiths, J. (2012). Using observation as a data collection method to help understand patient and professional roles and actions in palliative care settings. *Palliative Medicine, 26*(8), 1048-1054.

Yoneyama, S. (2012). Critiquing critical thinking: Asia's contribution towards sociological conceptualization. In X. Song, & K. Cadman (Eds.), *Bridging transcultural divides: Asian languages and cultures in global higher education* (pp. 231-249). Adelaide: University of Adelaide Press. Retrieved 14 April 2016 from www.adelaide.edu.au/press/titles/transcultural-divides.

Young, R. (1992). *Critical theory and classroom talk.* Bristol: Multilingual Matters.

Zielonka, J. (2015). Introduction: Fragile democracy, volatile politics, and the quest for a free media. In J. Zielonka (Ed.), *Media and politics in new democracies: Europe in a comparative perspective* (pp. 1-24). Oxford: Oxford University Press.

12

Standardisation and its discontents

John M. Swales

1. Prologue

In his earlier days, the 20th-century British novelist Graham Greene made a distinction between his serious novels, such as *The Power and the Glory*, and his 'entertainments', like *Orient Express*. The former often dealt with serious issues of Catholic theology and ethics; the latter often had as their subject matter depictions of espionage activities. However, these entertainments often also raised serious issues of human behaviour at social, moral and political levels, and were not simply 'lightweight' in the normal sense of this term. In this essayist piece, I offer a Greene-coloured entertainment, but one which will be seen, if the reader perseveres, to have a serious purpose or two.[1]

2. Introduction

As many will recognise, my title is a riff on the famous book by Sigmund Freud, originally published in 1930 in German and entitled in English *Civilization and its Discontents*. Freud argued that civilisation acted as a necessary curb on the hedonistic and instinctual Pleasure Principle. Without the rules, regulations and conventions that civilised societies promulgate and impose, human beings would succumb to parricide, war, rape, pillage and so on. Without civilisation, following Freud, life would be a series of ancient Greek dramas or Shakespearean tragedies.

In the academic world, we also have regulations and conventions, although their existence is designed to mitigate less serious crimes and misdemeanours than those

---

1 This essay is based on a talk with the same title that I gave at PRISEAL3 in Coimbra, Portugal in October 2015. I had not, in fact, planned to turn the talk into a written piece, but several of the people who heard it have urged me to do so.

Freud invoked. And, indeed, there are recognised crimes of writing, such as forgery, false authorship, child pornography, libel and bolder attempts to plagiarise (Stewart, 1994). So, in science, conventions have been established for the priority system for naming natural and scientific discoveries so that the field, in the famous phrase, 'be not thrown into confusion'. There are also conventions regarding plagiarism, although what exactly can be borrowed or copied, and where exactly lies the boundary separating permissible practices and unacceptable ones, have long been much disputed, and are now embroiled in questions of social constructionism, intertextuality, and diverse temporal and cross-cultural expectations (for example, Pecorari, 2003; Pennycook, 1996). Especially in literary worlds, widely varied opinions exist. On the one hand, the Roman philosopher and dramatist Seneca can write, 'What anyone has said well is mine', or T.S. Eliot can suggest, 'Good poets borrow, great poets steal'. On the other hand, we have John Donne, the leading metaphysical poet and celebrated Dean of St Paul's Cathedral in London with this trenchant couplet on being plagiarised:

> If one eat my meat, let it be known
> The meat was mine, the excrement is his own.

However, let's leave this difficult area and move on to something else, especially as I tend to find that my opinions about plagiarism are more liberal than most.

3. Imaginary authorship

Consider the following:

> C. Batich, E. Heilbronner, V. Hornung, A.J. Ashe, D.T. Clark, U.T. Cobley, D. Kilcast, I. Scanlan. (1973). Applications of photoelectron spectroscopy 41: Photoelectron spectra of phosphabenzene, arsabenzene, and stibabenzene. *Journal of the American Chemical Society*, 95: 928-930.

I believe (as, incidentally, does Wikipedia) that one of the authors in the above paper is imaginary; in other words, he (or just possibly she) does not exist. British readers will probably be in the best position to identify the interloper because of their possible familiarity with a 19th-century folksong from southwest England entitled *Widecombe Fair*. Here is the relevant section:

> Tom Pearce, Tom Pearce, lend me your grey mare.
> All along, down along, out along the lea.
> For I want for to go to Widecombe Fair,
> With Bill Brewer, Jan Stewer, Peter Gurney,
> Peter Day, Dan'l Whiddon, Harry Hawke,
> Old Uncle Tom Cobley and all,
> Old Uncle Tom Cobley and all.

In consequence, 'Uncle Tom Cobley' can still be occasionally heard as meaning 'and everybody else', or, in our own academic dialect, 'et al.'. Whatever the motive of Batich et al. for interpolating 'U.T. Cobley' into their list of co-authors, one likely scenario would be that it was designed to cover a rag-bag of otherwise unacknowledged and perhaps unacknowledgeable technicians, students and/or research assistants.

I have known about this U.T. Cobley case for some years, and I know of other instances of Old Uncle Tom infiltrating lists of authors, and have long harboured a slightly mischievous wish to keep the tradition going by attempting to publish an article with my venerable imaginary colleague 'U.T. Cobley'. Since Ken Hyland (2012) has done me the honour of writing a largely favourable article about my writing style, I think I would like to repay the favour with something like:

> U.T. Cobley & J.M. Swales. *Productive fluencies: An analysis of Ken Hyland's prose style.*[2]

4. Snarky acknowledgments

At the opposite end of an article to the title are the acknowledgments, tucked in before the references, typically set in smaller type, and usually not carefully and closely read. In fact, for these reasons, they may escape the eagle eyes of copyeditors and editors. In consequence, there may arise various opportunities for ingenuity and playfulness.[3] Or, in the following two cases, an opportunity to get back at (non-) funding agencies:

> I thank the National Science Foundation for regularly rejecting my (honest) grant applications for work on real organisms (cf. Szent-Gyorgyi, 1972), thus forcing me into theoretical work.

> This work was ostensibly supported by the Italian Ministry of University and Research ... The Ministry however has not paid its dues and it is not known whether it will ever do.

A further opportunity for being subversive occurs with the often fraught issue of the order of authors. Here are two examples that copyeditors may have taken as being purely descriptive:

> Order of authorship was determined by proximity to tenure decisions.

> Order of authorship was determined from a 25-game croquet series held at Imperial College Field Station during summer 1973.

Finally, we circle back to fictional characters:

> We thank Jim Coloso and Laura Smith who collected much of the data shown here and Jim Hodgson, Jon Frum for inspiration in writing this paper.

> (Jon Frum is a deity worshipped by a cargo cult in the south Pacific.)

---

2   In fact, my original title opened with 'The gift of the gab', but I subsequently decided that this opening formulation was a touch meretricious, a little tongue-in-cheek. If ever the piece gets written, it would be particularly nice if I could slip it under the radar and get it published in a publication edited or co-edited by Ken Hyland. (Provided, of course, he never reads this piece!)

3   Much of this section comes from an online piece by Meredith Carpenter and Lillian Fritz-Laylin and kindly sent to me by Christine Tardy of the University of Arizona. It was called 'The snarky, clever comments hidden in the "Acknowledgments" of academic papers', and appeared in 'Future Tense' (*Slate*), 27 December 2013 (pp. 1-3).

So, in the future I might assay something like this:

> I would like to thank the University of Michigan for leaving me a desk to rest my weary head on; my very occasional research assistant, Holly Golightly, for remaining occasional; and our cat, Atlanta, for sleeping on top of drafts of my most unpromising ideas.

5. Confessions from old hands

Up until now, the tenor of this paper has been lighthearted, and it is perhaps time for a change of tone. It has long been recognised that the smooth appearance of finished articles allied with the logical progressions of problems and solutions therein can give an impression, especially to junior researchers, that old hands have some mysterious capacity for 'getting things right'. Barton (2002), in particular, has stressed that we might be more explicit about our methodological uncertainties, missteps and confusions, so that the wandering paths of our research efforts are revealed — rather than concealed in method-section rational retellings devoid of all contingencies (Swales, 2004). So, let us consider the case of Deborah Cameron[4], a very senior scholar — and I have partly chosen Cameron because she is the other academic author whose prose style has been analysed by Ken Hyland (2012). Here she is revealing her reaction to a review:

> A few years ago, one of the peer reviewers of an article I had submitted to an academic journal upbraided me (or rather, 'the author') for making insufficient reference to the work of Deborah Cameron. The omission was, of course, deliberate: the journal's policy of anonymous reviewing required authors to minimize clues to their identity, including citations of their previous publications. But I was surprised, and slightly piqued, to know this strategy had worked so well. I like to think I have a distinctive voice; yet a reviewer who was clearly familiar with my work had not even suspected that s/he might be reading my words. My reaction made me realize that I had expected to be recognized, and that unconsciously I must have wanted to be. (As cited in Hyland & Sancho Guinda, 2012, p. 249)

So, here we have an open and confessional reaction to lack of recognition. But, more importantly, Cameron continues by opening up some important wider considerations:

> This story may not reflect well on me, but I tell it here because it illustrates a dilemma faced by all academic writers, and by teachers of academic writing: how to negotiate — and help students negotiate — the competing claims of self-assertion and self-effacement, individual creativity and institutional authority, personal commitments and community expectations. (p. 249)

In fact, I believe that these eloquently written extracts reflect — despite what Cameron has herself to say — exceptionally well on the author, not only for the points that she wants to make, but also for the way she articulates them.

---

4 Deborah Cameron is the Rupert Murdoch Chair of Language and Communication at the University of Oxford.

6. Two egregious texts

Cameron's 'Epilogue' is in part an essay about her reaction to a review of a paper she had submitted. Reviews of academic books are, of course, a regular feature of our field, and in nearly all cases they tend toward the descriptive, with elements of general praise as well as elements of typically more specific criticism. In fact, all the reviews I have seen of the books I have either authored or co-authored have, more or less, followed this pattern. Except one. Here are two extracts — one longer and one quite short — from the text of this outlier review (Marius, 1991):

> But literature profs believe with equal conviction that today's crop of writing teachers are not humanists at all. Rather, they look like technicians, absorbed like engineers in the mechanics of language but attuned to none of its pleasures. I shudder to imagine the effect Swales's book might have on anyone who loves English, for his graceless jargon can serve only to make the discipline of rhetoric look ridiculous to those who already lack faith in its practitioners.
>
> In hacking my way through this jungle of obfuscation, I find pools of wisdom. (459)

So much, then, for my attempts in *Genre Analysis* (1990) to craft a slightly more open and relaxed writing style (as noted by Hyland for one), as I am pinned by this reviewer as a purveyor of 'graceless jargon'. I do like, though, the John Bunyanesque character of the second extract; to *Pilgrim Progress*'s 'slough of despond' and 'thickets of despair', we can now add 'jungle of obfuscation'. This was the first printed review of *Genre Analysis*, and I was frankly taken aback by it; fortunately, a friend from the English literature field explained that the reviewer, Richard Marius, was a somewhat maverick director of the writing program at Harvard, as well as being a distinguished renaissance scholar, and I should not therefore be totally surprised.[5]

Marius concludes his 1991 review with this peroration:

> Most of Swales's examples come out of scientific or quasi-scientific disciplines; he neglects literary criticism and other humanistic endeavors. He has convinced himself that only jargon-riddled, obscure prose like that of the *American Sociological Review* can be taken seriously by other scholars. His book is therefore a Trojan horse, brought within the city of rhetoric. Deans and college presidents perusing it, imagining that this is the kind of prose we seek to teach students, might decide to save a lot of money by torching their writing programs. (460)

This egregious text (if it be such) I first read 25 years ago; my other selection for this section was received as recently as in 2015. In 2014, I published an article in the journal *Written Communication* on the citation practices of the biology students in the MICUSP corpus. After publication, I did an audio interview about the article with the journal's editorial assistant, which apparently they put on the website. End of story, I presumed. Sometime later, the publisher contacted me and asked if I would make a 10-minute

---

5 The fuller story of this review and for an account of why Marius might have reacted so violently can be found in Aull & Swales (2015).

video, giving the highlights of my findings. Somewhat reluctantly I agreed, but then they sent a document for me to sign, part of which is reproduced below (emphases added):

> [This publisher] is producing a video in which I perform, participate, am portrayed, or appear recognizably.
>
> *For good and valuable consideration, the receipt and sufficiency of which is hereby acknowledged*, I hereby authorize [this publisher], its affiliates, licensees, assignees, and authorized agents to photograph, record or otherwise reproduce and depict my name, voice, and visual likeness, and to exhibit, distribute, transmit and/or otherwise exploit any and all such reproductions containing my voice and/or appearance, *altered as [this publisher] may see fit*, in any and all media now or hereafter known.

I eventually worked out that the first italicised section meant that the publisher now or never in the future would be offering me any monetary reward for my efforts on their behalf. The second italicised section led me to believe that the publisher, if they wanted to, could change my appearance and voice into some transgendered munchkin. I declined with some heat, suggesting, *inter alia*, that they get a new lawyer, but, as you might anticipate, I never received a response.

7. Another dangerous Swales text

According to Professor Marius, *Genre Analysis* lurked as a serious potential threat to the continuing existence of traditional first-year writing programs in the United States. Another book I co-wrote was (rather more seriously) deemed to be hazardous to human health. (As far as I know, Paul Fanning, my co-author, and I have the distinction of being the only ESP material writers to have so far been accused of posing such a threat.) The book was *English in the Medical Laboratory*, and it was published in 1980 by Thomas Nelson in London.

We based this short textbook on materials we had developed over three years for teaching English to the trainee technicians in the Institute for Medical Technology, which was attached to the University of Khartoum's Faculty of Medicine. On Page 34, there is an illustration of mouth pipetting, a common procedure in the Sudan in the 1970s. Sometime after publication, the publisher received a letter from the registrar of a major London teaching hospital. I no longer have the letter, but I remember well the key part of its contents, which essentially said:

> The book contains an illustration of a technique (mouth pipetting) that is now banned in the United Kingdom. In the interests of public health, therefore, all copies of the book should be withdrawn from circulation and destroyed.
>
> Needless to say … [6]

---

6   By this time, Thomas Nelson had been acquired by the Thompson organisation, and a few years after publication, a new management team decided to cease publication of textbooks that failed to sell 'x' thousand copies a year. *English in the Medical Laboratory* fell into the category, so in a strange way, the hospital registrar soon got his way.

8. From a simple textbook to erudite footnotes

English in the Medical Laboratory was a simple 100-page textbook with no references or notes of any kind. In terms of scholarly apparatus, its opposite would be a scholarly humanities work with prolific and multifunctional footnotes and endnotes. The major historical study of footnotes is Grafton's 1997 monograph entitled, *The Footnote — A Curious History*. He discusses the double structure that extensive notes provides: the text persuades, while the notes prove; the text is superstructure, while the notes are infrastructure. Indeed, Grafton likens footnotes or endnotes to the hidden infrastructure of sewage systems that undergird modern towns and cities. Over the course of the book, he illustrates footnoting practice through history, but one of the footnoting mavens whom he most admires is Edward Gibbon, especially in his masterpiece, *The Decline and Fall of the Roman Empire*. Gibbon explains that the early Christian desert fathers attempted to remain chaste. He then says, 'The learned Origen judged it most prudent to disarm the tempter'. And then explicates this example with a footnote:

> As it was his general practice to allegorize scripture, it seems unfortunate that, in this instance only, he should have adopted the literal sense. (p.2)

(And if a footnote to a footnote is needed; 'Origen castrated himself')

Another entertaining and more modern use of notes occurs in Malcolm Ashmore's 1989 doctoral dissertation, which Stephen Woolgar, a leading sociologist of science, insisted be published 'as is'. This is the beginning of Ashmore's copious endnotes:

> 1. Welcome to the notes. I hope you will visit this section of the text regularly. Quite a lot will be going on here and it would be a shame to miss it all. But to get to the business of this particular note: May I ask you by which route you arrived at Chapter One, note 1? If you are a 'notephile' you were probably guided here directly by the note number in the text on page 15 — and quite right too. However, you might also have come to this reading by way of the reference to … (p. 227)

9. Non-standard imperatives

Although imperatives also occur in footnotes and endnotes, they tend toward standard — and rather tame — bibliographic linkages, such as 'See Chapter 2', or 'Note that McCauley (1872) makes a similar argument'. In contrast, other imperatives, such as 'Imagine … ', 'Notice … ', or 'Assume … ' are potentially a rather tricky move in academic prose because of their potentially face-threatening character. In fact, I first became aware of this (as I have written elsewhere; see Swales, 2004, p. 95) when, on a college promotion committee, I was reading an article by a philosopher and came across: 'And do not even attempt to argue that … '

'Whoa, you can't do that', I thought. 'Perhaps not even if you are a philosopher.'

So, recently, a group of us looked at professor and student uses of imperatives in their academic writing (Neiderhiser et al., 2016). In the course of this investigation, we interviewed a number of professors from those fields where we found imperatives in academic articles to be quite common. We discovered that our professor of philosophy informant, Professor Loeb, had in 2004 written the following as part of a complex argument about David Hume. It opens a new paragraph:

> *But wait.* What if sympathetic response to some groups is impeded by prejudice that is not supported or sustained by misinformation? (p. 349, emphasis added)

Intrigued by his usage, my research assistant[7] and I conducted a text-based interview with the professor, who explained his use of 'But wait' as follows:

> What that says to me is that it's an allegedly punchy way of saying we need to slow down here because, contrary to what you might notice, this argument went too fast, and let me show you why … This going to sound pretty uppity — to say that, there has to be a block of material that gives an argument that really looks good, but there's a subtle defect. And only if those conditions are satisfied would you be allowed to say, 'But Wait'. (Interview with Professor Loeb, March 2012)

Sometime later, I began to wonder whether Professor Loeb's use of 'But wait' was a single occurrence — a *hapaxlegomenon* in corpus speak — or whether other academics had adopted it for whatever dramatic reasons of their own. In fact, I soon found, thanks to Google Scholar, a piece that used several examples. This was published in 1988 in *Natural Language and Linguistic Theory* and written by Geoffrey Pullum. The topic was the history of the Unaccusative Hypothesis, a label apparently coined by Pullum himself.[8] He then explores its antecedents in the linguistic literature:

> A possible example is the … dissertation of Robert Fiengo, submitted to MIT on August 12, 1974: …
>
> *But wait.* Apparently unknown to Fiego, Donna Jo Napoli had presented a year earlier …
>
> *But wait.* The … dissertation of John Bowers, submitted to MIT in January 1972, analyzes …
>
> *But wait.* An earlier influence cited by Bowers … is Fillmore (1968) which clearly shows …
>
> *But wait.* Bowers also cites an even earlier work: the MIT dissertation of Barbara Hall [now Partee] from 1965.
>
> *But wait.* There is a yet earlier dissertation that introduces the idea …
>
> And who is this, advancing the UH in 1962. Surprise! None other than Paul Postal …
>
> *But wait.* Postal's dissertation … (pp. 582-4, emphases added)

---

7   Not Holly Golightly, but the excellent Kohlee Kennedy.

8   Geoffrey Pullum is a well-known linguist, albeit with a maverick streak in him. He, at the time of writing, is Professor of Linguistics at the University of London. The Unaccusative Hypothesis deals with structures like 'The ice melted', which can be shown to be related to formulations like 'The sun melted the ice'. In the latter, the ice is in the accusative, but in the former, original sentence, it is not. Hence, the Unaccusative Hypothesis [UH].

Pullum then argues that in the crucial period between 1962 and 1980 this earlier work on UH-style analyses went almost totally uncited. He then closes with this obviously heartfelt but ironic peroration:

> Given the trend of the times, and the difficulty of determining answers to vexed questions of priority from the literature I have surveyed, I recommend that anyone wishing to assume or discuss the UH should simply reintroduce it as their own, citing no one. For my part, I will certainly be attributing the UH to myself. Hell, I may even rename it. (p. 587)

10. The biodata puzzle

Often right at the end of articles, we can find, in 50 words or so, biodata summaries of their authors' careers. Although there has been some recent work on this mini part-genre (Tardy & Swales, 2014; Hyland, 2012; Tse, 2012), nowhere have I seen or heard anybody refer to the apparent anomaly of impersonal biodata statements following single-authored papers whose authors had opted for using, at least on occasion, the personal pronoun 'I'.[9] If I have used 'I' in the body of the text, I wondered, why do I have to become 'John M. Swales' in the closing biodata section? After all, I wrote the section, rather than somebody else, as, for example, in an obituary. So why cannot I be allowed to tacitly acknowledge this by continuing to use the by-now-established first-person pronoun? Nor can it be argued that these biodata statements are, in any real sense, impressive models of strict objectivity and impartiality and so therefore require third-person pronoun treatment. As Tse observes, 'Almost always, a bio is not a pure and plain account of oneself, but an account which puts its writer in a positive light' (2012, p. 71).

In a recent article published in *English for Specific Purposes*, I used several instances of the first person in the body of the article (Swales, 2015). After the article had been accepted — after the usual two tough rounds of reviews — I decided to challenge the orthodoxy by submitting this biostatement:

> I officially retired from the University of Michigan in 2007 as Professor Emeritus of Linguistics; although I continue to be research-active, as hopefully this article demonstrates. A fifth volume in the mini-textbook series (with Christine B. Feak as co-author) dealing with results and discussions is under review at the University of Michigan Press.

Readers will notice two instances of 'I'; they may also notice that the second and third clauses (starting with *although*) are not strictly correct grammatically. When I received the proofs, I found I could claim at least a partial victory:

> John M. Swales officially retired from the University of Michigan in 2007 as Professor Emeritus of Linguistics; although I continue to be research-active, as hopefully this

---

9   The anomaly does not apply to multi-authored articles, or to the consolidated biodata entries in edited collections.

article demonstrates. A fifth volume in the mini-textbook series (with Christine B. Feak as co-author) dealing with results and discussions is under review at the University of Michigan Press.

As can be seen, I lost the battle for the first, and arguably the more important, opening 'I', but was allowed to keep the second one, as well as my doubtful syntax.[10]

11. Fables and fantasies

The place of narrative in academic genres has been a lively topic of discussion in recent years, as perhaps best exemplified by the large edited collection, *Narratives in Academic and Professional Genres* (Gotti & Sancho Guinda, 2013). For one thing, we know that narratives occur in spoken academic genres (Thompson, 2002; Mauranen, 2013), in academic blogs (Luzón, 2013), in methods sections in research articles (Mur Dueñas, 2013), and in literature reviews (Feak & Swales, 2009). Elsewhere, they may be less common, unless circumstances suggested otherwise. For one instance of this, Fredrickson and Swales (1994) over 20 years ago showed that introductions to linguistic articles in Swedish often contained narratives because, in such a small discourse community, the primary aim of the authors was apparently to secure as large a readership as possible, rather than to establish a research space. However, my interest here is not so much to explore such anomalies, but to focus on narrative-like rhetorical extravaganzas that take us away from the standardised academic territory into a land of academic fable and fantasy. I have chosen three of these: the first tells the story of academic discourse in recent centuries through a set of elaborate personifications; the second offers a complex geographical metaphor to tell the history of ESL; and the third is a re-imagining of the recent history of the language sciences based on a crucial event that might have happened, but which in fact did not take place.

The first set of extracts is taken from Karen Bennett's 2007 paper entitled 'Epistemicide':

> Once upon a time, many years ago in England, a new discourse was born. His parents were both very old at his birth, and poor; although they were of illustrious lineage, they had since fallen on hard times. Moreover, the kingdom was ruled at that time by a tyrannical old discourse who claimed to have been put there by God, and who cruelly suppressed any that challenged his word. Consequently, the new baby discourse had to be nurtured with care and in secret, for fear he would be silenced before he was strong enough to fend for himself. (pp. 151-2)

Thus is described the emergence of the new scientific rhetoric in the second half of the 17th century. Bennett then goes on to show that Enlightenment discourse (and its

---

10   I did think of re-inserting the first 'I' when responding to the request for proof corrections. However, I thought I would tell the story as it was for my talk at PRISEAL3.

associated scientific method) became increasingly dominant, so that, in recent times, the old Catholic humanistic discourse that had long survived in the Iberian peninsula is now in danger of extinction, as indeed are other alternative discourses to Anglo-American paradigms. She concludes:

> So how does the story end?
>
> I'm afraid, dear Reader, I don't know, for it hasn't ended yet. Our discourse is today very rich and powerful, and he controls most of the western world. Many people from other parts of the globe are dazzled by him and so he attracts new supporters every day, who want to partake of his power and wealth. But he has lost supporters too, people who have become disillusioned with his methods and conclusions ...
>
> And so around the boundaries of his kingdom, small groups of protesters are mobilizing, some of them in the name of the god that he denounced so many years ago, others with a different agenda ... (p. 166)

As the reader might intuit, I have chosen this highly imaginative narrative not only for its ingenuity, but also because it is a story about standardisation and its discontents.

The second example comes from an article in *ELTJ* by Alan Waters of Lancaster University (2009). Here are two extracts from his 'geography lesson':

> Methodologia is an island in the ELT archipelago, surrounded by the Sea of TESOL. It is inhabited chiefly by large numbers of teachers and learners of EFL, who have migrated to it from all over the world. However, although each of these waves of settlers is familiar with its own part of the island, very few of them have visited the rest of it, and so they are often somewhat confused about its overall geography. The turbulent nature of its recent history has also left many feeling rather disoriented. This brief illustrated guide to the island has been provided in order to try and solve these problems. (p. 108)
>
> Our journey begins, appropriately, in the historical capital, Methodsville. Among the major sites of interest in the older parts of the city are the monuments to methods such as grammar-translation, audiolingualism and so on. It was the creation of these impressive structures that originally led to the rise of Methodsville ... The largest and most important part of the present day city is occupied by the Kommunikatavia sector. Its sprawling environs along the banks of the River Akademika encompass a wide range of different architectural styles. ...' (p. 110)

This is an imaginative and instructive re-telling of a history that most readers will have some familiarity with; notice, in particular the monuments to defunct methods!

The third and final exhibit in this section is a short piece I wrote myself in 1999. It can, I believe, tell its own story, except for pointing out that Bakhtin's *The Problem of Speech Genres*, although written in the late 1940s, did not appear in English until 40 years later. Now suppose ...

After exchange of the usual pleasantries, Professor Bakhtin[11] inquired both eagerly and nervously, 'Mikhailovich?' Patrick shrugged apologetically and said, 'Alas, Nikolai, I never got to Saransk, but I did give my lecture on E.P. Thompson and the British Working Class in Nizhniy Novgorod. Afterwards, in the lavatory, a young chap sidled up and said that he was one of your brother's student teachers in Saransk and could he give me a packet to bring to you. Well, to cut a long story short, here it is ...

'My brother says that he is quite well given his infirmities but goes on to say that he has no immediate hope of getting his latest work published in Russia, and wonders whether it might find a small audience in England ... if I translate it', he added with a wry chuckle ....

'It's called *Problema Rechevykh Zhanrov*, which I guess would be in English something like *The Problem of Discursive Genres* — whatever that might mean.' (p. 527)

...

A thoughtful Zellig Harris bustled across the MIT campus one bright if windy morning in late March. He was on his way to a meeting with his brilliant young student, Noam Chomsky, who had just finished his MA thesis on the Morphophonemics of Modern Hebrew. He was wondering what Chomsky would say about possible dissertation topics and about the carbon copy of a small monograph — apparently to be published later in the year by Oxford — that had been smuggled out of the Soviet Union and sent to him by Rupert Firth.

'Morphophonemics, schmorphophonemics' announced Chomsky, 'this is stunning stuff, and casts your article in *Language* on discourse analysis in a new light. Bakhtin is clearly correct that all utterances are in some way dialogic, and the future of linguistics depends on all of us recognizing this, including you, Sir'. (pp. 528-9)

...

Bakhtin's *The Problem of Speech Genres*, as it was finally called, was published in the same year and by the same press as Ludwig Wittgenstein's *Philosophical Investigations*, and these two seminal works have been linked in the thoughts of the world's intelligentsia ever since. They remain, despite the academic industries that have grown up around them, tantalizingly similar and tantalizingly different. However, Language Sciences really shot to its current pre-eminence with the appearance in 1964 of *Aspects of a Theory of Language and Social Life* by Noam Chomsky and Erving Goffman. Within a space of ten years, a Nobel Prize in Language Sciences had been

---

11   It is a fact not universally known that Michael Bakhtin had a brother, Nikolai, who became Professor of Slavic Linguistics at Birmingham University. At the time when the story opens, he and Rupert Firth were the only two professors of linguistics in the UK. I am grateful to Paul Hopper, now Paul Mellon Distinguished Professor Emeritus of the Humanities at Carnegie-Mellon, for help with the historical accuracy of the piece. In fact, he has been the only person I know who was ever enthusiastic about my little historical reconstruction.

established, and fittingly the first laureate was Mikhail Bakhtin ... Later laureates were, of course, Chomsky and then Halliday, the latter for his masterpiece *Context in Text and Text in Context*. There is doubtless more to say, but the hour grows late and the cat is scratching at the door. (p. 529)

I should now admit that one extra reason for including this *jeu d'esprit* was that, although published in *Written Communication* in 1999, it has never been cited, not even by me.[12] Until now. After it appeared, I did receive a couple of emails from two graduate students in US English departments, congratulating me on having produced a narrative rather than a piece of stodgy expository prose, but, alas, they both thought that my little fanciful story was, in fact, true.

12. Final thoughts

In this short chapter, I have dealt with several unconventional (or at least odd) aspects of academic writing. These have included an imaginary author, double-edged acknowledgments, a public confession of pique, a highly critical review, an egregious contract offer, a dangerous ESP textbook, unusual imperatives, an attempt to modify biodata conventions, and narratives in the form of allegories or alternative histories. While these have been mostly 'entertainments' in Greene's sense, since they deal mostly with the ludic rather than the agonistic side of the academic world, they can reveal potential openings for alternatives, and hence hold out prospects for change, for ways of wriggling out of the straitjacket of hallowed conventions. And while it is true that my focus has been more on matters of style rather than on those of topic and substance, we can express our discontent with the *status quo* also in this arena.

It is often argued that divergencies are only possible for senior authors, but I have seen over the years little evidence for this claim, and there is little evidence for it here. While Deborah Cameron is indeed famous, it was Ashmore's doctoral thesis that has its highly original elements. Karen Bennett was at the beginning of her academic career with her 'Epistemicide' essay, and Alan Waters never became a professor. As for my opening promise to close with serious thoughts, let me end with this appeal:

As academic and research English increasingly becomes a *lingua franca*, both in its forms and its varieties, as well as in terms of its participants, experimentation in both style and substance should be open to all the bolder-hearted, to all the malcontents of excessive and stultifying standardisation, whoever they are, and wherever they be.

---

12   This admission has, I hope, something of Deborah Cameron's frankness.

I hope you have been paying attention to the notes. Quite a lot has been going on here, and it would be a shame if you have missed it all.

References

Ashmore, M. 1989. *The reflexive thesis: Wrighting sociology of scientific knowledge.* Chicago: The University of Chicago Press.

Aull, L., & Swales, J.M. (2015). Genre analysis: Considering the initial reviews. *Journal of English for Academic Purposes, 19* (1), 6-9.

Barton, E. (2002). Inductive discourse analysis: Discovering rich features. In E. Barton & G. Stygall (Eds.), *Discourse studies in composition* (pp. 19-42). Cresskill, NJ: Hampton Press.

Bennett, K. (2007). Epistemicide! The tale of a predatory discourse. *The Translator, 13*(2), 151-169.

Cameron, D. (2012). Epilogue. In K. Hyland, & C. Sancho Guinda (Eds.), *Stance and voice in written academic genres* (pp. 249-256). Basingstoke, UK: Palgrave MacMillan.

Feak, C.B., & Swales, J.M. (2009). *Telling a research story: Writing literature reviews.* Ann Arbor, MI: University of Michigan Press.

Gotti, M., & C. Sancho Guinda (Eds.). (2013). *Narratives in academic and professional genres.* Bern: Peter Lang.

Grafton, A. (1997). *The footnote — A curious history.* Princeton, NJ: The University of Princeton Press.

Fredrickson, K., & Swales, J.M. (1994). Competition and discourse community: Introductions from *Nysvenska Studier. ASLA, 6,* 9-22.

Hyland, K. (2012). *Disciplinary identities: Individuality and community in academic discourse.* Cambridge: Cambridge University Press.

Hyland, K., & C. Sancho Guinda (Eds.). (2012). *Stance and voice in written academic genres.* Basingstoke, UK: Palgrave Macillan.

Loeb, L.L. (2004). Stability and justification in Hume's treatise, another look — A response to Erin Kelly, Frederick Schmitt, and Michael Williams. *Hume Studies, 30*(2), 339-404.

Luzón, M.J. (2013). Narratives in academic blogs. In M. Gotti, & C. Sancho Guinda (Eds.), *Narratives in academic and professional genres* (pp. 175-194). Bern: Peter Lang.

Marius, R. (1991). Genre analysis: English in academic and research settings. *Journal of Advanced Composition, 11*(2), 458-460.

Mauranen, A. (2013). 'But then when I started to think … ': Narrative elements in conference presentations. In M. Gotti, & C. Sancho Guinda (Eds.), *Narratives in academic and professional genres* (pp. 45-65). Bern: Peter Lang.

Mur Dueñas, P. (2013). Scholars recounting their own research in journal articles: An intercultural (English-Spanish) perspective. In M. Gotti, & C. Sancho Guinda (Eds.), *Narratives in academic and professional genres* (pp. 217-234). Bern: Peter Lang.

Neiderhiser, J.A., Kelley, P., Kennedy, K.K., Swales, J.M., & Vergaro, C. (2016). 'Notice the similarity between the two sets': Imperative usage in a corpus of upper-level student papers. *Applied Linguistics, 37*(2), 198-218.

Pecorari, D. (2003). Good and original: Plagiarism and patchwriting in academic second-language writing. *Journal of Second Language Writing, 12*(4), 317-345.

Pennycook, A. (1996). Borrowing others' words: Text, ownership, memory and plagiarism. *TESOL Quarterly, 30*(2), 201-230.

Pullum, GK. (1988). Citation etiquette beyond Thunderdome. *Natural Language and Linguistic Theory, 6*, 579-588.

Stewart, S. (1994). *Crimes of writing*. Durham, NC: Duke University Press.

Swales, J.M. (1990). *Genre analysis: English in academic and research settings*. Cambridge: Cambridge University Press.

Swales, J.M. (1999). Moments in the modern history of the language sciences. *Written Communication, 16*(4), 526-530.

Swales, J.M. (2004). *Research genres: Explorations and applications*. Cambridge: Cambridge University Press.

Swales, J.M. (2015). Configuring image and context: Writing 'about' pictures. *English for Specific Purposes, 41*(1), 22-35.

Tardy, C.M., & Swales, J.M. (2014). Genre . In A. Barron, & K. Schneider (Eds.), *Handbook of Pragmatics: Vol. III* (pp. 167-188). Berlin: De Gruyter.

Thompson, S. (2002). 'As the story unfolds': The uses of narrative in research presentations. In E. Ventola, C. Shalom, & S. Thompson (Eds.), *The language of conferencing* (pp. 147-167). Frankfurt: Peter Lang.

Tse, P. (2012). Stance in academic bios. In K. Hyland, & C. Sancho Guinda (Eds.), *Stance and voice in written academic genres* (pp. 69-84). Basingstoke, UK: Palgrave MacMillan.

Waters, A. (2009). A guide to Methodologia: Past, present, and future. *English Language Teaching Journal, 63*(2), 108-115.

Reflections and future directions in publishing research in English as an Additional Language:

An Afterword

Laurence Anthony

Academia has become a world in which scholars are being encouraged or pressured to publish more articles in higher-impact journals under increasingly stringent evaluation and review systems. In the UK, for example, the assessment of scholars' research outputs within the national Research Excellence Framework [REF] can affect individuals' promotions, departmental funding, and ultimately the ranking of the university within the country (Higher Education Funding Council for England, 2009; Parker, 2008; Martin, 2011). In countries where English is seen as an additional language, the pressures on scholars can be even greater. Not only do they have to reach the high standards of international journals in terms of content, relevance and novelty, but they also have to meet the often opaque and varying language requirements of these journals, while navigating through the sometimes cryptic, indirect suggestions and comments of reviewers (Paltridge, 2015).

It is within this demanding and challenging environment that the PRISEAL [Publishing and Presenting Research Internationally: Issues for Speakers of English as an Additional Language] and MET [Mediterranean Editors and Translators] organisations decided to hold a joint conference in 2015. The conference was held in the beautiful city of Coimbra, Portugal, and provided a unique forum for researchers on academic writing and research publication to meet with in-house and freelance professional editors, who receive daily requests from clients to edit or translate their work for publication. In this volume that emerged from the joint conference, we can see a strong reiteration of the growing pressure on scholars to publish in English and recognition of the challenges they face. However, the strongest message we can receive from the authors of these chapters is that the challenges faced by scholars using English as an additional language can be overcome through a greater understanding of the problems they face, instruction and supervision from academic faculty that is tailored to their particular needs and contexts, and discipline-specific, focused support from professional language editors and translation experts.

Clearly, the challenges faced by scholars who need to publish in English as an additional language are not just surface-level writing problems, such as verb tense and voice usage, modality, subject-verb agreement, article usage, hedging and punctuation, although without instruction, these may appear to many scholars as the aspects of their writing in most need of being 'fixed'. As we find in Cargill et al.'s study in Chapter 8, for example, the planning of writing is also a very important skill that scholars need to develop. Planning may include deciding on a suitable target journal, choosing which section of the research article to write up first, and understanding common conventions in the rhetorical structuring of research articles, such as the model presented by Martín and Pérez in Chapter 7 for the immunology and allergy sub-branch of medicine. Throughout the volume, we see the various methods employed by instructors, supervisors and professional editors to help scholars plan their work, including the use of the Research Writing Matrix presented by Cadman in Chapter 2, the CCC model presented by Linnegar in Chapter 5, the guiding comments of supervisors as discussed by DiGiacomo in Chapter 3 and Li in Chapter 9, and inline and margin comments of editors as discussed by Shaw and Voss in Chapter 4. It is also clear that support offered to scholars as they aim for publication needs to be tailored to the particular culture, context and language experience, a point emphasised by Burgess in Chapter 1 when describing how researchers are assessed in Spain, by Bennett in Chapter 10 when discussing how to understand and deal with academic plagiarism, and Cao and Cadman in Chapter 11 when explaining the challenges faced in developing an effective ELT training program in Vietnam.

One particularly difficult challenge faced not only by scholars hoping to publish internationally but also instructors and professional editors hoping to support them as they work towards this goal is that of language variation. A great body of work in the area of English for Specific Purposes [ESP] has shown that language varies considerably depending on the specific discipline (see for example Hyland, 2002, 2008). However, throughout the volume, we find other interesting examples of language variation. In Chapter 7, for example, Martín and Pérez show that the rhetorical structure of research articles can vary even with a narrow sub-discipline of medicine depending on the journal of publication. In Chapter 12, Swales shows that authors can sometimes be ingenious or playful in their writing, for example in their acknowledgments and footnotes, and that these divergences from journal conventions are made not just by senior academic scholars but also those beginning their careers. Of course, this does not necessarily mean that fledgling researchers should go out of their way to write in a divergent way from those around them. We should remember that Swales's work only reports on the examples of divergent language patterns that made it to publication, whereas there are likely to be many other cases where the divergent patterns were revised or 'corrected' through the review editing process, or where the papers were rejected outright. The cases raised by Martín and Pérez and Swales do, however, emphasise the point that language variation is real and that scholars learning how to publish in English as an additional language need strategies to assess what types of variability exists and what language choices are available to them.

One way to approach the issue of language variation in the classroom is through a data-driven learning [DDL] approach, where learners are given software tools to explore a target language corpus with guidance from an instructor (Anthony, 2016). Results of these explorations can reveal the most frequent words and phrases in target journals, common rhetorical devices to open and close journal article sections, idiosyncratic uses of tense, voice and modality, and a host of other language features that are normally inaccessible to scholars using EAL. The approach also lends itself well to heterogeneous groups of learners from different areas of specialisation or aiming to publish in different target journals. In these settings, each learner can acquire or build their own unique language corpus and then use common search and analysis techniques to probe their data and extract meaningful information from it that can guide their own writing practices. Indeed, a large and growing body of empirical research has demonstrated the effectiveness of DDL in a variety of settings (Boulton, 2012). However, an instructor considering introducing DDL into the writing classroom must still be sensitive to the culture and context of the learners as well as consider the practical limitations of the institution's classroom facilities and technical support staff.

The discussions on how best to guide and support scholars on publishing research in English as an additional language are still ongoing. However, there is no doubt that the current volume provides many very important perspectives on how to take those discussions forward and help both scholars and instructors to arrive at real-world, practical solutions to the challenges that they face.

References

Anthony, L. (2016). Introducing corpora and corpus tools into the technical writing classroom through Data-Driven Learning (DDL). In J. Flowerdew, & T. Costley (Eds.), *Discipline-specific writing: From theory to practice* (pp. 163-181). Abingdon, UK: Routledge.

Boulton, A. (2012). Corpus consultation for ESP: A review of empirical research. In A. Boulton, S. Carter-Thomas, & E. Rowley-Jolivet (Eds.), *Corpus-informed research and learning in ESP: Issues and applications* (pp. 261-291). Amsterdam: John Benjamins.

Higher Education Funding Council for England. (2009). *Research Excellence Framework*. Retrieved 28 March 2017 from http://www.csmc.scieng.ed.ac.uk/docs/open/PaperD_REF.pdf.

Hyland, K. (2002). Specificity revisited: How far should we go now? *English for Specific Purposes*, *21*(4), 385-395.

Hyland, K. (2008). As can be seen: Lexical bundles and disciplinary variation. *English for Specific Purposes, 27*(1), 4-21.

Martin, B.R. (2011). The Research Excellence Framework and the 'impact agenda': Are we creating a Frankenstein monster? *Research Evaluation, 20*(3), 247-254.

Paltridge, B. (2015). Referees' comments on submissions to peer-reviewed journals: When is a suggestion not a suggestion? *Studies in Higher Education, 40*(1), 106-122.

Parker, J. (2008). Comparing research and teaching in university promotion criteria. *Higher Education Quarterly, 62*(3), 237-251.

This book is available as a free fully-searchable ebook from
www.adelaide.edu.au/press

www.ingramcontent.com/pod-product-compliance
Lightning Source LLC
Chambersburg PA
CBHW081131080526
44587CB00021B/3834